NEWS
AS IT
HAPPENS

DEDICATION

To my adored and loving wife and best friend, Lyn. This is for you. It could not have happened without you. Your strength sustained me as my own waned. Together, in Kipling's immortal words, we filled countless 'unforgiving minute[s] with sixty seconds' worth of distance run'.

NEWS AS IT HAPPENS

An Introduction to Journalism

SECOND EDITION

Stephen Lamble

OXFORD
UNIVERSITY PRESS
AUSTRALIA & NEW ZEALAND

OXFORD
UNIVERSITY PRESS

Oxford University Press is a department of the University of Oxford.

It furthers the University's objective of excellence in research, scholarship, and education by publishing worldwide. Oxford is a registered trademark of Oxford University Press in the UK and in certain other countries.

Published in Australia by
Oxford University Press
253 Normanby Road, South Melbourne, Victoria 3205, Australia

© Stephen Lamble 2013

The moral rights of the author have been asserted.

First published 2011
Second Edition 2013
Reprinted 2015

National Library of Australia Cataloguing-in-Publication data

Lamble, Stephen, author.
News as it happens : an introduction to journalism / Stephen Lamble.

2nd edition.

ISBN 9780195520408 (paperback)

Includes bibliographical references and index.

Journalism.
Journalism—Authorship.

070.4

Edited by Kirstie Innes-Will
Cover design by Caitlin Ziegler
Text design by Ana Cosma
Typeset by diacriTech, Chennai, India
Proofread by Geraldine Corridon
Indexed by Jeanne Rudd
Printed by Sheck Wah Tong Printing Press Ltd

CONTENTS

ABOUT THIS BOOK

The years immediately after the first edition of *News as it Happens: An Introduction to Journalism* was written were marked by life-changing advances in technology, which had an enormous impact on how information and news are hunted, gathered, and disseminated.

Remember, if you can, a world before the iPad was released in 2010, a world without thousands of apps, when communication-savvy professionals used Blackberrys, the first iPhone was seen as a trendy tool for downloading music, and most other mobile phones had tiny screens that did nothing if you touched them and keys so small that texting was only for the most dexterous. And what of photography and video-recording? One-to-one or one-to-many video calling was still around the corner for many, and live-to-air video sent from smartphone to newsroom was uncommon. Facebook, Skype, YouTube and Twitter were gaining popularity but were yet to become virtually ubiquitous.

Think too of how the founders of *The Age* and *Sydney Morning Herald* would have turned in their graves if they had seen their broadsheet newspapers that had been two of Australia's most highly regarded traditional sources of 'quality' news and comment squeezed into tabloid formats in 2013. There were other momentous changes too, among them the major restructuring of sub-editing across most newspapers and magazines, staff reductions and redundancies in print and television newsrooms, and an almost do-or-die push towards online publishing, not just by newspapers but by broadcasters too—particularly the ABC.

In the same period and coupled with what were fundamental, even if indirect, technologically driven restructures and realignments, Australian news media, particularly print and online, also came under sustained attack from government. Threats emerged on two fronts. First, there was an unprecedented proliferation of spin doctoring by political Svengalis ('media advisers') bent on the manipulation of public opinion in favour of those who paid them. Second, and considerably more worrying, there were direct, poorly thought out but very determined attacks on freedom of speech and media freedom.

Those things and the fact that more journalists are employed than ever before, are discussed and explained in this new edition. So too are fresh approaches to journalism, writing and reporting demanded by our ever newer and faster communication technologies and a 24/7 news cycle in which deadlines have become instant as news providers compete to be the first to publish breaking stories on mobile devices.

As with the first edition, *News as it Happens* draws on the author's experience as a journalist, sub-editor, editor and photojournalist; on his academic research, the research of many others, his shameless curiosity about the ways of the world, passion for the profession of journalism, and love of teaching and learning.

The book was designed and written to serve as a companion across all different levels of journalism subjects, courses, units and educational programs, not simply an introductory course. It is a guide designed to be acquired at the start of journalism studies, to also inform postgraduate research, and to go with you into industry as a reference. How you read the book will depend to some extent on how your journalism curriculum is organised. Chapters and sections lead from one to another in a logical sequence and build on each other and specific themes, but each chapter was also written to stand alone and, where relevant, point to other chapters that contain related information. At the end of each chapter you will find discussion points and news practice points. The points were designed to challenge you to go beyond the information presented in the chapters preceding them—to reflect on issues and research more widely to find fresh ideas, knowledge and understandings.

You will also find practitioner profiles and tips from a diverse range of journalists. They are people who are passionate about their profession and the importance of journalism. Their diverse backgrounds, work and interests reflect the fact that journalism is a broad church and a rich field with many facets.

Also bear in mind that no book can cover every aspect of a topic or every nuance, angle or opinion. You should read widely about journalism and in other liberal arts disciplines. To help you do that, at the back of the book there is a list of recommended readings. Another appendix lists web links and points to a wide range of useful information for journalists. There is also a copy of the journalists' code of ethics, while another appendix contains the URLs of a range of organisations involved in media regulation.

Finally, enjoy studying journalism—it truly is a wonderful, challenging and rewarding vocation. It is a portable profession that can take you to amazing places, open hidden doors many do not even know exist, introduce you to fascinating people and fresh ideas, enable you to really make a difference for the better and enrich you intellectually.

ACKNOWLEDGMENTS

This, the second edition of *News as it Happens*, has been enriched by the generosity of many of the same people who contributed so much to the first edition. There have also been new contributors who offered fresh advice, comments, ideas and constructive criticisms. Among those who helped were friends, colleagues, journalists based in regional and metropolitan newsrooms, freelancers who work from home, academics, columnists, feature writers, editors, lawyers, sub-editors, camera operators, news producers, IT experts and photographers. Each of us had a common bond: a commitment to journalism, and to educating the generations of journalists who will walk in our footsteps.

While there are too many to name individually, I particularly thank Jane Fynes-Clinton and Pamela Edsall. They were rocks, valued sounding boards, remarkable friends to my wife, Lyn, and me, and delightful advocates of fun and frivolity as I battled cancer to complete this work.

I also specifically thank Peter English, Rosanna Natoli, Ross Dagan, Peter Owen, Reged Ahmad, Nancy Bates, Bob Bottom, Lyndal Cairns, Adam Carey, Lucy Carter, Peter Gregory, Liz Jackson, Caroline Jones, Roz Kelly, Gary Kemble, Nick McKenzie, Dina Rosendorff, Leigh Sales, Kathleen Skene, Hedley Thomas, Virginia Trioli, Jack Waterford and Daniel Ziffer. This book would have been poorer without your input. Each of you is a role model who has earned deep professional respect for your contributions to journalism and the communities you serve. We are richer for your wisdom, insights and advice.

In addition I acknowledge the Media section, which appears weekly in *The Australian*, and those who write for it, including Mark Day, Errol Simper and Nick Leys. Your work is valuable. It furthers the pursuit of quality journalism, helps protect media freedom, informs national debate and fosters public understandings of key issues in journalism and news dissemination.

I am also indebted to Kayt Davies for her commitment and expertise in preparing the online learning materials that complement this book. Kayt has a broad, refreshing and practical interest in journalism and journalism education. She is a leading journalism academic who has worked in business and magazine journalism in Perth and London and for an international news agency.

Also a special thank you to Oxford University Press Higher Education Division senior publisher and development manager Karen Hildebrandt for once again having faith in me and for her support, consummate and eagle-eyed copy editor Kirstie Innes-Will, and Higher Education project editor Estelle Tang.

Stephen Lamble, 2013

INTRODUCTION

Put it before them briefly so they will read it, clearly so they will appreciate it, picturesquely so they will remember it and, above all, accurately so they will be guided by its light. (Joseph Pulitzer, 1847–1911)

Journalism is a rich and rewarding profession that underpins much of our social, cultural and political fabric. The work of journalists helps us make sense of the world. Despite the critics, and there are many, it is impossible to imagine how 21st-century society could function without journalism and journalists. More than ever, ours is an information world. We are creatures of the Communication Revolution and Information Age—one of the most amazing and rapidly changing periods in history. Never has so much information been available to so many, nor been so easily disseminated and accessed. It is an exciting and challenging era for journalists, journalism educators and journalism students—a time in which the traditional roles and responsibilities of journalists to inform, educate and entertain are as important as ever, but one in which media landscapes and the tools we use to gather, then circulate news and information are being shaped and reshaped at unprecedented speed by ever advancing technologies.

It is a truism that news travels. How far and how fast depends on variables including the impact of an event or circumstance, how efficiently facts are gathered, how effectively a story is told, and the vehicle that transports it. In today's 24/7 rolling news cycle, news is regularly reported minutes after it happens, even while it is still happening. Stories appear online or are broadcast as soon as they are written. As discussed in Chapter 1, our demand for news is insatiable. As quickly as journalists hunt and gather it, we consume it. Our compulsion to know, not just about events in our own backyards, but nationally and globally is deep-seated and urgent.

As skilled news-gathering professionals and seekers of truth, it is journalists who gratify most of the world's demand for news and the interpretation of news and current affairs. They write for print, broadcast, online and the news apps on our mobile devices. Tablet computers and smartphones have become constant companions, our means of staying in touch with friends and family, sources of instant news, reassurance and information. Like a child's security blanket, we are only subliminally aware of their closeness but many of us feel lost and out of touch without them.

But because we are familiar with our generation's technology, we tend to take it for granted—to forget, or not understand, how things were in the past. Yet there is much to learn from those who paved the way for us—especially as the fundamentals of good journalism remain the same despite ever newer and better ways of disseminating information. At their most basic level, news and current affairs have always existed. Even in the most primitive societies information was passed from person to person by word of mouth—a process likely to have bred inaccuracy in the same way gossip and Chinese whispers do today. Much later, news was printed, one sheet at a time on hand operated presses. With the start of the Industrial Revolution in the late 18th century printing was mechanised and the demand for professional news hunters and gatherers grew. Newspaper publishers were in the business of making money. They did that by selling advertisements. The more popular their newspapers were, the more advertisements they sold, and the more they could charge advertisers. To make their newspapers popular, spaces around advertisements were filled with news and information people wanted to read. Links between journalism and technology strengthened. Along the way journalists, editors and media owners became collectors, traders and gatekeepers of information. Accurately reporting current events, probing beneath the surface—prying loose morsels of information about decisions, deals, and secrets—was profitable. There was money to invest in newer and better technology and just as journalism has been changed irreversibly by the invention of mechanised printing, it was revolutionised by development of the telegraph, telephone, radio, film, moving pictures, television, and computers. There was a spurt of innovation during World War II and in the decades that followed.

By the early 1990s, journalism and communication technologies were evolving more rapidly than at any other time in history. Much of that evolution was driven by the development of digital electronics. Few people realised at the time what lay ahead, but each new development brought increased efficiencies and greater accessibility. The pace of change accelerated bringing with it the internet, world wide web (the web), digital photography, email, social networking, mobile electronic devices such as smartphones, tablets and an almost endless string of apps.

One person who did forsee the future was an eccentric Canadian professor of English called Marshall McLuhan. He had a remarkable gift of foresight and still influences our vocabulary and view of the world today. In the early 1960s, many decades before it was technically possible to publish or access online news, McLuhan started talking about something he called 'mass media'. No one had spoken about that before, but McLuhan explained that mass media 'are an indication, not of the size of their audiences, but of the fact that everybody becomes involved in them at the same time' (McLuhan 1964, p. 348). What he meant was not masses of media, but media for the masses. McLuhan also discussed the idea of a 'global village', and a concept he dubbed 'electric technology'. Somehow, years before the internet, web, broadband and wi-fi, McLuhan foresaw them. He prophesied that: 'with instant electric technology, the globe itself can never again be more than a village' (McLuhan 1964, p. 343). Home computers and personal mobile devices were decades into the future and, if imagined at all, would have been dismissed as science fiction. The only computers in existence were huge machines housed in special buildings, yet remarkably McLuhan wrote:

> Our new electric technology that extends our senses and nerves in a global embrace has large implications for the future of language ... Today computers hold out the promise of a means of instant translation of any code or language into any other code or language. The computer, in short, promises by technology a Pentecostal condition of universal understanding and unity. (McLuhan 1964, p. 80)

McLuhan's 1960s predictions have become our 21st-century reality. The pace of invention and evolution in digital communications technology has been incredible. It continues to accelerate and change our lives. In today's global village we would think it strange if we could not go online to shop, bank, study, pay for holidays, research, arrange dates, share thoughts and images, keep in touch with family and friends, blog, tweet and obtain our news. McLuhan is long dead, but what might he have thought about the fact that more than 2.3 billion users worldwide relied on 'instant electric technology' to access the internet in 2012 (Miniwatts World Stats 2012a)? Further, in something of a reflection of McLuhan's 'Pentecostal condition of universal understanding and unity' (McLuhan 1964, p. 80), most of those users—27 per cent—communicated in English, followed by 24 per cent in Chinese Mandarin and 8 per cent in Spanish (Miniwatts World Stats 2012b). Interestingly from an Australian media perspective, while Australia, New Zealand and the Pacific Islands had only slightly more than 1 per cent of the world's internet users in 2012, our penetration rate—the percentage of our population with internet access—was the second highest in the world at 68 per cent, behind the US and Canada, 79 per cent, and ahead of Europe, 61 per cent, in third place (Miniwatts World Stats 2012c).

One implication for today's beginning journalists is that those who will have the best chance of employment and forging impressive careers must become multi-skilled and feel as comfortable working for online news sites as for at least one 'traditional' media platform—print, radio or television. They should be able to write for the web and portable devices as well as for print, or radio, or television—but preferably all platforms. They should also be able to shoot good-quality news photographs, use sound recorders, and confidently capture video images. To give themselves the best possible chance of a long and satisfying career, they should be capable of doing a stand-up for television and online video, a live cross for radio, quickly writing a breaking news story for the web and then a story with a different, perhaps explanatory, angle for tomorrow's online or print newspaper. None of this is as difficult or daunting as you might imagine. That is because the basics of all news stories, how they are gathered and written, is the same.

Those students who future-proof themselves for work as journalists able to adapt and thrive in the years ahead will be those who develop solid understandings, skills and knowledge directly related to the profession of journalism while enriching that base with a broad liberal arts education. An overriding aim of this book is to help you meet those challenges. It is a book that, as Columbia University's journalism PhD program designer, the late Professor James Carey, so aptly put it, is written through the lens of journalism (in McKnight 2000, p. 17). The focus is on doing journalism and understanding why journalism is a profession whose members have special responsibilities to the community and in helping foster and protect democracy. Despite its critics, journalism is an honourable profession as old as democracy and as new as the most recent news story posted online. Its academic pedigree, or methodology, is shared with history, law and literature. Journalists really can, and do, trigger changes that improve the lives of individuals and have tangible community benefits. They should not wear their hearts on their sleeves, but in many senses they are a society's collective social conscience and watchdog. As well as reporting on current events, news media are also a forum for ideas and opinions, a source of information about things to buy and places to go, a diary, a warning notice and a record of events. They mirror society, reflecting it back to itself. And, as discussed later in these pages, journalists also have a special role in helping to hold those who should be accountable, accountable.

To meet their obligations to society, journalists must learn how to hunt, gather, write and disseminate information in ways clearly understood by the educated, uneducated, under-educated, and highly educated. They must have open and receptive minds, be wise in the ways of the world, be thoughtful, well educated, responsible, ethical and professional in their dealings with others. These were things one of the most remarkable journalists who ever lived spoke directly to his readers about. His name was Benjamin Franklin. His truly amazing contributions to journalism, democracy and society are discussed in Chapter 1 and the Epilogue; but suffice it to say here that in the October 2, 1729 edition of his *Pennsylvania Gazette* newspaper, Franklin wrote:

> to publish a good News-Paper is not so easy an Undertaking as many People imagine it to be. The Author of a Gazette (in the Opinion of the Learned) ought to be qualified with an extensive Acquaintance with Languages, a great Easiness and Command of Writing and Relating Things cleanly and intelligibly, and in few Words; he should be able to speak of War both by Land and Sea; be well acquainted with Geography, with the History of the Time, with the several Interests of Princes and States, the Secrets of Courts, and the Manners and Customs of all Nations. Men thus accomplish'd are very rare in this remote Part of the World; and it would be well if the Writer of these Papers could make up among his Friends what is wanting in himself. Upon the Whole, we may assure the Publick, that as far as the Encouragement we meet with will enable us, no Care and Pains shall be omitted, that may make the Pennsylvania Gazette as agreeable and useful an Entertainment as the Nature of the Thing will allow. (Franklin 1729)

What Franklin was getting at was that journalists need to draw on much more than a specific set of professional skills. As mentioned previously, they should be informed and enriched by what is known as a liberal arts education. His thoughts were echoed almost 200 years later by Albert Einstein when he said: 'The value of an education in a liberal arts college is not the learning of many facts but the training of the mind to think something that cannot be learned from textbooks' (Einstein in Frank 1947, p. 185). The College of Letters and Science at the University of California, Berkeley, offers a more contemporary and pragmatic explanation. It says:

> a broad-based liberal arts education does more than prepare you for a job. It lays the foundation for a future career ... You learn to think independently and make sound judgments. You expand your horizons, discover new perspectives, and acquire the tools

to defend your point of view. To be liberally educated is to be transformed. A liberal arts education frees your mind and helps you connect dots you never noticed before, so you can put your own field of study into a broader context. It enables you to form opinions and judgments, rather than defer to an outside authority. (College of Letters and Science 2009)

So, in addition to your professional journalistic studies, seize the opportunity to broaden your vision of the world. Use your time wisely during what for many people is a once-in-a-lifetime opportunity to experience university life. Absorb what you can about history, law, geography, philosophy, politics, science, business, economics, health and medicine, music, sport, art and culture. Above all, be curious, value learning, and learn how to learn. Then, for the rest of your life, and as you follow your dreams and mature professionally and personally, you will be equipped to keep learning what your life dictates you need to learn.

It is also important to understand from the start of your journalism studies that there is a great deal more to journalism than news reporting. Many who study journalism will not spend their working lives employed by news organisations. Some will move into different fields. Some who start their studies with a burning ambition to become print journalists will find themselves drawn more to radio or television. A few who aim for radio might find they prefer print or online. Yet others will study journalism in combination with second degrees in disciplines such as law, science, business, education or sport. Some will write books, others documentaries. But no matter which path you take, studying journalism and learning how to write news and feature articles will help you become a skilled harvester of facts, a disciplined and effective writer, an informed and ethical professional, and a person expert in communicating with others. You should learn to find the people and information you need and to write quickly and effectively for radio, television, print, online and mobile devices, take your own photographs, understand the basics of media law, develop a strong sense of ethics, appreciate the vital interconnections between journalism and democracy, and develop a broad general knowledge and compelling interest in news and current affairs. This book will help you achieve those goals.

THE HISTORY AND THEORY OF JOURNALISM

1

THE HISTORY OF JOURNALISM

Knowledge is power. Information is liberating. Education is the premise of progress, in every society, in every family.

Kofi Annan 1997

OBJECTIVES

After reading this chapter you will understand:

» Why we need news

» The role of journalism in society

» The importance of free speech and free media

» How journalism and democracy are linked

» Links between technology and journalism

» That we live in exciting times in the evolution of journalism.

Humans crave news—we are addicted to it. We are curious creatures with an urge to know what is happening next door, down the street, in our suburb or town, other parts of the state or territory we live in, nationally and internationally. We have an instinctive compulsion to hunt, gather and consume news. It is such a valuable tool in our fight for survival, food, shelter and in living, that journalists are sometimes killed to stop them collecting or reporting it. Yet news is intangible— almost impossible to define.

When you think about it, asking what is news is like asking what is art, what is air, what is life? It is at once concrete and abstract. Qualitative and quantitative. From primary sources and secondary. We get news from words, pictures, sounds, smells, taste, touch—anything that arouses our senses or emotions. Primarily, news happens when an event, action or circumstance has an impact, or likely impact, on people or their way of life. It is knowledge, rumours, discoveries, jokes, predictions, revelations and analysis. It is our brightest hopes and our worst fears. Yet, while news is difficult to define, it is a commodity. It is bought and sold, given freely, and often stolen. It helps us make sense of our world by developing our understandings, learning and intuition. It is spread by word of mouth, in newspapers, online, in magazines, via radio, television, computers, wi-fi and personal mobile devices. It inhabits our memories, guiding us and helping us navigate our daily lives. But, as discussed in Chapter 3, news is different things to different people at different times and in different places. What is important, perhaps life-changing, news for one person in one place at one time might be only of passing interest—if relevant at all—to someone else, somewhere else.

News happens when an event, action or circumstance has an impact, or likely impact, on people or their way of life.

So where, when and how did ideas about news originate? The earliest medium humans used to transmit news was touch, followed by the language of gestures and grunts. Then came primitive drawings and diagrams scratched on the ground, rocks and cave walls. As humans evolved news came to be transmitted by word of mouth and much later through written language. At first, news would have been shared information about problems and basic survival issues—where to find food, avoiding dangerous wild animals, lighting fires, identifying poisonous plants, where good water could be found and so on. Often there would have been news about rival tribes and groups—if there was a fight looming, perhaps who killed who and why. There would also have been an element of gossip—who was on with who, who made his wives go and dig in the gardens more often than other men's wives, who went to sleep under a tree when she was meant to be fishing, who was moving into a new, more upmarket cave with a better view! About 3400 BC, while word of mouth was still important, news started to be transmitted as handwritten hieroglyphic inscriptions in clay. Much later, first in China and later in Europe, came paper-making and a massive leap forward with the invention of printing, inks and moveable type. That meant news could be printed on handbills, pamphlets, then in 'news' papers. For the first time, many different people were able to access the same news stories, told in the same way by the same person—mass media, or more correctly McLuhan's media for the masses,[1] had arrived (McLuhan 1964, p. 348).

Journalism, democracy and technology

Journalism and democracy each evolved in Ancient Greece. The two grew to be inseparably linked. Similarly, although there have been growing pains at times, advances in communication technologies have been inevitably linked to advances

---

1   See Introduction for an explanation.

in journalism and news dissemination. Over time, governments—legislatures, executives and judiciaries—came to develop an ambivalent relationship with mass media. On one hand, politicians relied on news media to help them win re-election or maintain their hold on power by providing the governed with information about the popular and benevolent decisions of government. On the other, those in power came to fear media and its capacity to hold rulers accountable. It is therefore significant when we look back from our current era in the first decades of the 21st century, that there has never been any previous period in history in which advances in information technology have allowed ordinary people to be so well informed about those who govern them and the decisions of government. The advent of the internet, web and mobile technologies has revolutionised the world and shaken information managers to the core. In no other era has so much up-to-the-minute news and news analysis been at the fingertips of so many citizens. Never has there been such a significant upheaval in the dissemination of knowledge and such a focus on the workings of governments. It is an upheaval that is only in its infancy: there is more and better to come. But change, even when for the better, is not always embraced. In fact many individuals and institutions still try to hold back the tide and restrict the flow of news and information. Some—such as the Taliban, which sought to outlaw internet access in Afghanistan, or the Communist governments in China and North Korea, which seek to shelter their people from learning about what they consider to be the evils of democracy—have struggled desperately to block or control internet access, censor the web and impede freedom of speech on social networking platforms. In that context it is instructive to reflect on the words of former United Nations Secretary-General and winner of the 2001 Nobel Peace Prize Kofi Annan when he said:

> … it is ignorance, not knowledge, that makes enemies of men. It is ignorance, not knowledge, that makes fighters of children. It is ignorance, not knowledge, that leads some to advocate tyranny over democracy. It is ignorance, not knowledge, that makes some think that human misery is inevitable. It is ignorance, not knowledge, that makes others say that there are many worlds, when we know that there is one. Ours (Annan 1997).

To understand the enormity of the upheaval still-evolving digital communication technologies have caused, and will continue to cause, in the realms of politics, journalism and news dissemination, it helps to view the current era from a historical perspective because, as one of Australia's most formidable investigative journalists, Bob Bottom (2005), said, 'the past conditions the future'.

Journalism and history intersect

It is generally accepted[2] that the first journalist was an Ancient Greek historian called Thucydides. He was born around 400 BC in Athens, a city that became the birthplace of a form of direct democracy in the fifth century. However, Thucydides and the great philosophers Plato and Aristotle were critics of early Athenian democracy. They thought it was not democratic enough because it was cumbersome, with those who were eligible to vote having to actually attend meetings of the governing assembly to cast their ballots. For the system to work effectively, voters needed to be well informed about current affairs and have a good grasp of relevant issues. But disseminating news and commentary about affairs of state was difficult. Printing had not been invented and all documents had to be handwritten and copied. One way people such as Thucydides worked around that problem was by writing speeches which they either delivered themselves to mass audiences or which were delivered by other orators. Over time, however, democratic rule evolved and changed. The system of direct voting, which had been criticised by Thucydides as 'the severest form of mob rule' (Richard 2003, p. 86), was replaced by systems of representative democracy in which a group of leaders who put themselves forward as 'the best' was elected to govern and make decisions on behalf of all people. One key element which allowed that evolution to take place was the spread of political information to citizens and the handing down of ideals and principles from one generation to the next. That dissemination of information and its handing down to later generations is where journalism and history intersect.

As well as being the first true journalist Thucydides is also regarded as the first true historian. This is significant because there are still close ties between journalism and history, particularly (as explained in Chapter 2) between the evolution of each as academic disciplines.

It is therefore significant that as well as being thought of by many as the first true journalist, Thucydides is also regarded as the first true historian (Richard 2003, p. 86). That link is notable because there are still close ties between journalism and history, particularly (as explained in Chapter 2) between the evolution of each as academic disciplines. As Windschuttle (1999) said:

> The origins of journalism lie in exactly the same place as the origins of history. The first true historian is widely acknowledged as Thucydides, the Athenian who wrote *The History of the Peloponnesian War* some time between 424 and 400 BC … This is all first-hand observation and, to my mind, there is no doubt it is journalism. In short, as well as the first

---

2   Although not by US media historian Mitchell Stephens (1997, p. 48)

historian, Thucydides should be recognised as the first journalist... (Windschuttle 1999, pp. 52, 54).

Much of *The History of the Peloponnesian War* is a running commentary on the course of the war as it unfolded. Thucydides described his methods as follows:

> with regard to my factual reporting of events of the war, I have made it a principle not to write down the first story that came my way, and not even to be guided by my own general impressions: either I was present myself at the events which I have described or else I have heard of them from eye-witnesses whose reports I have checked with as much thoroughness as possible. Not that even so the truth was easy to discover: different eye-witnesses give different accounts of the same events, speaking out of partiality for one side or the other or else from imperfect memories (Thucydides 1972, p. 48; also in Windschuttle 1999).

Thucydides was clearly seeking truth and doing his best to write fair, accurate and balanced reports. As de Burgh said, 'It is often said that journalism is the first rough draft of history ...' (de Burgh 2000, p. 3). Similarly, Startt and Sloan could have been referring to journalism when they said 'historical study contains at least three elements: (a) evidence, (b) interpretation, and (c) narrative' (Startt & Sloan 1989, p. 2). But, as noted previously, printing had not been invented—and neither had paper—so Thucydides could not circulate his handwritten reports to the masses.

It was to be about 1000 years before that problem was resolved. The invention of printing and moveable type happened first in China. It led to the earliest mass printing of documents in the period from 600 to 700 AD. From about 600 AD, China became the most advanced nation on earth. It gave the world paper, ink and printing—three essential ingredients in the development of newspapers— hundreds of years before similar technology appeared in Europe. In fact the first newspapers, which were just a single page, were published in China during the Tang dynasty, from 618 to 907 AD. A thousand years later, the Worcester Society of Antiquity reported:

> The Chinese, who were the earliest printers, issued the first newspaper printed. It was in the form of an Official Gazette, giving the political news, government changes, series of events and items of general public interest, and was continued for centuries (Worcester Society of Antiquity 1908).

Those first 'news' papers were printed with symbols carved into wooden blocks. Later, the wood was replaced with ceramics. Incongruous as it may seem today when news is so heavily censored in China, that nation was actually upheld for centuries as the model of a free press and freedom of speech, being described in 1766 by leading Finnish/Swedish scholar[3] Anders Chydenius as 'the richest kingdom in the world in population and goods' and 'the model country of the freedom of press' (in Lamble 2002). In essence, China was a benevolent dictatorship. It was governed by a succession of ruling monarchs or emperors, at least some of whom could be seen to parallel the philosophical ideals of Thucydides, Plato and Aristotle in their belief in a system of government based on 'rule by the best' in the interests of the people.

In the same era printing was invented, Chinese inventors also gave the world gunpowder, spinning wheels for making yarn, the magnetic compass, the abacus, suspension bridges, specialised ship-building techniques, cast iron, the toothbrush and toothpaste, silk, rice, printed books and tea. In his book *A Short History of the World*, eminent Australian historian Professor Geoffrey Blainey says paper came to be regarded as such a valued commodity that in 751 AD several Chinese papermakers were kidnapped and taken to central Asia, where they were forced to reveal their secret techniques (Blainey 2000, p. 284). Previously, writing had been preserved on parchment, which was made from animal skins, and Blainey estimated that a book of 200 handwritten pages 'might consume the skins of about 80 lambs' (Blainey 2000, p. 285).

Once the secret of paper-making was revealed, the process made its way to the Middle East and then Europe. In 1456 Johann Gutenberg[4] 'invented' a printing press with moveable type in Germany. Originally it was only used to print the Bible. That was partly because, just as the web and the internet are feared today by repressive rulers, printing was then regarded with deep suspicion and was closely regulated by governments. They feared it could be used as a tool to educate and inform the masses, thus leading to discontent, questioning of authority and civil unrest.

Over time, however, printing presses proliferated and technology improved. Governments were unable to restrain progress and presses were used to print many different kinds of books. Stationery was also printed, as were pamphlets and handbills. Many who wrote pamphlets were printers or would-be politicians. Gradually their pamphlets evolved, with some being published regularly and circulated among a growing proportion of the population who had learnt, or were learning, to read. Some pamphlets evolved into 'news-sheets' and

---

3   Finland was a part of the Swedish realm at that time.
4   Whose real name was Johann Gensfleisch

then 'news-papers'—literally, printed papers that carried news. The World Association of Newspapers (2005) said the first real newspaper, *Relation*, was printed in 1605 in Strasbourg by Johann Carolus, a writer who purchased a print-shop in 1604. The Worcester Society of Antiquity (1908) had a different interpretation. It said:

> The Germans are said to have been the first in Europe to issue a news-sheet, in the year 1563; their first issue in numbered sheets appeared in 1612. The first French paper was published in 1632. The first regularly published English newspaper appeared in London issued by Nathaniel Butter in 1622, a small weekly quarto of eighteen pages. It was called *Certain News of the Present Week*.

Most early newspapers were short-lived. Printing and paper were expensive, printers had yet to find ways to recover costs, and relatively few people could read. Journalism was also a risky business. Those in power did not welcome criticism or scrutiny—something British printer and pamphleteer John Gwyn discovered. He met a fate literally worse than death in 1663 after upsetting authorities. Described as 'a poor man, with a wife and three children', Gwyn was accused of printing an article criticising the conduct of government and magistrates (Thayer 1897, p. 152). Found guilty of threatening King Charles II, Gwyn was sentenced to be 'drawn to the place of execution upon a hurdle, and there hanged by the neck'. While still alive he was to be 'cut down, castrated, and disembowelled. And you still living … your entrails are to be burnt before your eyes, your head to be cut off, and your head and quarters to be disposed of at the pleasure of the king's majesty' (Thayer 1897, p. 153). Despite a plea for mercy, Gwyn was executed in accord with his sentence. His head and limbs were suspended over the gates of London as a warning to others.

Another English writer who fell foul of the rich and powerful was London bookseller Benjamin Harris, a pamphleteer who published a newspaper in 1679. Around the same time as his first newspaper hit the streets, Harris wrote a seditious pamphlet openly critical of the king and his connections with a supposed 'popish plot' (Ingelhart 1998, p. 71). Arrested and tried before Chief Justice Scroggs, who convicted and fined him, Harris did not have money to pay the fine. He was jailed, but later released because of a legal technicality. Bravely or foolishly, he then published a new pamphlet, this time criticising Scroggs. Arrested and charged again, Harris was described by Scroggs as 'a wretch who would set us all by the ears for a groat'[5] (Mott 1962, p. 9). This time, Harris was put in a pillory in front of his own office, where his friends prevented bystanders hurling rubbish at him. After being released, Harris gathered his wife, children and a collection of books and sailed to Boston. There, on September 25, 1690, he began what some consider was the Americas' earliest newspaper, *Publick Occurrences, Both Foreign and Domestick*. It was banned after its first issue. Harris then turned to publishing almanacs and other informative books. He returned to London about eight years later, published another newspaper, 'declined in wealth and fame', and turned to selling patent medicines (Mott 1962, p. 10).

The evolution of newspapers

Through the 17th and well into the 18th centuries, printing and education were regarded with equal suspicion by many in authority. For example, in the then British colony of Virginia, Sir William Berkley, the Colonial Governor for what must have been 38 long and dreary years, wrote a report to his superiors in Britain in 1671 in which he said:

> I thank God, we do not have free schools nor printing; and I hope we shall not have them these hundred years. For learning has brought disobedience and heresy and sects into the world; and printing has divulged them and libels against the government. God keep us from both (Mott 1962, p. 6).

Even Daniel Defoe, one of the most notable writers of his time and the person regarded by many as the father of English journalism, was punished by the courts as a result of his writing. A prolific writer probably best known as the author of the classic novels *Moll Flanders* and *Robinson Crusoe*, Defoe was also a pamphleteer. From 1704 to 1713 he published a pamphlet that came to resemble a newspaper. Originally a weekly, the paper later appeared three times a week, and although its main focus was on politics, it also included entertainment-orientated articles. But, like Harris before him, Defoe was literally pilloried for his writing. He was also jailed twice because he wrote articles that offended the government, and he was twice convicted of libel—written defamation.

---

5   A silver coin

But the journalism genie was out of the bottle. Printers and writers started winning converts in their quest for free speech and freedom of the press as an increasing number of newspapers appeared on the streets. In the US, the first continuously published newspapers were *The Boston News-Letter*, which was established on April 24, 1704; *The Boston Gazette*, established on December 21, 1719; *The American Weekly Mercury*, which appeared in Philadelphia on December 22, 1719; and *The New England Courant*, which was launched by James Franklin—an elder brother of Benjamin Franklin—in Boston on August 21, 1721 (Thayer 1897, p. 98). Writing about establishment of *The New England Courant*, which Benjamin Franklin later edited while still only a teenager, his biographer WM Thayer said:

> There was not a little commotion when James Franklin launched *The New England Courant*. It was regarded generally as a wild project. It was not thought that three newspapers could live in America. The field was not large enough (Thayer 1897, p. 98).

However *The New England Courant* thrived for a time, partly because the newspaper was cheeky and brash, often taking a swipe at those in authority. But trouble was looming for the Franklin brothers. In the early 1700s colonial newspapers were published 'by authority' of the British-controlled colonial government. James Franklin was a printer who had learnt his trade in England. Coincidentally or otherwise, he followed in the footsteps of Benjamin Harris and Daniel Defoe and offended the government of the Colony of Massachusetts Bay. He did so by publishing a letter ridiculing the government's 'dilatoriness' in dealing with pirates who were playing havoc with shipping. James and Benjamin, who was James's apprentice, were summoned to appear before the Legislative Council. Members of the legislature were determined to find out who wrote the letter, but James refused to tell. He was threatened with jail. He again refused, saying he was determined to defend the freedom of the press. He was convicted on the spot of 'a high affront to the Government', seized by the sheriff, and taken to Boston jail (Thayer 1897, pp. 148 & 149).

The New England Courant had supported moves for the North American colonies to break free from Britain, and it maintained that stance after James was jailed and Benjamin—then just 15—took over as editor. The jailing of James, who was released after four weeks, created great consternation in the colony and widened the rift between the colonial population and its British rulers. It was a rift James fuelled even further after his release from jail. He stepped up his attacks, particularly taking aim at the British Governor and members of the legislature who had voted to lock him up. Exasperated, the parliament passed a law forbidding James from publishing any more newspapers or pamphlets. That might have been the end of *The New England Courant* but the newspaper was popular. Benjamin, who had turned 16, was again appointed editor, and publication resumed under his name. Sadly however, while the fight for press freedom continued, and despite Benjamin's key role at the paper, he was bullied and mistreated by James. Forced to work 12 to 15 hour days, Benjamin was also physically beaten by his brother. Finally, in 1723, after eight months as editor, and at the age of 17, Benjamin ran away. He sailed to London and continued his own training as a printer. James never edited the *Courant* again in his own name. The paper closed in 1726 and James, too, left Boston—moving to Newport where he established the *Rhode Island Gazette*.

In 1726 Benjamin returned to the US. He went to Philadelphia, and in 1728 opened his own printing business. A year later he became sole owner and publisher of the *Pennsylvania Gazette* newspaper. As editor, he implemented three new policies. First, he dramatically improved editorial content, giving readers something to whet their appetites and make them want to buy the next edition. In doing so he adopted a snappy, simple and direct style of writing and reporting. Second, he became a pioneer of the idea of paid newspaper advertising. This was an extremely significant development and led to newspapers becoming profitable business enterprises. Franklin had realised that news and business could go hand in hand—that well-researched and well-written news, feature articles and informed comment made a newspaper popular, and if a paper was popular and circulated widely, businesses and individuals would pay to advertise in it. Third, he implemented a broad, largely non-judgmental, non-interventionist policy of editorial impartiality. This policy was clearly articulated in an editorial column in the *Pennsylvania Gazette* in 1731 titled 'An Apology for Printers'. Like Franklin, most early printers of newspapers were also journalists. The 'apology' was a defence of journalistic freedom as relevant today as it was then, in which Franklin wrote, in part:

> If all Printers were determin'd not to print any thing till they were sure it would offend no body, there would be very little printed… [and] Printers are educated in the Belief, that when Men differ in Opinion, both Sides ought equally to have the Advantage of being heard by the Publick; and that when Truth and Error have fair Play, the former is always an overmatch for the latter (Franklin 1731).

Franklin built his newspaper and printing business into highly profitable enterprises. He 'sold' them in 1748 but remained a silent partner in the printing business—something which provided him with an income for the next 18 years as he devoted himself to affairs of state.

In the meantime, pressure for press freedom and freedom of speech had mounted in Europe. One of the most influential advocates for those freedoms was a remarkable Finn called Anders Chydenius. An extraordinary person, who coincidentally shared many interests with Franklin, Chydenius became a medical doctor, among other things developing a vaccine to inoculate people against smallpox. He also performed cataract surgery. Medical practice aside, Chydenius was also a politician, economist, historian, Lutheran clergyman, writer and pamphleteer. He studied China and its system of newspaper publication and press freedom and, in 1765, wrote a pamphlet that said, in part:

> No proof should be necessary that a modicum of freedom for writing and printing is one of the strongest pillars of support for free government, for in the absence of such... learning and good manners would be suppressed, coarseness in thought, speech and customs would flourish, and a sinister gloom would within a few years darken our entire sky of freedom (Chydenius 1765).

A year later, Chydenius persuaded the Swedish and Finnish parliament, or Diet as it was then called, to pass a new law, the *Freedom-of-Press and the Right-of-Access to Public Records Act*. The legislation specifically aimed to create an open society and was framed in such a way that it became embedded in the Swedish Constitution. Today, a variation of the same law, the *Freedom of the Press Act*, remains in force as one of Sweden's four 'fundamental laws'. It guarantees freedom of speech, media freedom and freedom of access to government information.

Back in the US, Benjamin Franklin had become an influential leader in the push for independence from Britain and a member of the General Assembly of Pennsylvania. In 1776 he was one of the signatories of the American Declaration of Independence—a document he helped draft. In 1782 he helped negotiate the peace treaty that ended the War of Independence. In 1787, just three years before he died, he became a delegate to the Constitutional Convention which led to the creation of the US Federal Constitution—a document Franklin also had a hand in drafting, along with James Madison, George Washington and others. Two years later, in 1789, the US Congress ratified 10 amendments to the Constitution, and these amendments became known as the Bill of Rights. The first of those amendments protects the rights of free speech, free assembly, freedom of religion and press freedom. It says:

> Congress shall make no law respecting an establishment of religion, or prohibiting the free exercise thereof; or abridging the freedom of speech, or of the press; or the right of the people peaceably to assemble, and to petition the Government for a redress of grievances (US Constitution).

Thus, in a period of just 23 years, two remarkable individuals in two different continents—Europe and North America—who spoke different languages and had been educated in different ways, helped embed notions of freedom of speech and media freedom deep into the constitutions of their respective nations.

No guarantee of media freedom in Australia

Australians do not have a guarantee of media freedom, nor even a right to free speech embedded in our Constitution. There is little to stop our state and federal governments tinkering with media regulation and censorship laws.

Australia had neither an Anders Chydenius nor a Benjamin Franklin. We do not have a guarantee of media freedom, nor even a right to free speech embedded in our Constitution. There is little to stop our state and federal governments tinkering with media regulation and censorship laws. Writing in 1990 in his book *Sense and Censorship: Commentaries on Censorship Violence in Australia*, journalist, author and social commentator Michael Pollak lamented the fact that: 'The subjugation of thought in Australia through stringent censorship and draconian defamation laws has existed throughout the 200 years of white settlement ...' (Pollak 1990, p. 7).

Perhaps one reason we lack a guarantee of media freedom in Australia stems from our beginnings as a convict colony. Convicts had few rights or freedoms. Many were illiterate and only a handful would have had money to spend on luxuries like newspapers. It is hardly surprising then that although a printing press arrived with the First Fleet in 1788 it was not used to print newspapers. Instead, news was recorded on 'pipes': handwritten sheets that contained critical comment and were circulated from person to person throughout the colony of New South Wales. It was not until March 1803 that our first newspaper, the *Sydney Gazette and New South Wales Advertiser*, was published. At the time Sydney had a population of about 7000, but only 1000 were free citizens (Kirkpatrick 2003). The paper was 'published by authority' by the government printer, who was a convict named George Howe. Prior to being transported after a conviction for shoplifting, Howe had trained as a printer and worked on *The Times* and other English newspapers (Byrnes 1966, pp. 557–9).

The *Sydney Gazette* was heavily censored and mainly published government notices. By 1831 it was printed in three editions a week, but publication was suspended between August 30, 1807 and May 15, 1808 as a result of a dispute between the infamous Governor William Bligh and some of his enemies (Byrnes 1966, pp. 557–9). In 1824, restrictions on newspaper publication were lifted and the *Sydney Gazette* faced its first competitor with publication of *The Australian*, a newspaper not related to today's paper of the same name. Newspaper historian Rod Kirkpatrick (2003) said the first Tasmanian newspaper appeared in Hobart in 1810. *The Perth Gazette and West Australian Journal* was launched in 1833 and became the *West Australian* in 1877. The first paper in South Australia, the *South Australian Gazette and Colonial Register*, was actually printed in London in 1836 and shipped to Australia. Its editor and part-owner subsequently emigrated to Adelaide in 1837, where he printed the second and following editions of the newspaper in 'its own country' (Kirkpatrick 2003, p. 33). The handwritten *Melbourne Advertiser* arrived in 1838. *The Port Phillip Patriot and Melbourne Advertiser*, Victoria's first daily, was published in 1839. The *Sydney Morning Herald*, Australia's oldest surviving newspaper and its oldest daily, first appeared as a daily in 1840; the *Moreton Bay Courier*—the forerunner to Queensland's *The Courier-Mail*—in 1846; and Melbourne's *The Age* in 1854, by which time it was that city's third daily newspaper.

By 1860 Australia had more than 50 newspapers, although Mayer said the effective number at any one time was only about 12 because many of the new publications were 'ephemeral' (Mayer 1968, p. 10). One paper that became far from ephemeral was *The Ballarat Times, Buninyong and Creswick Advertiser*. Launched in March 1854 by Henry Seekamp—an Englishman who said he had an 'Arts Bachelor' degree when he emigrated to Victoria from Britain in 1852 (Seekamp n.d.)—and his Irish actress wife Clara, the newspaper was later accused of helping incite an uprising that was the nearest Australia ever came to a war of independence: the bloody rebellion against British colonial authorities at the Eureka Stockade, Ballarat, in December 1854.

The short-lived but bloody insurrection happened because gold miners were fed up with the colony's autocratic government and its decision to increase the tax on their licences to dig for gold. With the start of the Australian gold rush in 1851, three years after a similar rush began in California, thousands of Australian miners who had sailed to the US to dig for gold returned to their 'own valleys and creeks with new eyes' (Blainey 1980, p. 156). While in the US they had experienced life in a society which was no longer ruled from Britain by an oppressive colonial regime, but was controlled by a democratically elected federal government. They had worked beside people from many different nations and walks of life. In particular, they mixed with Americans who took it for granted that there was a free press, and that citizens had a right to bear arms. As noted previously, thanks to the efforts of people like Benjamin Franklin, the US had become a nation in which rights of free speech, petition and assembly were constitutionally guaranteed. Miners who subsequently returned to Australia from the US with the idea of finding a fortune in gold found British colonial rule and the lack of rights and freedoms stifling. That contrast, and the arrogance of petty officials—many of whom were former convicts employed by an unelected colonial government—contributed to the frustrations which erupted at Eureka.

Henry Seekamp—described as 'a dapper little man with a fierce temper'—was a former gold miner. He used his position as editor of *The Ballarat Times, Buninyong and Creswick Advertiser* to become 'a forceful advocate of reform' of the goldfields administration and a proponent of votes for diggers (Beggs Sunter 2005, pp. 335–6). Within months of establishing the newspaper, Seekamp became a foundation member of the Ballarat Reform League, a miners' group that called a public meeting attended by 10,000 people at Bakery Hill, Ballarat on November 11, 1854 (Clark 1962, p. 58). Among other things, the meeting resolved: 'That it is the inalienable right of every citizen to have a voice in making the laws he is called to obey. That taxation without representation is tyranny' (Clark 1962, p. 58). More public meetings were held. On November 30 a meeting erupted into a riot. Shots were exchanged between diggers and military—although no one was hurt—and the *Riot Act* was read to the diggers (Clark 1962, p. 60). The miners set up a stockade. Authorities called in two regiments of troops and 'two howitzers'. Early on the morning of December 4, the troops—redcoats—attacked the stockade (Clark 1962, p. 60). More than 30 miners, redcoats and police were killed. Pollak (1990) said government officials later 'snuffed out much of the comment relating to the incident'.

After the uprising, Victoria's then Governor, the unpopular Sir Charles Hotham, ordered Seekamp's arrest on a charge of insurrection because of the editorials he had written in support of the miners. Pollak said: 'Seekamp's "crime" was that he had urged citizens to mount a "vengeance deep and terrible" in retaliation against the "foul massacre" of innocent lives at Eureka' (Pollak 1990, p. 7). It is noteworthy that of the 13 people arrested and charged in the days after the uprising, Seekamp was the only one convicted. Found guilty of 'seditious libel', he served three months of a six-month jail sentence.

While Australia no longer has a colonial government and, as discussed in Chapter 14, we are supposedly a democratic federation of states and territories, journalists are still sometimes jailed and governments—especially those which fear criticism or are unpopular—meddle with media regulation. The reasons why are discussed in Chapters 15, 16 and 17. In summary though, our news media are more heavily restrained by our government and legal systems than media in many other nations.

Technology helps news travel further and faster

Consider the fact that 'the American Declaration of Independence was not reported in England until more than six weeks after the event' (Quinn & Lamble 2008, p. 9). Compare that time-lag with how quickly we can use mobile devices today and literally see news in the making as breaking stories are reported while they unfold, often with sound, photos and video.

US physicists Bill Brinkman and Dave Lang from Bell Laboratories said the foundations of communication technology lay in the discoveries of the first electromagnet in 1825, and independent discoveries in 1831 by Michael Faraday and Joseph Henry that electric current could be induced in wires moving in a magnetic field. In turn, that led to the invention of a telegraph system by Samuel Morse in 1837. By 1861, Western Union had built a transcontinental telegraph line that crossed the US. The first successful trans-Atlantic telegraph cable was laid in 1866 (Brinkman & Lang 1999, p. 2). Blainey said that by 1876 overland and undersea telegraph lines had connected nearly all the main cities of Asia, Africa and South America (Blainey 2000, p. 480), and:

> Nothing so far in the history of the world had done as much to unite all lands as this slender thread of wire crossing steppes and plains, jungles and icy valleys, factory suburbs and mountain villages, and the very bed of the sea (Blainey 2000, p. 482).

In Australia, Melbourne, Sydney, Adelaide and Tasmania were all connected by telegraph lines by 1860 but the southern network was self-contained. News could be sent from city to city within the network but ships were the only carriers of news from overseas. Sea transport was slow and it commonly took up to five months for news from Europe to reach Australia. It was not until October 1872 that the nation was first linked to other parts of the globe by a submarine telegraph cable. It came ashore at Darwin, but completion of the undersea link was only half the story. The other half was construction of the Overland Telegraph. In a remarkable engineering and logistical feat of enormous national significance, the 3000 km line was strung on 360,000 poles snaking south through the Outback from Darwin down to Port Augusta in South Australia. Work on the project had been started in 1870 and was completed in two years. At the heart of the system were 11 repeater stations dotted along the line at 200 to 300 km intervals. It was impossible for a telegraph signal to travel more than that distance, so every message was received at each remote station, then tapped out again in Morse-code and sent on to the next station. In many ways the telegraph operators, their wives and children shared much with isolated light-house keepers and their families. Stations were manned around the clock and telegraph operators worked in shifts because messages were constantly going up and down the line. Thanks in part to the work and dedication of the operators, a message sent from Adelaide would arrive in England only seven hours later—something of a miracle compared with the months it took ships to carry mail and news. And like most technology, there were constant improvements with Blainey noting that by the 1880s 'news was occasionally relayed across the world in less than two hours' (Blainey 1982, pp. 223 & 224).

The undersea cable and Overland Telegraph forever changed journalism in Australia (and later in New Zealand, after a cable was laid under the Tasman Sea). Access to the international telegraph network meant at least as much in its day as access to the internet, web, mobile devices and global satellite communication mean today. Newspaper reporting was brought into line with developments in Europe and North America. In his classic history book *The Tyranny of Distance*, Blainey explained the impact of the new technology on reporting thus:

> The main job of Australian newsmen had always been the boarding of incoming ships and the collecting of the latest English newspapers… however, the submarine cable replaced incoming steamers as the fastest carrier of news. In Australian cities, telegraph offices replaced the waterfront as the receiving centre for world news (Blainey 1982, p. 222).

Canadian media academic Marshall McLuhan said growth of the telegraph network marked the start of a new era which unchained news media. He said that in the UK, 'The telegraph freed the marginal provincial press from dependence on the big metropolitan press' (McLuhan 1964, p. 225). Further:

> By 1848 the telegraph, then only four years old, compelled several major American newspapers to form a collective organisation for newsgathering. This effort became the basis of the Associated Press, which, in turn, sold news service to subscribers (McLuhan 1964, p. 224).

What McLuhan was talking about was the first step towards development of what we know today as newswire services such as Australian Associated Press (AAP), which aggregate news and feed it to publishers and broadcasters. Apart from the telegraph, greater literacy and improvements in printing technology also contributed to the development of mass media in Australia, the UK and the US during the second half of the 19th century. Then came the telephone. It was patented in 1876 by US inventor Alexander Graham Bell, but voice transmission over long distances was complex and difficult at first. It was not until 1976 that Australians living in capital cities could directly dial overseas telephone numbers. In the 1970s and '80s, fax machines came into widespread use. Coincidentally, about the same time as Australians were getting used to the idea of direct dialling their international calls, a US college dropout called Steven Jobs, then just 21, and a friend, Steven Wozniak, 26, founded the Apple Computer Company in the Jobs' family garage. In 1977 the pair started selling the world's first mass-marketed personal computer. By 1980, both were millionaires. In 1981 IBM made its first PCs. Mobile telephones were invented in 1983, but were expensive and resembled a brick in a bag so at first they were more a curiosity than a necessity. Although the first email was sent in 1971, it was not until 1993 that email became available to the public. Internet service provider America Online (AOL) had its first customer in 1985. The world wide web was created in 1990 and the first Yahoo! search occurred in 1995.

Without these developments, the current era of news production and almost instant dissemination would not exist. There would be no Information Age or Communication Revolution, no internet, no web, no smart-phones nor tablet computers, no online news and no social networking. If it had not been for the invention of the electromagnet, followed by the telegraph, the evolution of the telephone, the invention and laying of trans-oceanic submarine cables, manual then automatic switching in telephone exchanges, concepts of digital encoding developed by Morse, the invention of the vacuum tube and its replacement with the silicon chip transistor, the invention of coaxial cables, microwave links, satellite repeaters and fibre-optic cables—to list just a fraction of the relevant technology—it would be impossible for today's journalists to connect to the web, to send and receive emails or SMS messages, search and research online, or for news organisations to publish online and to mobile devices. The implications for present generations of journalists of digital technology are enormous. Technology has given journalists an ability to circumvent political restrictions and new weapons to use in the continuing battle for greater media freedom and freedom of speech. It has enabled and empowered them to gather and report news as it happens, and for the public to access that news on demand.

DISCUSSION POINTS

1   How important is it for today's journalists to know about the history of journalism? Why?

2   Should Australian news media be as free to report, discuss and criticise as media in the US and Sweden? Why?

3   If US media are so free and that nation has such great guarantees of freedom of speech, why are US newspapers so boring?

4   Are today's bloggers the equivalent of what early pamphleteers were to journalism and the dissemination of news, or are they all just self-opinionated ratbags and ego freaks? Why?

5   Newspaper circulations in many parts of the world are falling and papers have closed. What are the key reasons why?

6   Where is information technology heading and what impact will that have on journalists and news dissemination?

7   Are online news publishers really going to help bring democracy and freedom to totalitarian regimes such as those in China, Afghanistan and North Korea, or will they just cause trouble by making people yearn for things they cannot attain?

NEWS PRACTICE POINTS

1 This chapter has touched on how Benjamin Franklin, Anders Chydenius and others created a legacy of media freedom and free speech. Make a list of six other people who are not named in this chapter, including at least one Australian, who helped create that legacy. Under each name write a sentence or two explaining what she or he did.

2 In Australia, those who oppose the introduction of a Bill of Rights argue that it would put too much power in the hands of judges as opposed to elected members of parliament. Is that argument valid? Why or why not?

3 What happened to destroy media freedom and freedom of speech in China? Explain in no more than 350 words.

4 Australia and the US originally inherited their media laws from the UK. How free are media in the UK today?

5 Find an online copy of Benjamin Franklin's 'An Apology for Printers'. Read it, discover the context it was printed in, and then discuss: a) the document's relevance today, and b) whether you think Franklin's opinions as expressed in the document were purely altruistic or whether he had a commercial motive.

6 Benjamin Franklin is credited with being one of the first newspaper owners to use advertising revenue to pay for the production of news. But ever since news has been published online, that recipe has started to fail. Other than charging for content, what can you find out about alternative revenue models for financing online news?

7 *The Ballarat Times, Buninyong and Creswick Advertiser*'s editor Henry Seekamp was charged with insurrection after the Eureka Stockade uprising. Have any other Australian news editors faced similar charges? If so, who?

8 Who—other than journalists, news media and industry bodies such as the Australian Press Council—are concerned about media freedom and freedom of speech in Australia? How effective are they?

2

THE METHODOLOGY
OF JOURNALISM

Covering the news is an infinite, impossible task. News is therefore an exercise
in imperfection, the product of a series of compromises
Tiffen 1989, p. 28

OBJECTIVES

After reading this chapter you will understand:

» Journalism as an academic discipline

» The role and place of journalism in society

» Journalism as a quest for truth

» Differences between reactive and proactive journalism

» Links between journalism, law and history

» The distinction between studying journalism and doing journalism.

Journalism as a university discipline has been described as 'a hybrid, interdisciplinary mix of the humanities and the social sciences'—partly professional in outlook and partly academic—straddling theory and practice (Reece 1999, p. 72). Much the same can be said of other professionally oriented disciplines. Medicine, for example, involves a blend of sciences, humanities and social sciences. It, too, straddles theory and practice. Engineering is based on a similar mix. Law and teaching also draw on humanities and social sciences and combine theory and practice. Yet, despite the parallels, only the brave or foolish would ask an engineer to excise a brain tumour or deliver a baby, or a medical doctor to design a bridge or build a ship! Most academic professional preparation programs and the vocations they inform are distinctive. Each has its own skillset, knowledge base, understandings and methods—its own 'pedigree', or, in academic jargon, its specific 'methodology'.

The word 'methodology' can be a little confusing. It sounds like the word 'method' but actually means something much more. It is an intellectual concept that should not be confused with words such as 'theory', 'argument' and 'method'. US journalism academic Margaret DeFleur explained the concept of methodology. She wrote:

> Developing a methodology… requires that the steps used in selecting and studying a problem be described and that justifications for using particular approaches be explained (DeFleur 1997, p. 212).

Quoting respected US philosopher and methodological researcher Abraham Kaplan, DeFleur continued:

> Kaplan summarised these points in this way: 'The word "methodology"… is one which is used for a certain discipline and for its subject matter. I mean by methodology the study—the description, the explanation, and the justification—of methods, and not the methods themselves' (DeFleur 1997, p. 212).

What Kaplan meant is that every discipline field has its own trademark methodology or 'brand'. For example, just as medicine and engineering have their explicit methodologies so do teaching, history, law, geography, economics and mathematics. Each methodology is a discipline-specific umbrella under which can be found a set of beliefs, concepts, ideals, methods, knowledge, skills and theories which in combination define a discipline and make it different from others. Understanding a little about the academic methodology of journalism helps us enhance our understandings of the profession and its place in society. It should also provide insights into the ways in which journalism is taught and studied.

As a starting point, it is helpful to understand that when those who work as journalists talk about research they are referring to the methods and techniques discussed in Chapter 6—things like interviewing participants and witnesses, finding documents, checking facts, finding statistics, quoting experts and so on. But when academics talk about research, they are speaking about methodology and research methods. Despite the differences in terms, however, both actually work in much the same way. There are many parallels between the methods of journalistic research that inform news stories, particularly investigative stories, and academic research. One hallmark of academic research is that findings must be described and presented (usually in writing) in such a way that they can be replicated and validated by others. Similarly, journalists should be able to demonstrate that researched facts supporting a particular story and their accurate representation in articles can be verified and justified—in a law court if necessary. Thus quests for true information that satisfies precise standards of proof, an accurate presentation of those facts in writing, and an ability to turn back if necessary to retrace past steps in order to replicate research outcomes are common threads woven into the fabrics of sound journalistic research and good academic research.

Another reason why it is important for journalists to understand at least the basics of academic research jargon is because many academics are experts in their fields and are therefore often quoted by journalists who have sought expert opinion. Self-preservation also makes it useful for journalism practitioners to understand a little about how journalism research works in academia. Further, discussed in greater detail in Chapter 4, which examines journalism ethics, professional journalists should be able to speak with authority about the purposes and practices of journalism. Just as a doctor, lawyer, architect or teacher should understand the underpinnings of his or her profession, journalists must be able to defend their profession from attack by ordinary citizens, politicians, business interests, hostile academics, lawyers and others—particularly those who fear, or do not understand, news media. Some of those individuals set themselves up as self-proclaimed media 'experts'. The worst of them make assumptions about and comment on journalistic outputs but do not actually know much about journalism, news-gathering and reporting. As respected US journalism scholar Professor James Carey said when referring to attacks on journalism by academics from another discipline field:

> Most social science studies of journalism—and they are studies *of* journalism; that is, they are conducted from the outside rather than from within—are seen through the lens of social science, not through the lens of journalism (Carey, in McKnight 2000, p. 17).

And:

> For me the question is: How do you study it [journalism] in a way which is both intellectually sound and scholarly and yet at the same time that attends to it, in terms of what it is: a social practice, a historical phenomenon, part of the political discourse of a nation and a people, and a piece of narrative art—that is a form of the art of storytelling which it takes in modern industrial conditions (Carey, in McKnight 2000, p. 19).

Carey made key points. They lead to questions such as: What, then, is journalism? What makes its methodology distinctive and different from other methodologies? What do journalists actually do? What are their methods—what actually happens before and during the process of an article being written for publication or broadcast?

Seeking and reporting truth

One overriding aim of journalism, and a key part of its methodology, is to discover truth and report it. In doing so, journalists deal with things that have happened— concrete occurrences such as events and incidents—and with people's reactions to those things: their observations, thoughts and interpretations. Reporting therefore involves seeking answers to questions. Whether a journalist or an academic, questions are an aid to finding and telling truth in fair, accurate, balanced, and ethical ways. As Kaplan put it:

> the domain of truth has no fixed boundaries within it. In the one world of ideas there are no barriers to trade or to travel. Each discipline may take from the others techniques, concepts, laws, data, models, theories, or explanations—in short, whatever it finds useful for its own inquiries (Kaplan 1964, p. 4).

Leaving aside philosophical discussion about what truth is and accepting the fact that one person's truth may not always be the same as another's, a next step is to ask how journalists discover the truths they report, describe, discuss, interpret, analyse and comment on. Traditionally, they do that by attempting to answer basic questions of *who, what, when, where, why* and *how*. Those six words are like signposts on a voyage of discovery. Answering them guides a journalist as she or he finds the way through a story. That is a truism immortalised by one of the world's great early journalists, Rudyard Kipling, when he wrote:

> *I keep six honest serving-men,*
> *(They taught me all I knew);*
> *Their names are What and Why and When*
> *And How and Where and Who.*
> *I send them over land and sea,*
> *I send them east and west;*
>
> (Kipling (in 1902) 1986, p. 291)

As Medsger said, many journalists have paid the ultimate penalty over the years for asking those questions: 'killed because, in one way or another, they were asking: Who? What? When? Where? How? Why?' (Medsger 2002, p.1). Further:

> We should all remember that people pay a high price for asking those often complex and hated questions, simple though they may sound. Who did what, when and where they did it, how and why it happened... these

One overriding aim of journalism, and a key part of its methodology, is to discover truth and report it. In doing so, journalists deal with things that have happened— concrete occurrences such as events and incidents—and with people's reactions to those things.

are, in fact, the very essence of the most courageous acts of journalism throughout history. They require a journalist's knowledge and a journalistic understanding of the matter at hand (Medsger 2002, p. 1).

Kaplan, likewise, recognised the methodological significance of attempting to answer fundamental questions such as *what* and *why*. Talking of questions, descriptions and explanations, he said:

> descriptions may themselves be explanatory—the 'how' may give us the 'why' and not just a 'what'. For instance, we may describe certain prior events, and thereby provide a causal explanation, or we may describe certain immediate events to explain why one produced another (Kaplan 1964, p. 329).

Reactive and proactive journalism

Kaplan's observation leads to the obvious point that, just as there are different branches of medicine or law, not all journalism is the same. Most forms of journalism actually lie between two extremes; the simplest being very shallow, often formula-based, opportunistic and/or reactive—merely involving reporting on events and/or the outpourings of others as, when and where they occur—while complex forms are generally highly meaningful and proactive and involve deep investigation and research followed by careful writing to explain and describe in depth and detail. As Weinberg observed:

> It would be wonderful to say every journalist *is* an investigative journalist, but it would be untrue... Some reporters and editors must be available to produce features about how cats now outnumber dogs, service pieces on how to purchase an energy-efficient refrigerator... (Weinberg 1996, p. xv).

The point is that there are two broad categories of journalism: reactive and proactive. Reactive journalism is the bread and butter of news reporting—something happens, one or more journalists find out about it, and a news item is generated. Examples include: reports about accidents, fires, media conferences, staged public relations events such as openings or product launches, political meetings, and natural disasters such as cyclones, floods and bushfires. Proactive journalism is different—a journalist discovers or is told about something, conducts research and then makes news happen by developing an article or news item. Examples include: investigative articles, stories based on leaked information, 'campaign stories' in which a news outlet promotes a topic or cause, stories based

There are two broad categories of journalism: reactive and proactive. Reactive journalism is the bread and butter of news reporting—something happens, one or more journalists find out about it, and a news item is generated. Proactive journalism is different—a journalist discovers or is told about something, conducts research and then makes news happen by developing an article or news item.

on information from exclusive sources, profiles, and explanatory or analytical feature articles or reports.

Higher-level proactive journalism—and particularly investigative journalism—generally involves much deeper intellectual involvement and commitment from journalists than shallower reactive reporting, because the former requires forward planning and may rest, for example, on extreme persistence, complex research methods such as painstaking document analysis, diplomatic cultivation of shy sources, access to databases, freedom of information searches, computer-assisted statistical analysis, careful and sustained interpretative research, and even elements of personal danger—all leading to the publication or broadcast of high-impact, often agenda-setting, public interest/benefit stories. Closely related to that point, but distinct from it, is an observation by Johnson (1994) that journalists and the news outlets they work for (arguably also, by extension, journalism academics and managers in media companies) can be broadly categorised into being 'A-team' or 'B-team' players:

> The A-level publications and broadcasters generally exhibit a richer version of the complex issues for the community, nation and world, and they are willing or able to devote the resources to reporting them... The 'B-level' news producers are all those who do not cover the news with the depth, imagination and intellectual grounding as the 'A' producers. In similar fashion, editorial staff members in any newsroom are informally classified as being on the 'A' team or the 'B' team. The 'A' reporters are brighter and more intellectually aggressive... The 'B-team' journalists are, at best, pedestrian... (Johnson 1994, pp. 57–8).

Journalism, history and law

When thinking about the methodology of journalism and what journalists actually do, it should be understood that journalism as an academic discipline and as a profession cannot be viewed in isolation. Journalism must be seen in different political, social, cultural, legal and historic contexts. Making a point related to the historical perspective discussed in Chapter 1, Carey, for example, defined journalism 'concretely' as:

> a vernacular form of literature, an imaginative practice that emerged at a given historical moment (roughly the 17th century) in relationship to

the growth of literacy and above all, the social movement of republican democracy (Carey, in McKnight 2000, p. 18).

Knight offered a different but related interpretation:

> Journalism could be said to be non-fiction writing (news) which relies on identifiable sources. Investigative journalism might be defined as finding important news someone does not want the public to know. Journalists… have professional and ethical responsibilities to look beyond what they have been told by those in authority (Knight 2000, p. 48).

As noted in Chapter 1, there is a close relationship between the methodologies of journalism and history. Historians too look beyond what they have been told by authorities. Famously, Philip L Graham, a former publisher for the *Washington Post* newspaper, reportedly told his staff:

> I am insatiably curious about the state of our world. I revel in the recitation of the daily and weekly grist of journalism … So let us drudge on about our inescapably impossible task of providing every week a first rough draft of a history that will never be completed about a world we can never understand (Graham, in Simpson 1988).

Meyer described journalism as 'history in a hurry' (Meyer 1979, p. 14), while back in 1949 (in the days before gender equity and at a time when journalism was an almost exclusively male-dominated vocation), Wilkerson observed:

> the journalist is himself (sic) the historian of the present, and the record which he puts together will, when used with critical discretion, furnish valuable source material for the scholar of the future who delves into the history of our times (Wilkerson, in Nafziger & Wilkerson 1949, p. 11).

Much of the work of journalists is informed by Kipling's 'six honest serving men' and discovering what, when, where, why, who and how. It is about developing and refining your skills and understandings as a writer, becoming a good interviewer, an exceptional listener, learning where and how to hunt and gather information, being ethical, curious, fair, persistent, objective, balanced, and seeking truth.

The methodology of journalism is also linked to the methodology of law—something of a common thread for the many students who study combined degrees of journalism and law. In fact, pointing out that legal research is one of the 'oldest areas of communications research', Gillmor and Dennis (in Stempel & Westley 1989, p. 333) said methods of history, and other disciplines such as philosophy, have been applied to the law over many years. Obvious connections between the academic disciplines of law and journalism inspired one of the earliest attempts to identify a methodology of journalism. Writing in 1949, US journalist, academic and media studies theorist Frederick Siebert suggested research in the field of law fell within the ambit of the 'immediately related fields' of journalism, law and political science (Siebert 1949, in Nafziger & Wilkerson 1949, p. 34).

Ericson (1996) is another who implied there were close methodological links between law and journalism, or 'law and news' as he put it. He said:

> Both legal operatives and journalists work in terms of an event orientation, conflict resolution, individualisation and personalisation of problems, and realism… Both legal officials and journalists have similar procedural norms, including especially conceptions of objectivity and fairness, through which they practice their craft and achieve legitimacy (Ericson 1996, pp. 196–7).

Academic discussion aside, there is also a much more practical and immediate mutual dependency between law and journalism. As discussed in Chapter 16, by reporting on courts, law, crime and punishment, journalists play an active role in helping law maintain legitimacy, both as a profession and a discipline. They also help hold the judicial system accountable. As Bentham said in 1825:

> Publicity is the very soul of justice. It is the keenest spur to exertion and the surest of all guards against improbity. It keeps the judge himself, while trying, under trial. It is to publicity, more than to everything else put together that the English system of procedure owes its being the least bad system as yet extant, instead of being the worst (Bentham 1825, p. 67).

And just as journalism gives legitimacy to law and the courts, the process also works in reverse—with law and its dependence on publicity helping legitimise the methodology of journalism. Further, as Breen put it: 'Journalists, like historians, are concerned with fact, and how to make sense of "the real world"… As well as having this kinship with history, journalism is also within the domain of literature' (Breen 1998, p. 170). Academic discussion about journalism's links with other methodologies aside, Windschuttle (1998), had definite ideas about the scholarship of journalism. He said:

> There are three characteristics of journalism that any education program in the field should uphold. First, journalism is committed to reporting the truth about what occurs in the world … Journalism, in other words, upholds a realist view of the world and an empirical methodology. Second, the principal ethical obligations of journalists are to their readers, their listeners and their viewers. Journalists report not to please their employers or advertisers nor to serve the state or support some other cause but in order to inform their audience… Third, in the print media, journalists should be committed to good writing. This means their writing should be clear and their grammar precise (Windschuttle 1998, p. 17).

US journalism historian Frank Luther Mott pointed out many years ago that one advantage 'natural to research in journalism' and its place in academia relates to the way the outcomes of journalistic research are presented:

> While some of the [academic] investigations result in reports designed for a highly specialised audience and therefore are not easy reading for the general public, most of them may be, and should be, presented in forceful, unpedantic, readable prose. The idea that a doctoral dissertation must be dull, sesquipedalian, and so recondite that it requires translation into good English to be comprehensible to Tom, Dick or Harry, is a superstition of which no journalist should be guilty. We [journalists] should not renounce our birthright, which is fresh and effective English, for the pedant's mess of pottage (Mott, in Nafziger & Wilkerson 1949, p. 129).

The outcome of all journalism research, whether for publication in an academic setting or for consumption by those who access their news on mobile devices, via newspapers and/or newspaper websites, television, radio or converged media is that stories and reports must be clear and communicated in plain English. As discussed in later chapters, much of the work of journalists is informed by Kipling's 'six honest serving men' and discovering what, when, where, why, who and how. It is about developing and refining your skills and understandings as a writer, becoming an effective interviewer, an exceptional listener, learning where and how to hunt and gather information, being ethical, curious, fair, persistent, objective, balanced, and seeking truth. They are the things that make journalism a distinctive profession and define its unique methodology.

DISCUSSION POINTS

1   Should journalism students really concern themselves about the academic basis of the profession when there are so many practical skills to learn before they are let loose on the public? Why?

2   In simple terms, what is journalism? How can it be defined?

3   Which of Kipling's 'six honest serving men' are the most important? Why?

4   What specific qualities would distinguish an 'A team' journalist from one in the 'B team'?

5   If interviews, documents, surveillance and surveys are the tools of a proactive investigative reporter, what are the tools of a reactive news reporter?

6   Do judges, lawyers, citizens and courts really need journalists? Would it matter if court and legal stories were not reported?

7   How important is it really that journalists' 'writing should be clear and their grammar precise'?

NEWS PRACTICE POINTS

1   Search online and through academic journal articles to find two specific attacks on journalism as an academic discipline. Briefly outline the details of each.

2   In no more than 500 words, critique the two attacks on journalism you found in Practice Point 1. Specifically, did the criticisms seem justified, or were they ill-informed? How?

3   In your own words, explain what you think Carey meant when he said most social science studies of journalism are conducted from the outside, and not through the lens of journalism.

4   In about 250 words, explain what qualified Rudyard Kipling to set himself up as an expert on journalism who could tell others what questions they should ask.

5   Use a dictionary to find at least one definition of the word 'truth' that you consider to be accurate and logical. Discuss how that definition relates to what journalists do, or should do, when they report news.

6   Find five newspaper reports (either published in print or online) about different topics that were literally first rough drafts of history.

7   Explain, using examples of each, what is meant by qualitative and quantitative research.

8   Define the words 'sesquipedalian' and 'recondite'. Then find one separate example of writing that illustrates each definition and translate each into clear English.

REGED AHMAD _____

Reged Ahmad spent about seven years in community radio working as a volunteer presenter and journalist and then as a talks coordinator and news editor. She then went to ABC Central West in NSW as the morning show producer, but eventually made her way back to Sydney to work as a producer at 702 and producer/presenter at ABC News Radio. She settled in the ABC Sydney Radio newsroom as a reporter and sub-editor, and also dabbles in online producing, radio current affairs and television reporting.

---

1 How did you get your first job as a journalist?

I spent about four years in community radio working as a volunteer broadcaster and two years before that coediting student university publications. So it was about six years all up before I finally started to get paid a living wage for what I was doing. Mind you, other journalists have moved much more quickly into the mainstream. I meandered through a few community radio positions first because I loved the freedom the sector gave me to report on whatever I wanted to in whatever format. As for my first paid position, I won it in the time-honoured tradition of buzzing around long enough. When the studio manager left, I started acting in the position and then competed for it when it was advertised.

2 What advice would you offer a beginning journalist?

Just start doing it. I'm a big fan of working in community radio for a few years. Operating outside of the mainstream media for a while means you can critique it from the outside before diving in. If you start off inside the bubble it's very hard to see what shape it is. Often the brief in community radio is to offer an alternative service. That can act as a challenge to a new journalist to push boundaries, choose creative angles and report underreported stories using alternative sources. It really pushes you to learn and develop research skills and do everything yourself. It can be a bit tough because there

often isn't someone directing every element of your story, but it also means the sky's the limit. Whereas mainstream radio or television reporting can be about paring down an angle to only one aspect and what's new or conflicting within that aspect, community radio reporting gives you the freedom to report a side of the story not often heard, or to lead with what you perceive to be the most important angle, rather than the sexiest. Then it's up to you to find a format to report the story that will be most engaging to the listener. It also means you can take historical context into account, whereas there often isn't the space to do that in a mainstream format where there's a strict story length. You can really explore issues and find your niche.

It's also good to monitor sources of news other than the mainstream. A lot of employers will want you to monitor the bigwigs in media and that's great, but more and more there is an emphasis on journalists reading blogs and news websites that aren't published by the usual suspects. Try for a job with the BBC and that's the standard question they will ask you—which blogs and alternative news websites do you monitor? Journals are also fantastic for edgy and fresh story ideas that aren't just being recycled in the mainstream. *Overland* is my favourite.

Analysis, analysis, analysis. By reading analysis and other opinions it can give you a framework to understand what's going on around you in politics and other sectors. You can spend a couple of days watching a few news bulletins and getting up to speed, but constant reading of analysis gives you that deep background that you can only get over time.

3 What is the role of journalism in 21st-century Australian society?

I think the role of media is and always has been to act as the fourth estate. I see it as a pillar in a healthy and functioning democracy. A healthy democracy doesn't just happen by accident because people go to the polls once every few years. It takes a level of understanding of the issues among the public and an engagement with the political landscape and I think journalism is there to facilitate that and seek out the truth. I don't think that has changed in the 21st century—but it is getting harder. There are fewer permanent journalist positions than in the past and we are outnumbered by people in public relations. There is also more of a demand to deliver large amounts of content more quickly, with the emphasis tipping away from the quality of reporting as well as the time to research, find underreported or breaking news and craft our stories well. Journalists need time and resources to do that and both are something of a rare commodity these days.

4 Journalism is being changed and challenged by technology. What are your thoughts about the future of journalism in Australia?

Whereas before a reporter needed to fly in to wherever the story was happening and put a microphone in front of someone's mouth, now, depending on the level of technology available in a country, all we need to do is log on. The web and mobile phones as well as cheap cameras and video recorders have meant journalists don't need to leave the office for eye-witness accounts and amazing pictures. That is having enormous implications for the immediacy of news and the level of awareness of what's happening in the world, or in our own backyard. It's been an exciting development. It's helped to redefine the way journalists and mainstream news organisations operate, challenging how the media sees its role and allowing the

public to be more involved in what the media covers and how it reports on stories. But there are problems.

Interestingly, as newspaper sales decline and some argue the public is disengaging, there's also a demand for more content: more online stories and articles to fill the endless cyberspace, more television news bulletins (both Channel Seven and Nine now have 4.30pm bulletins as well as the 6pm news), SKY's 24-hour news channel; this on top of radio's hourly bulletins. Now, the ABC has a new 24-hour news channel. So there's more content to be found across more mediums. But does this necessarily guarantee quality of content and an increase in the number of stories being covered? I think as the demand to fill broadcast and online space grows, it's going to be harder for journalists to find new stories and to spend time on quality reportage and analysis. Instead, it's often the same stories reworked and repackaged.

For journalists on the ground, it also means an increased workload. Whereas radio reporters used to be able to just worry about their hourly deadline and a newspaper reporter could write their piece for the day, now there's extra demand for radio reporters to file more information for a longer online story. Newspaper journalists are sometimes expected to write an online piece with their deadline being 'right now', instead of for the next day's edition. While this is great for the immediacy of news and offers reporters a chance to put in some of the extra information we painstakingly (sometimes heartbreakingly) leave out, it's changing the emphasis of our role. That's because the more time we spend filing the same sort of content in multiple mediums with extended grabs, the less time we have to craft our stories, and to research and hunt around for stories to break. The emphasis has changed across all media outlets from more depth to greater quantity. I also fear it will change the type of stories we pursue: ones that are easier to report, simpler and easier to understand, easier to make interesting and easier to gather information on. It means we have less time to perform our key task—working hard to make an important, complicated story interesting to the public.

5 What are the key things a journalism student should learn during their studies?

Journalism is a craft. If you know how to do the basics well—such as writing for different mediums, researching, planning and shaping a story—then this frees you to report well on any story you like. The hardest thing for a new journalist to do is to make the intention or story angle in mind manifest itself in the final product. The trick is to learn to define your lead line and angle at the beginning, rather than meander through a story and hope you hit on it eventually.

There are also basic rules for writing in each medium. For example, in radio we write in the active tense; we have a short lead that has only the bare essentials of information and which defines the angle. Learn the basics and be disciplined about them, and they'll guide you every time.

Another 'must' is having an understanding of the court system. That includes training in the rules of legal reporting and an understanding of what angle journalists look for in a court story. Also learn the basics of the electoral/political system. The basics of election reporting and reading and understanding polls can make life much easier.

I also think it's vital that journalists learn how to ensure their stories are accurate. This may not be as simple as it sounds. Often facts are nuanced and learning to ask the right questions and enough of them can make sure you understand the story and report it accurately. This often avoids problems down the track when you start to write your story and find you're struggling to convey the meaning. Problems like this almost always come down to not asking the right questions and collecting enough information to begin with. Learn to be sceptical, but not cynical.

6 Is there anything else you would like to say to journalism students and/or about journalism as a profession?

If you're deliberating over whether to study another major such as science, history or politics in addition to your media major—do it. Having another focused background or skill along with your media degree is priceless.

CAROLINE JONES ⸺⸺⸺⸺⸺⸺⸺⸺⸺⸺⸺⸺⸺⸺⸺

Writer and broadcaster Caroline Jones has worked at the ABC for more than 40 years, on current affairs programs such *as This Day Tonight* and *Four Corners* and on Sydney morning radio. On ABC Radio National, Caroline presented *The Search for Meaning* programs, in which hundreds of Australian men and women told stories of their lives. These programs were an inspiration for ABC TV's *Australian Story*, which Caroline has contributed to and presented since its inception in 1996.

In 1988 Caroline Jones was made an Officer of the Order of Australia and in 1997 she was voted one of Australia's National Living Treasures. She is the author of the best-seller *An Authentic Life: Finding Meaning and Spirituality in Everyday Life*.

1 What is the role of journalism?

To reflect back to the public. The job of the journalist is to record the facts—the stories of what is happening in our society now as faithfully and fully as possible, so that the public at large can be more enlightened about the big picture. That does not mean every story has to be about the big picture. I think much of it can be told and illuminated through the story of a person's personal experience.

I was trained to get underneath what is happening on the surface so that we can truthfully and faithfully report. Journalism should really be about trying to find out; to record what is actually happening. And to get underneath what is happening in politics and business and inside people. That takes time and diligence, patience and persistence—all those qualities. But while we might have those skills personally and we try to encourage them in ourselves, our work is still going to be framed around how much time our editor or producer wants to give us.

I suppose the difficulty about doing incisive and in-depth reporting is that time is a factor and most producers and editors are going to put a time limit on it. Maybe that's one of the reasons why journalism is not pursued in the depth it should be, because time is a factor. But also there is so much spin-doctoring. That's like a blanket you have to push aside, or work your way through, to actually get to original sources. That is something that has changed so tremendously since I worked on *Four Corners*, but that's going back 30 years.

It seems to me that in the evening current affairs programs there used to be much more face-to-face interviewing by the presenter of politicians—much more challenge. But now there's often an intermediary. There are barriers now to jump over and I think the manipulation of news is a real problem for journalists—manipulation of news by the public relations people.

I am quite often frustrated as a viewer or a reader. I don't always feel that I am getting information from the horse's mouth and that's what I want. But then you get a few older-style investigative journalists and you think, I know you, and I know you've done your utmost. I suppose reputation builds up over the years... as a reader or viewer we take our time to build up trust in a certain writer or reporter.

2 Some people become journalists to make a difference. Does that still matter?

Students have to decide whether they become a crusader and have a point of view; or whether they really want to use the principles of journalism and explore a problematic subject from every point of view and look beyond that to find people who can speak about a possible solution to a particular problem. I think that's a very valuable way to go—to try to portray to the public, in the public interest, the fullest possible picture. Then let people make up their own minds. I think that's what we are supposed to be doing.

There are many ways of doing it. You can find and interview—in depth—people who have solutions to a certain problem. Let's say you have a passion about a particular issue, but you want to use journalistic principles. It is quite okay to find people who have solutions to burning current problems and to interview them. Let them put that point of view. But you should properly present that problem, too, as truthfully as you can. I think there are many ways of doing it honourably, faithfully, and objectively—and to still make a difference because you are putting constructive information out to the public who will, of course, have their own responses and reactions.

The law has to work in with our journalistic principles too. I'm thinking about some of the whistleblowers in recent times who have been brave people in the community who have been prepared to go public to talk about something wrong in a government department, or the way something has been administrated or run, and what a terrible road that can be. I think it is important for journalism to give them a platform, but then again we have to have regard for the law and how far we can go with that too.

3 What more should be said about the journalist in society?

You have to be brave and have courage.

I got into a good deal of trouble reporting on some of the activities of the Labor Party branches in NSW, and that became dangerous for not only myself as the subject of threats in the parliament, but also for my researchers, which is much worse, because you are very vulnerable to being scared off, as it were, when someone close to you or working close to you is being threatened.

Sometimes you realise that you are dealing in very murky waters as we were in reporting on things that were associated with organised crime in NSW.

So I suppose you have courage for a certain number of years but then you might back off for a certain number of years to have a rest from it. You hope there are other journalists still with the spirit and gumption and the energy and courage to keep doing it because it does matter.

LEIGH SALES

Leigh Sales is an award-winning journalist and author, who hosts the ABC TV current affairs program *7.30*. From 2006 to 2008, she was the ABC's national security correspondent and from 2001 to 2005, Washington correspondent, covering the momentous years after the September 11 terrorist attacks. She has won two Walkley Awards—the first in 2005 for her coverage of issues surrounding Guantanamo Bay and the second in 2012 for her interviews on *7.30*. She is also the author of two books, *Detainee 002: The Case of David Hicks* (Melbourne University Press, 2007) and *On Doubt* (Melbourne University Press, 2009).

1 How did you get your first job as a journalist?

I basically went up to Channel Nine one day per week to work for nothing. Eventually, the most junior person moved up a rung and I was employed in that position. It involved doing a bit of everything—rolling the autocue for the anchor, printing and distributing scripts, answering the phone, writing research briefs, doing pick up interviews for reporters, organising the crew roster. It was a great beginning as it allowed me to observe the diverse aspects of a TV newsroom and how all the different parts work together.

2 What advice would you offer a beginning journalist?

Take whatever media job you can get, even if you think it's not what you want. The important thing is to get a foot in the door. Also, you know nothing when you start your career—no matter how much of a star you may have been at university—so keep your mouth shut and learn from people who are good at what they do.

3 What is the role of journalism in 21st-century Australian society?

Given the rise of opinion in the media over traditional objective journalism (mostly because opinion is cheap to produce and easier to do than old-fashioned shoe leather reporting), it's very important that newsrooms keep producing journalists who can actually report, not just commentate.

4 What are your thoughts about the impacts on journalism of changing communication technologies?

The pace of change seems to be speeding up all the time. Digital editing has been the most profound change for me. The ability to drop things or change the order of a TV or radio story without having to cut from scratch or drop a generation is fantastic. The advent of Twitter has been momentous too, both in terms of keeping across news and finding original sources.

5 What key things should a journalism student learn?

The most important thing to learn is how to think critically and to develop a love of learning and a natural curiosity about the world. The rest of it you can learn on the job, as long as you're working with good people.

6 Is there anything else you would like to say to journalism students and/or about journalism as a profession?

Even though I think it is the best job in the world and I love it, I actually feel anxious these days about recommending it as a career choice. That's mostly because it's an industry in a state of flux. It was extremely difficult to get a job in journalism when I was starting out 20 years ago; today it's even harder. If somebody came to me and said they were tossing up about whether to be a doctor or a journalist and they didn't have their heart set on journalism, I'd say be a doctor. It saddens me enormously to say that but I think this industry is very tough currently.

WHAT IS NEWS?

2

NEWS VALUES 3

*It is a newspaper's duty to print the news,
and raise hell.*
Wilbur Storey, Editor, *Chicago Times*, 1861

OBJECTIVES

After reading this chapter you will understand:

» How news is selected for publication and broadcast

» The main functions of news media

» Definitions of news

» News values and how they can be categorised

» How reactive and proactive news are both important

» The inverted pyramid and news values

» Why public relations blurb is rarely news.

How does an editor, editorial director or news producer decide which stories will be featured most prominently on a continuously updated digital news site, become the front page lead in a newspaper, the first in a radio or television news bulletin, or the cover story in a magazine? And how does a chief-of-staff decide which stories should be pursued at all costs, which are not quite so significant but should still be worked on or followed up, and which will never see the light of day?

The answers are complex. Most news editors, directors and producers have an instinctive 'feel' for news. They understand their readership and audience. In bigger news organisations they also respond to market research, to the types of stories members of the public and focus groups have identified as the most compelling, and to the categories of stories that attract the most hits online and on mobile devices. Sometimes their choice is influenced by the availability of high-impact photos, sound or video that will enhance the work of journalists. At other times a story is simply so big it overwhelms everything else. The terrorist attacks on the World Trade Center towers in New York and the Pentagon in Washington on September 11, 2001 are examples of such stories. So were the killing of Osama bin Laden in 2011, the horrendous 2011 Japanese earthquake, tsunami and subsequent meltdown of the Fukushima nuclear reactor, the 2011 Queensland floods, the February 2009 Black Saturday bushfires in Victoria, the 2009 crash of an Air France jet into the Atlantic Ocean, and the 2011 Madeleine Pulver collar-bomb extortion attempt. But, fortunately, big stories like those do not happen every day.

News media are generally regarded as having three functions: to inform, educate and entertain. A news story may do all three at once. Yet, as mentioned in Chapter 1, news is difficult to define. With the exception of relatively few stories which have the potential to affect all humanity, what is defined as news depends to some extent on where you are geographically in relation to a particular event. If a newsworthy event happens near you, or is likely to have some sort of effect on you, it will be of more interest than a story that happened in another part of the globe and is unlikely to have a bearing on your life. Whether we like it or not, most of us—although some more than others—tend to be egocentric and ethnocentric. Where we live, the culture we live in, our climate, our beliefs, our way of life, work, hobbies, level of education, health system, and a myriad other factors combine to colour our view of the world. The same factors also influence journalists, editors and news producers. Thus, when editors, editorial directors, news producers, chiefs-of-staff and other news executives make seemingly instinctive decisions about what news is, they are actually making decisions influenced by their own backgrounds and their unique perceptions of the world. This helps explain why one media outlet might give top priority to one story, while a different outlet in the same market or region might downplay that same story and give precedence to another. It also helps explain why news is so hard to define and why it is difficult to explain what makes interesting stories that will attract readers and audiences—and keep bringing them back to a particular news outlet day after day, week after week, year after year, as they seek more of the same.

> If a newsworthy event happens near you, or is likely to have some sort of effect on you, it will be of more interest than a story that happened in another part of the globe and is unlikely to have a bearing on your life.

Attempts to define news

It was noted in Chapter 1 that news happens when an event, action or circumstance has an impact, or likely impact, on people or their way of life. It was also explained that news is a difficult concept to define. One of the earliest references to 'newes' was in 1551, when the word originally meant 'novelties' (Mott 1962, p. 48). It becomes evident when considering attempts to define 'news' that, like 'beauty', 'news' is often in the eye of the beholder. At different times, it has variously been described as:

— 'The first rough draft of history'—Philip Graham, a former publisher of *The Washington Post* (cited by Bradlee, in Hough 1984, p. 60)

— 'Anything that makes a reader say, "Gee whiz!"'—Arthur MacEwen, a former editor of the *San Francisco Examiner* (cited in Boorstin 1961)

— 'Anything you can find out today that you didn't know before'—Turner Catledge, a former editor at *The New York Times*

— 'Anything that will make people talk'—Charles Dana, editor of the old *New York Sun*

— 'New or interesting information, fresh events reported'—*The Australian Concise Oxford Dictionary*

— 'When a dog bites a man, that is not news because it happens so often. But if a man bites a dog, it's news'—John Bogart, city editor of *The New York Sun*.

One of the best definitions of news comes from US journalism educator Melvin Mencher (1997). He said there are two general guidelines:

— 'News is information about a break from the normal flow of events, an interruption in the expected'

— 'News is information people need to make sound decisions about their lives' (Mencher 1997, p. 58).

In those two senses, news is still very much the same commodity today as it was when passed on by word of mouth in the days of cave-dwellers. They too would have been concerned about breaks in the normal flow of events and interruptions to the expected in their immediate locality. They would also have needed information to make decisions about how they lived and how they could survive. We have similar concerns today, although our priorities would be things no cave-dweller would have dreamed of! One of the other big differences between then and now is that today we have people in our communities whose job it is, and whom we pay, to go out and hunt and gather news on our behalf and then disseminate it to a wide—at times global—audience. They are journalists. As professional news gatherers and disseminators, journalists are relied on by doctors, lawyers, truck drivers, judges, labourers, computer nerds, politicians, preachers and the community generally to tell them what happened (or was predicted to happen) in the world while they worked, slept, played or were otherwise occupied.

Six functions of journalism

Within the broad framework of informing, educating and entertaining, journalists and news media have six specific and often overlapping functions:

1   acting as a mirror reflecting a society to itself. In so doing, they highlight good and bad—warts and tragedies as well as peaches and cream; from wars and disasters to frippery and fashion parades!

2   helping keep influential and powerful individuals and institutions honest and accountable by exposing them and their actions to the sometimes harsh light of public scrutiny

3   an advocacy role—being an agent for the good of society by providing a voice, sometimes a voice of last resort, for individuals who have not been able to attain redress or have wrongs righted in other ways. Much investigative journalism and some political journalism fits into this category, especially when journalists step in and investigate matters authorities have ignored or covered up.

4   protecting, informing and promoting democracy and democratic ideals

5   telling people in one part of the world what is happening in the rest of the world. What would we know, for example, about major international events (such as those mentioned earlier in this chapter) and more recent events without journalism and news media?

6   protecting the public interest—raising questions, informing and educating readers and audiences about things which affect, or could reasonably be expected to affect, their lives, and which it is in their best interests to know about.

In fulfilling those roles, journalists seek truths and then explain those truths in ways individuals and the public collectively can understand. They must tell those who rely on them about Mencher's breaks from the normal flow of events and interruptions in the expected while providing accurate and unbiased information people can use to help make sound decisions about their lives (Mencher 1997, p. 58). In performing their duties—and journalism is as much a vocation as a job— journalists have a crucial function in the life of a nation. Among other things they:

— try to keep governments honest and help us decide who to vote for

— help us view our world in context by examining events on a local, regional, national and global scale

— warn of dangers and deceptions

— help right injustices

— expose hypocrisy

— promote health and safety

— help us make informed choices about products, services and other people

— allow us to express our opinions and feelings about events

— draw communities together in times of trouble and disaster.

If you take the first part of Mencher's definition of news—that it is information about a break from the normal flow of events, an interruption in the expected—you will see it is a broad description of what journalists report on when they cover stories about accidents, fires, natural disasters, terrorist attacks, epidemics, assassinations and other things out of the ordinary. The facts they gather and descriptions they provide often link to the second prong of Mencher's definition—that news is information people need to make sound decisions about their lives. If, for example, we hear or read a report about a bushfire, flood or cyclone and we know we have to leave a particular place or region, or stay away from it, then news has helped us make an informed decision. Similarly, if we become aware of a report about an airline with a history of crashes, we will probably make an informed decision not to fly with that airline.

The 'big six' news values

A key point to understand about news values is that commonly there are no right or wrong answers. Something you personally consider red-hot news might not interest others. Conversely, something boring to one group might spark outrage, fear and loathing in another. Similarly, it would be wrong to imagine that news editors and producers sit down with lists of stories and work through them as if they were following a recipe in which the ingredients for their particular news outlet were based on a set mix of news values. Nothing is as complex as that—most judgments about newsworthiness are intuitive. But there has been considerable research into news values, much of it focusing on analysis of news content published and broadcast by different media outlets on different platforms in different markets.

One early study of news values was conducted by Norwegian academics Johan Galtung and Mari Ruge in the 1960s. They examined foreign news published in four Norwegian newspapers and hypothesised that there were 12 news 'factors', including such obscure concepts as 'reference to elite nations', 'reference to persons', 'unambiguity' and 'threshold' (Galtung & Ruge 1965, pp. 65–71). In 1995, after surveying thousands of journalists in 67 nations, New Zealand journalist and journalism academic Murray Masterton formulated a much clearer explanation. He found there were:

> Three essential elements which allow information to become news and six truly international criteria—news values if you like—which can be used to assess the level of newsworthiness of that information. Most importantly, they are the same everywhere (Masterton 1995).

Masterton's three 'essential elements' which *differentiated* news from information were: interest, timeliness and clarity. He said news items must interest many people, they must contain new or newly known information, and the information must be presented in an easily understood form. After the basic criteria of interest, timeliness and clarity were satisfied, Masterton's 'big six' news values in descending order of importance were: significance, proximity, conflict, human interest, novelty and prominence (Masterton 1995), each of which we now consider in some detail.

SIGNIFICANCE (SOMETIMES ALSO KNOWN AS 'IMPACT')

Significance relates to the number of people affected in some way by a newsworthy event. One notable example happened on February 7, 2009—Black Saturday—when 173 Victorians lost their lives, more than 2000 homes and other buildings were destroyed, and about 43,000 hectares were burnt (Bushfire Authority 2009). News reports of the fire tragedy were graphic. There were also significant impacts from a series of major natural disasters which hit Queensland in December 2010 and January and February 2011. Floods in the December–January period resulted in more than 78 per cent of Queensland (an area bigger than France and Germany combined) being inundated. At least 33 people died in the floods (some bodies were never found), more than 2.5 million people were affected, about 29,000 homes and businesses were flooded, mines filled with water, roads and railway lines were washed away and the damage bill was estimated to be more than $5 billion (Queensland Flood Commission of Inquiry 2012). Then, in February 2011, Category 5 Cyclone Yasi slammed into the town of Mission Beach in Far North

Queensland with winds gusting to about 285kph and a 5m storm surge. Homes, businesses and whole towns were flattened in a 500km radius from the cyclone's eye. It was one of the worst storms in recorded history to hit Australia. The combined impacts of floods and the cyclone resulted in more than 99 per cent of Queensland being disaster-affected by March 2011, with about 7000 people accommodated in 74 evacuation centres across the state and about 136,000 residential properties damaged (Department of the Premier and Cabinet Queensland 2011).

Internationally, the March 2011 Japanese earthquake and tsunami were examples of events which had major news significance. While it is unlikely the total death toll will ever be known, it was estimated in mid-2012 that at least 15,854 died and a further 3271 were missing (Ryall & Demetriou 2012). The impact of that tragedy became of even greater significance after radiation leaked from the Fukushima nuclear power station reactors, which were damaged by the earthquake. In terms of sheer numbers of people killed, one of the most significant events this century was the terrifying Indian Ocean tsunami disaster on Boxing Day 2004, in which an estimated 227,000 people died.

Each of these events attracted saturation media coverage. The earthquake and tsunami stories were of major significance in Australia—a nation in which most of our population is clustered around an often low-lying coastline and a country in the same global neighbourhood as the nation worst-hit by the tsunami, Indonesia.

Stories about major disease outbreaks, taxes, employment, pensions, bushfires, cyclones, education, riots and civil unrest, interest rates, earthquakes, electricity charges and petrol prices are all likely to have high significance because they affect many people at once. But unless other news values come into play, we hear much less about stories that impact on relatively few people at one time, or people we do not identify with. Individual tragedies such as road crashes are an example. They too take lives in the most frightening and tragic circumstances, shatter families and leave many survivors permanently disabled, but they do not attract the same news coverage as mass tragedies.

To help understand significance as a news value, imagine for example the news impact of a single event that killed more than 1200 Australian men, women and children at one time. It would be a huge story. But spread that number of deaths geographically across every region in Australia over a whole year and the significance decreases, as does the news coverage—something reflected in the fact that there was only cursory reporting of many of the separate road crashes that claimed close to 1300 Australian lives and left a shocking toll of injury and permanent disability around the nation in 2012 (Department of Infrastructure, Transport, Regional Development and Local Government 2012).

PROXIMITY

As a news value, proximity not only relates to news that happens close to us geographically, but also events close to us emotionally, culturally, historically and socially. In this sense, the 2009 Black Saturday bushfires, 2011 Queensland floods and Cyclone Yasi, February 2011 Christchurch earthquake which killed more than 180 people and flattened the city, and 2004 Indian Ocean tsunami involved proximity as well as significance. But if each event had happened further away— say in Argentina, the Congo or Russia—there would not have been anything like the same news coverage in Australia. Similarly, while we hear plenty about medical conditions such as Alzheimer's disease and breast and prostate cancer, which have big impacts in our own region and on people we know or know of, we hear relatively little news about the more than one million men, women and children in other parts of the world who die each year from malaria (International Federation of Red Cross and Red Crescent Societies 2009).

Proximity obviously relates closely to egocentricity and ethnocentricity. For example, as Moeller observed in relation to US journalists:

> In the US media, all international crises are Americanised… The premium on news gathering is to select such details from an event as can give a reader a sense of identity with the topic. Americans are terribly preoccupied with themselves (Moeller 2004, p. 58).

Much the same can be said of Australians and Australian news media. If, for example, a Russian-made aircraft crashes in Kazakhstan killing all 250 people on board, reporting of the story in Australia is likely to be minimal, if it is reported at all. But if one or more of the dead passengers was an Australian, or the aircraft had been made in Australia, news coverage here would be intense. Similarly, if a boatload of asylum seekers arrives in Greece from North Africa, the event hardly rates a mention in an Australian-based news outlet other than SBS. In contrast, however, there is extensive reporting across Australia when boats carrying asylum seekers are intercepted in our territorial waters—with even greater coverage when lives are lost, a boat sinks, explodes or is wrecked.

Proximity is also the mainstay of regional and local news media. We like to know what is happening in our backyard (or at least the backyards of our neighbours): who is doing well, or not so well, who had a baby and who died, about our local heroes and villains, and about our roads, rates and rubbish. As Kirkpatrick (2000) pointed out, local news content is everything in regional media and 'the glue' that holds regional newspapers together (Kirkpatrick 2000, p. 100). To that end, many news outlets go to almost ridiculous lengths at times to develop proximity in a story that happened in another part of the world by desperately seeking a local angle—all too often the home-town 'hero' or 'heroine' who was coincidentally holidaying and on the very spot whenever whatever it was happened!

CONFLICT

News stories dealing with conflict cover a wide spectrum, from physical life-and-death struggles in wars and rebellions to mere differences of opinion, such as political conflicts in parliamentary debates, rows between neighbours, sporting clashes, spats involving movie stars, and court reports. We see and hear daily news stories about conflict in the Middle East and Afghanistan, and about riots, rebellions and coups. We are told about conflicts between sporting clubs, individuals and nations. We have conflicting issues, values, priorities and demands for our time and our attention. Super-bugs and cancers conflict with our fight for survival; so do droughts, floods, fires and famines. There are intense arguments over politics, religion, gender and equality—or the lack thereof. Vested interests have conflicts of interest, unions conflict with employers, developers with environmentalists, miners with farmers, criminals with police, dogs with cats. Sometimes journalists short of a story or struggling to find a news angle succumb to temptation by exaggerating and exploiting conflict. It is not unknown, for example, for a television journalist or camera operator to ask protestors to push against security guards to create 'better' footage, or at least suggest protestors might get their point across more effectively if they chant and wave placards for a camera. Similarly, some journalists and television presenters deliberately annoy and verbally provoke an interviewee in a bid to elicit an angry response.

In many ways conflict, even more than money, can be seen as the root of all evil. Unresolved conflict lies at the heart of all terrorism. It fuels wars and despotic political regimes. It underlies abuses of trust and power. It shatters nations, families, friendships and lives. It results in killings, torture and shocking inhumanity. On the other hand, not all conflict is bad. Sometimes conflicting tensions result in new scientific discoveries, new technologies, and new ways of seeing and doing things. There can be lasting peace and giant steps forward for societies when conflicts are resolved and new understandings emerge. Most of those things are newsworthy.

HUMAN INTEREST

Humans have a passion for knowing what other humans are doing. We are inveterate stickybeaks—especially those of us who are journalists! We like to know what our neighbours get up to, which movie star is on with which pop idol, what the latest sporting bad boy or girl did that landed him or her in so much strife, why that elderly lady down the street has a bad limp and a bad temper, and what really attracted the prime minister to his or her partner. As well as having an interest in the intimate, often salacious, details of others' lives we also like to have heroes and heroines—role models we can look up to. It can be inspiring and uplifting to know what makes a sporting icon tick, what makes one politician a great leader who stands out, or a gifted doctor a much-loved medical genius. We also feel great sympathy for many of those who have suffered. We admire individuals who make sacrifices so others can have better lives, and marvel at ordinary people who do extraordinary things in response to extraordinary circumstances.

Human interest stories tend to be based on emotion and the provoking of emotion. Moeller says children in particular arouse human interest:

> Children at risk have become a default way for journalists to capture the interest of their readers and listeners… children command our sympathies and our engagement. They keep our attention. Injury to them provokes our outrage (Moeller 2004, p. 61).

Although not 'human' in their own right, much the same can often be said of 'humanised' animals and the relationships some people forge with them.

NOVELTY (SOMETIMES ALSO KNOWN AS 'THE UNUSUAL')

As Masterton (1995) explained:

> Novelty can also be called the strange, odd-ball, bizarre, or 'Gee-Whiz' journalism. This is where the man-bites-dog item fits, or anything else which is reported because it is rare or unusual or not done before (Masterton 1995).

This is also where Mencher's break from the normal flow of events particularly stands out. Examples abound, with some news outlets actually having special sections for publishing bizarre stories. On September 23, 2009 for example, Reuters India published articles on its online news site about a US woman who was jailed for a year and a day after being found guilty of keeping her dead mother's body hidden in her house so she could continue collecting her age pension. Another article on the same site reported that a special 18-kilometre walking trail had been developed in Germany for people who wanted to walk in the nude (Reuters India 2009). In 2012 a live television chat show in Greece erupted into chaos when a spokesman for a far-right wing political party repeatedly slapped a female left-wing politician, threw a glass of water at another woman and called her a 'tart'. He was overpowered and locked in a room but later escaped and was last seen running away (ABC News—Offbeat 2009). Closer to home, there was a wonderful ABC News Online report in 2009 about Northern Territory police responding to a noisy and apparently violent disturbance only to find the cause of the commotion was a couple having sex (ABC News—Offbeat 2009).

Such stories are often fun to gather and fun to write, but a word of warning. Ask yourself: how unusual is too unusual? Is someone exaggerating or joking at your expense? Whenever you can, double-check unusual information, preferably with a credible source or authority. Also be careful of the language you use in reports—can you be certain something really is the 'biggest', 'oldest', 'first', 'last', 'unique', 'only' or 'heaviest'? And remember, if something seems to be too good to be true, it probably is!

PROMINENCE

People who regularly feature in news reports tend to develop a certain notoriety, or prominence. Sometimes what they actually said or did is not of any real consequence. What is more important to quite a few is that they are photographed, interviewed or are the focus of a triumph or disaster. This news value helps explain why there are so many reports about entertainers, royalty, high-profile politicians, notorious criminals, sporting personalities, pop-psychologists, religious leaders, fashion models, television and radio presenters, and others who have a need to constantly push themselves into media spotlights. Prominence is closely related to human interest and novelty as news values. It can come to be attached to people we admire, those we like to dislike, people we envy, and those we revile.

Some individuals who thrive on living in the limelight have trouble understanding that prominence can be a double-edged sword. On one hand, they invite journalists and media into their lives and seek positive publicity to promote an image and build their careers. On the other, in the process they become blind to the fact that the more they allow their lives to become public property, the more they relinquish their privacy. Problems subsequently arise if journalists probe beyond the edges of a carefully cultivated media image, or if a prominent individual behaves badly. It is too late then to turn against journalists and media, saying in effect: 'Yes, I want you to report on the good things I do. But respect my privacy; you have no right to report on embarrassing things I did or said that might harm my image or damage my reputation!'

Values tend to blend together

While some stories are clearly dominated by one strong news value, say conflict or the unusual, others involve combinations of values. But whether dominated by a single value, or drawing on a subtle blend of less obvious values, news usually also reflects Masterton's three basic elements of interest, timeliness and clarity. People lose interest if told repeatedly about events they already know about, particularly if those events happened some time ago and fresh angles have been exhausted.

Interest, timeliness and clarity have become even more important since the move to online and mobile news platforms. Stories that are not interesting, timely or clear drop off news sites quickly, but interesting stories about developing or continuing issues remain current, with updates and links published regularly and new angles pursued over hours, days and weeks. In essence, a strong news story will reflect one or more news values: it will be about something that readers, listeners or viewers find interesting; it will be about something that has just happened, just come to light, or something that might happen soon; and it will have been written by a journalist who has understood the relevant issues and information and presented it in clear, easy-to-digest chunks. Journalists sometimes talk about such news as being a story that was so strong it virtually wrote itself.

Kipling's 'six honest serving men'

Journalists use specific tools when they write news. Once they become aware of a newsworthy event or issue, they must discover all they can, then write the story. They will need to interview people, ensuring all sides are covered if a topic is controversial, and maybe seek comments from authorities or experts. Journalists must be particularly careful to get facts and names right, to find the most important information, perhaps do some quick background research, and finally pull everything together while the information is still timely to write a story that is interesting and clear. As noted in Chapter 2, the keys journalists use to gather information they will report, describe, analyse and/or comment on are found in six simple but crucial words: *who, what, when, where, why* and *how*. Discovering the answers to those questions—words Kipling (1986) described as his 'six honest serving men'—will unlock any news story. They are signposts that direct and guide your writing. They aid your quest to find and report truths while helping you explain a story clearly to your readers or audience.

If you are to catch and hold the interest of readers, viewers and listeners, you must tell them what happened, to whom, when and where. It helps if you can also explain how whatever it was happened, and why. A good rule of thumb is to do your best to tell a story in the way you would want it explained to you.

The inverted pyramid

Remembering how important it is for a story to be clear, many journalists first harness the power of Kipling's six honest serving men, and then use a tried-and-tested format to present information they gathered. This format amounts to a recipe for writing news; it is known as the inverted pyramid.

An approach that falls in and out of favour in some news organisations and among journalists, editors, news producers and journalism educators, the inverted pyramid structure is something every journalist should understand; whether they use it or not. As discussed in Chapter 8, many believe other approaches make stories more interesting and help keep news consumers with a story longer, but the inverted pyramid is a useful starting point—especially for beginning journalists. It also provides an invaluable fallback if an alternative approach gets messy, and is particularly useful when writing complex stories. As explained in Chapter 10, it also the best approach when writing news for publication online or via mobile devices.

The idea of the inverted pyramid is to provide the most newsworthy information first, and least important last. A story written to the inverted pyramid formula starts with an introduction, which is generally referred to as an 'intro', or 'the lead' in the US. As explained in Chapter 8, a good intro explains in one short, sharp sentence of up to 25 words what a story is about. It should encapsulate the main news value and usually explains *what* happened *where*. It might also contain information about *who* was involved, especially if prominence is one of the main news values. Subsequent sentences and paragraphs should explain *when* and, if possible, *how* and *why* whatever it was happened. The last part of the article or news item should contain non-essential details that, while interesting, have the weakest news values and are not crucial to the story. The aim is to build interest and ensure clarity. In doing that, however, do not try to explain everything and answer all Kipling's questions in an intro! Trying to explain too much too quickly creates confusion. It turns readers, listeners and viewers off.

A story constructed around the inverted pyramid framework has the advantage of appealing to news consumers who are in a hurry. They can scan, or listen to, the first part and pick up key facts. If the intro arouses their interest, they will hopefully keep reading, listening or viewing. If not, they will go to another story— or maybe flick a button and go to another radio station, television channel, website or app. In newspapers and magazines the approach is also useful because it allows an article to be cut from the bottom, or end, to fit a particular space on a page, or news hole, without losing all meaning. The concept of the inverted pyramid is represented in Figure 3.1.

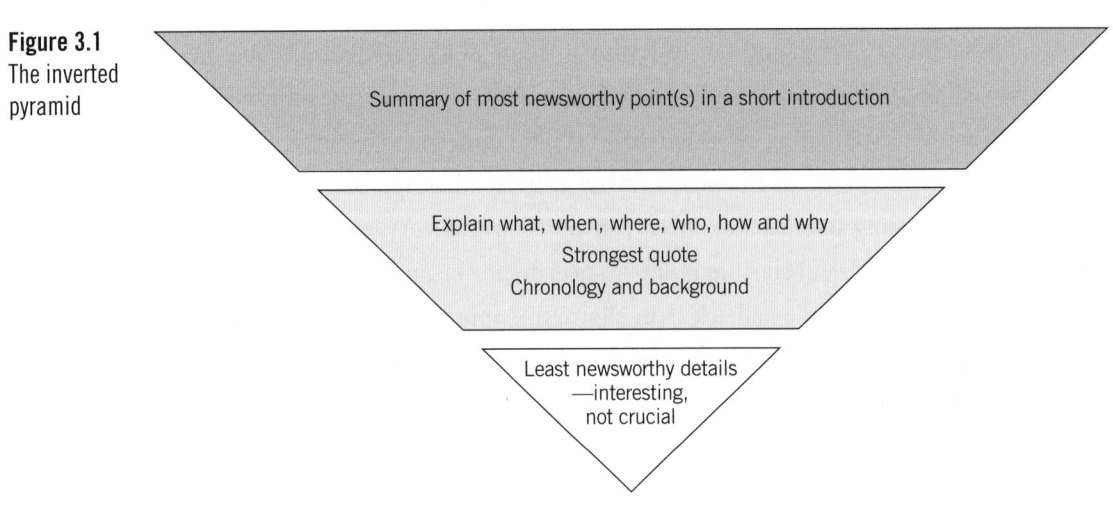

Figure 3.1
The inverted pyramid

Summary of most newsworthy point(s) in a short introduction

Explain what, when, where, who, how and why
Strongest quote
Chronology and background

Least newsworthy details
—interesting,
not crucial

Although a valuable concept, Mencher (1997) warned that the image of the inverted pyramid might be misleading and should be interpreted with care because it is an 'unbalanced monolith', which belies the fact that the top of a story 'should be deft and pointed' (Mencher 1997, p. 124). Conversely, however, you can view the diagram as demonstrating that the top of the pyramid has the broadest news values, and the base the narrowest. Combining the two interpretations, we have a diagram that can be seen to demonstrate how a news story should start with news values with the widest appeal by presenting them in a 'deft and pointed' intro, followed by more substance and more answers to what, when, where, who, why and how—perhaps including the strongest quotes—then background, and finish with interesting but not crucial information with the least news value.

Reactive and proactive news

As noted in Chapter 2, there are two basic categories of news produced by journalists: reactive and proactive. A reactive story is one that starts with an event or circumstance—something interesting and newsworthy happens, leading one or more journalists to report on it. A proactive story often starts with an idea—a journalist sets the news agenda by producing an interesting and newsworthy story as the result of research, a tip, a leak, a discovery or an approach by a whistleblower. Proactive stories include investigative reports, exposés and exclusive interviews, and can contain unique photographs, vision and images of documents. Reactive news is best suited to radio and online because it can be reported and published quickly—even while a story is still happening. Proactive news is particularly well suited to newspapers or serious television news and current affairs programs, although it is growing in importance online. Aligned to these general points is the fact that while news outlets publish reactive news online as soon as they know other news organisations have obtained a story too—even if online publication means scooping their own newspapers or news broadcasts—they still tend to keep their proactive news exclusive. Truly agenda-setting articles and unique photographs or vision are often kept for presentation as major news in traditional media such as newspapers or television news and current affairs, often before being aired online.

If you consider the first part of Mencher's definition of news—that it is information about a break from the normal flow of events, an interruption in the expected—it is a broad description of what journalists report on when they cover reactive stories about accidents, fires, natural disasters, terrorist attacks, chemical spills, epidemics, assassinations and other events that are out of the ordinary. Elements of reactive news also sit well with the second prong of Mencher's definition—that news is information people need in order to make sound decisions about their lives. If, for example, we hear a reactive report about an approaching bushfire or storm we could decide to leave a particular place or region or stay put. Similarly, when we learn about a highway we intended travelling on being blocked by an accident, we might delay a planned journey or take an alternative route. A reactive story from overseas about a disease outbreak, natural disaster or terrorist act might lead us to change our travel plans. Proactive news can have similar impacts. If, for example, a journalist gathers statistics and crunches numbers that reveal a particular vehicle make and model has a history of crashes, we will probably decide to purchase a different brand or model. Similarly, we make decisions about how we will live our lives when journalists write proactive research-based articles about health, consumer products, climate change, investments, wars, politics, etc.

Journalists must distinguish between news, comment and opinion

Journalists never write for themselves, only their readers and audiences. Similarly, journalists should clearly distinguish between news, comment and opinion—both when they write and when they read and hear reports by others. Apart from the fact that journalistic comment is not news—and as explained in Chapter 15, muddling news and opinion in the same article or broadcast can be legally dangerous—mixing the two can also damage a journalist's and news outlet's credibility. As discussed in Chapter 4, journalists should present an unbiased, fair and balanced view of the world so their readers, listeners and viewers can make up their own minds about issues. It is not part of a journalist's role to peddle their own personal views. Would-be journalists who are on a mission to change the world by telling others what to think, which political party to vote for, or which issues are the most important are likely to have spectacular but short newsroom careers.

They would be much better suited to spin-doctoring jobs in public relations, or to becoming politicians. Further, despite the boring pomposity displayed by a gaggle of bloggers, some air-headed Twitterers, and a few radio and television presenters, many of whom are obviously uncommonly fond of themselves, the public is likely to become annoyed with, and ignore or turn against, commentators and interviewers who push their own personal views. That is especially so if those views are not perceived as impartial or rational.

Commentators whose opinions are respected are specialists. The best are experienced journalists who have earned their spurs news reporting and feature writing. They have built respect during a distinguished career and become expert analysts in highly specialised fields such as federal politics, economics, business, law, finance, property, media and information technology. They draw on years of experience gained, and contacts developed, while working their specialised rounds. They have acquired wisdom, knowledge and understandings that equip them to interpret often complex news and analyse it in terms ordinary people can understand. Their approach to what are often difficult and partisan issues is balanced and fair-minded. They also go out of their way to ensure their comments and analysis are clearly labelled as such. Further, they do not mix news reporting with comment and analysis in the same article or item.

> Journalists never write for themselves, only their readers and audience. It is not part of a journalist's role to peddle their own personal views, and would-be journalists who do so are likely to have short but spectacular newsroom careers.

Smoke, mirrors and frightened rabbits

Globalisation and moves by news media to publish online and on mobile devices have resulted in huge changes in the ways news, or what sometimes passes as 'news', is selected and presented. Newspaper publishers, in particular, were affected— especially after major industry restructures in 2012 and 2013. Their revenues had plummeted since the mid-1990s because classified advertising, which was traditionally their bread and butter, dried up after a massive shift by the public to online advertising on websites such as eBay, Gumtree, and specialised sites for cars, real estate, and employment. The problem was exacerbated because print circulations were declining at the same time as advertising revenue was falling. Despite those threats to their existence, newspaper publishers were slow at first to react to the internet, web, online and mobile device publishing as the new era of paperless communication evolved. As former editor-in-chief of *The Age*, Michael Gawenda, confessed in 2012:

> We were like rabbits in the spotlight, aware that we faced challenges but unable to act, frozen with fear … there were frightened rabbits in newspaper companies everywhere … it seemed to me that while managers and editors talked about quality journalism, cost cutting was seen as the only solution to challenges facing newspapers (Gawenda 2012, p. 32).

Once print media companies did wake up to the challenges, one approach to cost cutting was to dump broadsheet formats in favour of tabloids. Another was to get rid of hundreds of journalists and production staff while replacing individual sub-editing sections in separate newspapers with centralised sub-editing hubs. Further, from about 2010, Australia's major newspaper companies started encouraging readers of their print editions to sign up for paid online and mobile delivery. The cost benefits of electronic delivery were obvious—printing presses could be shut down, printers and delivery truck drivers made redundant, the cost of newsprint slashed and payments to newsagents cut. All the while, quality and depth of reporting were sacrificed as many print products were dumbed down.

Commercial television, and to a lesser extent radio, newsrooms also felt the impacts of online and mobile device delivery of news. As competition between traditional commercial broadcasters and electronic delivery intensified there was greater pressure on broadcast newsrooms and broadcast journalists. One highly significant consequence of cost cutting and staff reductions by both print and electronic news media was an increased reliance on public-relations-inspired media releases. Ironically, while the ranks of newspaper journalists thinned dramatically as a result of cost cutting between 2011 and 2013, the number of public relations professionals increased. In 2012 it was reported that there were about 23,000 journalists and writers in Australia and 21,500 public relations staff. The number of PR operatives was predicted to match or outnumber journalists by 2013 (Jackson 2012, p. 3). That trend reflected a 2008 warning by the Australian Press Council that newsroom cost cutting at that time was coinciding with 'formidable growth' of media management teams whose aim was to protect senior executives and organisations while 'getting the company's story published' (McKinnon 2008, p. 2):

> All of which leads to an unfortunate trend, as yet anecdotal and unquantified, in which the pressures of the newsroom (or according to some, laziness, or inadequately trained journalists) result in everyday reuse of press releases without re-writing, checking or analysis. Checking the reliability of press

release information, or of unattributable 'spin', lies at the heart of good journalism (McKinnon 2008, p. 1).

Apart from the obvious point that the purpose of media releases is to promote or protect the vested interests of those who issue them, the vast majority are little more than spin and have no real news value. Often the aim of those who prepare and issue media releases is to use smoke and mirrors to manufacture 'news' even if it does not meet definitions of news and does not reflect Masterton's three elements of interest, timeliness and clarity (Masterton 1995). Another goal is to cheaply promote products or services without paying for advertising. But Professor of Public Communication at the University of Technology, Sydney, Jim Macnamara said research indicated that between 30 and 80 per cent of media content was sourced from, or significantly influenced by, public relations practitioners (Jackson 2009). A former president of the Public Relations Institute of Australia and a former journalist, Macnamara had warned years ago that 'ironically, the media themselves have contributed to the growth of public relations. Economics have forced the shrinkage of reporting staff in most media' (Macnamara 2003).

Discussions about newsworthiness and public relations spin aside, journalists and news outlets face at least one other obvious practical danger of dressing media releases up as 'news': if two separate news organisations simply publish articles or 'news items' based on the same media release without obtaining their own fresh information, and particularly if they publish on different days, the outlet which publishes second will appear to the public to be plagiarising from the first.

The purpose of media releases is to promote or protect the vested interests of those who issue them. The vast majority are little more than spin and have no real news value.

Thieves and copycats

In addition to an unhealthy dependence on media releases, some journalists and news outlets also attempt to cover their own news-gathering deficiencies by shamelessly 'lifting', or stealing, each other's stories, particularly in the online and mobile delivery environment. In the days before news was published online and on mobile devices it was usually newspapers that set the news agenda, with print stories being seized on and followed up by radio and television. Today, however, it is not uncommon to see a print story which includes lines like: 'Mr So-And-So told ABC Radio …', or 'said on talkback radio that …', or 'was reported on Channel Nine's *Today* as saying …', followed by a direct quote taken from the broadcast or text story. But rehashed news lacks timeliness and interest. Its news value is diminished. Thieving stories, or parts of them, from other news outlets also sends an obvious message to audiences and readers that the original source is better at gathering news than the outlet that copied from it. There are also implied messages about credibility and reliability—with the outlet lifting its 'news' from another outlet potentially being seen to endorse the credibility and reliability of a competitor's news reports, something that implicitly says news consumers would be best to simply get their news from the original news outlet and not bother with the copycat. Copying and pasting direct quotes from newspaper or online text articles also carries with it a danger of repeating an original quote that was inaccurate—something that could result in the copying outlet being drawn into any subsequent legal action(s). If done without attribution it also constitutes plagiarism.

A change in the balance from news with strong news values to tabloid pap, public-relations-driven spin, entertainment and items lifted from competitors' outlets has produced other unforeseen consequences for newspaper and magazine publishers. Commenting on the trend to add 'more and more sections in a bigger core product', Wilkinson (2004) reported that when the Paris tabloid *Liberation* added an extra 36-page supplement to its 72-page newspaper in the belief that 'more is always better', there was a 'spectacular reaction' from readers as 'circulation fell sharply from 200,000 to 140,000' (Wilkinson 2004, p. 77). An international expert on newspaper marketing, Wilkinson said:

> I believe for every page you add to today's newspaper you'll lose readers who don't have time to read it, feel guilty they can consume only 10 per cent of it, and while they enjoy a good buffet... they can't fathom the idea of a buffet every day (Wilkinson 2004, p. 78).

This is a point that publishers of Saturday newspapers could reflect on. How many people buy newspapers because they want to read real news, and how many really read all the lifestyle and infotainment sections, many of which are little more than public relations blurb or advertorial? And how about those who do not buy a Saturday paper because doing so would make them feel guilty about not having time to plough through it all, let alone worrying about the trees and carbon used in producing unread newsprint carrying information that was not newsworthy or interesting? Reflecting on points such as those, Gawenda said:

> The great revolution in newspapers 20 or so years ago was sectionalisation, designed to attract both advertisers and readers. And so papers added

sections for food, entertainment, television, education and personal finance among others … but it has proved to be a failed revolution. There is no evidence that I know of that shows readers in great numbers came on board and stayed on board. The advertising response was mediocre at best. Today, sectionalisation is an anachronism. Every newspaper section can be produced online, with all the advantages and at much lower cost (Gawenda 2012, p. 32).

In a 2009 address to the National Press Club in Canberra titled 'The future of journalism', former News Limited Chairman and Chief Executive John Hartigan had expressed a not dissimilar view. He asked:

How many journalists in this room have written a story recently that was original, exclusive, highly relevant and genuinely useful to your audience? I'm not saying there haven't been stories like this. But, there have been too few. And I reckon it's much the same in general news, business and sport, even the lifestyle sections (Hartigan 2009a, pp. 1 & 2).

Hartigan said the future of journalism would be assured if journalists and newspapers (or news outlets) did two things:

One. If you want to attract readers, break stories people want to read.

Two. Give them something they can't get anywhere else, make it relevant and useful and let them get involved (Hartigan 2009a, pp. 1 & 2).

Attempting to define 'quality news' Hartigan (2009a) said it should be 'well researched, brilliantly written, perceptive and intelligent, professionally edited, accurate and reliable'. He said 'great journalism' would tell news consumers 'something they did not know' and that 'they need to know'. He said journalists must listen to their public, answer their questions and inspire and entertain them. In a further echo of Mencher's definition of news, he said: 'Give them what they need to make decisions and equip them to act on those decisions' (Hartigan 2009a, p. 13).

DISCUSSION POINTS

1 Is Mencher's definition of news adequate? Do any news stories come to mind in which its two prongs would not apply?

2 It was only in the mid-1990s that Masterton identified his three essential news elements and six news values. How did journalists, editors and news producers decide what was news and what was just information before then?

3   Masterton listed the six news values he identified in descending order of importance. Is that order still valid today? Should the list be rearranged? And should new values be added?

4   It has been suggested in this chapter that there is probably a link between the declining circulation of print editions of newspapers and falling quality. Is that suggestion valid? What other factors might also be relevant?

5   And what of the quality of news and current affairs reporting by other media? Is quality really an issue across the board, not just for newspaper outlets?

6   Does it really matter if a 'news' story is sourced from a media release? Surely some media releases are written for altruistic reasons and are newsworthy.

NEWS PRACTICE POINTS

1   Find a 'news' article that does not contain a single news value listed in this chapter.

2   Find a news article that reflects at least four of the news values discussed in this chapter. Highlight the relevant parts of the article and label each with its associated news value.

3   Find a news article that reflects one or more of Masterton's six news values but which is let down because it is not interesting, or not timely, or not clear.

4   Find an online news story on a newspaper's website that contains information lifted from a broadcast story. How strong are the news values in the lifted story?

5   Find a news story on a broadcast outlet's website that is based on a proactive, agenda-setting print story.

6   Does the term 'tabloid' necessarily equate with poor quality? Identify three highly significant news stories that have been broken by tabloid newspapers, or on the websites of tabloid newspapers, in the past year.

7   Find a story that has obviously been sourced from a media release. How many different media outlets can you identify that carried the same story within a two-day period? Does the story carry Masterton's three news elements? If so, which of his six news values, if any, can be attached to it?

8   Should journalism and public relations students study in the same schools and complete overlapping courses at universities? Make a dot-point list of six reasons for and six against. Which list is more convincing?

JOURNALISM ETHICS 4

That was a lie, but you know that was a lie to a journalist, I didn't quite feel the same obligation, if you don't mind my saying so.

Marcus Einfeld, former Federal Court judge, 1986–2001

OBJECTIVES

After reading this chapter you will understand:

- » Contradictory public perceptions about journalists and news
- » Links between ethical decision making and the preservation of free speech
- » Why it is essential for journalists to be ethical and accountable
- » The MEAA *Journalists' Code of Ethics*
- » Industry codes of conduct and self-regulation
- » The need to balance privacy, public benefit and journalistic integrity.

It is rare for a journalist to send a judge to prison, but that was effectively what happened when former Federal Court judge Marcus Einfeld was sentenced to three years' jail for lying to a court in a bid to avoid paying a $77 traffic fine. The founding president of the Human Rights and Equal Opportunity Commission, and a former judge of the Federal Court and the NSW Supreme Court, Einfeld had been awarded an Order of Australia medal, was a Queen's Counsel, and had been honoured by the National Trust as 'a national living treasure' (Pelly 2009b).

Einfeld was released from jail on parole in 2011 after serving two years of his sentence. The seeds of his downfall were sown on January 8, 2006, when his silver Lexus was photographed by a speed camera travelling at 60km/h in a 50km/h zone. The penalty would have been a $77 fine and loss of three demerit points (Pelly 2009a, p. 3), but the judge had broken road rules before and his tally of demerit points was close to the limit. He feared he would lose his licence. He decided to fight the fine in court and wrote a letter saying he was out of town that day and had lent his Lexus to a female friend, Professor Teresa Brennan from Florida, who had since died. On August 7, 2006, Einfeld appeared in court, took an oath to tell the truth, and swore his statement before a magistrate (Ferguson 2009). The court dismissed the case against him. That evening, an assistant editor at Sydney's *The Daily Telegraph*, Michael Beach, was putting the finishing touches to the next morning's paper when young court reporter Viva Goldner filed a three-sentence article about Einfeld's court appearance and alibi. Beach later told *Four Corners*:

> I thought I'd make a couple of quick checks and I was intrigued about who is Teresa Brennan? I think one of the first checks that came up was the International Association of Literature and it referred to her dying in February 2003. And remember Marcus Einfeld had said in the court case that she'd died in early 2006 (Ferguson 2009).

Beach had done a basic Google search. He then asked Goldner to telephone Einfeld. She asked the former judge how it could be possible Teresa Brennan was driving his car if she was dead. Goldner later told David Penberthy of *The Australian*:

> And he paused and then said it was the other Teresa Brennan. I asked him if there were two of them, and he said yes. I asked if she was also from Florida as it said in his statutory declaration and he said, 'Yes, yes, I think so', and then he said he wasn't sure if it was Theresa with an h or Therese (sic), but that there were definitely two of them. He didn't know where she was now, and then he said 'I have nothing more to say' and hung up... he sounded like a bit of a bullshit artist (Penberthy 2009).

The next day, August 8, 2006, *The Daily Telegraph* ran a major story headlined 'The respected judge, the dead professor and a speeding fine' (Goldner 2006, p. 9). The story began:

> He's a respected former Federal Court judge and a top civil libertarian. But Justice Marcus Richard Einfeld's appearance at a Sydney court yesterday seems to have raised more questions than answers (Goldner 2006, p. 9).

The article sparked a police investigation. It was revealed that mobile telephone records showed Einfeld was in the area where his Lexus was photographed by the speed camera on the day the photograph was taken. Einfeld told more lies, but his pretence fell apart and he was charged with perjury and perverting the course of justice. He pleaded guilty. Sentencing Einfeld, NSW Supreme Court Judge Bruce James said his 'deliberate premeditated perjury' was 'part of a planned criminal activity' (Pelly 2009b). Enfeld subsequently admitted that in addition to committing crimes he had also been morally and 'communally' wrong (Ferguson 2009).

In a pre-recorded *Four Corners* program broadcast after Einfeld was jailed, ABC investigative journalist Sarah Ferguson revealed Einfeld had avoided earlier traffic fines by offering similar false excuses and had used Teresa Brennan's name previously (Ferguson 2009). She asked Einfeld why he lied in court and if he had 'a habit of dishonesty' (Ferguson 2009). Einfeld replied: 'I don't want to be offensive but that's a bit offensive and I don't think I'm in the slightest bit dishonest. I just made a mistake' (Ferguson 2009). Later in the program, Ferguson asked the former judge why he lied to Viva Goldner when she asked how Professor Brennan could have been driving his Lexus when she was dead. His reply was dismissive: 'That, that was a lie, but you know that was a lie to a journalist, I, I didn't quite feel the same obligation, if you don't mind my saying so' (Ferguson 2009). The comment raised the ire of journalists. It was the subject of an editorial opinion piece in *The Australian* headed 'Truth is paramount' which said:

> Einfeld's contempt for journalists is one thing, but his contempt for the public, who rely on accurate reporting for information, is quite another. To lie to a journalist is to lie to the broader community, and that is a serious matter ('Truth is paramount', April 6, 2009).

Society is ambivalent about journalists and journalism

A stark irony of Einfeld's fall from grace was that he deceived a court but not two nosy journalists—members of a profession he felt no obligation not to lie to.

Einfeld's attitude highlighted a wider social ambivalence about journalism and journalists. On one hand, society hunts for and devours the news, entertainment and educational information journalists produce. It needs journalists to warn it, inform it, educate it and entertain it. As discussed in Chapter 14, it also relies on journalists to fill a watchdog 'Fourth Estate' role when systems of governance, law and accountability fail. On the other hand, repeated surveys show journalists rank with real estate agents, politicians and used-car salesmen/women in terms of low status and limited public trust. Journalists are sued, abused and despised. Governments and criminals fear them. Too often—and literally as well as figuratively—journalists become targets for those who would shoot the messenger. Yet we all need journalism. It is a vital ingredient in our democratic way of life and it helps us make sense of the world.

Journalists' central functions are to seek truths and pass them on to their communities. In doing so, journalists often must decide what is in the public interest—what it will benefit the public to know—compared with what the public might be interested in and want to know.

In the preamble to the *Journalists' Code of Ethics*, the Media, Entertainment and Arts Alliance (MEAA) says:

> Respect for truth and the public's right to information are fundamental principles of journalism. Journalists describe society to itself. They convey information, ideas and opinions, a privileged role. They search, disclose, record, question, entertain, suggest and remember. They inform citizens and animate democracy. They give a practical form to freedom of expression. Many journalists work in private enterprise, but all have these public responsibilities. They scrutinise power, but also exercise it, and should be accountable. Accountability engenders trust... (MEAA 2013a).

In a nutshell, journalists' central functions are to seek truths and pass them on to their communities. In doing so, they often must decide what is in the public interest—what it will benefit the public to know—compared with what the public might be interested in and want to know. The two can coincide, or be vastly different. In reality, despite their often negative public image, journalists are much like any other professionals. They live in the community and, like judges and lawyers, the vast majority are ethical, honourable and decent people who take their responsibilities to the public they serve very seriously. Most are proud of their profession—rightly believing they fulfil a significant role in society and can make a difference for the better. Most abide by the MEAA *Journalists' Code of Ethics*—see Appendix 1—even if they are not members of the MEAA, which administers it.

Pragmatic reasons to be ethical

Moral, professional and altruistic motivations aside, there are sound pragmatic reasons why journalists work within the MEAA *Journalists' Code of Ethics*. As Sheridan Burns (2002, p. 65) said, 'All professions face ethical conflicts, but journalists publish the results of theirs. The journalist's decisions about the public interest are open to wide scrutiny'. Therefore, despite the bad behaviour of a few who give news media a bad name, the majority of employers expect journalists on their staff to behave ethically.

So do other journalists. There is strong peer pressure to be ethical, and those who are not are ostracised. Decent journalists with pride in their work are well aware of the poor public perception of their profession. They understand that just as the image of judges and lawyers was diminished a little by Einfeld's unethical and hypocritical conduct, journalism is tainted every time an individual journalist behaves badly, so they have a vested interest in ridding the profession of rogues. There is also the point that journalists' two most important assets are their contact book and their good name. Without a solid reputation as a responsible and ethical professional whom sources, employers and the public can trust, a journalist will find that his or her contact book contains few names. Without a full contact book, that journalist will not last long in the profession—or not, at least, in responsible mainstream media. Word of mouth is everything when it comes to reputation. It truly is a remarkably small world and, as many have found to their cost, our sins really do have ways of finding us out.

One watchdog that has specialised in making journalists pay for transgressions is the ABC's *Media Watch*. Since its first broadcast in 1989, the program has focused on journalistic 'stuff-ups, beat-ups and barneys' (Media Watch—20 Years 2009). The program's motto 'everyone loves it until they are on it' is an added incentive for journalists to avoid ethical breaches and consequent on-air naming and shaming. *Media Watch*'s philosophy is explained on its website:

> The media provides the information we need to make decisions about our lives, but how reliable are the media reports that shape our views of the world? *Media Watch* turns the spotlight onto those who literally 'make the news': the reporters, editors, sub-editors, producers, camera operators, sound recordists and photographers who claim to deliver the world to our doorsteps, radios, computers and living rooms. We also keep an eye on those who try to manipulate the media: the PR consultants, spin-doctors, lobbyists and 'news makers' who set the agenda (ABC 2012).

Rogue journalists threaten media freedom

In 2011 Rupert Murdoch closed his British Sunday newspaper *News of the World*. It had been published for 168 years and was one of the oldest papers in the UK. When it was shut down its circulation was about 2.8 million copies a week (BBC 2012).

A News Corporation paper on the lower end of the British tabloid scale for sleaze, sex scandals and gossip, its popular colloquial nickname 'News of the Screws' (BBC 2012) pretty much said it all. But it wasn't drugs, sex or rock 'n' roll which brought the publication down. It was the hacking of mobile phones by an editor, journalists and a private investigator paid by the paper. The issue first attracted widespread attention in 2006–07 when a *News of the World* royal editor and a private investigator were convicted of intercepting voicemail messages left for staff of the royal family. The pair were jailed. Their editor, Andy Coulson, subsequently quit, saying he took responsibility for what happened (BBC 2012). However, instead of learning from past mistakes, the staff culture inside the newspaper was so dysfunctional that the phone hacking continued. The BBC reported that:

> By September 2010 a string of well-known people began legal moves to have their claims looked at … amid mounting suspicions that phone hacking had been more widely used. The turning point came in January 2011 when the Metropolitan Police launched Operation Weeting, a fresh phone hacking investigation which included looking at the original 2006 case. The investigation slowly widened to include allegations of improper payments to public officials and separate claims of computer hacking (BBC 2012).

Then came news, reported in the *Guardian* newspaper in July 2011, that *News of the World* had hacked into a mobile phone owned by schoolgirl Milly Dowler, 13, who had been murdered in 2002. Other targets were claimed to include politicians, celebrities and relatives of dead soldiers. The public was so outraged and disgusted that Murdoch had little option other than to shut the paper. The scandal also sparked a political backlash, with British Prime Minister David Cameron announcing the appointment of Lord Justice Leveson to examine the ethics of Britain's press (Cusick & Milmo 2013).

In a report published in November 2011 the Leveson Inquiry found press behaviour had been 'outrageous' and 'wreaked havoc with the lives of innocent people'. To ensure accountability in future it recommended establishment of a strict new independent regulator backed by legislation (BBC 2013). The government responded with plans for a 'royal charter' to control newspapers but the concept was condemned by human rights groups, media organisations and freedom campaigners around the world who perceived any government control of news media as threatening freedom of speech and democratic government.

Although the *News of the World* mobile phone hacking scandal had nothing to do with Australian journalists or editors, and although there is a totally different culture among newspaper journalists in Australia from that which perverted the *News of the World*, the Gillard Labor Government, backed by the Greens, established two reviews in 2011 to examine news media regulation and ownership in Australia. The role of the first, the *Convergence Review*, was said to be an examination of:

> a broad range of issues, including media ownership laws, media content standards, the ongoing production and distribution of Australian and local content, and the allocation of radio-communications spectrum (Department of Broadband, Communications and the Digital Economy 2012, p. vii).

The second inquiry, *The Independent Inquiry Into The Media And Media Regulation*, which became known as the 'Finkelstein Inquiry' after its chairman, Ray Finkelstein, QC, was established to make recommendations about 'media codes of practice in Australia', impacts of technical change on 'quality journalism and the production of news', 'strengthening the independence and effectiveness of the Australian Press Council', and 'any related issues pertaining to the ability of the media to operate according to regulations and codes of practice, and in the public interest' (Finkelstein Inquiry 2012 p. 13).

The Finkelstein Inquiry recommended establishment of a government funded 'news media council' to make 'news media more accountable to those covered in the news, and to the public generally' and to have 'power to enforce news standards across all news media outlets' (Finkelstein Inquiry 2012, p. 13). It was proposed that the new regulator take over the functions of the Australian Press Council (APC) and Australian Communications and Media Authority (ACMA) and be chaired by a 'retired judge or other eminent lawyer' (Finkelstein Inquiry 2012 p. 291). The inquiry also recommended that:

> There should be a legal requirement that if a regulated media outlet refuses to comply with a News Media Council determination the News Media Council or the complainant should have the right to apply to a court of competent jurisdiction for an order compelling compliance. Any failure to comply with the court order should be a contempt of court and punishable in the usual way (Finkelstein Inquiry 2012 p. 298).

The recommendations of each inquiry were seen by journalists, media organisations, advocates of free speech and many members of the public as a direct assault on media freedom and free speech. Their response was summed up in an editorial opinion column in *The Australian* thus:

> To hand government a direct or indirect role in controlling editorial content and enforcing sanctions against journalists is to throw a wet blanket over

freedom of speech. Much of the accountability and freedom we have come to enjoy and expect through our liberal democratic system will be placed at risk, and inevitably be diminished, if press freedom is eroded. Governments do not like scrutiny—they like power (*The Weekend Australian* 2012, p. 23).

After lengthy consideration of both reports federal Communications Minister Stephen Conroy introduced legislation into the parliament in March 2013 which, among other measures, provided for the government to appointment a 'public interest media advocate' who would oversee 'news media standards' and have power to decide if media mergers 'of national significance' could proceed (Conroy 2013b). Conroy attempted to ram the enabling legislation through parliament by declaring that if it was not passed in just 11 days he would withdraw it. His approach was widely condemned, even by members of Conroy's own party and independent members of parliament who the minority Gillard Government depended on to retain power.

The proposed legislation, and extreme haste of its introduction, also drew vehement criticism from industry, journalists and the public. As an example, News Limited chairman Kim Williams described the proposed new laws as 'Stalinist', Seven West Media chairman Kerry Stokes said he was 'trying for the life of me to understand what we could possibly have done to warrant such intrusive laws' and Fairfax chief executive Greg Hywood said the proposal to establish a public interest media advocate was 'dangerous' because the appointee would 'have too much power and could be pressured by a minister or a government to shut down critical media reporting' (Griffiths 2013).

Without direct inside knowledge one can only speculate if the two Australian media inquiries in 2011–12 and subsequent attempt by the Gillard Government to regulate news media was related to the *News of the World* hacking scandal. Perhaps it was, as some commentators suggested, a ham-fisted attempt to control what some in the government regarded as a hostile news media—specially News Limited's *The Australian* and *The Daily Telegraph*. That was certainly the view of an editorial comment writer at *The Australian*, who said:

> The impetus has come from former Greens leader Bob Brown and the Communication Minister, Stephen Conroy ... Brown has described News Limited as the 'hate media' and Senator Conroy has accused it of running an agenda against the government. They saw the shocking revelations about phone hacking at News Corporation newspapers in London as an opportunity to escalate their media war and delegitimise their critics [in Australia] (*The Weekend Australian* 2012, p. 23).

Conversely, the government's motivation in attempting to strengthen Australian news media regulation might have been genuinely altruistic. Announcing his government's response to the Convergence Review and Finkelstein Inquiry, Senator Conroy said:

> The government passionately believes in freedom of the press as a cornerstone of our democracy. At the same time, the government believes that in a democracy a diversity of voices within the media is essential. The government's reforms seek to ensure no further reduction in media diversity and requires no change to existing media standards. The government also understands that there is community concern about media quality and how press complaints are handled. The government will bring to the parliament legislation that will promote diversity and fairness in the media for the public (Conroy 2013a).

Whatever the motivation, the intense focus on media accountability and journalism ethics in Australia in the aftermath of the *News of the World* scandal was at least a wake-up call for media organisations, their managers and journalists—a salient reminder not only that it is in their own best interest to think and behave ethically, but also of the overwhelming public importance in protecting freedom of speech and resisting government interference in news gathering and reporting.

Codes of ethics and codes of practice

Codes of ethics and industry codes of practice are separate from the legal constraints discussed in Chapters 15, 16 and 17. Links to the different codes discussed in this chapter can be found in Appendix 3. The MEAA *Journalists' Code of Ethics* is enforced to a limited degree by a judiciary committee of the journalists' section of the MEAA—a union representing entertainers, advertising professionals, radio announcers, book editors, clowns and website producers as well as journalists. In addition to the MEAA code, Australian journalists are held accountable to some extent by specific codes of industry practice.

The Australian Press Council is governed by its own self-regulating Standards of Practice (as distinct from a code of ethics) governing content of newspapers and their associated websites (Australian Press Council 2013). One problem the council faces is that because it is a self-regulating industry body, membership is voluntary. Another relates to funding. The council was reasonably well supported by major publishers, and particularly News Limited, until 2009 but in that year its members slashed funding by 20 per cent. This led to a decline in services and a weakening of the council. Coincidentally, or otherwise, funding was restored in 2012–13 after the convergence and Finkelstein inquiries. The council also introduced new rules which meant members would have to give four years' notice if they wished to withdraw their membership. Prior to implementation of that rule, Seven West Media, which owns *The West Australian*, a number of regional papers, and the Pacific Magazines group, which publishes *New Idea*, quit the council and established its own complaints handling body, the Independent Media Council.

Radio and television stations are self-regulating through codes of practice but are ultimately answerable to the Australian Communications and Media Authority (ACMA), as are internet content providers. The only codes that have statutory backing are the broadcast and internet codes associated with the ACMA. In addition the ACMA is responsible for enforcing Australia's anti-spam laws and regulating fixed line and mobile telephone services (ACMA 2013).

Lack of external accountability in relation to the MEAA and press council codes has led to criticism. It was argued in the Finkelstein Inquiry, for example, that voluntary codes administered by journalists and industry groups tend to be self-serving and ineffectual. One obvious issue is that journalists who breach the MEAA *Journalists' Code of Ethics* can only be censured and fined if they are MEAA members. The union has no power to punish non-members, and a member can evade penalties by resigning. On the other hand some journalists who have faced union action over ethics matters have likened the MEAA judiciary committee to a kangaroo court. They have accused it of paying too much attention to vexatious complainants instead of supporting and protecting union members from harassment.

Similarly, there has been strident criticism of the broadcasting and internet codes of practice, which are registered with the ACMA. The ACMA only steps in if complaints are not resolved satisfactorily by the relevant broadcast outlet. When dealing with complaints, the ACMA does not distinguish between journalists, presenters and announcers. Even though some of the most outrageous breaches of broadcast codes of practice have been committed by radio talkback hosts— so-called 'shock-jocks'—not journalists, the public tends to perceive both as being tarred with the same brush.

Imperfect as Australia's media self-regulation is, it is preferable to state control of media and journalists. Delivering the 1999 AN Smith Lecture in Journalism at the University of Melbourne, journalist and lawyer Paul Chadwick made points that resonate even more strongly today:

> Many people associate better media accountability with some kind of statutory scheme, underpinned by parliament's will, administered by the executive and refereed by the judiciary. I do not. I stake my all on self-regulation. History and experience tell me that, whatever the flaws of a media free from detailed content regulation, media subject to such regulation would be worse. Politicians of all complexions would be drawn irresistibly into the use of such regulation to manipulate, to intimidate and to suppress. All roads from a so-called independent statutory tribunal lead back through a parliament to a cabinet room. (Chadwick 1999)

MEAA *Journalists' Code of Ethics*

When members of the then Australian Journalists' Association—the forerunner to the MEAA—first adopted a code of ethics in 1944, their stated aim was to better serve the community and their motivation was seen as being altruistic. But there was also an ulterior motive—journalists hoped the code would protect them from employers who pushed staff to behave in ways they found morally uncomfortable. Mayer (1968) said proprietors saw the code as an 'interference' with their businesses. He said its adoption by the union implied:

> proprietors and executives would not or could not fix and enforce such standards; at the extreme, it implies that before the code, such standards did not exist owing to the policy of employers (Mayer 1968, p. 203).

The situation is different today, with major media organisations actively promoting the current MEAA *Journalists' Code of Ethics* to staff. News Limited, for example, includes a copy of the code in its own training materials (Cameron 2007, pp. 86 & 87) and *The Sydney Morning Herald* incorporates the code in its own code of ethics (*The Sydney Morning Herald* 2009). *The Age* also promotes the alliance's code within its code (*The Age* 2009).

The MEAA *Journalists' Code of Ethics* commits journalists to honesty, fairness, independence and respect for the rights of others. It contains 12 provisions which, among other things, say that journalists should:

— not distort facts

— not allow gifts or benefits to undermine their independence or fairness

— identify themselves when seeking interviews

— not exploit people's ignorance of media practices

— respect grief and privacy

— do their best to correct mistakes

— never plagiarise

— not use their positions for personal gain

— not allow advertising considerations to undermine their independence

— attribute whenever possible

— not put undue influence on personal characteristics

— allow opportunities for reply

— use fair and honest means to obtain material for stories

— disclose payments for stories, pictures or information (MEAA 2013).

Richards (2005) said the code has three different types of provision: those that benefit journalists' audiences, those that benefit journalists' sources, and those that benefit the subjects of journalists' stories (Richards 2005, pp. 60 & 61). He criticised the code 'because most of its clauses contain concepts—"fairness", "honesty", and "independence", for example—which are unclear to say the very least' (Richards 2005, pp. 61 & 62). Nonetheless, Richards said codes of ethics are useful because they highlight potential ethical dangers before they are encountered, and they publicly express values and ideals of journalism. In doing so they 'serve as a reminder of the moral point of the sorts of activities in which journalists are involved' (Richards 2005, p. 60).

Every aspiring journalist must become familiar with the MEAA *Journalists' Code of Ethics*, understand it and adhere to it if they wish to build a successful professional career. While most clauses are self-explanatory, there are sections students should be particularly aware of. First, when working on a story as a student journalist you must introduce yourself properly to those you interview by saying something like: 'Hello, my name is Fred/Freda So-And-So. I am a journalism student at XYZ University and I am working on a story about... The story could be published in...'. If you were participating in a formal internship with a news organisation, you could introduce yourself by name and say you are working on a story for that particular publication, website or broadcast outlet.

Second, as a student you are not well placed to offer to protect the identity of a source. For a start, you do not have the backing of a large media organisation that might be prepared to pay for potentially expensive legal representation if it is needed. Even then, as explained in Chapter 16, this is a vexed area in which something that seems like a good idea at the time can come back to haunt you. Point 3 of the code says: 'Aim to attribute information to its source.' It then warns: 'Where a source seeks anonymity, do not agree without first considering the source's motives and any alternative attributable source. Where confidences are accepted, respect them in all circumstances' (MEAA 2013). That warning is for a good reason. If on one hand you decided to protect a source, and were later asked in a court who that source was and you refused to reveal her or his identity, you could be jailed for contempt of court. On the other hand, if you did bow to pressure from lawyers, a magistrate or judge and reveal the source's identity, your name would be mud—not only with the source, but within media generally and probably also with the public—making it unlikely sources, your peers, news executives, or your readership or audience would trust you ever again.

Also, as a student journalist, unless confronted with extraordinary circumstances, you would be wise to avoid invoking the guidance clause at the end of the MEAA *Journalists' Code of Ethics* that says:

> Basic values often need interpretation and sometimes come into conflict. Ethical journalism requires conscientious decision-making in context. Only substantial advancement of the public interest or risk of substantial harm to people allows any standard to be overridden (MEAA 2013).

Deciding to invoke this clause is a serious step. It is usually only done by an experienced professional journalist in consultation with her or his editor, chief-of-staff, director of news or news producer. Unless there is an exceptional circumstance in which a journalist must make a snap decision, the clause should only be relied on after careful consideration. Issues involved in a story must be balanced against the implications of breaching the code—not just for the journalist, but also for his or her media organisation, the public and sources. As a general rule, this is not a decision you should make as a journalism student, and certainly not without seeking guidance from senior journalism staff at your institution. If you are in an internship or work-experience situation, you should consult your immediate supervisor and also the editor, chief-of-staff or news producer.

If you decided to protect a source, and were later asked in a court who that source was and you refused to reveal her or his identity, you could be jailed for contempt of court. But if you did bow to pressure and revealed the source's identity, your name would be mud.

There are two other sections of the MEAA code that can be particularly challenging. In some senses they are at opposite ends of the spectrum: one relates to dealing with death and disaster, and the other with offers of gifts and favours. Each is discussed in the following pages.

PRIVACY AND PUBLIC BENEFIT

Point 11 of the MEAA *Journalists' Code of Ethics* says: 'Respect private grief and personal privacy. Journalists have the right to resist compulsion to intrude'. Journalists are sometimes faced with conflicting obligations with respect to private grief and personal privacy. There are times when balancing the public's desire— or need—to know against an individual's desire for privacy can be a difficult judgment to make. As discussed in Chapter 17, there is no all-embracing right to privacy in Australia. There is also a difference in how private citizens who go about their lives and jobs without fanfare or seeking glory are treated, compared with those who live much of their life in the public eye. Overall, Australian journalists tend to be reasonably conservative in their treatment of grief and privacy, leaning more towards protecting privacy and respecting grief than aggressive reporting supposedly conducted in the public interest. Journalists in some other nations take the opposite approach. In the US, for example, the balance is weighted more heavily on the side of public interest than protection of personal privacy, so interviewing and reporting are considerably more intrusive.

Hurst and White (1999) said 'news media are never welcome at the scene of a tragedy', but 'tragedy is news, and it is the media's job to report it' (Hurst & White 1999, p. 111). One thing not generally well understood by the public in that context is that while journalists learn to cope when dealing with tragedy, most do not feel comfortable doing so. As discussed in Chapter 5, many journalists dread 'death-knocks'—literally being sent to knock on the doors of relatives and friends of people killed in accidents, crimes, or uncommon circumstances. Point 11 of the MEAA *Journalists' Code of Ethics* implies that employers cannot compel journalists to do this, yet there are times when interviews with grieving relatives and friends do result in stories with strong public benefit.

In the writer's experience there are two dimensions involved in making ethical decisions about personal grief and news. The first is to ask yourself: what potential public benefit could there be in approaching a grief-stricken person for an interview? If there is absolutely no foreseeable benefit, do not make the approach.

But if there is a potential public benefit, then make contact. When doing so, the key to ethically and sensitively dealing with grieving family and friends lies in the word 'respect' in the first sentence of point 11 of the code. If you approach bereaved relatives with respect and they say they do not want to talk, then simply go away and leave them alone. Do not argue or try to convince them otherwise. Even if they are angry and abusive, as grieving people sometimes are, do not argue back. Accept their decision, but do try to leave a business card with your contact details. Then, if on reflection they change their mind, as does happen sometimes, they can contact you.

A second dimension in which there can be a fine line ethically is in deciding at what point personal behaviour ceases to be private and becomes news. Often matters relating to the personal lives of politicians, sporting identities and celebrities, which are known to Australian journalists, are never reported. It is only when private behaviour or interests start impacting on public duties, if hypocritical public utterances conflict with private activities, or there is potentially criminal behaviour that a line is crossed and public benefit is seen to outweigh personal privacy.

Questions about when private behaviour impacts on public political duties and allegiances were faced by Canberra media gallery bastion Laurie Oakes before he decided to go public about an affair between former Labor government foreign minister Gareth Evans and former leader of the Australian Democrats Cheryl Kernot. Oakes' 2002 revelation has become a landmark example of where ideals of privacy and public benefit intersect. Information about the relationship was reported after Kernot defected to the Labor Party. Oakes said there was no mention of the affair in a book Kernot had released in 2002, but if there had been, people would have viewed her defection to the Labor Party in a different light (AAP 2002). There was intense debate at the time about whether Oakes should have disclosed what he and others in the Canberra press gallery knew, or if he should have kept quiet. Evans and Kernot subsequently left politics. Oakes was reported as saying the five-year affair ended in November 1999 after a 'long period of recrimination' (AAP 2002).

At what point does personal behaviour cease to be private and become news? Often, it is only when private behaviour or interests start impacting on public duties, if hypocritical public utterances conflict with private activities, or there is potentially criminal behaviour that a line is crossed and public benefit is seen to outweigh personal privacy.

Commenting at the time, the then *Canberra Times* editor Jack Waterford said:

> The primary rule involves hypocrisy. If you are not on record as opposing it, it is unlikely that you will be exposed for doing it. Most public figures in Australia are allowed a reasonable private life, and I can think of scores of well-known ones whose sexuality, friendships and habits of drug or alcohol abuse are not referred to in the media because reporters generally do not

see how it impinges on the performance of their public duties. But there are buts. The obvious one is where it does impinge on your public duties (Waterford 2002).

PERSUASION AND INFLUENCE

Dealing ethically with gifts and freebies can be another awkward area for a journalist. There is an old saying that there is no such thing as a free lunch, and that is often the case. Gifts tend to be offered by two separate types of people— those genuinely grateful to a journalist for some reason, and those who seek to manipulate or bribe for their own ends.

Three points in the MEAA *Journalists' Code of Ethics* come into play here:

— Point 4: 'Do not allow personal interest, or any belief, commitment, payment, gift or benefit, to undermine your accuracy, fairness or independence.'

— Point 5: 'Disclose conflicts of interest that affect, or could be seen to affect, the accuracy, fairness or independence of your journalism. Do not improperly use a journalistic position for personal gain'

— Point 6: 'Do not allow advertising or other commercial considerations to undermine accuracy, fairness or independence' (MEAA 2013).

Issues arise if business, political, corporate, public relations and other interests attempt to influence and/or compromise journalists. One key point to remember when dealing with professional manipulators of opinion is that while journalists have a duty to serve the whole public and report in the public interest, a public relations operative, real estate agent, political spin-doctor or business representative ultimately serves a single master or mistress—the person with a vested interest who pays them!

Attempts to influence journalists are sometimes blatant—examples of tempting inducements include gifts, money, sex, alcohol or holidays in return for favourable coverage, or indeed no coverage. Accepting just one offer can forever compromise you because acceptance means becoming indebted. The person who made the offer will most likely want a greater return on investment in the form of more favourable treatment next time. If the person does not get her or his own way, that person might threaten to reveal details of whatever compromising inducement you accepted. The threat might be to tell your boss, police, colleagues or competitors, a girlfriend, boyfriend or spouse. Common sense—not just the code of ethics—says the smart thing is to politely but firmly decline any offer of a gift or potential inducement from any vested interest, no matter how seemingly innocent. This might even mean returning gifts delivered to your office or home with a polite note explaining how acceptance would be contrary to your professional code of ethics—something an ethical public relations professional or corporate employee should understand anyway.

As noted in Chapter 11, journalists who write travel features have special responsibilities to openly reveal any sponsorship of travel, meals and accommodation. They must also be totally honest with readers and audiences in their assessments of resorts and destinations. The same applies to motoring writers, information technology reporters and restaurant reviewers, with the latter being well advised to walk in off the street without a booking and without revealing the reason for their visit if they plan to review a particular eatery.

At a different level, journalists sometimes have to decide how to deal with gifts genuinely given by people whose stories they have told, and who seek to do no more than express gratitude. Some journalists and some news organisations have a blanket policy that all gifts must be returned. Others are more flexible. As a general rule of thumb, it is wise to politely return gifts from anyone who has been the subject of an article you have written or broadcast if you are likely to write or broadcast about that same person again, or any organisation they represent. But if you had worked on an article that genuinely helped someone—perhaps even changed their life for the better—and it is highly unlikely you would ever be writing about them again, it would seem churlish not to accept an appropriate heartfelt gift.

Overall, it is wise to think ahead about ethical decision making before you are actually confronted with difficult or awkward situations. That way you can consider potential scenarios and decide how you might best deal with them. Doing this should help you make sensible decisions later and avoid spur-of-the-moment mistakes.

Industry codes

As noted earlier in this chapter different media organisations have their own in-house codes of practice, guidelines or statements of principles which are over and above the MEAA, Australian Press Council and ACMA codes. The ABC and SBS, for example, each have Codes of Practice which deal with complaints, principles and standards. News Limited and Fairfax also have in-house codes of conduct. Journalists who work for those organisations are expected to be aware of and abide by both the internal and external codes. Links to the main industry guidelines are listed in Appendix 3.

Chequebook journalism

The Australian Press Council warns that paying money to sources in return for stories is fraught with danger. Writing in *Press Council News*, former council member Chris McLeod concluded:

> there are great dangers in waving the cheque book around. The obvious risk in some cases is that the story-teller may feel obliged to enhance the story. It also devalues good journalism… It's not much of a journalistic boast to say the story was won because 'we outbid the rest'. Journalists become less relevant in cheque book journalism (McLeod 2005, p. 1).

In its 2008 *State of the News Print Media in Australia Report* the council said:

> Most instances of paid interviews—the term 'chequebook journalism' isn't really appropriate because the practice often has little to do with journalism at all—come in the highly competitive world of 6.30pm TV programs. That's peak viewing time… The cut-throat magazine industry is also active with the chequebook… TV current affairs programs and glossy gossipy magazines include themselves in the press or news media when more properly they are engaged in the entertainment business (Australian Press Council 2008b).

An obvious potential weakness of paid stories is that interviewees could be tempted to enhance versions of events, or even fantasise, in order to make a story seem more interesting and hence 'worth' more money than it really was. Another is that it is a form of media control in which a source usually commits to dealing exclusively with a single outlet—something which limits dissemination of a story and also places the source at the mercy of the outlet and how it decides to portray her or him.

There is also a copycat effect, by which members of the public develop an expectation that they will be paid for stories because others have been paid. And what of the morality of paying for stories about criminals? The council has said: 'being in the news it seems has become a ticket to fame for many who have fringe connections to criminal activity, though they themselves have not been found guilty of anything' (Australian Press Council 2008b, pp. 5–8). The council said that in one week in 2008, television current affairs programs 'shelled out around $100,000 for interviews' with a Melbourne gangland lawyer and the wife of a gangland figure, as well as $30,000 paid to a former staff member who had worked for a prominent politician (Australian Press Council 2008b). The council also said:

> Eyebrows were raised when a Logie award (for most outstanding public affairs report) was presented to the Nine Network for an interview with Terri Irwin against the background of Nine making a donation to her late husband Steve's foundation to secure exclusivity (Australian Press Council 2008b).

The council said online journalism, and particularly sporting journalism in which sporting organisations were seeing coverage as a 'potential cash cow', resulted in a disturbing trend in which media were expected to pay for publication and broadcast rights. The council said sections of media that paid for stories should disclose the fact, so the public could make judgments about the authenticity of interviews. It said:

> Undoubtedly, the integrity of journalism will come under more challenges. Journalists and publishers alike will have to ensure that legitimate news coverage survives, free of chequebook controls, so that the public continues to have timely access to legitimate news coverage... The public, after all, is entitled to the truth. And to honest journalism (Australian Press Council 2008b).

Journalistic integrity

Journalists, like judges, have a key role in keeping others honest and accountable. And, like judges, journalists must be honest and accountable themselves because they occupy a position of power and influence. Otherwise, like Einfeld, they would be hypocrites. An honest journalist is one who presents all the facts as he or she understands them as fairly, accurately and objectively as possible. Journalists must not suppress facts or fail to report opinions they disagree with. That is an ethical stance with a long and honourable tradition. Benjamin Franklin explained the concept to readers in his 1731 'An Apology for Printers' when he wrote:

> it is unreasonable to imagine Printers approve of everything they print, and to censure them on any particular thing accordingly; since in the way of their Business they print such great variety of things opposite and contradictory.

> It is likewise as unreasonable what some assert, 'That Printers ought not to print any Thing but what they approve;' since if all of that Business should make such a Resolution, and abide by it, an End would thereby be put to Free Writing, and the World would afterwards have nothing to read but what happen'd to be the Opinions of Printers (Franklin 1731).[1]

Franklin's 'apology' is as relevant today as it was the day he wrote it. There should be no clues in a journalist's work about her or his political leaning, religious affiliation or other personal interests. As former Managing Editor of *The New York Times* Clifton Daniel said, a journalist's role is to 'serve the public, not the profession of journalism, not a particular newspaper, not the government, but the public' (Daniel, in Mencher 1997, p. 641). It should also be understood that mistakes are a fact of life—we all make them. What is important, is that we react ethically when we do. Will we own up, apologise and learn from what happened? Or will we emulate Marcus Einfeld—bluff, bluster, lie and misrepresent our case to the public? Asked by *Four Corners* journalist Sarah Ferguson why he perjured himself and perverted the course of justice, Einfeld replied:

> I don't really know. I've searched my conscience and my mind about this for a long time as you might imagine, I think of very little else. I got myself into a deep hole and I didn't know how to get out of it (Ferguson 2009).

As a journalist it is imperative that you avoid digging yourself into deep ethical holes—doing otherwise will harm you, your readers or audience and your news outlet, diminish the profession of journalism, and be an abuse of your privileged position as an agent of free speech.

DISCUSSION POINTS

1   What are the real reasons why the public has such a poor perception of journalists?

2   Would you ever lie to a journalist? Why or why not?

3   Was Einfeld right about not feeling the same obligation regarding lying to a journalist as lying to others? Or is it true that when a person lies to a journalist, they lie to the broader community?

4   A member of the public contacts you and points out a major error in one of your stories. You feel sick in the pit of your stomach about the mistake. What will you do?

---

1   Remember that, as explained in Chapter 1, printers and journalists were often one and the same in the 1730s.

5   Should governments regulate and control media and journalists to ensure issues are reported properly and individuals are treated fairly? Why? Why not?

6   Occasionally, police may ask journalists not to report on a specific issue, or to hold off reporting until a particular crime has been solved. Sometimes those requests have a legitimate public benefit, but at other times they might simply be because a police officer is trying to cover up a mistake, or is corrupt. How would you discover if such a request was legitimate or if it was not? Is it your decision, or should you just ignore the request and report anyway?

7   Does the nature of news mean all people involved in newsworthy events automatically forfeit their privacy? Does it make a difference if those events occurred in public, or if they happened in situations such as a home in which one might reasonably expect privacy?

NEWS PRACTICE POINTS

1   You are the court reporter on a major regional newspaper. A teenager is convicted of a prostitution offence. During the hearing, it is revealed that her partner is terminally ill and that she is supporting him financially and emotionally in the last days of his life. He thinks she works in a bank. The girl's father approaches you and begs you not to run the story, but your newspaper normally reports all such cases. List three reasons why you would report the story and three reasons why you would not. What is your final decision? Will you discuss the story and the father's request with your chief-of-staff or news producer? Why or why not?

2   Identify a controversial print or online story that concerns an individual. Either clip or print the story, then go through it and use contrasting colour highlighter pens to mark the sections that present the different sides. Was the story fair and balanced, or not? In what ways?

3   Find an advertising feature article in a newspaper or magazine that was not labelled as such, and also an advertisement in the same edition of the same publication to which the article appears to be linked. Compose a letter of complaint that refers to the relevant section(s) of the MEAA *Journalists' Code of Ethics* and send it to the publication's editor. What response, if any, did you get?

4   Sometimes it can be relevant to report on a person's race, sexual orientation or religious affiliations. Make a list giving an example of when it might be relevant to report on each one of those three characteristics, and a parallel list giving examples of when it would gratuitous to do so.

5   Go online and find a copy of the 2012 Convergence Review report. List five significant points in the report which you consider to be sensible and reasonable and five which could be construed as being threats to media freedom.

6   Following on from Practice Point 5, in no more than 750 words explain how you think the report could have impacted positively or negatively on media freedom and freedom of speech in Australia if its recommendations had been adopted and become law.

7   Details of the affair between Gareth Evans and Cheryl Kernot were made public by journalist Laurie Oakes. List six reasons why the story should have been reported as news, and six reasons why the story should have been suppressed. What would you have done if the information had come to you?

8   If doctors or lawyers are exposed as having behaved unethically, they can be de-registered and will no longer be permitted to practise. But if journalists are shown to have behaved unethically, they cannot be de-registered. Write a balanced article of about 650 words setting out the pros and cons of whether or not journalists should have to be registered to practise.

THE NEWSROOM 5

The recurring dilemma for news organisations is the regular production of an irregular and unpredictable commodity. This organisational feat can only be sustained through institutional routines...
Tiffen 1989, p. 4

OBJECTIVES

After reading this chapter you will understand:

» The chain of command in a newsroom

» Different jobs in newsrooms

» Newsroom etiquette

» How to find news stories

» Approaches to difficult stories

» How to protect yourself as a journalist.

The newsroom is the engine room of every news media outlet. When the engine is well oiled and ticks sweetly, so does the news product. But if the engine is neglected, it runs rough and the product breaks down. As in most organisations, the tone and culture of a newsroom is set at the top and flows down. In larger news outlets there is a clearly defined pecking order. Structure varies a little between organisations and media platforms, but is basically similar.

— At the top of the online, mobile and print editions of major newspapers there is traditionally an editor-in-chief, or editorial director, and an editorial manager. In a television station the equivalent of the editor-in-chief will usually be known as the director of news.

— Next in the chain of command is usually a general editor or news editor (in print, radio and online), or an executive producer of news (in television). In a large newspaper organisation there will probably be a night editor and section editors in charge of areas such as sport, features and business.

— Then comes the chief-of-staff (print and online) or the news producer (television and often radio).

— In charge of visuals are the photographic editor or chief photographer (print and online), or the senior video editor or senior video camera operator (television).

— After that there are senior journalists and senior sub-editors; journalists assigned to particular news rounds such as courts, police, health and education; a range of sub-editors; video editors; general journalists; floor managers; video camera operators; photographers; casual journalists and sub-editors.

— Finally, there are often junior journalists, known as 'cadets' in some organisations or 'graduates' in others.

Newsroom structures have changed, sometimes dramatically, since the start of the 21st century. Some changes resulted from the move to online and mobile device news publishing and others from quests for efficiencies by newspapers such as the establishment of centralised sub-editing and news production hubs. Although details vary a little inside different organisations it is important for journalism students to have a broad understanding of newsroom structures before they undertake an internship or work experience, and/or before they graduate and apply for their first job. Different roles are examined in detail in the following pages.

The chain of command

EDITOR-IN-CHIEF, DIRECTOR OF NEWS AND EDITORIAL MANAGER

These positions are a bridge between corporate management and newsrooms. The editor-in-chief is responsible for the overall editorial direction of a newspaper's print and online publications. The director of news (sometimes called the head of news and current affairs) has the same role in relation to broadcast news, current affairs programs and online policy. In many instances—and depending on the individual and how much she or he delegates—the editor-in-chief/director of news has a limited role in day-to-day news selection and production, although in some organisations he or she would have the final word on which stories run on front pages, are featured online or at the top of news broadcasts. An editor-in-chief/ director of news is usually the public face of a news organisation and the person who takes final responsibility for rises and falls in online readership, circulation or ratings. In some organisations, the editor-in-chief/director of news is responsible for a single news product, but in others the person in this role can be responsible for a group of products.

An editorial manager usually has a different role. He or she is likely to be responsible for the financial management of a newsroom or newsrooms. That responsibility often involves things such as setting and meeting budgets, hiring and firing staff, staff promotion, purchasing equipment, corporate forward planning and so on. Depending on the organisation, its editor-in-chief, director of news or editorial manager also has responsibility for dealing with legal issues such as defamation and contempt, handling industrial matters and representing the organisation in its dealings with external bodies, including those which set standards and deal with complaints, such as the Australian Press Council and agencies that monitor broadcast media.

GENERAL EDITOR, EXECUTIVE PRODUCER OF NEWS AND SECTION EDITORS

While a smaller online, print or broadcast news outlet may have only a single editor or news producer, most larger news organisations—particularly print and online newspaper publications—have several editors who are accountable to a general editor (in print and online; also called a news editor) or an executive producer of news (in television). In turn, the general editor/executive producer is usually directly accountable to the editor-in-chief/director of news and the editorial manager.

A general editor/executive producer is responsible for the news content of a print publication, website or broadcast outlet. He or she will usually consult and liaise with the chief-of-staff/news producer to decide which are the most important stories to pursue as a day unfolds; how those stories will be treated; where they will be placed in tomorrow's newspaper, the next news bulletin or on the website; and the prominence stories will be given. A general editor/executive producer will call at least one—and often several—news conferences each day. The first conference is held in the morning. In some organisations all journalists will attend and each will be expected to contribute several ideas for possible stories. In other organisations only the general editor/executive producer, section editors, the chief-of-staff/news producer and senior sub-editors will attend.

General editors/executive producers need to be flexible, able to think quickly and make decisions on the run. They will have to refocus many times during a day as news stories break and unfold—dropping some stories and story ideas, and replacing them with breaking news or other stories with stronger news values. In this environment, they must be able to trust their staff. They need to know their journalists will do what they said they would do; that they will try their hardest to get stories and find relevant people to interview; that they will be persistent, ethical, work quickly and accurately, balance their work, recognise and deal appropriately with potential legal issues; and that they will remain pleasant and level-headed in what tends to be a stressful environment. In newspapers and television, that stress tends to peak later in the day as the evening news broadcast and deadline for tomorrow's paper approach, but in radio and online newsrooms stress is more constant because there is intense pressure to be first with breaking news.

Newspaper section editors face similar (if in some ways different) stresses to general editors. In some areas—particularly sport, entertainment and business—things can move rapidly and change frequently during a day. But in other areas—such as pre-planned features, education, health, arts and fashion—while the immediate pace may not be as intense, there are other demands. One is ensuring the work of photographers, graphic artists, designers and journalists is co-ordinated. Another is planning well ahead: for example, knowing when articles will be needed to commemorate anniversaries of important events, ensuring obituary files for significant individuals are up to date, timing features to coincide with the finalisation of interesting court cases, and organising timely interviews with individuals who are likely to be in the news in future when particular events (such as conferences on climate change or terrorism) occur. Section editors are also likely to have responsibilities for aspects such as working out ways in which features, analysis and commentary can be developed to support, expand on and explain major news stories.

Most, but not all, news executives are professional and ethical—one simple way of picking the difference is to look at the product(s) they produce. The majority have made their way up through the ranks and know the news business inside out. Sometimes they make decisions journalists on their staff disagree with, or may not understand, but in most instances there are good reasons informing those decisions.

CHIEF-OF-STAFF AND NEWS PRODUCER

To continue the analogy between a newsroom and engine room, the chief-of-staff in a newspaper organisation (or news producer in a television newsroom) is the person with her or his hands on the levers and eyes on the dial. The chief-of-staff/news producer makes things happen. He or she is directly responsible to the general editor/executive producer and, depending on the size and complexity of an organisation, the editor-in-chief or director of news. Chiefs-of-staff/news producers assign stories to individual journalists, consider story ideas proposed by journalists, deal with news tips from the public, ensure photographers or camera operators and journalists work together, watch the clock and hurry journalists along as deadlines approach, draw teams of journalists together if necessary to cover major breaking stories, liaise with section editors, balance staff assignments on pre-planned stories against the demands of breaking news, decide what breaking news should be reported immediately on the organisation's online news site, and organise for legally difficult stories to be sent out for legal advice prior to publication.

The job of chief-of-staff/news producer is the most difficult and demanding role in a newsroom. It is stressful and can be like juggling a hundred balls in the air at once, none of which can be let drop. In larger news organisations, there may be two or three chiefs-of-staff/news producers who work in rostered shifts. As a shift unfolds, a chief-of-staff/news producer will monitor radio and television news broadcasts and news websites of competing media outlets to ensure no major breaking stories have been missed by her or his own journalists.

The job of chief-of-staff/news producer is the most difficult and demanding role in a newsroom. It is stressful and can be like juggling a hundred balls in the air at once, none of which can be let drop.

PHOTOGRAPHIC EDITOR AND CHIEF PHOTOGRAPHER

Staff in these roles nearly always have a wealth of experience. They know what shots will work in print and online and what will not, and when images are essential to a story or will dramatically improve it. They usually work closely with the chief-of-staff.

In addition to ensuring photographers travel with, and work directly with, individual journalists on some stories, they must also ensure photographers and journalists who are travelling separately meet at prearranged times and places for scheduled interviews and events. Then there are stories that a journalist does not need to attend—perhaps because they have conducted a telephone or email interview—but photographers must still be sent to get shots. Conversely, there are many stories when the journalist who covers it shoots his or her own photos and/or video. These images must also be considered during editing processes so decisions can made about placement and publication.

SUB-EDITORS

Sub-editors are known as copy editors in the US because their basic function is to edit—correct, improve and fit to a specified length—the copy, or stories, of journalists. Sub-editors, or 'subs', must be experts in house style (which is discussed in Chapter 8), grammar, spelling and punctuation. They must have an amazing eye for detail. In addition to tidying up journalists' work and picking up mistakes which could make a journalist or news organisation look silly if published or broadcast, they write headlines and captions, design and lay out pages in print publications, repurpose print and broadcast stories for publication online, and check facts. Most also have a strong sixth sense about the veracity of sources and stories, and a nose that sniffs out potential legal problems.

Good sub-editors will generally improve stories. Bad ones can wreck them. One thing sub-editors must be particularly careful not to do is introduce errors into a story or cause legal problems by writing inappropriate headlines, online headings or captions. Experienced News Limited reporter, columnist, feature writer, sub-editor and journalism educator Jane Fynes-Clinton understands the importance of relationships between writing and sub-editing. She said it is sometimes necessary for a sub-editor to rework a journalist's copy, but she stressed the significance of a team approach:

> It is essential that if time allows, the subeditor should check any rewrites with the reporter. It is also common courtesy, as it is the reporter's byline that appears on the story and their neck that could be on the line if an error is mistakenly introduced in the rewriting process (Fynes-Clinton 2009).

Fynes-Clinton believes senior sub-editors should help promote a climate of mutual respect by being sensitive to a journalist's feelings and aims, and explaining changes she or he has made. She said:

Too often, there is a prickly tolerance between reporters and subs—the relationship can easily become acrimonious. But subs should promote themselves as guides and point out to reporters that often they are all that stands between them and public ridicule, or worse, legal action (Fynes-Clinton 2009).

VIDEO EDITORS, AND VIDEO CAMERA OPERATORS

No television news broadcast could go to air, nor could any professionally presented video be published online, without video editors and video camera operators. Theirs are key roles in a newsroom and on the road. Out on assignments, camera operators, or 'camos' as they are known, work with journalists to ensure vision and words match and complement each other to tell a story. Back in the newsroom, editing begins and camera operators and journalists decide which grabs of sound and vision are important to a story and which are not. Often, especially as deadline approaches, video editors work under tremendous pressure. They are highly skilled, proficient users of editing software and tend to have an intuitive understanding of news values and how to cut and stitch sound and vision for maximum impact.

Newsroom presentation and etiquette

When you first arrive in a newsroom—whether for an internship or in your first job—it will take time to find your feet. Journalists and senior staff will be sizing you up. They will expect you to have a broad knowledge of, and genuine interest in, news and current affairs—something that would seem like common sense and a given for every journalism student but, amazingly, a basic point too many students do not grasp. In fact *The Canberra Times* editor-at-large Jack Waterford said he was 'astounded' at the number of would-be journalists who do not read newspapers or books and who do not keep abreast of current affairs on radio, television or online (Waterford 2004). It will also be assumed that by the time you arrive at work each day, that as a minimum you will have read the publication you work for, online and in print if there is a print edition, or have watched or listened to the latest news broadcasts of the television channel or radio station that employs you, and you will be abreast of that organisation's latest online offerings. You must also have listened to, watched and read the offerings of other media outlets, especially those of competitors, and have a solid grasp of latest current affairs issues.

Similarly, you will be expected to show respect for those you work with, and those you work for—that is, your readership or audience. Sadly, editor-in-chief of *The Australian* Chris Mitchell expressed concern about a tendency by university journalism graduates to 'look down their noses' at newspapers, media owners and readers (Mitchell, in Day 2004, p. 22). Mitchell said 'many students from journalism courses' exhibited a degree of condescension, implying they were superior to readers of tabloid newspapers that reflect the concerns of less educated or less well-off readers (Mitchell, in Day 2004, p. 22). Also be aware that you will be expected to arrive in a newsroom with your own original story ideas. You will certainly be assigned stories by the chief-of-staff/news producer, but the more ideas of your own you can come up with, the better it will be for you, and the more quickly you will build a positive reputation.

As you ease your way into a newsroom you will notice that like any office setting there will be banter at some times, tension and stress at others. Over time you will start to get a sense of the workplace politics—who gets on well with whom, and who does not. There will be those who respect the chief-of-staff, general editor or director of news, and those who do not. Some people will be happy and gain great job satisfaction but there will probably be some who are miserable and toxic. As the new kid on the block, there are two things you would be well advised not to do. First, do not allow yourself to be drawn into newsroom politics—it is a sure way to make enemies. A wise newcomer will watch, listen, be cheerful, polite, and treat everyone with the same degree of respect. Second, while you might see or hear things you do not understand and may not agree with, at all costs avoid telling people higher up the pecking order how to run their newsroom. The fact is, they have all been at it longer than you have. Sometimes they will make real mistakes but most of the time there are probably good reasons informing a decision that you or others may disagree with. Besides, bosses do not like being told what to do!

Tips for finding stories

Some people are naturally highly self-motivated, while others have to work on making motivation a habit, and some are naturally shy and reserved. No matter where you fit in that spectrum, remember that it is an essential part of the journalist's job to find fresh new stories. Another essential quality is to have a genuine interest in people and what makes them tick. A good journalist is someone who can relate to and empathise with individuals from many different backgrounds and walks of life.

When you arrive in a new newsroom, do not sit around waiting for stories to come to you—literally go out and find them. If you have moved to a new area, as many beginning journalists do when they take up their first job, use your eyes and ears. Before you even start work, drive around the area and really look at and think about your surroundings. Even if you know the locality well, look for things that are new, different or changed. In the first few weeks drop in and introduce yourself to local police, fire and ambulance staff. Get to know publicans, clergy, teachers, local councillors and politicians—and talk to them. Be inquisitive—ask questions… and more questions. Overcome feelings of shyness and do not feel intimidated—it is your job to be upfront and out there! You need to know what makes the area tick and you must start filling your contact book. Also, gather business cards and keep them in an organised collection. As discussed in Chapter 4, a journalist really only has two assets: a good name—a reputation built on ethical and responsible professional conduct—and a contact book. Without one, you will not have the other. Being well informed, staying informed and behaving ethically at all times will help you develop and build both. And just as your good name is your personal property, so is your contact book. The longer you keep adding to the book, the more valuable it will become. So never share it—not even if a chief-of-staff, news producer or other more senior person tells you to—and do not lose it.

Journalists tend to move around, especially in the early phases of their career. As quickly as you can after moving to a new city, town or district—but without making rash judgments—you need to discover who the movers and shakers are. Who are the con artists, eccentrics and quiet achievers? Go to courts and local council meetings and talk to staff (often the people who know most about an organisation are the cleaners, security staff and maintenance workers). Attend media conferences, and accept invitations to functions such as openings and launches—even if it is in your own time at weekends or after work. In short, get yourself noticed and make a good impression. Think about how you look, how you dress, your grooming, your manners, how you speak and how you smell—there are few turn-offs greater than putrid body odour and bad breath, or someone who reeks of enough perfume or aftershave to kill a horse! To do your job well, you

Present yourself as someone professional, trustworthy and authoritative. It should be clear from your presentation and manner that you are genuine, ethical, compassionate and professional, but not smart or a know-all. Remain pleasant and polite, even if people are rude to you—you never know when you might need a comment from them again, or when they might tell you something interesting.

need to make a good impression and present yourself as someone professional, trustworthy and authoritative. It should be clear from your presentation and manner that you are genuine, ethical, compassionate and professional, but not smart or a know-all. Remain pleasant and polite, even if people are rude to you— you never know when you might need a comment from them again, or when they might tell you something interesting. Also be aware that how you behave in your private life outside work is also important to how you are perceived—especially in a smaller community. Similarly, be extremely careful of online social networking sites—many a professional has lost their job and/or been humiliated by stupid and thoughtless things they posted themselves, or allowed others to post, on Facebook, Twitter and other sites.

When you can, try to interview people face-to-face instead of by phone, SMS or email—that way they get to know you. In turn, you can observe their body language and form an impression of them. Become the world's best listener. If you have an interest in a sport, hobby or some other activity, think about joining a club or group. That way you will meet people, chat, listen and hopefully pick up stories and story ideas. Shop regularly in the same places and talk to people behind the counter. It is also sensible to move outside your comfort zone and mix with people from different social groups and walks of life. Make it known to everyone that you are a journalist and are always hungry for stories and interesting snippets. Make sure you hand out your business card at every opportunity and be accessible— return all phone calls, answer all emails and cultivate sources. You will be surprised what people tell you and what you overhear.

But a word of warning here. Do not allow yourself to become too close to your sources. The relationship should be professional, but not personal. This is for several reasons. Among them is the point that if a relationship with a source becomes personal it means you will have a conflict of interest that could place you in a difficult situation in relation to the Media Entertainment and Arts Alliance (MEAA)'s *Journalists' Code of Ethics*. Also be aware that sources commonly have their own axe(s) to grind and own agendas. Journalists are in a position of power in a community and what can seem like genuine friendship may be no more than manipulation of a relationship by a source determined to score points for his or her cause. There is also a risk that by becoming too close to a source you could compromise yourself, your job and your other relationships—and this is particularly true if a source is involved in illegal or amoral activities. If she or he goes down, and you are too close, you might be dragged down too. Also be especially wary about what you put in writing when dealing with sources—an indiscreet comment in an email or text message could well come back to haunt you, even years later or if revealed in a court case.

Apart from sources, among your most useful story-finding tools will be online telephone books—especially the *Yellow Pages* listings for things like clubs, hobbies, gardening and sporting groups. Other useful leads can come from local directories, notice boards at shopping centres, school newsletters, roadside development application signs, real estate signs, court lists, local government meeting minutes, and the advertisements and letters to the editor or comments on stories in print and online versions of your local newspaper—even if it is the one you work for! Keeping a regular eye on the paper and its website will help you find contacts for business groups, community organisations, schools, playgroups, preschools, universities, retirement villages, tourist attractions, TAFE colleges, local history, and unusual businesses and people—each of which can be sources of stories or provide sources who can comment on stories. Over time you will also come across online, print and broadcast stories in which contributors, or even other journalists, have missed the real point or failed to recognise a potential lead or news angle within a story. In such instances a follow-up story is just begging for your attention!

Also regularly conduct web searches for names and topics relevant to your area. Particularly keep an eye on the websites of councils, water boards, environmental groups, churches and key industries. Routinely visit websites such as the Australian Bureau of Statistics and federal and state government to search for information relating to your town or area.

It pays to think outside the square. Consider stories about odd weather events, the environment and strange behaviour by animals. Keep a forward file listing of coming events and reminders about anniversaries of past events. Also think about Masterton's 'big six' news values discussed in Chapter 3 and how they apply to the area you work in. For example:

— Significance—what issues and events are important in this community?

— Proximity—what is happening or planned nearby that might affect this community?

— Conflict—who and what are contentious individuals and issues?

— Human interest—what would people like to know about other people?

— Novelty—what strange, different, outrageous, spooky, mysterious or unexplained things are going on around here?

— Prominence—who are the movers and shakers and what good works or hijinks have they been up to lately?

If you see something new in the community it is also useful to think of Kipling's 'six honest serving men' and ask yourself questions such as:

— What is it?

— Why did that happen?

— Why was that road/house/shopping centre built there?

— Who is behind it?

— Where can I find out more?

— Who can tell me more?

— How did this happen?

— Why did this happen, or why was it allowed to happen?

— When did work start/was approval given/will it be finished?

— What went wrong?

— Why did it go wrong?

— Who is responsible for it going wrong?

Finally, when it comes to looking for stories and story ideas, hone your curiosity, be a stickybeak. Never take anything for granted or at face value—quietly, and without getting people offside unnecessarily, question everything and everyone. Remember, you are the eyes and ears of the community—it is your job to find out and then explain to others. Above all, be persistent.

When the spin-doctors spin out

As noted in Chapters 4, 6 and 12, journalists should be wary of spin. Early in their careers journalists discover that governments and many politicians are masters of deception. Our state and federal governments in particular, but also many local governments, employ small armies of public relations staff and media advisers: 'minders' whose sole responsibility is to do their utmost to portray their government and its members—especially ministers and public service department heads and party officials—positively to the public. This involves a two-pronged approach: minders blowing the trumpets of those who employ them, and targeting journalists with a deluge of media releases; and deflecting criticism of their bosses or departments, preferably by heading it off before it hits news media. Some public relations people become expert in specialist areas of public relations known as issues management and crisis management ('Crisis? What crisis?'). But on the positive side, media releases can sometimes provide great story leads, particularly if those leads are picked up by an intuitive journalist who senses a release is actually designed to cover something up, rather than promote something else. To that end a key rule in dealing with a media release is to become a little paranoid and ask yourself: Why was it really sent out? What was the underlying motive? Is there a hidden agenda? Who wrote the release and why? What sort of issue might be being managed here? Who has most to gain, or the most to lose? Seeking answers to questions such as these can sometimes help a journalist turn the tables on crafty public relations spin-doctors and, in doing so, pull a good story out of thin air.

Reporting on protests and riots

Crowds, whether involved in street demonstrations, at music festivals, sporting events or New Year celebrations, can be dangerous. Emotions tend to run high. Protesters sometimes become angry and crowds turn ugly. So too can crowd controllers and police. Fights sometimes erupt and in worst-case situations people become frightened, panic and stampede. When this happens individuals can be overwhelmed and unable to escape. Some are crushed, swept off their feet and trampled to death. If you, as a journalist, become caught in such a situation you will be carried along with the throng. You could be killed or injured yourself or, at best, be unable to get away to file your story. Also bear in mind that large gatherings are potential targets for terrorists. Street-smart journalists therefore stay well away from the centre of a crowd. It is safer—and more practical, particularly if covering protests and mass rallies—to stay on the edge, or to watch and listen from a vantage point. It is essential to ensure you have at least one clear escape route—several alternative routes are better—not just for your own safety, but also so that you can extricate yourself quickly when you need to write and file your story or send an

Crowds can be dangerous. It is safer to stay on the edge, or to watch and listen from a vantage point. It is essential to ensure you have at least one clear escape route, not just for your own safety, but also so that you can extricate yourself quickly when you need to write and file your story or send an update back to the studio.

update back to the newsroom or studio. Also remember that many people dislike and fear journalists—some become angry about being photographed or when a video camera points in their direction.

Photographers and camera operators can be particularly vulnerable because they must focus on what they see through the lens and may not have a broad view of a developing situation. When photographers or video camera operators ('camos') and journalists work together on difficult or dangerous assignments, they should be a team, looking out for each other and warning the other of dangers. They can also improve each other's work by talking and pointing things out. For example, there are times when images are visible through a lens that a journalist cannot see. At other times a journalist will see things a photographer or camera operator cannot.

Finally, be particularly careful if anyone has weapons. If you hear shooting (it frequently sounds more like a popping noise than loud bangs), seek cover first and find out where the gunfire is coming from second. Whether in Australia or overseas, people with guns in a crowd situation, including police and military, will generally be extremely edgy and nervous themselves. If you are ever unfortunate enough to be bailed up at gunpoint, do *exactly* as you are told, do your utmost to appear calm, be polite, never joke or make smart comments, and do not make any sudden or unexpected movements.

Reporting on death and tragedy

Before you start work in a newsroom you will probably have already discovered that while some stories virtually write themselves, others are particularly difficult. In a newsroom you will find journalists often compete to cover the former but do all they can to avoid the latter. As discussed in Chapter 4, one particular type of story journalists dread is what are known as 'death-knocks'—contacting relatives or close friends of a person who has died in the immediate aftermath of the death to ask for an interview as the basis of a story.

While the MEAA's *Journalists' Code of Ethics* makes it clear that a media organisation—or at least a chief-of-staff/news producer as the person who usually directs reporters and assigns them to stories—cannot compel journalists to literally go and knock on the doors of surviving relatives, there are times when there is clear public benefit in doing so. For that reason at least some experienced journalists will tell you that a death-knock, while uncomfortable and something they do not like doing, is not inherently a bad thing. It is not uncommon for relatives and friends to be willing to speak to a journalist so they can have a story told. This can be anything from a simple tribute to the person who died, to a story that galvanises communities and governments into action to remedy problems, or at least search for solutions. Such stories emerged in the aftermath of the tragic 2009 Black Saturday bushfires in Victoria and 2010–11 floods in Queensland. Among other things they helped raise awareness of the need for new building and planning codes, new rules about evacuation, and improved warning systems. There are numerous other examples of death-knock stories that led to positive change, new safety precautions, better security, new procedures, widening and realignment of roads, new air safety rules, public awareness campaigns and other positive outcomes. Often they are stories that draw communities and families together, united in their grief, but positive in their outlook.

AT THE SCENE OF A TRAGEDY

Accept that you did not cause whatever it was that happened, but be aware that emotions will be in overdrive—as well as victims and their friends and families being upset, sometimes even the most hardened emergency workers, including police, will be too. Remember that just as emergency services personnel have their jobs to do, your job is to tell the community about what happened, and often why. Also understand that just as emergency service professionals must learn to put personal feelings, fears, revulsion and anger aside if they are to do their jobs, so must you. Remain outwardly calm—it will help you do your job better and may also help soothe others.

Overall, approach slowly, taking time to develop an overview of the whole scene. Initially at least, you must concentrate on the big picture. In doing so, be careful not to get so involved in gathering information that you put yourself or others in danger. Above all, keep out of the way of emergency service personnel and obey the instructions of emergency services staff. Also, be aware that a tragedy could cloud your own judgment, so be careful and considered in what you say and do. Be especially careful not to engage in black humour—comments by emergency service workers and other journalists that are inappropriate, but which are made as a means of helping them hide or deal with their own over-stretched emotions.

ACCIDENTS

Road accidents, industrial accidents, aircraft accidents and boating mishaps often have tragic outcomes. Your first priority when arriving at an accident scene must be to ensure that you do not become the next victim. Beware of passing traffic, look for fallen power lines and other dangers such as leaking fuel or gas, and keep a safe distance. Above all, ensure that electrical equipment like camera lights, flashes and even mobile phones do not literally spark an explosion. Look carefully around the scene and make notes so you can describe it later. If possible, look for the cause or causes: ask yourself 'how' and 'why' questions. Do not stay longer than you have to at the scene—get your story, then go and write it—but do ensure you get all the information you need before you leave because it will usually be impossible to go back and get it later. If appropriate, try to get the names and contact details of key emergency workers—usually police—so you can follow up with them. Once you have written and filed your original story, you will then have the option of being able to contact them by telephone to see if there is more information that can be added in an update. As with all violent incidents in which people are injured and/ or killed, do not identify victims until their names have been released by police. Family members should not learn about the death of a loved one, or of serious injuries to a loved one, from a news report.

MURDER

Unlike accidents, natural disasters or illnesses involving loss of life, a murder is a deliberate killing. Reporting on a murder, especially if there are children killed or it happened in a domestic situation, is always difficult. If the murderer has not yet been apprehended, your first priority should be to ensure your own safety—after all, if you become the next victim it will be one story you will not report! If there is a siege situation, police will normally keep journalists a safe distance away, but even so your safety is ultimately your own responsibility. So be extremely careful, especially if high-powered weapons or vehicles are involved. In the rare event that a journalist arrives at a murder scene before police, she or he should not attempt to get too close. For your own safety and the safety of others, never do or say anything that might provoke the killer if they are still at the scene or nearby. It is also vitally important not to do anything that could contaminate the scene or destroy evidence.

When reporting, stick with the facts. There is no room for speculation or opinion. Also be aware of the laws of *sub judice* contempt. These are explained in Chapter 16, but in essence mean that after an arrest a journalist must not report anything that could potentially influence future jurors. In most situations, police will be the best source of information and will usually hold a media conference, especially if they want media help in finding a killer.

SUICIDE AND MENTAL ILLNESS

Suicides are probably the most difficult event those who are left behind will ever have to cope with. Unless there is a strong public benefit reason, or unless a high-profile personality takes her or his own life, the majority of suicides go unreported. Media are usually careful never to convey any impression that suicide is an acceptable way of dealing with a problem, or to provide details of method. If for some reason a suicide is reported, media outlets should always include information about where depressed people can find help. They include Lifeline (www.lifeline.org.au; phone 13 11 14) and Beyond Blue (www.beyondblue.org.au; phone 1300 22 4636).

News media are usually also sensitive about how mental illness is reported. People who suffer a mental illness are not 'mad', 'insane', 'lunatics' or 'stupid'; they are ill. Reporting, if necessary and relevant, should convey this. It should also be borne in mind that mental health issues of one sort or another will affect nearly all of us at some time in our lives and the vast majority of people who suffer a mental illness recover, or learn how to manage their problems. Further, there are some conditions affecting the brain—for example, acquired brain damage, epilepsy and many congenital disorders—that are not mental illnesses. There are excellent online resources, links and contacts for journalists about suicide and mental health issues at the Mindframe website (www.mindframe-media.info/for-universities).

Acknowledging your own feelings

While you must control your feelings when interviewing people who are bereaved and traumatised if you are going to do your job properly, it is important to understand that trauma can, and does, affect journalists too. Interviewing those who have been involved in traumatic and/or tragic events, or those who are dying as the result of medical conditions such as cancer, can lead journalists to reflect on their own humanity and mortality. The US-based Dart Centre for Journalism and Trauma said:

> Because of the nature of news, it is likely that a journalist will have to interview trauma victims in the course of his or her work. Interviewing someone who is under psychological stress is difficult for both the interviewee and the interviewer. As interviewers, journalists can help victims and survivors tell their stories in a way that is constructive (Dart Centre for Journalism and Trauma 2005).

The Dart Centre quotes psychiatrist Frank Ochberg as saying:

> Good listening requires hearing not only the words that are spoken and making sense of them but also noticing gestures, facial expressions, emotions, and body language. Take the other person fully into account, then remember and make sense of what that person heard and saw (Ochberg, in Dart Centre for Journalism and Trauma 2005).

Death knocks, or interviews with survivors and relatives of injured survivors, victims of crime, sufferers of terminal illnesses, and witnesses to traumatic events are often confronting and upsetting. Stories you are told, and must then write and report, can be harrowing. After you have done the best you can with such a story, it is vitally important that you talk with someone else about it and about your feelings. That person can be a colleague, friend or maybe a counsellor. The Dart Centre has online resources at http://dartcenter.org/ that have been specially designed to help journalists deal with the personal impacts of reporting on trauma, death and disaster. The centre advises that when selecting someone to talk with about a difficult interview or story, it is best to:

> Find someone who is a sensitive listener. It can be an editor or a peer, but you must trust that the listener will not pass judgment on you. Perhaps it is someone who has faced a similar experience. [And] learn how to deal with your stress. Find a hobby, exercise, attend a house of worship or, most important, spend time with your family, a significant other or friends—or all four (Dart Centre for Journalism and Trauma 2009).

There are also good resources on the Mindframe website. Under the 'For Universities' tab there are special sections related to journalism and trauma, and student well-being. The site highlights the importance of recognising and dealing constructively with your own stress, including seeking help if needs be. Under the heading 'Journalism and trauma' is a warning that:

> Reporting on distressing events and working with the survivors of trauma can have a personal effect on the journalist. It is important to recognise that journalists, like other professionals, need to safeguard their own wellbeing in these situations. This may run counter to the culture in some media organisations and among some journalists, but unresolved stress can have a significant impact (Mindframe 2013).

Making mistakes

Obviously no one likes making mistakes—probably least of all journalists, because our mistakes are made in public. But if there is one overriding rule of reporting news—apart from the obvious need to be fair, accurate and objective in your quest for truth—it is that the art of journalism is to do the best job you can within the time that is available, and to then move on and do the same again with the next story. During your career, and as noted in Chapter 4 in relation to ethics, you will make mistakes. We all do. However, as Mencher said:

> It is important to learn from mistakes and not to be discouraged. Although mistakes can be embarrassing and humiliating, they are unavoidable... Don't live in fear of making a mistake; that will cut down your range. Do the best you can. That's all anyone can ask of you (Mencher 1997, p. 30).

DISCUSSION POINTS

1   Who really controls the newsroom agenda: the editor-in-chief/director of news, general editor/executive producer, chief-of-staff/news reporter, journalists, shareholders, board members or the public?

2   You are working on a sizzler of a story you generated yourself, and your chief-of-staff or news producer tells you to drop it and work on another story you are being assigned to cover. What will you do?

3   How far would you go to get an exclusive story? At what point does the price become too high?

4   Is it a good idea for journalists to join clubs and community groups in order to build contacts so they will hear about stories? Or is it wiser not to be a joiner because being a member of a club or community group could place you in a difficult position ethically in which you could be seen to have a conflict of interest?

5   You are sent to death-knock the parents of a two-year-old boy who has been hit by a ute driven by a hoon in a busy suburban street. You arrive at the address with a photographer and find the distraught young parents in the street building a shrine with the boy's teddy and other toys. The police have been and gone. The father is stabbing the ground repeatedly with a large carving knife and the mother is so distressed she can hardly breathe. They tell you they want you to write a story about how their child ran out of the driveway after his cat and how the hoon, who is well known in the neighbourhood, was going too fast to stop. As you talk, you discover the couple has no family in the state and has had no offers of counselling or help. They blame themselves for the accident and are talking of making a suicide pact so they can be with their child. What will you do?

6   You are talking to your chief-of-staff or news producer about the death-knock described in Discussion Point 5 and you mention how upset you feel yourself for the toddler and his parents. She tells you to 'get over it' and 'we all have to cope with stuff like that'. Now you feel even more upset. What can you do to help yourself deal with: a) your feelings about the tragedy, and b) your feelings about your immediate boss?

NEWS PRACTICE POINTS

1   See what you can discover about the background of the editor-in-chief or network director of news for three major news outlets. Who among the three has the most experience as a news-reporting journalist?

2   List five key attributes you would expect to find in a chief-of-staff or news producer. Now see if you can identify a real person in one of those roles who has all five attributes.

3   A good example of a newsroom structure is what is known as 'line management'. In a few words, explain your thoughts about why this has evolved as the most common management structure in news organisations.

4   You have just been appointed to your first job as a journalist on a daily newspaper and its online news site. List which, if any, of the news-finding tips discussed in this chapter you would use in your first few weeks to help find your own stories.

5   Following on from Practice Point 4, you have just been appointed to your first job as a journalist with a regional television network. List which, if any, of the news-finding tips in this chapter you would use in your first few weeks. Are there any significant

differences in your two lists? If so, what are they and what are the reasons for the differences?

6   Visit the Mindframe website and take time to work your way through the 'For media' section. Was there anything in what you read that surprised you? And/or was there anything that changed your perceptions? If so, what? If not, what did you think of the site generally? Explain your answers in an article of about 750 words.

7   Go online and find a news report and images of an uprising, some sort of civil unrest, or a crowd out of control. Look carefully at the images—either still photographs or video—and read the report. Now make a list of the potential dangers, if any, faced by the reporter, and a separate list of dangers faced by the photographer/camera operator. Did it appear the two were working together or apart? Did it appear they were actually in the crowd, or on the edge of it? How dangerous did the crowd really seem to be?

8   Define each of the following words or terms: psychologist, psychiatrist, paranoid, psychopath, depression, schizophrenia, bipolar, autism, attention deficit hyperactivity disorder and post-traumatic stress.

6 JOURNALISM RESEARCH

It's not that I'm so smart, it's just that I stay with problems longer.
Albert Einstein

OBJECTIVES

After reading this chapter you will understand:

» Why journalistic research must be thorough
» Research traps to avoid
» Traditional journalistic research
» Computer-assisted research
» Ways of verifying online information
» How to extract information from statistics.

On April 15, 1912 the *Christian Science Monitor* newspaper in Boston carried the headline 'Passengers Safely Moved and Steamer *Titanic* Taken in Tow' above a story which included statements that 'bulkheads hold' and 'officials of White Star company confident steamer is unsinkable'. The next day, April 16, London's *Daily Mail* reported '*Titanic* sunk. No lives lost... all passengers taken off'. In fact, the sinking of the *Titanic* was one of the worst maritime disasters in history. More than 1500 lives were lost. A century later, news outlets are still fallible and still making embarrassing mistakes. These blunders damage the credibility of news media and the reputations of journalists.

One of the more spectacular slip-ups in recent history happened in 2009 when the weekend before a Queensland state election, in which former One Nation founder Pauline Hanson stood as an independent, and lost, Sydney's *The Sunday Telegraph* and many other News Limited newspapers around Australia published photographs of a near-naked woman they said was Hanson. *The Sunday Telegraph* could not disguise its glee. Front-page headlines 'Please Explain' and 'Hanson's nude photo betrayal' pointed to an article that said:

> Pauline Hanson's political comeback has been derailed with the emergence of nude photographs taken 30 years ago by a boyfriend she met in a Brisbane shop. The photographs were taken in the mid-1970s and show Hanson, who was roughly 19 at the time, posing seductively in various states of undress (Leys 2009a, p. 1).

The article said the former boyfriend, who it named as Jack Johnson, had been in the army and was a commando when he took the photos. Similar articles also appeared on News Limited websites. Hanson subsequently denied the photos were of her. She said she would sue for defamation. In the days that followed, *The Sunday Telegraph*'s editor Neil Breen revealed he had paid Johnson $15,000 for the photographs. Breen said he was certain they were of Hanson; he had spent a day checking them, and was convinced they were not 'doctored'—digitally manipulated (Feneley 2009). A week later, *The Sunday Telegraph* published a grovelling apology. Under the headline 'Pauline: we're sorry, they weren't you', Breen wrote: 'Pauline, I'm sorry. We should never have published them [the photos]... we accept that decision was made on a flawed premise' (Breen 2009, p. 35). In the same edition it was revealed that five face recognition experts had been asked to examine the photographs in the week after they were published and a majority concluded they were not of Hanson (Leys 2009b, p. 14). A separate article in the same edition attacked Jack Johnson. It alleged he was 'a conman' who was 'a desperate figure who lives in a public housing estate' and who had 'a tenuous hold on reality' (Leys & Sexton 2009, pp. 14–15).

The moral of the story? Journalists—and editors—must do their research *before* a story is published, not afterwards. But like so many before him, Breen let himself and his readers down—not to mention Pauline Hanson—because he did not do proper research. Instead, he made fundamental mistakes. With the help of experts he had decided the photographs had not been digitally manipulated, but he did not call on face recognition experts until after publication. Similarly, Breen paid for the photographs but failed to thoroughly research Jack Johnson's background, despite admitting later that 'all along he [Johnson] has claimed cancer treatment and painkillers have played havoc with his memory' (Leys & Sexton 2009, pp. 14–15). There is also the point that a little simple mathematics would have revealed Johnson would have been only 17 and Hanson 19 when the photographs were supposedly taken—something which surely begs questions about whether a

17-year-old could have had time after joining the army to have completed basic training then trained further as an elite commando.

All journalism involves research in a bid to find and report truths. The depth of research depends on the type of story to be told, its complexity, ethical constraints, legal risks and the medium in which it is presented. It is also relevant that there are many different types of journalists and journalism. They range from reporting hard news, to feature writing, sport, photojournalism, sub-editing and specialised rounds such as police, courts, education and health. Journalists work for a wide array of publications, from free weekly community papers, through regional daily outlets, to major state-wide and national dailies, broadcast outlets, and online, as well as varying combinations of converged media.

To some extent, where journalists work tends to govern the type of work they do. In Chapter 3 it was explained that there are two main categories of articles journalists produce—reactive, in which an event happens and journalists report on it; and proactive, in which a journalist actively sets out to make news by investigating, unearthing hidden information and data, and linking facts and events. Researching reactive news stories is usually relatively simple. Journalists interview witnesses and authorities in a bid to find answers to basic questions of what, when, where, who, how and why. They might also visit the scene of whatever it was that happened and describe what they saw and heard. Proactive journalism also sets out to answer questions about what, when, where, who, how and why, but it nearly always involves much deeper research and digging—there might be money trails to be traced, documents to be discovered and examined, data to be unearthed and aggregated, timelines to be constructed, people to be found, and potentially helpful sources to be identified and cultivated.

As well as researching to find truths so they can report accurately to readers and audiences, sound research and considered judgments based on research help journalists avoid making fools of themselves and can save them from making expensive legal mistakes.

In many senses good journalistic research is similar to the rigorous due diligence process conducted by lawyers before complex business deals are signed—the idea is to discover as much detail as possible prior to putting your name to a document. How much research will be involved and the direction of that research is usually a matter of common sense. As well as researching to find truths so they can report accurately to readers and audiences, sound research and considered judgments based on research help journalists avoid making fools of themselves and can save them from making expensive legal mistakes. Further, as experienced journalists will tell you—and contrary to public opinion—it really does happen sometimes that facts do, and must be allowed to, get in the way of a good story!

Getting the basics right

When researching for a reactive story, the key is to ensure that you gather all relevant details and that the information you collect is accurate. Check things such as names and their correct spelling, ages if possible, times, distances, weather conditions if relevant and precursor events. If possible, a journalist should interview at least some of those involved, and whenever possible at least one key person in authority, such as a police officer. You should collect mobile phone numbers from those you interview so you can follow up if a story continues unfolding or takes a new twist. Often a reactive story is based on not much more than basic facts fleshed out with comments from interviewees. But if you have more time, or there are opportunities to update an unfolding story, you can add depth by seeking expert opinion, checking to see if other similar events have happened before, and getting back to authorities and/or others to seek updated information and fresh quotes.

Researching for proactive articles is different. With investigative articles, for example, interviews often come last—after relevant facts have been gathered, sorted and evaluated, and an overall picture has emerged. As discussed in Chapter 12, proactive research also typically involves things like searching for documents and financial details, and finding relevant statistics. Often it is useful to check archives for earlier articles relevant to your research, to interview a range of on-the-record and off-the-record sources, conduct company searches, find people, access court records, build chronologies, analyse data, examine old photographs and video recordings, seek expert opinion and advice, and even conduct covert observation. Whenever possible, research for proactive articles should involve finding and copying primary data and documents because it is much safer to rely on your own research than the sometimes poorly conducted or incomplete research of others.

Traditional approaches to research

Journalists tend to be pragmatic and to use basic 'real-world' research methods. As noted in Chapter 2, they must always be able to retrace their research steps and replicate findings. This becomes particularly important if a story becomes the focus of a court case or its accuracy is disputed. And as explained in Chapter 7, it can be vitally important to do background research before you conduct an interview for anything much more than a basic reactive news story.

Journalists' most important research tools are:

— their own contact books

— on-the-record interviews

— telephone books—both online and in hard copy, although online is often best because it is updated daily, while the print edition is only updated annually

— checks of their own news organisation's archives, and sometimes the archives of competitors, for background information—although be careful not to repeat mistakes made by others

— quick web-based searching to find people, background information and data

— documents such as court records and company searches

— electoral rolls—which can be viewed at Australian Electoral Commission offices in each state and territory

— off-the-record information from sources—but ensure the information is reliable and do your best to discover if a source has an axe to grind

— information from colleagues

— computer-assisted research techniques, including deep searching of the hidden web

— statistical analysis

— their own eyes, ears and sense of curiosity!

When conducting research, always use the key questions of what, when, where, who, why and how as your guide. If possible, get out of your office and talk to people—some of the things they tell you and comments they make will amaze you! Write notes—never put all your faith in your smartphone, or a voice recorder or video camera. Date and keep those notes, not just so you have an accurate record when you write your story, but also so you can go back over them later if the story moves in a new direction and you have an opportunity to update it. When dealing with contacts and interviewees be assertive if necessary, but never rude. And be persistent—if at first you don't succeed, do not give up. Research can be frustrating at times but good researchers keep trying; they think outside the square, mull things over, look for different angles and different people to talk to; they prod and poke, seek expert opinion, and look at how similar problems have been resolved in the past. Good journalists tend to gather and hoard small morsels of information and painstakingly put them together over time. Eventually, fragments that might be meaningless in themselves connect over time until ultimately there is a 'Eureka' moment when pieces of the jigsaw fall into place and a meaningful picture emerges.

Journalists also need to understand the difference between primary and secondary documents and other source materials. Primary documents are original materials. Secondary materials are documents and other matter based on primary materials. A court transcript would be an example of a primary document, while a newspaper report based on that document would be a secondary document. As discussed in Chapter 12, you will avoid the risk that those who prepared secondary source material made mistakes in their interpretation of primary documents if you base your stories on primary source material. Obtaining primary documents and other resources should be a major aim. That is one reason why you should not trust Wikipedia—it is virtually all secondary material.

> Journalists must understand the difference between primary and secondary documents and other source materials. Primary documents are original materials. Secondary materials are documents and other matter based on primary materials.

How not to research

Readers, audiences and newsroom bosses do not respect journalists who are ignorant, lazy or stupid. They expect journalists to check facts and present accurate, reliable information. If you hope to earn respect, you would be well advised not to do any of the following.

— Ask others to provide basic information you could have easily gathered yourself—for example, phone numbers anyone could have found on a website or an address you could have looked up in a telephone directory.

— Be rude or demanding of contacts, other journalists, public relations people or the public—they might help you once, but will not go out of their way again.

— Throw discretion to the wind—for example, by telling one source about things another source told you.

— Only seek one side of a story—especially if it is controversial or political.

— Allow yourself to get too close to sources.

— Behave unethically.

Laziness and stupidity aside, journalists should be wary of taking information and people at face value. Just as it is dangerous to believe everything you read, it is important to understand that not everyone is trustworthy. There are some strange people in this world, some of whom try to fool others with things like 'doctored' documents, photos and emails. Sometimes 'urban myths' and gossip circulate widely and are repeated by apparently sincere sources, so they seemingly get a life of their own. One of the best defences against being fooled is to listen very carefully to things people tell you. Ask yourself: does it make sense, is it too good to be true, how can I double-check? Above all, trust your own sixth sense: if something feels wrong or unlikely—even if you only feel a vague sense of unease— the chances are that something is wrong and you will need to do more research.

Beware of online traps

Journalists often use a quick Google or Wikipedia search for checking facts. A Google search occasionally results in a ground-breaking story, but unless handled with care, a simple search can also be a recipe for disaster. The problem is that the web and internet are simultaneously a gold mine and a minefield—anyone can put anything online. Even if an online publication is well intentioned, information might or might not be accurate—or if it is accurate, might still convey a false impression because relevant key facts were omitted. There are also grave dangers in using sites such as Wikipedia and Answers.com. While they were founded by people with good intentions, anyone can 'edit' the vast majority of Wikipedia entries and anyone can submit articles. As a result, non-experts who do not know how much they do not know, can 'correct' the entries of real experts. Consequently, Wikipedia is riddled with misinformation and half-truths, plagiarism is rampant, some entries are defamatory, and others advertise products or promote causes including those of political extremists, perverts, terrorists and religious zealots.

Wikipedia is also a haunt of jokers, hoaxers and satirists. Its problems are compounded by the fact Wikipedia entries tend to rank highly in Google searches, often coming right at the top. One better-known Wikipedia hoax occurred in 2009 when Irish sociology student Shane Fitzgerald, 22, 'edited' the supposedly biographic entry of French composer Maurice Jarre immediately after the musician died. As part of his handiwork, Fitzgerald invented a quote he attributed to Jarre which said:

> One could say my life itself has been one long soundtrack… Music was my life, music brought me to life, and music is how I will be remembered long after I leave this life. When I die there will be a final waltz playing in my head and that only I can hear (Fitzgerald 2009).

Fitzgerald's fictitious 'quote' was subsequently copied and used in stories by unsuspecting journalists around the world. But it was not long before they learnt they had been fooled in an experiment conducted by a university student. Imagine how silly those journalists must have felt when Fitzgerald owned up in an article he wrote for the *Irish Times* under the headline 'Lazy journalism exposed by online hoax' (Fitzgerald 2009). In the article, Fitzgerald said he knew journalists relied on finding information on the web and:

> I wanted to prove that this was indeed the case, and show the potential dangers that arise… I was shocked that highly respected newspapers would use material from Wikipedia without first sourcing and referencing it properly (Fitzgerald 2009).

Social networking sites can also be dangerous. In 2012 a rumour that started as a joke on Twitter about the death of Rowan Atkinson, aka Mr Bean, went viral. Within a short time, and even though Atkinson was very much alive, his Wikipedia entry listed his date of death (Gardiner 2012). A key point to remember is that your best defence against online traps is to develop a healthy scepticism—to understand that web hoaxes, hoax emails, counterfeit websites and fake YouTube and Facebook photos and videos abound. It is also relatively easy for jokers and deceivers to establish a Twitter or Facebook presence in a false name—even the name of someone powerful and famous. There was a good example of that in 2012 when Twitter verified a false account set up in the name of Wendi Deng, the wife of News Corporation Chief Executive Rupert Murdoch (Adegoke 2012). So be wary of running with the pack. Do not become so eager for a story that you only see what you want to see. It is much better to check facts and not be taken for a sucker.

One classic example of a gullible journalist who failed to heed the warning signs and fell into a carefully baited, multi-pronged online trap occurred in 2009 when *The Sydney Morning Herald*'s Caroline Marcus reported on a too-good-to-be-true 21st-century fairy tale. Under the headline 'A lost jacket and a stolen heart', Marcus's article began:

> Heidi Clarke could be a modern Cinderella. But instead of a glass slipper, she has a tuxedo jacket and rather than knocking on doors to find her Prince Charming, she has YouTube. The 24-year-old retail worker from Elizabeth Bay launched an extraordinary quest to find a mystery man she met briefly at a city cafe last week (Marcus 2009a).

The article explained how 'Miss Clarke' had a brief conversation with a mysterious male stranger after a waiter muddled their orders. She said she felt 'a connection' with the man, who she described as '6 foot, tall, toned—and hot'. Explaining that he left his jacket on the back of his chair when he left the café, Miss Clarke said her aim was to find the man so she could give his jacket back. As part of her quest, she subsequently created a website and made a YouTube video. Denying she was a stalker, Miss Clarke said she hoped to go out with the man on 'a few old-fashioned dates' (Marcus 2009a). In fairness to Marcus, she did report that 'sceptics' had asked if Miss Clarke's search was an example of the internet being used for self-promotion and that 'some' had even suggested the YouTube video was a fake, 'but Miss Clarke says she is sincere' (Marcus 2009a).

Imagine then how humiliated Marcus must have felt the following day when she had to report 'Heidi Clarke is a fake' and 'an actress hired for a viral marketing campaign to promote a jacket' (Marcus 2009b). At is turned out, Marcus and *The Sydney Morning Herald* were conned into promoting a brand of men's jackets. In the process they had ignored clear warning signs—something rival publisher News.com.au was only too happy to remind its readers when, under the headline 'YouTube Heidi Clarke lovelorn plea wears thin', it reported:

> Within four days, more than 60,000 people had watched the pretty blonde put her heart on the line and plead for the handsome stranger to come forward. In that time, close to 200 people—most of them men—have left comments on the site or emailed 'Clarke' with propositions, accusations of a 'set-up' or claims that they are 'the man in the jacket' (News.com.au 2009).

While it could be argued the hoax was relatively innocuous and did little more than make a newspaper and a journalist look silly, it could equally be argued that every mistake by a journalist negatively impacts on all journalists because each error reinforces perceptions that news media and journalists collectively are not to be trusted.

One of the worst web hoaxes a journalist has fallen for—and one of the most heartbreaking for the ordinary people who were among its innocent victims—happened in December 2004 when the BBC broadcast an interview with a man who said he was a 'company executive' with Dow Chemical. A huge multinational corporation, Dow, had taken over a large chemical plant in Bhopal, India, from Union Carbide Corporation after a 1984 gas leak killed thousands of people and left more than 100,000 others with permanent injuries in one of the world's worst industrial disasters. During the interview, the 'Dow executive' pledged $US12 billion to compensate 120,000 victims who had survived the initial accident but who had continuing health problems and whose life expectancy was reduced (Yes Men 2005). The BBC broadcast the interview twice on television and repeatedly on its radio news.

But one of the world's most respected news services had been cruelly hoaxed—as had the Bhopal victims. As it turned out, the 'Dow executive' the BBC interviewed was really an activist with Yes Men, an anti-globalisation group that takes pride in impersonating government officials, 'criminals' and corporate leaders 'who put profit ahead of everything else' 'in order to publicly humiliate them' (Yes Men 2012). The group had cloned the real Dow website and set up a fake site which fooled the BBC producer who was looking for a Dow Chemical spokesperson to interview. The ensuing embarrassment was almost palpable. An internal BBC inquiry later found that:

> A producer on BBC World [news] had been asked to book a representative from Dow for the 20th anniversary of the disaster, which has claimed the lives of 20,000 people. He went to the fake Dow website, and was directed to the media relations section (BBC NewsWatch 2004).

The preceding examples are the tip of an iceberg. They should not put you off using the internet and web as research tools, but they should encourage you to be careful and to become web-savvy. The keys are to learn how to pick the good from the bad and to fine-tune, then trust, your intuition.

Computer-assisted research

An understanding of how to use computer-assisted research techniques will help you sift the credible and legitimate from the smoke and mirrors. It will also do much more than that. Computer-assisted research—a concept often referred to in the past as computer-assisted-reporting, or CAR—is concerned with ways of finding, collecting, sorting and interpreting information and data. As Paul Adrian (1999) said:

> [it helps journalists] hold officials' feet to the fire. When they dismiss your question by saying, 'that one just fell through the cracks', you can come

back at them and say, 'actually we looked at the records and found 46 more examples of the same thing' (Adrian 1999, p. 12).

Computer-assisted research is a brilliant tool for developing exclusive proactive news stories. Among other things it can be used to quietly work away on backburner stories—researching on rare slow news days over a considerable period, when intuition suggests there is information to dig for, but the research is not urgent and it will take time to build a story. It is an approach to research that can be as simple as a Google search or as complex as deep investigative news-gathering searches of what is known as the 'hidden web' for computer-linked, stored or generated information and databases, and the subsequent analysis of that information (Garrison 1998, p. 11). It is also an invaluable aid in finding and interpreting statistics. In essence computer-assisted journalistic research involves searching for information, both online and in specific databases, and also using computers to sort, group and analyse statistics and other potential sources of information in order to build news stories (Garrison 1998, p. 11).

There is virtually no article—from a simple picture story to a complex investigative report exposing multi-million dollar fraud, or a political scandal—that cannot be enhanced by using online resources. The most important skills to acquire in relation to computer-assisted research are learning where to look, how to look, and developing an ability to assess the legitimacy or otherwise of what is found. That said, it should be understood that using a computer as a research tool does not supersede traditional tools such as going out and talking to people, it just adds to them.

There are also two websites which were specially built as aids for Australian journalists and journalism students using computer-assisted research techniques: http://ComputerAssistedReporting.Com, which was established by the author of this book, and the OZguide to internet sources for Australian journalists: www.journoz.com. As with everything in the online world, there are no infallible guarantees, but these sites do contain lists of links that have been reviewed and judged reliable, accurate and plausible—at least in terms of being what they say they are—by academic researchers who have been prepared to attach their names to them.

Key aspects of computer-assisted research are considered in the remainder of this chapter.

Verifying online information

To restate an important point, the first thing to remember when you search the web for information is that anyone from a High Court judge to the village idiot can put just about anything online. Early in the history of the web, a group of US journalism educators known as the Missouri Group specifically warned that:

> Databases aren't infallible. The information in them is entered by humans, who are susceptible to mistakes. Some material is even deliberately misleading. Databases occasionally are doctored in an attempt to prove a position or promote a cause (Brooks et al. 1996, p. 157).

Verifying information is essential. So how do you do search safely? You start by being sceptical about everything you find online, and by understanding that you need to probe it and test it. Ask yourself if a website 'RAPs': is it *reliable*, *accurate* and *plausible* (Quinn 2001, p. 130)? The following checklist will help:

1 *Look for authentication and attribution*:
   Start by examining the address, or URL (Uniform Resource Locator) of a website. If it includes '.gov', it is reasonable to expect that you have found a government site and the information it contains is reasonably credible, although there will probably be plenty of public relations spin. Similarly, '.edu' indicates a site is owned by an educational institution such as a university, school or college. There are strict rules about the registration of websites containing '.gov' or '.edu' which mean they can only be used for legitimate government and educational sites. But it is a different story when sites have URLs containing suffixes such as '.com', '.net', '.org' or '.name'. These have been registered by individuals, groups and businesses.

   Also look for extensions, such as '.au', '.ca' or '.uk'. No extension usually, but not always, indicates a site was registered in the US; otherwise the extensions are a guide to where it is likely a site has been registered—for example '.au' = Australia, '.ca' = Canada and '.uk' = United Kingdom. Be suspicious about sites with URLs indicating they have been registered in tax haven nations such as Vanuatu, '.vu'; the Bahamas, '.bs'; or the Seychelles, '.sc', to name a few. URL extensions are, however, only an indication of where a site was registered. They do not guarantee anything, because it is relatively simple for a person in one nation to register a site in another.

Looking carefully at details in the URL should help you identify spoof sites. For instance, the legitimate website address for the US White House is www. whitehouse.gov, while there is a parody site at http://whitehouse.gov1.info/. The giveaway is in the suffix, with the '.gov' site being legitimate and the one ending with '.info' being the fake. Also note, and do not be fooled by, the '.gov1.' in the middle of the joke site URL.

2   *Ask yourself a series of questions*:

   a) Who put the information online?

   b) Is the author mentioned on the site?

   c) How can I be sure the author is who they say they are? Is there some way of checking?

   d) Is the site up to date?

   e) Are there any potential legal problems such as defamation, *sub judice* contempt, or obvious breaches of copyright? (These issues are considered in Chapters 15, 16 and 17 of this book.)

3   *Look carefully around the site*:

   a) Does it include a real telephone number and street address, or provide any other way of contacting the author other than via email or an anonymous post office box address?

   b) Is what is written on the site consistent and its style appropriate, or does it look as though bits and pieces have been copied and pasted from different sources? Are the spelling, grammar and punctuation consistent? Is the font uniform?

   c) Look at the overall effect of the website. One would be suspicious, for example, of a site purporting to be a government site if it featured dancing girls, pop music and spangles!

   d) Are there links to the site from other credible websites? To check, you could put the site's title or the name of its author into several different search engines and see what, if anything, comes up. Maybe the author is listed in a staff profile of an organisation such as a university or government department? If, for instance, there is a link to the site from a government department, it is probable that whoever created the link would have satisfied themselves about its credibility. Similarly, a link to the site from the website of a credible organisation such as the Australian Medical Association, the Law Society, the Australian Journalism Education Association, the Royal Flying Doctor Service, a university, the CSIRO or a major company means the site is more likely than not legitimate.

4 *Check to see if an online 'expert' really is an expert:*

a) Once satisfied a website is legitimate and an author is who they say they are, then check to see if that person really has the authority or credentials to be saying whatever it is they have put online. Are they an expert or a fraud? Maybe they have relevant academic qualifications or years of experience? Perhaps they have been published in another form, such as a book or refereed academic journal articles? Do they belong to some recognised professional, industry or hobby group?

b) If the person claims to have qualifications, ask yourself where they are from—is it a well-known academic institution where they could be verified, or a high-sounding but dubious 'university' where anyone can buy a 'degree' or 'doctorate' for a few dollars?

5 *Trust your intuition.* If everything appears to be legitimate but you still feel unsure about a website, or the information on it, try to verify the information via other sources:

a) Perhaps the author's name, or the organisation's name, is listed in another type of directory, such as the telephone book? Check.

b) If there is a telephone number, call it and ask about the information online— but remember how the BBC was fooled by the Yes Men.

c) Check who the site is registered to by examining details of the site's URL registration. That can be done relatively easily through free web-based searches of the WHOIS US database, which can be accessed at http://whois.domaintools.com/, or for Australian registered sites search through www.mywebname.com.au. Lists of international registrations can be found at the Norid website: www.norid.no/domenenavnbaser/domreg.html. Registration details found through these sites should reveal the name and contact details of the person or organisation that registered just about any website. However, be aware that unscrupulous operators frequently lodge false information when they register a URL and in some jurisdictions it is possible to register websites anonymously.

Newspaper archives

Journalists working for major newspaper companies are most likely to start, and perhaps finish, searching for information in their own organisation's computer archive. Access to the archive allows journalists—whether reporters, sub-editors, feature writers or columnists—to literally call up every news story or feature article published in the past two decades or longer about a particular person, issue or place. But, as touched on earlier in this chapter, there is a danger in relying on an in-house archive that you might perpetuate an error made by another journalist. Old stories may contain errors of fact, wrongly spelt names of people and places, inaccurate corporate data, or wrong dates and times. Even in cases when an apology has been published in a newspaper, the story it referred to can sit uncorrected in the archive. For instance, as can be seen in the following extracts from a story dated February 21, 2002, which was recalled from the archive of *The Daily Telegraph*, there would be problems for a journalist attempting to find how to spell the surname of the then Governor-General because it was spelt in two different ways in the same story:

> Anglican Archbishop of Sydney Dr Peter Jensen yesterday said 'it's just intolerable' that Governor-General Peter Hollingsworth would state that a 14-year-old girl could lure a priest into a sexual relationship…

> Prime Minister John Howard was studying Mr Hollingworth's defence last night before deciding on the Governor-General's future (Kamper & Gearing 2002, p. 5).

Some years ago Brisbane's *The Courier-Mail* found itself in a terrible tangle after problems in an archived story caused it massive embarrassment. Its troubles started when a court reporter took the unusual and dangerous step of filing a story based on a prediction that a particular piece of evidence would be given during a coronial inquest. But the evidence was not given. The next day, a different journalist attended the inquest and reported. The second journalist subsequently returned to the newsroom, called up the previous day's article from the newspaper's archive and included some of the predicted 'information' that was not actually given in court as background in her own story. The paper initially apologised to a witness at the hearing for reporting she gave evidence which she did not give. Later, after being roasted by the coroner, it printed a grovelling 525-word apology to a hospital mentioned at the inquest. The apology said, in part:

> *The Courier-Mail* regrets the factual errors in the articles and its failure to correct them when they became apparent and after the coroner had made criticisms. *The Courier-Mail* apologises to the Mater Hospital and its staff for the distress and injury to reputation caused by the publications (Apology 2002, p. 3).

One of the basic lessons to be learnt from this mess is that it is unwise to rehash information found in predictive articles that have been archived. It is also prudent to search for the most recent files and additions to the archive as well as older ones, because doing so increases the chances of discovering apologies, retractions or corrections.

Another way to protect yourself is to cast your net as widely as possible. Try to discover everything you can about a person or issue from as many different sources as you reasonably can. That way, if there is a problem somewhere, hopefully somebody else will have mentioned it or, if researching online, you will discover a discrepancy that rings alarm bells and needs investigation. So if there is even the slightest doubt about information in an archive, go back to primary sources—for example, by telephoning the Governor-General's office to check spellings, or asking the subject of a previous story if earlier details were correct when you interview them for a new story. This way you are unlikely to repeat the mistakes of others, and if you do find yourself in trouble, at least it will have been your own mistake and you will not have been made a fool by parroting errors of others.

Not all journalists work for mainstream news outlets with in-house access to story archives. Some, often smaller, news outlets do not have searchable archives. Their journalists must rely on the web for background information. In addition to using search engines, they can search News Limited and Fairfax archives through web portals such as Newstext—www.newstext.com.au—or the Fairfax Digital News Store: http://newsstore.theage.com.au/apps/newsSearch.ac. There is an upfront fee to access the Newstext archive but access to the Fairfax archive is free.

These two portals provide access to the majority of metropolitan and some major regional newspapers across Australia. In addition, Newstext allows searches of News Corporation's newspapers in other nations, including New Zealand, the UK, Papua New Guinea, Fiji and the US. The downside is that accessing the archives becomes expensive if there is a need to download many articles. Another point to remember is that online newspaper archives did not exist until the mid-1980s and early 1990s because computerised archival systems simply did not exist before then, so there is a limit to how far you can go back unless you go to capital-city state libraries where you can access copies of earlier newspapers on microfiche. Digitised copies of many historic newspapers dating from about 1800 to the 1980s can also be accessed via the Australian National Library's Trove archive website at http://trove.nla.gov.au.

Searching the web

While Google is the dominant search engine, there are others—some of which are better for some tasks. Among the others are what are known as meta-search engines, which search groups of other search engines, for example www.metaeureka.com or https://ixquick.com. A simple, superficial search is as easy as typing keywords in a search box. It might not return any 'hits'—web pages a search engine has decided are relevant to your keywords—or it may return literally millions. Deeper searching is more complex but results will be more specific.

All good search engines have an option for 'advanced' searching in which you can specify how they look for keywords and phrases. One major benefit of advanced searching is that it allows you to save time and avoid having to scan pages of search results, by filtering out search words and terms you do not want. An alternative to using advanced searches which is preferred by some researchers is to use Boolean searching, which is a way of controlling a search. For instance, putting AND or a + symbol between words tells a search engine to find both words (or as many words as you have inserted AND or + between) in the one website. Inserting OR between words instructs a search to find one word or another. Including NOT or a minus sign—as in 'road NOT highway' or 'road – highway'—will tell a search engine to find references to all roads except highways. The NOT or – option does not work with Google but words can be excluded using Google's advanced search. Most search engines also allow users to refine a search by putting a "search term" or terms "of several words at once" between double quotation marks that instruct the search engine to find those exact words or exact phrase. The default for major search engines such as Google is to assume AND has been inserted between each word typed into its search box, so it will try to find web pages containing all the words.

In addition to conducting searches with different search engines, journalists can find a wealth of information in what is known as the hidden web, or invisible web—websites within websites that are not readily searched by Google and other general search engines, but which often reveal their secrets when searched internally from their 'mother site' or portal. Government websites are a great example. Digging down into them by using searches, and particularly Boolean searches or advanced searches, can produce surprising results. There are also sites on the web which help users work their way around the hidden web. Just entering the term "hidden web" in Google will return at least 500,000 entries. Another good tip is to enter the word 'database' and a keyword related to a particular topic you are interested in. Doing so will reveal surprising results—at least 1.4 billion search results for the word 'database' on its own at the time of writing! This is largely because much of the web is constructed around databases—aviation databases, health databases, nuclear explosion databases, climate change databases, to name just a few.

Another very useful place to look for information on the web is the Internet Archive's Wayback Machine: www.archive.org. It is an invaluable resource when searching for web pages that for one reason or another have disappeared. It is also useful for researching the history of a particular website and seeing how it has evolved, how people associated with a specific site have come and gone, or even how information on a site has been sanitised or corrected. Google Earth can also be a useful tool, especially when working on environmental, planning or land development stories. At a different level, visiting the websites of competing news organisation is a useful way for journalists and chiefs-of-staff to keep an eye on what rival media outlets are up to.

Government websites

Local, state and federal government websites in Australia carry an enormous amount of information, although some sites are better and easier to navigate than others. There is also a wealth of information about Australia—and about how people in other nations perceive Australia—in foreign websites. Some of these sites, especially if they are US Government sites, can be sources of better behind-the-scenes information about the activities of Australian governments than can be retrieved from our own government websites. For example, the US Federal Aviation Administration (FAA) publishes information on the web about Australian-based commercial aircraft. It also lists details of incidents such as near misses in international airspace involving aircraft flying to and from Australia. Or enter the words 'Australia' or 'Australian' in the US Government's official web portal—www.usa.gov—and it will return close to 4 million results! Similarly, there is plenty of information about Australia in government sites in the UK, Canada, New Zealand and many other nations.

It is also a fact that while Australia has some of the least effective and most government-abused freedom of information laws in the English-speaking world, our governments, and particularly the federal government, have put a remarkable amount of information on the web (Lamble 2004, pp. 5–9). This is not just for altruistic reasons. Making information available online saves governments a small fortune in wages for staff who would otherwise attend counters, and in paper and printing costs, because users of government web services pay to download and print their own documents on their own paper and with their own printers instead of governments paying for the printing and delivery. It also saves government departments adding more and more paper to an ever-growing document-based archive.

Government information on the web falls into several categories. One is public relations blurb. Governments love telling us about all the supposedly good things they do, or at least they try to put a good spin on everything they do. Then there is government information designed to help people deal with government. You can access many government services online—even a do-it-yourself divorce kit if you feel so inclined. There are also transcripts of many court hearings, information and reports from government committees, daily Hansard reports, and things like travel warnings and health information.

Government and corporate information

Governments also use the web to provide specialist regulatory information relating to business. The Australian Competition and Consumer Commission, for example, publishes much useful information about how business is regulated and controlled. Similarly, the Australian Securities and Investments Commission provides valuable information about business and company registrations, and its website is an important starting point for investigating the business dealings of companies and individuals. You can search information about companies and their directors and shareholders, including dates and places of birth of company officers. Searches will also reveal the names of individuals banned from holding responsible positions in companies or from working as investment advisers.

Basic searches for company information are free, but if you want detailed information you must access it through an information broker and pay a fee. Large media companies have accounts with information brokers, and in that case the chief-of-staff can authorise journalists to do particular searches the company will pay for. Journalists who work for smaller media outlets, however, might have to pay for searches themselves using a credit card. There is a list of accredited information brokers on the Australian Securities and Investments Commission's website. A full company search is likely to cost about $50, while searching the name of an individual for all the companies they are associated with will cost a little more. These might not sound like great amounts of money, but if a journalist is following a money trail or trying to find a shonky business operator who hides behind a string of company names in something like a pyramid structure, the costs quickly mount.

Some information brokers provide access to other government information, all through the same web portal, and journalists can also pay for land title searches and searches of motor vehicle registers. If they are authorised, they can also gain access to some police information. Both the Australian Competition and Consumer Commission and the Australian Securities and Investments Commission are federal government agencies, but some commercial activities—such as control of real estate agents and car dealers—are subject to state control.

Other good sources of government information can be found on websites such as those of the Australian Bureau of Statistics, Civil Aviation Safety Authority, Federal Health Department, Department of Foreign Affairs and Trade, the Commonwealth Parliamentary Library (where you can access Hansard) and State Parliamentary sites. Many other sites are useful on a day-to-day basis. As noted earlier in this chapter, they include Telstra's WhitePages.com.au, which is updated daily, making it a helpful tool in finding someone who has recently moved. Similarly, there is excellent information—including online radar and satellite images, as well as latest storm warnings and also historic weather data—on the Bureau of Meteorology site.

As Weaver (2000) said, a web-savvy journalist should be able to quickly find company annual reports, trade statistics, demographic information, full-text legislation and treaties, a vast range of reference tools, drug and clinical databases, online directories, media release archives, aviation crash statistics, election results, political contacts and cost-of-living calculators.

Social networking sites and blogs

Journalists working a particular round, conducting a special investigation, monitoring unfolding stories, or seeking to find particular people to interview can harvest valuable information from joining internet discussion groups such as Twitter, establishing a presence on personal networking sites such as YouTube, Facebook and LinkedIn, or accessing blogs—but be very careful. Again, the problem is that you often have no idea who is actually posting information. There have been countless news hoaxes traced back to those sites. They thrive on unconfirmed rumour and gossip. Also bear in mind that blogs generally deal with opinion, not news. Some blogs are valuable sources of tips and expert opinion, but many are written by individuals whose egos are much bigger than their intellects. Similarly, be careful of the work of so-called 'citizen journalists'. They can contribute invaluable information from the scenes of breaking stories, but few of them are actually trained journalists. Consequently they may not have a professional journalist's understandings about ethics; the journalistic imperatives of fairness, attribution and balance; fact checking; or the law. They may not understand news values, and could have made false assumptions and jumped to ill-informed conclusions.

> Some blogs are valuable sources of tips and expert opinion, but many are written by individuals whose egos are much bigger than their intellects.

Email and text messaging

Just as anyone can put anything on the web, anyone can send an email or text message. And just as websites may not be all they seem at times, emails and text messages may harbour hidden dangers. Apart from the obvious risks posed by unsolicited spam and attachments carrying viruses, worms and trojans, emails and SMS texts can have particular dangers when used for news-gathering—especially in relation to defamation. For that reason, and as discussed in detail in Chapter 15, journalists should be careful not to write things in emails or text messages that could be construed as defamatory—something you should consider when framing questions for email interviews or asking questions via text message.

On the other hand, a major advantage of email and other electronic messaging is that they produce a preservable text record—a feature which makes it difficult for a source to claim you have misquoted him or her. There is also the benefit of using a means of fast communication in which sender and receiver do not both have to be available at exactly the same time—something especially useful when communicating by email across time zones because it gets around the problem of having to wake in the early hours or stay up late to telephone sources overseas. Email and messaging also helps avoid the problem of 'telephone tag'. Further, email and text messaging allows simultaneous one-to-many communication, in which the same message can be sent to a group, or groups, at the same time. Email and other forms of messaging can also serve as carriers to which documents, photographs, video, sound and data can be attached—something of immeasurable benefit when filing stories back to newsrooms from remote locations.

On the downside, just as you need to verify websites, it is important to know who you are really talking to by email, on Twitter, Facebook, LinkedIn, or via SMS. If not, there is the same potential for disaster as there is in taking information from websites, online discussion groups or blogs at face value. These issues aside, the nature of email and text messaging gives rise to another potential problem in that emails and text messages are easy to ignore. A busy person will receive tens of emails and text messages a day. One from a pesky journalist asking questions which need thinking about is likely to be bypassed, put aside or deleted. Even if a recipient intends answering, other more pressing matters often get in the way and eventually the email or message is forgotten. Similarly—and unlike telephone or person-to-person interviews—a subject is not going to be caught off guard by a difficult or unexpected question asked in an email or text message. There is little scope for an instinctive, and perhaps revealing, reply. For reasons like these, and as discussed in Chapter 7, electronic interviews may not be a good option unless you have previously contacted an interviewee personally and she or he has agreed to provide written answers to questions. Also be aware that many people, especially those who are older, find text messaging annoying and are not proficient at typing replies on small keypads or touch screens, so they may not reply to you or they might ask another person to do so on their behalf.

The magic of number crunching

A fear of mathematics might be a reason why many journalists study Arts and Humanities, not Science at university, but journalists cannot escape maths. It sneaks up when you need to compare things with other things. And maths is particularly relevant to events such as elections and when reporting on figures to do with the economy, tourist numbers, occupancy rates, interest rates, population growth, demographics, newly released census data, and even marks and grades. Maths is also useful when dealing with statistics. A wonderful thing about number crunching is that it can help journalists perform seemingly high-class conjuring tricks to literally pluck stories out of thin air—developing good, strong articles from statistics in ways few people realise is possible.

One advantage of computer-assisted research is that it can employ software such as Excel to painlessly crunch numbers, leaving it to journalists to interpret the results for readers. Many students arrive at universities with a good working knowledge of Excel because they learnt about it at school. Those who do not can find free tutorials on the web, or they can buy a self-help book. It is beyond the scope of this book to explain how to use Excel, but it will help you enormously—if you are interested in unleashing its power as a journalist—if you brush up on a few basic mathematical concepts first.

One of the most important laws of maths, and one which Excel assumes those who use it understand, is what is known as the order of operations. It says that multiplication should be calculated first, then division, addition and subtraction in that order. If the order is not followed without deviation, the result will be wrong. Next is brackets. Operations enclosed within brackets must be completed first and in the correct order as per the order of operations. Operations outside the brackets follow, also in order.

Another concept all journalists should understand is how to present comparative figures in terms of population. There are two generally accepted ways of doing this: as percentages, or in terms of prevalence per 100,000. Each approach allows meaningful and easily understood comparisons of instances—or prevalence, or impact—of similar events or occurrences in communities of different sizes. It is important to develop an understanding of how percentages work and how they are used to present data in terms of occurrences per 100 (hence 'per cent'). Percentages can be a little confusing at first, but they are not really difficult once you understand the idea of expressing numbers as a ratio of 100. Again, there is excellent information on the web, where there are calculators which will work out the figures for you, as does the calculator on your computer or a simple electronic calculator.

As mentioned earlier, the other common way of presenting comparisons is to convert figures into a rate per 100,000. To do this, you simply divide the number of whatever is being compared—say the incidence of Ebola virus—by the number of people living in a particular area and then multiplying the result by 100,000. As an example, we can take a hypothetical case and say there are 192,000 people living in City A and there have been 12 cases of Ebola virus reported in the past month. In the same period there were nine cases in City B, which has a population of 90,000 people. How do we compare the rates? Simple:

— To work out the incidence in City A, divide the 12 cases by the population—12 divided by 192,000—and multiply by 100,000. The result: 6.25 cases of Ebola virus per 100,000.

— To work out the incidence in City B, divide the nine cases by the population—9 divided by 90,000—and multiply by 100,000. The result: 10 cases of Ebola virus per 100,000.

It can now be reported that there is a much higher incidence of Ebola virus in City B than in City A. In other words, even though the population of City B is much smaller than that of City A, a larger proportion of City B's population was infected. From there you would contact medical authorities, maybe also victims, employers, university experts and others. The result is an excellent story. The same concept can be used to express comparisons in terms of times, distances, and practically anything else that can be measured.

As an aside, many are unaware that there is a handy desktop calculator to be found in Windows-based computers. In Windows 8, 7 or Vista, click on the start button at the bottom left of the screen, type 'calc' into the search box and click on 'calculator'. In Windows XP click on 'start' and then 'run'. Type 'calc' into the box that says 'open' and click on 'okay' or hit 'enter'. Apple Macs also have a maths calculator widget and there is a free iPad app. Similarly, most mobile phones and smartphones have built in maths calculators. As with simple maths, journalists really only need master a few basic concepts in relation to Excel in order to use it to extract extremely useful information. Excel spreadsheets are formulae driven and the most important of those to learn how to use are SUM and AVERAGE, plus the 'logical' functions of AND, FALSE, IF, NOT, OR and TRUE. It is also necessary to become familiar with sorting, 'greater than' and 'less than' filters, and different ways of setting up formats for cells, columns and whole sheets.

The raw material for extracting story material from Excel is statistics. These can come from practically anywhere credible, but the Australian Bureau of Statistics and official state and territory government websites are good starting points. Often the figures can be downloaded into a spreadsheet, or highlighted then copied and pasted from a website. Figures from paper copies of information can be typed in, but be careful not to make mistakes. It is possible to combine statistics obtained from different sources into the one spreadsheet as long as they are compatible and like things are being compared with like—apples with apples!

Even leaving aside the calculating and sorting functions of Excel, the software can be useful for journalists because it allows you to enter figures and represent them graphically in different forms—such as graphs, charts and tables—to make them easy for readers to understand.

After meaning is extracted from statistics by sorting and grouping them in a spreadsheet, a journalist can flesh out what has been revealed by seeking appropriate comment. A major advantage for journalists in working with statistics in their own right and in working from raw figures produced by an official government statistician is that it becomes difficult, if not impossible, for a politician or anyone else to refute the final result. Spin-doctors cannot claim a story based on statistics collected and published by their own department was not accurate. That does not mean, however, that some public servants, public relations practitioners and politicians might not try! You should also be aware that the proper figures might come as an unpleasant surprise to some people you interview. They may have seen dodgy 'official' figures which were sorted and grouped in a different way to convey a sanitised impression.

Another point to understand is that many public servants are treated as much like mushrooms as the rest of the community—the only statistics they see are those released by government public relations staff. Sometimes the 'real' statistics are as much news to those public servants as to anyone else. But even if there is denial, there would be a good story in the fact that a particular government department was using data which made it smell like roses, but which failed to reflect a true picture. Something like that happened in the US in 1985 when journalist Elliot Jaspin discovered statistics he had crunched painted a very different picture from information published by a government housing authority. An investigative journalist with the *Providence Journal* in Rhode Island, Jaspin discovered that instead of exclusively providing special low-interest home loans for disadvantaged families, as it said it was, the housing authority had also provided low-interest loans for the well-off families of government officials and even its own employees, some of whom subsequently rented the houses they had purchased at nominal interest rates to disadvantaged people too poor to purchase their own homes. About 25 officials were later charged with corruption-related offences (DeFleur 1997, pp. 3–5).

DISCUSSION POINTS

1   Newspaper editors are busy people, so could *The Sunday Telegraph*'s editor Neil Breen be excused for things going so badly wrong over the nude photographs that turned out to be of a woman who was not Pauline Hanson?

2   Should journalistic research always be about trying to find the truth, or is that sometimes an impossible quest?

3   It has been said that a journalist only has two assets, a contact book and a good name. But surely it would be possible to have a contact book without having a good name.

4   What are the main differences and similarities between researching for reactive and proactive news?

5   To what extent is a sixth-sense feeling that something is not what it seems to be—particularly when researching online—really a useful tool for a journalist?

6   I found information on Wikipedia and used it in my research for a story, but it turns out after publication/broadcast that the information was wrong and so was my story. Who is really to blame: me, Wikipedia, the stupid sub-editor who did not spot the mistake, the idiot who put the information on Wikipedia, or all of us?

7   What are the pluses and minuses of using social networking sites such as Facebook and Twitter as sources of information for news stories?

8   A basic understanding of statistics is important for a journalist, but many journalism students actually chose to study journalism and arts subjects because they did could not cope with maths and science! What should they do now?

NEWS PRACTICE POINTS

1   Find a proactive newspaper article, read it carefully and make a list of as many sources of information as you can identify that were used by the journalist who wrote it.

2   Find a reactive newspaper article, read it carefully and make a list of as many sources of information you can identify that were used by the journalist who wrote it.

3   Which of the articles you considered in relation to Practice Points 1 and 2 above would have been the most difficult to research and write? Why?

4   Go online to Wikipedia. Search for and open an entry about a hobby of yours, a recreational activity you enjoy, or a sport you play. Is the information you have found totally accurate? See if you can find the same information on another website. If you can, ask yourself which came first—the entry in Wikipedia or the entry on the other site?

5   Go back to the Wikipedia entry you opened in relation to Practice Point 4. Now edit the entry to improve it. Revisit the same entry the following day and see if your corrections are still in place or if they have disappeared.

6   Find a website that RAPs—is reliable, accurate and plausible—and one that is not. What specific factors make the first site credible? What are three warning signs that the second site is not credible?

7   Go online and find the name and contact details of the person who actually registered the website of the institution where you are studying.

8   There were 2463 cases of Icelandic influenza in the city of Wog and 9657 cases in the city of Lurgie. The population of Wog is 12,500 and the population of Lurgie is 32,250. What is the incidence of Icelandic influenza in each city? Who would you contact to seek informed comment relating to your statistical findings?

NANCY BATES _____

Nancy Bates was the second female editor of a daily newspaper in Australia, and during her 21-year tenure the *Fraser Coast Chronicle* regularly topped circulation growth in Australia. Her daily journalism career of 45 years spanned court, police, local government, general and feature writing. In a 2009 retirement tribute in State Parliament, Queensland Premier Anna Bligh described her as a trailblazer and an 'Australian newspaper legend' known for her fiery words and colourful turn of phrase.

---

1 How did you get your first job as a journalist?

I was hovering between leaving school and continuing studies, with little idea of what career I wanted. My mother was a country correspondent for a couple of newspapers and I had high English marks. That was enough in the mid-1960s. I was offered a cadetship at the *Bay of Plenty Times* in New Zealand.

2 What advice would you offer a beginning journalist?

Be curious, be courageous, be courteous and beware of spending too much time in the company of other journalists. Seek the benefit of experience and inside knowledge, but be aware that journalists who write to impress each other squander their freshness. Be careful not to become a courtesan at the courts of councils, parliaments and crime authorities; avoid being drawn into the flatteries and indulgences of inner sanctums where your role to report to the people is compromised.

3 What is the role of journalism in 21st-century Australian society?

Modern journalists are challenged by the dichotomy of shrinking resources and surging spin-doctoring. Dilution of the advertising base has inevitably led to trimming of newsroom budgets. Pressure on fewer journalists to do more means they rely too heavily on skilful media managers, most of whom have emigrated from the newsrooms to higher paying jobs. They know which buttons to press. Sifting through the blancmange of slanted spin to discover the truth is one of three great challenges for the modern journalist in Australia.

The second challenge is the constant battle to maintain reputations of independent, trusted newsrooms against the churning mayhem of twittering, blogging and pseudo-reporting. The third challenge is to inject awareness of serious threats to society into a population debauched by infotainment. Piquing the interest of people who work frenetically, eat well and have infinite entertainment at their fingertips is no easy task for a journalist today. Salacious scandal wins every time over exposure of evil in government. Corpses of persecuted whistleblowers litter our country, but attempts to arouse interest in the pursuit of justice are left in the dust of SUVs heading for the coast.

4 Journalism is being changed and challenged by technology. What are your thoughts about the future of journalism in Australia?

Australians consider it their right to have free, instant news and new technology makes every linked person a disseminator of news. Journalists must strive to separate themselves from the amateurs with quality reporting and insightful articles that provide succinct understanding of the big issues. They should understand that the endless space provided by the internet is not a licence to ramble. Our customers are now conditioned to quick grabs and small pictures: fitting into the new parameters will require honed talent. We can put flesh on the bones of our reports but each bite should be tasty; a mouthful of fat will prompt readers, listeners and viewers to flick elsewhere.

5 What are the key things a journalism student should learn during their studies?

- English—our readers and listeners might not have a great grasp of English but they sense when a journalist is breaking grammatical rules.

- Economy of words—modern Australians have no time in their lives for waffle or repetition. Lean is powerful. Abraham Lincoln's legendary Gettysburg Address contained 256 words uttered in two minutes. Edward Everett wrote 13,607 words and spoke for two hours. No one remembers what Everett said.

- Multi-skilling—a 21st-century soldier can be a one-man army, carrying all the equipment needed to wage modern war and having the technological skills to use it. A contemporary journalist should be skilled in all aspects of writing, photography (video and still), audio, editing, research, production and dissemination.

- Interviewing empathy—a great journalist is a great interviewer, armed with thorough research and equipped with the capacity to put a subject at ease and then on edge.

6 Is there anything else you would like to say to journalism students and/or about journalism as a profession?

Our world needs bona fide, courageous, unfettered and talented journalists today more than ever before. Technology has created Big Brother: he is watching and constraining us more each day. Databases are growing; intrusive tracking is entrapping us. Our freedoms are being sliced away in seemingly innocuous legislation that no one bothers to examine closely because it is easier to report on (and easier for the populace to comprehend) political sideshows and celebrity foibles that will have no effect on our lives. We need to re-awaken citizens' sense of responsibility to democracy and prise them away from the frivolous stories that have replaced weightier contemplations. Too many top journalists are lured away by the dollars of spin-doctoring, the shallow charms of sport or the perks of travel and glamour journalism.

LIZ JACKSON

Liz Jackson joined the ABC in 1986, presenting the *Coming Out Show*, *The Law Report* and *Background Briefing* on ABC Radio National, before joining ABC Television's *Four Corners* program. She has worked as a reporter/presenter at *Four Corners* since 1994, with the exception of one year as presenter of the ABC's *Media Watch* program in 2005. Liz has won seven Walkley Awards for excellence in Journalism, including the Gold Walkley Award in 2006.

1 How did you get your first job as a journalist?

I did no formal studies in journalism, instead studying Arts and then Law. I worked as a philosophy tutor, a community lawyer and a public servant before applying for my first job as a journalist, at the age of 36. At the time I was a policy adviser on women's issues within the NSW Public Service.

At the same time I had been volunteering for more than two years at a Sydney community radio station, 2SER. I was a regular contributor to the station's weekly two-hour current affairs show, *Razors Edge*, which involved interviewing, presenting and producing both live and pre-recorded material. I loved it, and devoted lots of time to it.

I heard there was a job going at the ABC, co-producing a weekly 45-minute radio show broadly covering women's issues, *The Coming Out Show*. I had been advising on women's policy for two years, and had gained confidence, a body of work and radio skills from community radio work. It seemed that if I was ever going to be able to break into the ABC, this was going to be my best chance. I applied and got the job.

2 What advice would you offer a beginning journalist?

Pursue what interests you down every rabbit hole, as your first choice.

Approach all subjects with an open, critical and questioning mind, and respect that the media consumer has a mind of their own as well.

Your credibility is your most critical asset. Check every fact, and take care that you are not cherry-picking the facts that suit your outlook.

Research widely using all the fabulous tools now available, but never neglect the telephone. Internet searches are no replacement for one-on-one conversations. Make that extra phone call. Even better, go out and talk face-to-face with people. Get out of the office, and mingle.

Be clear about the storyline, the issue, the question that is at the heart of whatever you are writing, the person you are interviewing, why you are filming this event, why you are doing this piece.

Don't be afraid, and if you are, do your best to hide it. Remember, no one ever died from being asked a question.

Storytelling is often the most engaging way to present a subject, and is a skill to be respected. Don't lecture, tell a story.

3 What is the role of journalism in 21st-century Australian society?

The basic role of journalism is to provide accurate information on which members of the community can rely to form an informed view about what is going on in the world. Right now there is plethora of information and spin that is in the public domain. The journalist's role is to assess and analyse that information, investigate its truth, and to seek out further information that is not in the public domain.

Beyond straight reportage there is an important role for the media in providing review, opinion and analysis. The complexity of subjects such as climate change demand time and research from the media, not simply the reporting of hotly contested points of view.

The most important role of journalism is to hold individuals, companies, institutions, agencies, government departments, politicians and governments accountable for the way they use power. The more power they hold, the more important that they be held accountable.

LYNDAL CAIRNS

Lyndal Cairns is an online editor and social media strategist working in Melbourne. She has dedicated much of her career to community news and non-profit work. She is partial to terrible puns and met her fiance on Twitter.

1 How did you get your first job as a journalist?

Through determination and balls-out arrogance. I pretended I already had a job and would sidle up to businesspeople and politicians, identify myself as a journalist and just start asking them questions.

They never asked until the end of the interview what publication I was writing for. When my CV landed on the desk of Merilyn Vale, editor in chief at Quest Community Newspapers in Brisbane, it was full of the kind of stories her papers would run, and she knew I was a sure bet.

2 What advice would you offer a beginning journalist?

Learn from the old hands while they're still around. Ask a thousand niggling questions of the sub-editors. They may be gruff but they're a brains trust and they will secretly love you for asking. Compare the raw copy or rough cuts that you submit with the finished product and try to work out why the changes have been made. Be proud of your work, your role and your publication. And start building your brand from day 1. If you have a business card, you should have professional social media accounts.

3 What is the role of journalism in 21st-century Australian society?

Readers are desperate for reliable, timely and useful information. Journalists need to fill that role, especially online, or it will be filled by people who don't use journalistic inquiry and ethics. But I also think journalism has to step up and take back the community-building role it once had. We can't afford to report from the sidelines—we should get among it and help people take an active role in their news, and thus their democracy.

4 What are your thoughts about the impacts on journalism of changing communication technologies?

I am supposed to say something naff here like 'new technologies present great opportunities as well as challenges' but I won't. The truth is, journalism has never been about the technology and I don't think the journalism will or should change based on platform. Journalists and news organisations have to be flexible enough to give their audience their news in the way they want it.

5 What key things should a journalism student learn?

Curiosity is your finest skill, so take the time to wonder. It's not about writing, it's about communicating effectively. Read widely and voraciously. Eavesdrop—people can't help but tell others where the stories are. Go into every interview with questions you need answered but also with an open mind. Make sure you get your questions answered. Engage readers and contacts about your stories before, during and after they're produced.

6 Is there anything else you would like to say to journalism students and/or about journalism as a profession?

For goodness sake, leave your desk. Stories are out there on the streets and in your Twitter feed, not in your email. Nobody talks like they sound in press releases. Times are tough, particularly in newspapers, but it won't help you or the industry to do a sloppy job. You have to enjoy it. Chutzpah helps.

NEWS WRITING

3

INTERVIEWING

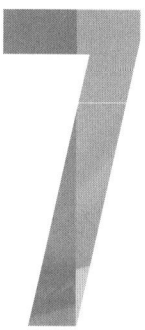

One must spend time in gathering knowledge to give it out richly.
Edmund Clarence Stedman, 1885

OBJECTIVES

After reading this chapter you will understand:

» The importance of interviewing

» How to prepare for an interview

» Alternatives to face-to-face interviewing

» Different types of interview questions

» How to structure an interview

» Why journalists must be excellent listeners

» Journalists' relationships with sources.

Two essential elements of journalism are information gathering and story-telling. Journalists gather information in the field by observation and interviewing. Interviewing is usually the best way to flesh out what has been observed. Asking questions of witnesses, participants, experts and those in authority is sometimes the only way to gather details—especially for reactive news stories. An 'interview' can be as simple as asking someone 'what happened?' or 'how did it happen?', but an in-depth interview for a personal profile, feature story or documentary can take hours. Sometimes information flows freely, but at other times extracting it can be as hard as getting blood from a stone. To be an effective interviewer you must gain people's confidence and entice them to talk to you. Then you must ask questions that draw out information. Journalists who best achieve those goals are professionals who convey an image of being well educated, informed, polite, confident and trustworthy.

Convincing people to talk to you

Some people love to talk, others do not. Some who normally talk other people's heads off will be dumbstruck in the presence of a journalist. Others who would not normally say boo to a goose become voluble when they think their words will be reported. Convincing individuals to talk can come down to an intuitive sixth-sense understanding of what buttons to push when. With some people, and in some circumstances, it works if you are a little assertive. In other cases being assertive is the worst approach and will cause interviewees to shut down and withdraw. Generally, an empathetic, calm and courteous approach will make the best impression and draw the best responses. But bear in mind that no one actually has to talk to you—it is your job to get them to.

First impressions are everything when approaching a potential interviewee. If conducting a telephone interview, those impressions will be based on your voice and how you introduce yourself. In an email interview, the appearance of your email, its grammar, punctuation and spelling are all important. So too is your email address—an address like 'hottotrot@hotmail.com' will not inspire confidence. Similarly, when making a direct personal approach to a potential interviewee it will be how you are dressed, your bearing, your grooming, your speech, and the way you smell that colour the first impression. Imagine how you would react if a journalist who arrived to interview you had garlic breath, foul body odour, greasy hair, dirty clothes, and so many body piercings he or she jangled! Stinky perfume, aftershave and deodorant are also repulsive.

When thinking about how others perceive you, it helps if you understand the image you wish to project. To convey a professional image a good starting point is to dress appropriately for the area you work in and the people you interview. A female journalist who turns up in a tight skirt, skimpy top and high heels to interview a farmer in a horse paddock about an outbreak of Hendra virus is unlikely to make a confidence-inspiring first impression. And what impression is a bearded male journalist wearing holey jeans, sneakers, a dirty shirt, and sporting a mullet going to make when he arrives to interview the governor of the Reserve Bank? If possible, especially if you have prior warning you will be interviewing a particular person in a particular role and environment, it pays to dress for the occasion. If that is not possible, a good rule of thumb is to dress conservatively in tasteful, practical, and clean clothes and footwear. Some journalists even regard first impressions as so vital they change clothes between interviews—the writer once worked with one who changed her outfits so often between interviews she ran an account with a local op-shop!

Body language, bearing, manner and voice also make an early impression on potential interviewees. A positive, but not bone-crunching, handshake makes one impression—a limp one another. Good manners and careful speech are obviously preferable to slang and a superior or aloof demeanour. Inappropriate laughter, swearing, and approaching strangers as if they are your long-lost best mate are turn-offs. Standing straight and looking an interviewee in the eye—although breaking the gaze, too, so that you do not appear to be staring—conveys confidence and authority. Wringing your hands, staring at the ground, shuffling, mumbling and an apologetic air have the opposite effect. Continually looking around, tapping a foot, jiggling a leg, yawning, tapping fingers or a pen, and asking silly questions reflect disinterest or boredom.

The best way to obtain an interview is usually a direct approach. At the scene of an unfolding incident or event, simply approach people, introduce yourself and your news organisation, and start asking relevant questions. Handing out a business card can also help—it implies you are a professional. It also gives interviewees a reference point, especially if they already know your byline or name, and provides contact details if they want to contact you again.

After introducing yourself, it is a good idea to ask a couple of ice-breaker questions. They help put the person at ease and also convey a sense that you already have a broad understanding of what has happened. Sometimes, especially in a tense situation and when reporting a reactive news story, it is better to cut straight to the chase—but do so without being abrupt. Intuition will help you decide which approach is most appropriate.

Irrespective of the approach, what you need to discover when gathering information for a reactive story is what happened, when, where, how many were involved, who was involved or affected, how did it happen, and why? It is unlikely that one individual at the scene will have all the information you need, and even if he or she does seem to, it is wise to cross-check with another source if possible because people's perceptions vary. Some will have heard and seen certain things, but not others. Some might have been there at the time, others arrived later. Therefore you should talk with a range of people including witnesses, those involved, authorities, and maybe others such as nearby residents or workers.

Similarly, if researching for a more feature-oriented or documentary story, you often need to go out, chat to people, introduce yourself as a journalist, explain a bit about the story, and lead them into an interview. If for some reason you cannot make a direct face-to-face approach, contact by telephone is the next best tactic. A carefully written email or text message may be effective—but if attempting to set up an interview by email or text message, avoid slang and texting 'shorthand' otherwise your approach could be viewed as discourteous. Once contact is established, the routine is basically the same as face-to-face: introduce yourself, explain the nature of the story and ask for information.

Less often, when reporting general news or researching for a feature or documentary it will be necessary to make an indirect approach through a third party in the hope that she or he can arrange an interview for you. This commonly occurs with celebrity interviews. Celebrities tend to be stage-managed by public relations practitioners and promoters who arrange for those they represent to be available in person, by telephone, or online at a set time. Many politicians work in similar ways. It is not uncommon in these circumstances for media minders or political spin-doctors to demand you submit a list of questions first. When this happens, the minders usually sit in on the subsequent 'interview' and will cut you off if you attempt to move away from the agreed topics.

Breaking the ice as a student

Journalism students frequently have trouble obtaining interviews. The problem is that interviewees fear you might make mistakes and feel they would rather speak to a 'real journalist' than a novice. They might be dubious about being interviewed in the first place and fear a student would misunderstand or misquote them. Others—especially if they are devious and have been caught doing something their mother would not be proud of—will bully and bluster in an attempt to intimidate a student when they would not dare be as rude to a hardened professional. Some potential interviewees are simply condescending and rude to students, perhaps thinking they are much too important or too busy to be interviewed by a trainee. An issue that can exacerbate the problem is that there is often a lower chance students' work will be published or broadcast than if they were a journalist employed by a media outlet.

But on the bright side, there are plenty of interviewees who will go out of their way to help you. They will be patient and understanding, perhaps remembering their own student days. And you can help yourself. It is understandable that you will be nervous at first, but a timid, self-effacing, apologetic approach will not inspire confidence and encourage people to believe they can trust you. Even if you do not feel like it, make like a duck—calm and serene above the surface, and paddling like a threshing machine underneath. As Sally Adams explains in her excellent book *Interviewing for Journalists*:

> If you are worried about approaching strangers, it's likely they'll refuse to talk to you. This is evidence of one of the great laws of interviewing, that of reciprocity: you get back what you send out (Adams 2001, p. 10).

Whatever reactions you get from potential interviewees whom you approach as a student, there are four key points to remember:

— First, keep your cool and remain polite—among other things you are more likely to talk a reluctant interviewee around if you do.

— Second, be persistent. Ask again, and if one person will not agree to an interview, find others.

— Third, work on not feeling intimidated—even if seeking interviews with powerful figures such as prime ministers, judges, employers or crooks. The fact is that you have every bit as much right to walk on this earth, to ask questions, and do your job as any person you interview.

— Fourth, you will find that once you are a fully fledged and employed journalist, people will respond differently. In other words, do not be discouraged: the most difficult time you will ever have in convincing people to be interviewed will be in your student years, but things will improve, so hang in there.

Background research

It will help break the ice with interviewees, and also lead to quality interviews, if you have done relevant background research. It is clearly not possible to conduct much—if any—research before covering a breaking story for a reactive news report, but in many other circumstances there will be an opportunity. Being knowledgeable about a relevant topic and/or an interviewee's background inspires confidence in interviewees because it conveys a sense of empathy and indicates you understand the topic you are asking questions about. It also improves your own self-confidence. If, for example, you seek an interview with a tennis ace, it is common sense to check her background before you contact her so that you can learn what championships she has won: Wimbledon, the US Open, Australian Open, French Open, or all four? Who did she beat? Were the games closely fought? How did her tennis career start? Who is her coach? At what level is she seeded in the current tournament? Similarly, a movie star would expect a journalist who interviews him to know which movies he acted in. A politician would expect you to know what party she represents, the name of her leader, her portfolio if a minister or shadow portfolio if in opposition, details of the latest political ructions, and above all to be conversant with the issue(s) you want to interview her about.

People, especially well-known people, *expect* journalists to know all about them. If you go into an interview unprepared (if you get that far), a lack of background knowledge is likely to make you look stupid. In extreme cases it can result in an interviewee walking out. And even if the interview concludes, the interviewee— although too polite to tell you to your face that you are a fool—would probably not agree to speak to you again, especially if your lack of background research results in an inaccurate or out-of-context story.

Background research is rarely difficult. Even if you only have a few minutes, a brief background check is better than none—you do not have to memorise a person's whole life story. If you work for an organisation that has its own news archives, they are a good starting point. A Google search is also worthwhile, although ensure the information you find is from a reliable source and is accurate—do not forget that, as explained in Chapter 6, anyone can put anything online! It can also be useful to ask others in a newsroom, particularly an old hand, what they know.

RESEARCH ON THE RUN

As noted earlier, it is unlikely you would be able to do background research before covering a breaking story and interviewing people at the scene. In these circumstances you are on a fact-finding mission. The aim is to observe and gather information as quickly as possible while relevant people are still around and events are fresh in their minds.

But even as you approach the scene of an unfolding story, you should be researching. Approach slowly, observe, listen, smell, try to work out what happened and why, and identify people to target for an interview. All these things help.

If you have an opportunity after the first breaking story is written to go back and value-add with an update, you can of course do more in-depth research before conducting follow-up interviews.

The arranged interview

You have made an appointment for an interview and done background research. At this point it is good to write a few general questions in your notebook. This will help you focus on the reason for the interview, what you really must find out, and provide basic guide posts and fall-back questions. Next, check you have the 'tools' for your interview. They must include:

— several pens—never trust just one or two not to run out of ink

— at least two notebooks, one of which is empty—running out of paper to write notes on is not good

— a quality sound recorder with plenty of spare memory and a full set of unused spare batteries—if batteries can die at the wrong time, they will

— a reliable digital camera (see Chapter 13) and a spare fully charged camera battery.

Make a habit of leaving the office in time to arrive early. Flat tyres really do happen, and so do police checks, traffic congestion, bad weather, and GPS navigation devices that decide to take you across a swamp or the long way around! Arriving a little early also allows you time to think of last-minute questions, check your appearance, and take a few deep breaths to relax.

As you introduce yourself to your interviewee, sum them up in the same way they will be summing you up. Consider their appearance and the immediate environment. What does it tell you about them? It is also important to build rapport quickly. Commenting positively on something you noticed in the room or immediate vicinity is a good starting point, but do not prattle. You should now turn off or mute your mobile phone. As well as preventing distractions, it sends a message to your interviewee that they have your undivided attention. If the interview is to be video recorded, chat to the interviewee—generally referred to in television or radio as 'the talent'—while the camera operator gets the camera ready. If the interview is for print, radio or online, chat as you turn on your sound recorder and ready your pen and notebook.

While television and radio interviews are almost always exclusively recorded and television reporters cannot take notes and appear on camera at the same time, some radio journalists do also take notes while using a voice recorder. The reason they do both is so that they will still have a story they can voice themselves if the recorder fails. Wise print and online journalists use the same approach. Taking notes while also using a sound recorder will save you from enormous embarrassment the day you return to your office and find the recorder has failed. With no recording and no notes you could not directly quote anyone in a story. And what about other details? What if there were several people talking, arguing or discussing an issue? What would you tell a chief-of-staff or editor, especially if they were counting on you for a major news article?

For reasons such as those, some old-school print journalists and editors frown on the use of sound recorders. They argue that learning to use shorthand is better because there is no technology involved that can break down. They also point out that transcribing from a recording takes extra time. But few beginning journalists today are competent at shorthand. While most will develop at least some form of shorthand over time—often one of their own making, or by completing a Teeline shorthand course online—using a voice recorder does help ensure accuracy and that you do not miss vital details while you are distracted by writing notes. Using a digital recorder has the added benefit of allowing you to skip backwards and forwards through an interview once you have downloaded a file to a computer. Having a sound recording also allows publication of voice grabs online and on mobile devices. Furthermore, as long as an interview is transcribed correctly, a recording serves as evidence you can use to defend yourself if an interviewee alleges you misquoted them.

No matter which medium you are interviewing for, start by getting the formalities out of the way. Always ask the person to spell their first name and surname. It may be 'Jon', not 'John'. Even if you think you already know, ask about their title and preferred form of address. Doing so indicates you are thorough and concerned about accuracy—and titles can change over time as people marry, divorce or acquire new qualifications or roles. Examples include: Mr, Ms, Mrs, Miss, Senior Constable, Sergeant, Captain, Lieutenant, Doctor, Sister, Professor, Father, Councillor and Justice. It is essential for your credibility and the credibility of your story that you get the title right—especially as titles can carry with them connotations about the potential expertise or otherwise of the individuals they are attached to. Further, if an interviewee represents an organisation, what is her or his position in the organisation? What is the correct name of the organisation? How is it spelt? Is the person speaking on behalf of the organisation, or expressing personal views?

Aim to get the interviewee chatting; asking about themselves and something familiar to them like their home, work, garden or an obvious interest can be a good start. If you have found background information and want to draw on it in your article, now is a good time to check if it is accurate. Then get specific and to the point of the interview. If you do not understand the reply to a question, say so and ask for clarification. Generally it is best to keep questions simple. Asking more than one question at a time, or framing a question as part of a long rambling statement, is likely to throw an interviewee off track, confuse them, or lead to a response that relates to only one part of the question. As you take notes, it works well to write down fresh questions or note points you want to come back to later—your interviewee will not know if you are taking notes or writing follow-up questions. If interviewing for a print or an online text article, focusing on writing in your notebook can also help shift the focus from a sound recorder and make an interviewee less self-conscious. Journalist Rosanna Natoli says that compared with a print or radio journalist, a television journalist has one more task to complete before an interview can begin:

> He or she must ensure the talent is comfortable in front of the camera—
> or better still that they've forgotten it's even there. A good reporter will
> empathise well and allow the interviewee to relax, thereby producing the
> best grabs, whether that's short and punchy or longer, emotional tear-jerkers
> (Natoli 2010).

One of the most important qualities a good interviewer develops is intuition— an understanding of when to probe and when to pull back, when to ask a follow-up question and when to move on. It is important to avoid the temptation to talk across an interviewee, or to answer your own questions! Also, avoid being drawn into an argument with an interviewee. Your role is to report what an interviewee says—no matter how much it might offend you personally—and not to defend your own opinions and values. And, as noted in Chapter 15, there are also legal reasons related to defending defamation actions which make it unwise to be seen to take a particular side in an argument or to become aggressive in questioning.

That said, do not be a wimp either—do not shy away from asking awkward or embarrassing questions if they need to be asked. The fact that someone might

One of the most important qualities a good interviewer develops is intuition— an understanding of when to probe and when to pull back, when to ask a follow-up question and when to move on.

explode with real or mock anger can add colour to your story, or at least help you convey a sense of the person you interviewed. As Mencher said: 'Do not be reluctant to ask an embarrassing question. After going through all the preliminaries you can think of the time finally arrives to ask the tough question. Just ask it' (Mencher 1997, p. 345).

Beware of liars, fantasists and comedians

As a general rule, people will not deliberately distort what they tell you. But some will blatantly lie. Others will not deliberately mislead, but their replies to questions will be coloured by their past experiences and attitudes—thus two people who witness the same event might describe it quite differently. It is therefore important not to take everything you are told at face value. Maintaining a healthy scepticism will help you serve your readers and audiences better and also protect you from making silly mistakes. Body language—rapid blinking, an inability to look you in the eye, blushing, touching the face, nodding the head while saying 'no', and changes in voice pitch—can help us sense another is lying or exaggerating. But body language can be deceptive too. Many habitual liars have learnt how to mask their deceptions. One technique that can be used to check if a person is lying or not is to ask them a question you already know the answer to, or a question that draws an answer you can check later. It is also worthwhile remembering that practised liars, especially confidence tricksters, compulsive liars and fantasists, often concoct a story that intertwines facts and falsehoods so tightly it becomes difficult, if not impossible, to determine what is true and what is false. As discussed later in this chapter, being an effective listener can help you detect such people. And, as Stovall suggests:

> If possible, a reporter should check important information that the source has given you with another source to verify it. Many reporters have been taken in by sources who sounded as if they knew exactly what they were talking about (Stovall 2005, p. 162).

On a lighter note, there will be times during interviews when you must literally force yourself to keep a straight face. Occasionally you will encounter an interviewee who tells you outrageous, obscene, intimate or disgusting things without really being aware of what they have said. You will find some comments offensive or shocking, and some hysterically funny. But if you react, your interviewee will feel humiliated and the interview will most likely end—so do not bat an eyelid, maintain a poker face, and keep your shock, horror or laughter for later!

Conversely, some interviews will be sad. Again, while we are all human and genuine empathy will help you tell a story better, breaking down and sobbing with an interviewee is unlikely to help them or your story. It is much better that you do your job as journalist and, if necessary, arrange for the interviewee to be helped by someone qualified to do so.

Telephone and video interviews

Telephone interviews save time and travel. They are particularly common when reporting for radio because interviews can be recorded, edited and broadcast within minutes. They are also frequently used when value-adding to reactive stories by topping them up with extra information from different sources, or for updating stories. Many people can be contacted on a mobile telephone when away from home or work, and telephone, Skype or FaceTime interviews are also one of the only ways of obtaining information from people in distant places whom it would be impractical to interview otherwise.

A big disadvantage of telephone interviewing is that a journalist cannot observe an interviewee's body language or surroundings. It can also be difficult to establish rapport over the telephone, and in addition an interviewee has the option of dealing with a difficult question by simply ending the call. Potential interviewees can be protected by personal assistants who filter calls, or they may be busy and forget to call you back. But a Skype or FaceTime interview with video, or a smartphone video call, can go a long way to overcoming at least some of those disadvantages, at least as far as facial expressions go.

One major turn-off when being interviewed by telephone, Skype or FaceTime is the sound of a keyboard clacking in the background as a journalist types responses to questions directly into a computer. Typing while interviewing is also distracting for journalists and can result in them asking silly questions or sounding vague and disinterested.

Email interviews and SMS dialogues

Email is an especially useful tool for interviewing people in different time zones in other parts of the world. When an interviewee replies to questions, those replies provide a ready-made transcript that can be copied and pasted directly into a story—something which makes it difficult for a source to claim they were misquoted. Email can also be used to send material—such as complex reports—to experts so they can express opinions about it. And sometimes, if you are lucky, an email or a text message to a mobile phone can be a way to communicate directly with a potential source whose office telephone calls are screened by a protective personal assistant.

But email interviews can be even more limiting than telephone interviews. And attempting to conduct an 'interview' by text messaging can be still more problematic—among other things, many people are not proficient at texting and text messages can be difficult to read and reply to on some devices. There is no tone of voice in an email or text message, questions cannot be asked spontaneously, many people are less likely to answer an email or SMS message than a telephone, and it is impossible to ask surprise questions. Further, as explained in Chapter 15, there is a need to be cautious about how you frame written questions because of potential legal problems. Overall, if you are going to attempt an email interview, you are most likely to get a good response if you keep questions short and simple, and limit them to one or two. You may also find that after getting your foot in the door with an email or text message, a potential interviewee might agree to a telephone or face-to-face interview.

As a final point here, telephones, emails and to a lesser extent text messages can work together. Emails, for example, can be exchanged with a source as a means of setting up a telephone or face-to-face interview. Similarly, emails and/or text messages can be used to clarify points made during telephone interviews, or to clarify difficult technical points.

Different types of questions

Interview questions can be grouped into broad categories: closed questions, open-ended questions, fact-finding questions, surprise questions, personal questions and confronting questions.

CLOSED QUESTIONS

Closed questions can be answered with a bland 'yes' or 'no'. A question such as: 'Do you approve of the government locking asylum seekers in detention centres?' is a closed question that invites a 'yes' or 'no' response. Journalists should try not to ask closed questions unless specifically seeking confirmation or denial of a particular point. For example, asking a politician: 'Is it true you leaked details of the budget?' would allow a journalist to write that the politician admitted—or denied—leaking budget information.

OPEN-ENDED QUESTIONS

Open-ended questions invite an explanatory response. For example, the question: 'How do you feel about the government locking asylum seekers in detention centres?' invites a detailed reply that can often be further drawn out with a simple follow-up such as 'Why?' Similarly, if a politician admitted leaking budget details, you could ask an open-ended 'why did you do it?', or, if the politician had denied leaking, an open-ended follow-on which might generate an interesting response could be something like: 'Why do you think the finger is being pointed at you as the source of the leak?'

FACT-FINDING QUESTIONS

Fact-finding questions are really a subcategory of open-ended questions but are more focused because they are designed to quickly gather specific information. Often used when reporting reactive news, fact-finding questions centre around asking what, when, where, who, why and how? The aim is to rapidly gather essential basic information.

SURPRISE QUESTIONS

Surprise questions are not an everyday interviewing tool but can be productive in the right circumstances. They work best if you have discovered facts in pre-interview background research or have been tipped off about information that an interviewee has attempted to suppress. Say, for example, you interview a prominent politician whom your research indicated was a member of an opposing party in her youth. Your interview is not going well because the politician is being obstructive, or is intent on getting a single message across by 'answering' questions you have not asked. Suddenly throwing in a question such as: 'Tell me how your membership of the XYZ party when you were at university is influencing your current stand on the issue of ABC?' is likely to pull the interviewee up in her tracks. The result might be explosive, or it might be dismissive but it will almost certainly be interesting and result in a better story than the one the politician wanted you to tell! The technique can also be useful when interviewing criminals and obstructive officials.

PERSONAL QUESTIONS

Personal questions can be tricky. They are particularly relevant when interviewing for profile and feature articles, but can also be important when reporting news. Stovall said such questions should be approached carefully and 'most experienced interviewers agree they should be left until the middle or end of an interview' (Stovall 2005, p. 160). That way if an interviewee becomes offended and walks out, at least you still have enough of an interview for a story.

Sometimes it helps to preface a personal question by saying something like: 'I do not like having to ask this, but...'. At other times it is better to use an element of surprise and just pop the question.

CONFRONTING QUESTIONS

Confronting questions are best kept as a last resort. It is better to gain an interviewee's trust and cooperation if you can. However, if an interviewee is hostile, obstructive, lies, or is evasive, a confrontational question such as: 'Why are you being evasive?', 'Are you aware that what you are saying now is inconsistent with XYZ?', or 'Why won't you answer—do you have something to hide?' will sometimes pull them up and get an interview back on track. At the least it might allow you to report something such as: 'Mr X said he had nothing to hide. He declined to answer questions about...'.

If you do decide to ask a confronting question, then as mentioned earlier in this chapter, do not under any circumstances be drawn into an argument with the interviewee or become rude or aggressive. And do not put confronting questions in writing because, as explained in Chapter 15, doing so could invite a defamation writ.

Where to conduct interviews

Face-to-face interviews are usually conducted in an interviewee's workplace, home, a journalist's office or in-house interview room, a television or radio studio, or in a public place. Circumstances and the nature of an interview will usually dictate the location. Sometimes, particularly when interviewing for investigative stories, an interviewee, especially a protected source, will not want to be seen talking to a journalist so an interview will take place in an out-of-the-way location. White (1996) says the location of an interview can affect the outcome, for example while 'the interviewee on home ground has a slight psychological advantage', a journalist should bear in mind that the 'home territory' she or he sees may not be genuine because the interviewee has had an opportunity to 'put the whisky bottles away, evict the smelly dog and plump up the cushions' (White 1996, p. 80).

When arranging an interview, a journalist should consider his or her own personal safety. Journalists have been attacked by interviewees. Rarely, they are the victims of hoaxes in which prospective interviewees lure them into attending a particular location but never arrive themselves. So be careful where you meet people. Busy but not-too-noisy public places such as coffee shops, outdoor cafés or your own office are safest. When going out, always tell someone reliable where you are going and when you expect to return. Take a mobile phone with a charged battery. Avoid meeting people who are obviously intoxicated, affected by drugs or alcohol, or who are intent on meeting at remote locations at odd hours. If you must meet a prospective interviewee at a location you feel uneasy about, take another person with you—even if he or she waits outside in the car, telling an interviewee you cannot be long because someone is waiting for you outside can offer a degree of protection.

The art of listening

In addition to having a well-honed sixth sense, good interviewers are excellent listeners. They are alert for the 'throw-away line'—an unexpected response or comment from an interviewee—which can potentially take an interview, or whole story, down a new, different, and more interesting path from that which was expected.

There is great wisdom in a quotation attributed to acclaimed US journalist and Nobel Prize–winning novelist Ernest Hemingway, who reputedly said: 'I like to listen. I have learned a great deal from listening carefully. Most people never listen' (Hemingway n.d.). Journalists must listen intently. If you are not naturally a good listener you should train yourself to become one. As White said: 'Good listening yields better and more accurate stories. It requires both self-knowledge and sensitivity to others' (White 1996, p. 90). Mencher said: 'Good listeners will have in their notes the quotations that give the reader or listener an immediate sense of the person being interviewed—what are known as high-quality quotes' (Mencher 1997, p. 356).

> If you listen carefully to an interviewee, one question will often lead you to the next. You are also likely to learn things you did not know, were not obvious, or which an interviewee might have not intended you to know.

If you listen carefully to an interviewee, one question will often lead you to the next. You are also likely to learn things you did not know, were not obvious, or which an interviewee might have not intended you to know. The writer once wrote a profile of a medivac helicopter pilot. He had flown an Australian Army helicopter during the Vietnam War. He spoke about the war and his experiences in general terms, but kept turning the interview back to his job flying a medivac chopper and how the rescue service it was part of had been established. I subsequently spoke to his wife, making a passing reference to the pilot's war service. 'Did he mention what he did?' she asked quietly. 'Yes, we talked about that,' I said, ready to move on. Then something, perhaps the tone of her voice, made me pause. 'What do you mean, what he did?' I asked. 'Rescue those blokes,' she replied. 'No, tell me about it,' I said. It emerged that the pilot, retired Major Jim Campbell, had landed his helicopter in a minefield to rescue trapped and injured troops and fly them to safety. He had not mentioned it when I interviewed him, I had not found any mention in my pre-interview background research, and no one in the wider community he lived and worked in knew what he had done. But as it turned out, Major Campbell is a remarkable Australian who was awarded a Distinguished Flying Cross (DFC) for his bravery. The helicopter he flew in the rescue[1] was subsequently preserved in the Australian War Memorial in Canberra. His DFC citation said, in part:

> there were 32 members trapped in the minefield. At great personal risk Captain Campbell flew a medical officer to the scene of the mine explosions, and landed in the minefield knowing full well that he and his helicopter could be destroyed by a mine explosion triggered by the helicopter's skids or the down blast of the rotors. He chose to do this so that by quick evacuation the lives of the more seriously wounded might be saved. With complete

---

1   A Bell 47G-3B-1 Sioux Helicopter: A1-404

disregard for his own safety, Captain Campbell landed time after time in the minefield in order to evacuate the wounded (Honours and Awards 1967).

At the opposite end of the spectrum, careful listening together with a couple of apparently innocent but probing questions and direct observation during an interview led to the undoing of another pilot. The man was involved in establishing a memorial for RAAF air aces. He organised an opening ceremony for the memorial and gained support from the RSL, a former Queensland governor, former prime minister John Gorton, the RAAF, a brass band, members of parliament and other dignitaries. During the interview the pilot said he had been with the RAAF pilot and had flown F111 fighter bombers during the Vietnam War. He also said he was a senior pilot for an Australian commercial airline, that he had miraculously landed a fully laden passenger jet after an engine fire on take-off, and he had top-secret information about pilots in northern Australia who were smuggling drugs and guns. During a mid-morning interview the day before the memorial was to be officially opened, I noticed that his pilot's uniform was worn and dirty and he smelled of alcohol. After the interview I contacted the RAAF and my suspicions that the Australian air force had never flown F111 aircraft in Vietnam were confirmed. A check with the airline the pilot said he was employed by revealed he had never worked for it. A check via a source revealed that the only pilot's licence he had ever held was a low-level training licence. The opening ceremony went ahead as planned— there was even a fly-past of F111 fighters. But while other journalists reported on the ceremony and speeches made by the dignitaries who attended, I wrote an article about how the pilot had tricked so many important people. After publication I was contacted by readers from around the nation. Information they provided revealed that as well as being a conman known for cadging free beers and meals from people he met in pubs, the pilot was a convicted bigamist, he had been 'married' at least five times, and had once been in trouble with the law for stealing food from the Tasmanian governor's kitchen—all of which made for a wonderful follow-up story!

The sounds of silence

Just as observation and sensitive listening are vital, a pregnant silence can truly be golden at the right moment. Do not overuse the technique, but sometimes pausing longer than you normally would after a person answers a question and before you ask another results in them instinctively 'filling the gap' with a telling comment. The technique can work well during a difficult interview and in interviews with people who naturally speak slowly because your unexpected silence carries with it an expectation you are waiting for more information. As Bartimus said:

> Most people abhor silence. It makes them nervous... often an interviewee, in an attempt to fill a silent void, will volunteer information that astounds both the talker and the listener. 'My God, I've never even told my husband that,' said one shocked interview subject (Bartimus, in Weinberg 1996, p. 86).

Closing an interview

As an interview draws to a close, there are things you should do. First, check names again and ask for follow-up phone numbers just in case there are points to be clarified as you write the story. Second, always ask a safety net question such as: 'Is there anything else you would like to say or would like me to add? Are there any points we haven't covered?' Then finish with a 'thank you'. Not only is it polite, you might have to interview the same person again one day. Finally, as White said, 'you should not close your ears when you close your notebook' (White 1996, p. 89). It might be that as you take your leave an interviewee drops a magical throwaway line that leads to fresh questions and a better story. Conversely, it is sometimes difficult disentangling yourself from an interview and getting away—especially if the interviewee is lonely or seeking a sympathetic ear. When this happens, it is useful to have another 'urgent appointment' you must go to. In reality, it is wise to get back to your office as soon as possible after an interview and to get your story written while information and impressions are still fresh. Your story will be better as a result, and you will be able to move to the next story with a clear mind.

Another difficult moment that can arise during or at the end of an interview for a print or online publication is a request by an interviewee to review your article before it is published. Most news organisations have a policy of refusing those requests unless an article deals with complex technical or scientific information which needs checking. The main reason is practical—journalists and news organisations simply do not have time in a deadline-driven industry to go back and rehash details of an interview that an interviewee might want changed. Doing so would create havoc with production, particularly in online publications in which a story is published literally as it is written. There can also be problems if people's opinions are not given the weight they believe they should be, if they are balanced by quotes from others with different beliefs or perspectives, or simply if an interviewee gets cold feet about what he or she said and wants to withdraw or change a comment.

Journalists and sources

As a journalist you will develop a contact list, or contact book, of sources you interview regularly. You will learn which sources you can trust and rely on, and which you need to be wary of. As a general rule, when reporting news it is safest if you interview official sources, qualified and experienced experts, and those in authority. In its style book for journalists the ABC says:

> We use information from reliable sources—people who are in a position to know what they're talking about. Reliability may be assured by the person's official position, or it may not. These are judgements for each journalist to make, in consultation with his or her editor.
>
> When reporting domestic news, the onus is on us to confirm information independently. If we can quote a source, especially for important breaking news, we should. For example, 'the Prime Minister's office has announced the death of the Governor-General'.
>
> ... There are no prizes for being first and wrong—so check and attribute (ABC 2008, p. 16).

You will also interview many people in one-off situations as you gather information for news, feature articles and documentaries. As noted in Chapter 6, if uncertain about the accuracy of what you have been told, or the credibility of a source, always do your utmost to verify information by contacting another source or cross checking in some other way. If you become involved in investigative research and reporting you are also likely to develop a network of unofficial or off-the-record sources and contacts. It is wise to verify information from those sources by cross-referencing with other—if possible on-the-record—sources.

Overwhelmingly, before agreeing to protect the identity of a source a journalist must understand she or he is making a potentially momentous undertaking. As discussed in Chapters 4 and 16, it could potentially see the journalist in court defending charges of contempt for refusing to divulge the identity of the protected source. Journalists can also quite literally hold a source's life, job, health and welfare in their hands. Sources whose identities have been revealed by journalists have been murdered. Others have lost jobs, families and their health. The responsibility can be heavy.

It is extremely unwise to allow yourself to become too close personally to a source, protected or otherwise. A journalist's relationships with sources and contacts should be professional and at arm's length. Be aware that journalists are seen by many as occupying positions of power—the power to sway public opinion, make or break personal and professional images, and influence the outcomes of decisions which have major financial and political implications. Sometimes sources will go to extraordinary lengths to carefully cultivate journalists they believe can help them or their cause. As noted in Chapter 5, one danger of allowing yourself to be drawn too close to a source is the risk that if the source becomes tarnished, you and your career will fall into disrepute too. Another is that the journalist loses objectivity and is drawn into sharing a source's obsession, thus becoming an advocate instead of an impartial reporter. There is also the fact that when you eventually realise you have been used and compromised by a source, you will feel personally let down and embarrassed and wonder why you were such a fool! So if you do find yourself becoming uncomfortably close or overly reliant on a source, or if a person keeps coming back to you even though he or she has no new or relevant information to share, cool the relationship, step away and move on.

DISCUSSION POINTS

1   You are interviewing a source and you sense he is lying to you. Should you report what was said even if you believe it was a lie? What else could you do?

2   Who is the best interviewer on free-to-air television? What are his or her strong points?

3   Who is the worst and most annoying interviewer on free-to-air television? What does she or he do wrong?

4   You are going to interview the prime minister about a controversial new government policy. You feel nervous because you have never interviewed such an important or media-savvy person before. What can you do to calm down before the interview?

5   It has been a busy day and you arrive late at the scene of what was a major reactive news story. Everyone who was involved has gone. Your editor is insisting you report

on the story because all the other media outlets in the area had reporters there and will be covering it. What will you do?

6   What are some of the worst potential dangers that could come back to haunt a journalist who becomes too close to a source?

NEWS PRACTICE POINTS

1   It is said that everyone has a story to tell. Interview a member of your family or a close friend and get them to tell you something about themselves you did not know previously, then write a 500-word article highlighting the main points of the interview.

2   Give the person you interviewed and wrote about in Practice Point 1 a copy of the article you wrote about them and ask what she or he thinks about you work. What, if anything, can you learn from the response?

3   Watch and analyse an in-depth television interview conducted by an experienced interviewer. Make a list of five things the interviewer does well during the interview and five things you believe could have been done better.

4   Read a selection of personal profile feature articles and identify one article in which it is obvious that the journalist managed to get the subject of the article to reveal surprisingly frank information about themselves. In no more than 350 words, explain what that information is and which questioning techniques were likely to have drawn it out.

5   Interview a person you do not know anything about and make a sound recording of the interview. During the interview, ask six closed questions, six open-ended questions, two surprise questions and one confronting question. Listen to the recording and keep a tally of the questions that drew the most interesting responses. What did you learn? What did your interviewee think about the experience?

6   There is a person you need to interview for an important story but she refuses to speak to you. List six things you could do that might cause her to change her mind and agree to an interview.

7   A person you have approached for an interview has agreed to speak to you, but only if you meet in a hotel and conduct the interview over lunch. There is no other option so you agree. List three potential advantages of conducting the interview in that way, and three potential disadvantages. Who should pay for lunch? Why?

8   You conduct an interview with a well-known local councillor. During the interview you start to feel uneasy because you suspect that the man has been lying for years about his past and, among other things, that he might have a criminal record. In no more than 400 words explain how you would try to verify your suspicions before the interview ends.

9   You interview the brother of a notorious mass murderer. Police have long suspected the brother was an accomplice in at least some of the murders, however they have not been able to prove it. But during your interview the man confesses. Later he retracts what he said and tells you it was off the record. Your voice recorder has been running throughout the interview and you leave it running.

a) What will your next three questions be?

b) Assuming you leave unharmed at the end of the interview, what will be two key things you do as a direct follow-up?

c) Who else would you interview for your story?

WRITING NEWS FOR PRINT

Words sing. They hurt. They teach. They sanctify. They were man's first, immeasurable feat of magic. They liberated us from ignorance and our barbarous past.

Leo Calvin Rosten, teacher, academic and humourist, 1972

OBJECTIVES

After reading this chapter you will understand:

» Changing trends in print and text news publishing

» How news writing differs from other forms of writing

» The importance of finding exactly the right word

» Key elements of news writing style

» Why good grammar, punctuation and spelling are essential

» How and why news writing styles and approaches vary.

Print journalism is the only form of journalism that can be consumed without relying on technology. A radio or television news story is gone the instant it is broadcast. If it is to be listened to or viewed again it must be recorded or saved in a computer archive for retrieval later. An online news story or one published on a mobile device such as a tablet, smartphone or netbook might or might not be archived, but unless printed, can only be viewed on a video screen. A newspaper, on the other hand, does not need batteries, mains power or a broadband, Bluetooth or telephone connection. It can be read practically anywhere, can be folded, read bit by bit over days, reread repeatedly, and handed around. Newspapers are also better suited to grouping stories together. They do not make a noise, are not subject to viruses, trojans or worms, and are recyclable.

Despite their advantages, newspaper circulations have been falling steadily in many, but not all, parts of the world. In Australia, for example, in the early 1980s there were almost four million metropolitan newspapers sold daily. By 1998 that number was about 2.5 million (Henningham 1999), and despite a burgeoning population it was less than 2.3 million by 2008 (Australian Press Council 2008b) and about 2.1 million by 2012 (Day 2012). Despite the decline, print and text-based journalism still have a bright future. Commenting on declining newspaper circulations and major restructures of News Limited and Fairfax newspapers in Australia in 2012, media commentator and former newspaper editor Mark Day (2012) said:

> Raw sales statistics fail properly to identify the role newspapers play in our society. They continue to set the daily news agenda. Radio and television talk programs could not exist without the daily ideas bank and discussion points provided by papers. The conversation world of Twitter and Facebook would not exist without the thought-starters in newspapers (Day 2012).

And:

> Certainly newspapers will have to change. They may not perform their traditional roles of being all things to all people. And they may not be printed on pulped-up trees… in time, logic says they will be delivered electronically rather than by diesel-powered trucks (Day 2012).

It is also important to remember that while News Limited and Fairfax traditionally dominated the national and state-wide newspaper markets in Australia, there are many other print publishers—especially in regional areas and those catering to specific interest groups. As editor of the multiple Walkley Award–winning *Bendigo Weekly* Anthony Radford said in 2012:

> Doomsday talk about the death of newspapers is out of control and being pushed by commentators who have little knowledge of the media landscape in regional Australia. Regional papers are both profitable and a real part of the community… the business model in suburban and regional areas is working, is making money, is sustainable and is in no way threatened by the web… as well as having journalism that bites, these papers attract readers (Radford 2012).

And Day's point about newspapers and newspaper journalists setting the news agenda is also highly significant. It reflected a 2010 study conducted in conjunction with the Pew Research Centre's Project for Excellence in Journalism in the US, which concluded that 95 per cent of all local news stories in the US which had eventually made their way across all media platforms—print, radio, television and online—originated as newspaper articles (Pew Research Centre 2012a). The study was a snapshot of how news organisations, bloggers, Twitterers and locally based websites in Baltimore reported news across one week. A separate study revealed that over a 30-day period more than 75,000 websites had reused at least one US newspaper article without obtaining permission from the newspaper (Newspaper Publishers' Association 2010). The same research found that US newspaper organisations and their affiliated websites broke 61 per cent of breaking or original news stories, and television news only 28 per cent. Radio, which was traditionally the source of breaking news before the advent of online news, broke only 7 per cent of stories, while non-newspaper websites accounted for just 4 per cent (Newspaper Publishers' Association 2010). More recently, the Australian Federal Government's media Convergence Review Committee, which was established in 2011 to make recommendations about communications and media regulation in Australia, noted in its final report that:

> news and commentary consumed by Australians across all platforms is still overwhelmingly provided by the news outlets long familiar to Australians. What has changed most dramatically is how Australians access their news— the source largely remains the same. For example, someone may read a news story on Facebook, but the originator of the article is a newspaper publisher (Department of Broadband, Communications and the Digital Economy 2012, p. ix).

The foregoing observations mirror two trends that emerged in the 1920s and 1950s when first radio, then television threatened newspapers in two almost diametrically opposite ways. First, broadcast outlets stole newspapers' thunder by taking advantage of the relative immediacy of radio and television transmissions to report breaking reactive news stories well before details could be published in tomorrow's papers. Second, the broadcasters started stealing story ideas, if not content, from newspapers by 'lifting' proactive newspaper stories from that day's paper and either broadcasting them as their own 'news', or using information from the articles as fodder for on-air debate and discussion. Until the advent of the web, internet and mobile publishing apps, newspapers were powerless to stop the plunder. But, as discussed in greater detail in Chapter 10, electronic news publication on newspaper websites and via mobile apps has turned the tables. It has allowed print—or more correctly text-based—journalists who work across platforms to break the majority of reactive news when they write it, for immediate publication online. Print journalists also continue to break the vast majority of proactive stories—stories other media subsequently follow like sheep.

Traditionally, print versions of newspapers and magazines have always been solid platforms for investigative reports, analysis, explanation and comment. That is still the case, with print publications remaining ideal platforms to support the three functions of news media: to inform, educate and entertain. Readers look to newspapers and their electronic editions for information and discussion that provide insights into factors underlying news, such as evolving political debates, international events, legal decisions, national security, social and cultural issues, health and welfare, and unusual events. In that context it is interesting that the 2012 Pew Research Centre's Project for Excellence in Journalism Report noted that in the US:

> more than a quarter of the population, 27 per cent, now get news on mobile devices. And these mobile news consumers are even more likely to turn to news organizations directly, through apps and home pages… mobile is adding to, rather than replacing, people's news consumption. Data tracking people's behavior, for instance, finds that mobile devices increased traffic on major newspaper websites by an average of 9 per cent (Pew Research Centre 2012b).

Building a relationship with words

To become a print journalist it is obviously necessary to be an effective writer. When you start work in a newsroom it is expected that you will write quickly and proficiently in a single draft to a set word length. Some people find writing comes naturally, others find it difficult. Fortunately, good writing can be learnt. Naturally gifted writers can become better, while those who struggle at first can learn to write beautifully. The keys are to persist, to keep wanting to improve, and to build an enduring relationship with words. That relationship must be founded on an understanding that words are not just a writer's tools, they are also the end product. Savour them, play with them, enjoy them. Words and punctuation are to a writer what notes are to a musician, or different coloured paints to an artist. Blend them one way and they convey one image, rearrange them, and the image changes. We must choose words carefully, not take them for granted nor abuse them. There are many good ways to improve your writing and word use. Three of the best are to read, read and read. The more you read, particularly if you read critically, the better your writing will become. So devour books. Read newspapers and magazines, but particularly newspapers. Read them critically and analytically. Look at how articles are constructed and the words used. Consider articles that read well and those that

The keys to becoming an effective writer are to persist, to keep wanting to improve, and to build an enduring relationship with words. That relationship must be founded on an understanding that words are not just a writer's tools, they are also the end product.

do not, and ask yourself: why, what is the difference? There are also many excellent resources on the web that can help build writing skills—although be selective and beware of US and other sites that use words, punctuation and grammatical structures which differ from those informing Australian writing and language.

Obviously, you should also write regularly—you could even rewrite badly written news articles you find with the aim of improving them. After you have written, read your work aloud to yourself. If it sounds good, it is probably all right. If it sounds bad, it will be awful. In that case, go back and write it again, then read it aloud again. If it sounds good this time, pat yourself on the back. If it sounds bad, write it again. Similarly, if you have time, put what you have written aside for 24 hours, then read it again and improve it if it jars, but leave it alone and move on if it reads well.

That said, be aware that unless working on a major feature article with a deadline several days ahead, journalists are unlikely to have the luxury of being able to rewrite. Contrary to the practice in many school and university subjects in which drafts can be submitted for review before rewriting for final submission, news articles must be written and filed immediately. As a rule, the only time an article will be rewritten is if an irritated sub-editor or editor returns it with a comment such as: 'this is rubbish (or worse), fix it'! It should also be understood that journalists simply do not have time—and neither do their editors—for the mysterious 'writers' block' that occasionally afflicts students, poets, academics and the odd creative writer.

As your writing develops and you learn to write in journalistic style, it is essential to remember who you are writing for. Journalists never write for themselves—writers who feel a need to do that should join a navel-gazing creative writing group! Journalists write in order to explain things to other people. They write for the uneducated, the undereducated and the highly educated—for those who can barely read, and for the most erudite. They must write in a style that is attractive at each end of the spectrum and all points between. They must also learn to explain complex issues and concepts in simple terms. This does not mean dumbing down your writing or being condescending. Quite the contrary—there is great skill in cutting to the heart of a complex issue and then explaining it in plain English. Many famous writers who have been both journalists and novelists have had those skills: Charles Dickens, George Bernard Shaw, Mark Twain (Samuel Clemens), Rudyard Kipling, George Orwell, Henry Lawson, and Banjo (Andrew Barton) Paterson to name a few. Each had an ability to connect with readers, explain complexities in everyday language, and hold readers with them. These are the keys to print journalism. There is no point having a great story to tell if you cannot tell it in an interesting way that readers can understand. You must attract readers to your story, give them something in return, and keep them with you as long as possible. The same can be said of many other forms of writing from literary works to scientific journal articles and books such as this. The fact is that learning to write news in the disciplined journalistic style(s) employed in print publications opens many doors other than simply those of newspaper offices!

Journalistic writing style

What is it that makes journalistic writing different from other forms of writing? Part of the answer lies in the fact that journalistic writing is highly disciplined. Journalists use words economically and efficiently. Space in newspapers costs money. Newspaper pages are expensive to produce, print and deliver. Papers earn the largest proportion of their income from selling advertising, not from the cover price, which rarely even covers the cost of the paper they are printed on. The price of advertisements is related to the space they occupy. Advertising and articles compete for space. Stories also compete with each other for space. Thus the best articles from a newspaper company's perspective are those that get to the point, have a strong impact on readers, and provide enough information to succinctly and effectively inform, educate and/or entertain in as small a space as possible.

A crucial step in learning to write in the same way as an experienced professional is to master style, grammar and punctuation. When combined with the other tenets of good journalism—such as fairness, balance and attribution—the application of sound news writing style, or its absence, is the most noticeable difference between the work of a professional journalist and that of a would-be-if-they-could-be amateur. The rules of grammar and punctuation, although often abused, are pretty much standard. Style is different. It has a range of generic meanings. For example, there is academic style, poetic style, discursive style, narrative style, scientific style, chatty style or formal style.

When journalists talk about style they are really talking about two different things. The first is *writing* style, which involves such things as the selection of particular words to convey a mood or feeling. For example, the writing style of an SMS message would be totally different from the style of an academic essay. Imagine writing to your maiden aunt Doris or uncle Cyril in the same sizzling style as you would to your lover! Journalists employ different generic styles for different types of articles such as news, features and sport.

The other sense meant by journalists when talking about style is what is known as *house* style. House style gives uniformity to newspaper articles, online articles and news broadcasts. It is about laying down a set of clear rules that all journalists who work for a particular media organisation should abide by. The idea can seem strange at first, but it works well and provides a sense of certainty for writers and readers. One way of thinking about house style is to consider it as being a little like road rules: there would be many more crashes without them. Similarly, we have a standardised currency, which is better than some people trying to pay for their groceries with shells, while others pay in gold or silver, chooks or yams!

House style helps readers feel comfortable. It means that even though different articles in the same publication are written by different journalists, there is a sense of uniformity and reading comfort. It can also help create a sense of uniformity across different titles and media platforms. The most commonly used house style in Australian journalism is that adopted by News Limited. The company publishes a style guide, *Style*, which spans all its numerous print mastheads and online publications. As well as being a guide for company staff, the book is also commercially available from bookshops. The book's introduction explains:

> The language used by journalists—and their publishers—must be simple and unambiguous… the aim of the style guide is to promote accuracy and consistency, and to strike a balance between brevity and clarity… it is not a rule book, and it does not seek to stifle good writing. English is a dynamic language and there is no place for inflexible rules that do not recognise the changing practices of readers (McLeod & Lockwood 2009, p. 5).

The News Limited guide has been adopted as the standard in many university journalism courses. It is also the style adopted for the body of this book. But it is only one interpretation of house style and other media organisations have their own. Some, for example, might require journalists to write 'per cent' as two words, others say it should be written as the single word 'percent', yet others require use of the symbol '%'. Specific differences aside, the basics of house style are the same across most newspaper and magazine companies. The overriding aim is to help journalists keep their writing tight and to choose words wisely.

House style helps readers feel comfortable. It means that even though different articles in the same publication are written by different journalists, there is a sense of uniformity and reading comfort.

Near enough is never good enough when it comes to words—you must find the right word for a specific purpose. Comparing the development of his own writing style with constructing a building brick by brick, Mark Twain famously wrote:

> The difference between the *almost right* word and the *right* word is really a large matter—'tis the difference between the lightning bug and the lightning. After that, of course, that exceedingly important brick, the *exact* word (Twain, in Bainton 1890, pp. 87 & 88).

There are common conventions about word use which inform different versions of journalistic house style. Some of the most important are as follows:

— Never use two or more words where one will do. Tautologies waste words and clutter your writing. Do not, for example, write 'at this point in time' when you mean 'now' or 'each and every one' when you mean 'all'.

— Never use a long word when a short word will do. 'Dog' is better than 'canine', 'flat' or 'unit' is shorter than 'apartment', 'end' is preferable to 'finalise'.

— Avoid words such as 'lot', 'got', 'lovely' and 'nice'. They do not tell a reader enough, if anything. It is better, for instance, to say 'The truck was carrying about 50 beer barrels when it was side-swiped and crashed' than 'The truck was carrying lots of beer barrels when it got in an accident and crashed'. Saying 'Flossy got a nice new dress' tells readers little. How did she get it? Did someone give it to her? Did she shoplift it? Or pay a fortune for it at an upmarket boutique? How is it 'nice'?

— Some words are old-fashioned or pompous. Why write 'upon', when you mean 'on', or 'utilise' when you mean 'use'. It is preferable to use 'while', not 'whilst'; 'among', not 'amongst'; and 'about', not 'approximately'.

— Do not repeatedly repeat the same or similar words repetitiously over and over again. Doing so is boring and amateurish. If needs be, use a good thesaurus, but take care to find the right substitute word.

— Never qualify absolute words such as 'unique' or 'dead'. Something is either unique—the only one of its kind in the world—or not. It cannot be 'very unique' or 'almost unique'. Similarly, things are either dead or alive. They cannot be 'very dead' or 'nearly alive'. And a woman cannot be 'a little bit pregnant'—she may be in the early stages of pregnancy, but she is either pregnant or not.

— Be careful of words that sound the same but are spelt differently, especially when using a computer spell cheque! For example 'where', 'wear' and 'we're';

'to', 'two' and 'too'; 'their', 'there' and 'they're'. The News Limited *Style* book has a good section on difficult words.

— Be consistent in spelling and use a set house style, especially with words like 'honour' and 'honor', or 'program' and 'programme'.

— Do not misuse, or abuse, words. We can seek 'advice' from someone and then 'advise' others. A 'memorial' is an object or occasionally a place like a park that commemorates something or someone. A memorial service or ceremony is something quite different. Someone injured in an accident does not 'receive' injuries, they are simply injured or 'sustain' injuries.

— Be careful of collective nouns. The government/team/club/company (singular) *is* going to do something, not 'are'. But members (plural) of the government/team/club/company *are* going to do it.

— As a general rule, avoid word contractions. It is better to write 'it is' than 'it's', or 'she is' rather than 'she's'. Spell out contractions such as 'couldn't', 'wouldn't', 'didn't' and 'can't'. An exception is in direct quotes. If someone uses contractions in their speech, quote them that way.

— Write in the language, and/or specific form of English, of the publication you are writing for. In Australia it is Australian English so avoid Americanisms and US spellings. For example, Australians put 'petrol' in their vehicles, not 'gas' and Australians have 'mobile' phones, not 'cell' phones. Also be careful of words which contain 'z'. US writers commonly use a 'z', where Australians would use an 's'. Australians, for example, would use 'realise' and 'organise', but Americans would use 'realize' and 'organize'. In that context be aware that many computer programs and apps for mobile devices default to US English.

— Avoid euphemisms. Many of them are dreadful in their deliberate obscurity. Why, for example, do you hear people say they are going to 'the bathroom' or 'the rest room' when they mean they are going to a public toilet—a facility unlikely to contain a bath or to be a pleasant place to rest? And what of people 'passing away', 'passing on' or 'passing over' instead of dying? Passing to where? Heaven? Hell? Somewhere else? What did they pass through: a gate, door, brick wall? And away from what: the family dog, annoying relatives, life? How much clearer is it to explain to readers that Fred died in a public toilet than to say Fred passed away in a restroom?

In addition to careful word use and good spelling, punctuation and grammar, there are other important conventions of journalistic style. Among them:

— Use active voice, not passive, when writing. Active voice is more direct and has greater impact. 'The crocodile ate the man' is active, but 'The man was eaten by the crocodile' is passive—it is also more words. Inclusion of the word 'by' is often an indicator of passive voice.

— Newspaper news stories are most often written in past tense because they are about events that happened 'yesterday' by the time a paper is delivered or purchased. That said, feature articles are commonly in the present tense. And news intros are sometimes written in the present tense, with the body of news articles nearly always reverting to past tense.

— Always attribute what you write. If the premier, Mrs Media Tart, said something stupid, make it clear she said it, otherwise readers are likely to think you, the journalist, said it.

— Do not write more than you need to, and do not include irrelevant facts or quotes. Use enough words to tell a story clearly, but no more.

— Do not include your own opinions or comments in a story. Unless you are a columnist, you are paid to report facts and information. Readers will not usually care what you think. Give them the facts and credit them with enough intelligence to form their own opinions.

— Avoid jargon, clichés, and trendy expressions. They detract from a good story and many less literate readers, or readers outside particular interest groups, may not understand. Whenever possible convert jargon—particularly occupational jargon such as 'police speak'—into plain English. For example, a police officer who says 'A person of interest decamped on foot from the immediate proximity of the said location where an offence was detected just as a police vehicle arrived on scene' actually means 'the suspect ran away before we could catch him'.

— Unless house style dictates otherwise, do not use symbols in place of words. Use 'and' instead of '&', 'per cent' in place of '%', 'plus' not '+' and 'at' not '@'.

— Do not overuse capital letters. Many amateur writers use capitals to add emphasis, but journalists minimise their use because they Disrupt The Flow of Text and Distract Readers' Eyes.

— Ensure you use honorifics and give people their correct titles, such as Mr, Mrs, Ms and Dr. Use surnames—do not write 'Flossy Smith said' then write 'Flossy said'. After including the first name in a reference to a person it is better to say 'Mr Smith' or 'Prof Smith'. Be aware that some women become infuriated if referred to as 'Mrs' when they prefer 'Ms' or 'Miss' and vice versa. Similarly, there are specific honorifics associated with rank and professional standing in certain occupational groups. Some publications have a house style in which honorifics are not used when sport reporting, or for the names of convicted criminals, or journalists! Making mistakes and being careless with honorifics not only offends sources you might want to quote again, it also damages your credibility in the community.

— Related to the foregoing point, it is a golden rule to ensure you spell names correctly. Is it 'Browne' or 'Brown'? 'Gillian' or 'Jillian'? Double-check. If you have names wrong, what will readers think about the accuracy of the rest of your story? There could also be legal implications.

— Ensure you understand how and where to use apostrophes. They either denote a word contraction—for example when two words such as 'he is' are contracted into 'he's', or 'it is' becomes 'it's'—or they are used, often with an added 's', to denote possession, for example the 'boy's bike', meaning 'the bike owned by the boy'. Be particularly careful of 'its' and 'it's' because 'it' never takes an apostrophe 's' to denote ownership—it only takes an apostrophe when abbreviated from 'it is'. Thus, if writing about a dog's bone, you would write that it—the dog—'took its bone to its kennel'. Inserting apostrophes would change the meaning and result in a nonsense clause meaning 'the dog took it is bone to it is kennel'!

— Unless an acronym is so well known it is virtually part of the language, as in the case of ANZAC, spell it out at first use. Avoid using acronyms that only have meaning for a small group—use full words instead.

— Do not join separate words into one. For example, write 'all right', not 'alright', and 'thank you', not 'thankyou' and 'any more', not 'anymore'.

— There are generally accepted conventions that apply to numbers and numerals. One is to spell out all numbers between one and nine but to use numerals for 10 and above. There are exceptions for percentages, for example 5 per cent; money: $4; and measurements: 5ml. Another convention is to never start a sentence with a numeral—either spell out the number, or rearrange the sentence to move the number. For example, you would not write: '100 horsemen rode over the ridge'. Acceptable alternatives would be: 'One hundred horsemen rode over the ridge' or 'Over the ridge rode 100 horsemen'.

— Never assume anything. Just as Murphy's Law says that if anything can go wrong it will, there is an immutable law of journalism that says an assumption will always be wrong!

— Avoid ambiguities. What, for example, do you make of this lead paragraph from Fox News: 'A woman reported missing for several days was found stabbed to death in a minivan by family members...' ('Talking turkeys' 2008, p. 36)?

Sentences and paragraphs

Well-written news stories are composed of short, sharp sentences and paragraphs. Often you see paragraphs in newspaper news reports that are just one sentence. But that does not have to be the case, unless an editor rules otherwise. Apart from an intro—which ideally is one sentence of no more than 20 to 25 words, and certainly no more than 30 words, in a stand-alone paragraph—other paragraphs can contain several sentences. But vary their length. A short sentence often has more impact than a long one. In a world struggling with information overload, your readers want to garner as much information as possible as quickly and easily as possible. If a story holds their attention by presenting interesting fact after fact, they are likely to read on. Alternatively, they might read enough to arouse their curiosity then pick up your article again later when they have more time. You increase the chances of both if you make your work as clear and effortless to read as possible.

As discussed in Chapter 11, feature and magazine articles are slightly different. They tend to have longer paragraphs and a different construction, but the overall idea remains the same—to deliver as much information and have the most impact in as few words as possible.

> In a world struggling with information overload, readers want to garner as much information as possible as quickly and easily as possible. If a story holds their attention by presenting interesting fact after fact, they may read on.

Introducing and quoting sources

There are two different ways of handling quotations. Direct quotes are an exact reproduction of what a person said and are placed inside 'quotation marks'. Indirect quotes are a summary, or paraphrase, of what a person said so there are no quotation marks. But an indirect quote must still maintain the meaning and sentiment of what was said. It is important to understand that a direct quote—exactly what someone said—can be paraphrased into an indirect quote but the process is strictly one way. A journalist must *never* attempt to convert an indirect quote to a direct one—legal and ethical issues aside, it would be impossible to do it accurately anyway. News Limited tells its journalists that when working with direct quotations:

> It is acceptable to tidy up people's minor grammatical faults and interpolations such as 'y'know', but be careful not to change the meaning of their statements... if more work is needed turn them (direct quotes) into indirect speech (McLeod & Lockwood 2009, pp. 19 & 20).

A strength of direct quotes is that they can add colour to a story and offer an insight into the character of the person being quoted. Among the better known quotes from 43rd US president George W Bush, which would have been lost if a journalist had 'cleaned up' his words, were offerings such as: 'They have mis-underestimated us', 'Too many good docs are getting out of the business. Too many OB/GYN's aren't able to practice their love with women all across the country', and 'Our enemies are innovative and resourceful, and so are we. They never stop thinking about new ways to harm our country and our people, and neither do we' (BBC 2009).

If a direct quote contains crass swear words, obscene or blasphemous language, or is in bad taste in other ways, it should as a general rule be paraphrased. An exception would be if the quote indirectly implied something significant to readers about the character of the person being quoted or if there was something notable about the circumstances in which the person said the words.

Two elements of journalistic style many students find tricky at first are formatting direct quotes and introducing speakers. The following tips will help:

— When attributing an indirect quote, the name of the person being quoted should be placed *before* the actual summary of what was said and be followed by the word 'said'. Thus an indirect quote would follow the format:

Ms X *said* blah, blah, blah.

— With a direct quote, the person's name should be placed at the end of the first sentence of the quote and be followed by the word 'said'. For example:

'Hoo, hoo, ha, ha,' Mrs X *said*.

— A direct quote should start a new line and new sentence—a sub-editor may change this later as a way of saving space but that is his or her prerogative, not yours as a journalist.

— The final quotation mark in a direct quote should be outside the final comma. For example:

'Always start a direct quote in a new line and put the final comma inside the final quotation mark,' Mr Styles said.

— A direct quote that continues for several sentences, often over several paragraphs, is known as a running quote. Writers should not close a running quote by inserting a final quotation mark until the quote actually ends. When it does end, insert a full stop inside the final quotation mark. For example:

'We do not think it is right that we have to pay to come to university by bus,' Ms Slack said.

'If the bus company wants us to ride on its buses, it should not charge us fares.

'There's six bus drivers who agree with us. They have been picking us up and not making us buy tickets.

'It is all the others who are the problem.'

— Always introduce a speaker before you quote them for the first time. This is commonly done with an indirect quote. For example:

Free Bus Travel Australia president Flossy Slack said the group was established for the sole purpose of convincing bus drivers to let students ride free.

'We're fighting to have all university students exempted from paying bus fares,' Ms Slack said.

— When introducing a person who speaks in an official role, on behalf of an organisation or group, or whose credibility you wish to establish, there is a set order in the way the introduction is structured. First, you name the organisation: Free Bus Travel Australia. Second, the person's position: president. Third, the person's first name, then family name: Flossy Slack. Thus, as per the earlier example, you would write:

Free Bus Travel Australia president Flossy Slack said...

— Do not use honorifics when you introduce someone but use them in subsequent quotes. For example:

People for Trees spokesman Terry Sly confirmed his group was stealing trees from the gardens of rich people and replanting them in the backyards of poor people.

'We're the Robin Hoods of the green movement,' Mr Sly said.

— When quoting a quote within a quote, use quotation marks different from those used for the main quote. Here are two alternatives:

'In my book about news writing I wrote that students should "use proper house style or you will look like amateurs",' Mr Styles said.

Or:

"In my book about news writing I wrote that students should 'use proper house style or you will look like amateurs'," Mr Styles said.

— If it becomes necessary to delete a word, or words, from a direct quote you should insert an ellipsis like this... as a signal to readers a cut has been made.

— If, for clarity, you need to insert a word or words into a direct quote, place the inserted words in brackets (like this), or in some publications [like this], as a signal words have been added.

— Only introduce a quote with a colon (:) if it is taken from a transcript or report. Unless quoting from a transcript, it is *not* generally acceptable to use the following structure:

Mr Smith said: 'Blah, blah…'

— It is unwise and unethical to beat up a paraphrase. If, for example, someone said they were 'concerned' about an issue, do not suddenly have them being 'disgusted' or 'outraged'.

— Although newspaper journalists normally write in the past tense, they use the tense a speaker used when they report a direct quote. For example:

Ding Dong Shire Council mayor Janet Jones said she was appalled when she learnt Mr Sly's group had stolen trees from the gardens of rich people.

'I am disgusted and outraged, not merely concerned, about what Sly and his group of deranged tree-snatching thieves are sneaking around doing in the dead of night,' Mrs Jones said.

— When used properly, direct quotes add colour and feel to a story. But if used too much, or if quotes are too long, they make a story boring. So do not fall into the trap of simply typing up a transcript of an interview. Paraphrasing saves space, omits unnecessary detail, and actually helps direct quotes stand out and add emphasis.

The following extract from a page two story in *The Age* of February 13, 2010 is an example of how many of the style points discussed in this chapter are applied, including its intro, which was written in the past tense:

> Melbourne has enjoyed its wettest summer in four years, with this week's storm adding to an encouraging six months of rain.
>
> Thursday's downpour delivered up to 50 millimetres to some parts of Melbourne and cut the power to about 40 000 customers in the city's west.
>
> ... State Emergency Service spokesman Tim Wiebusch said people should not swim or drive through floodwaters.
>
> 'We're quite concerned with the images we've seen,' he said. 'We've seen in other states such as Queensland and NSW that people die as a result of swimming in flash floodwaters.'

The following, from page two of *The Daily Telegraph* of February 13, 2010, is an example of how an intro and introduction to a person about to be quoted can be rolled into one:

> Environment Minister Peter Garrett yesterday insisted his job was safe, despite a soaring tally of disasters from his ceiling insulation program increasing demands for his dismissal.
>
> 'I'm not going anywhere at all except back to my office. I've got my sleeves rolled up. I intend to get on with work,' he said.

The following, from page 17 of *The Weekend Australian* of January 12 and 13, 2005, is an example of how tenses were changed from present in the intro, to past in the rest of an article:

> In a unique case of life imitating Monty Python sketches, an indignant Israeli is suing a pet shop that he says sold him a dying parrot.
>
> The *Ma'ariv* daily reported that the owner of the ex-parrot, Itzik Simkowitz, of the southern city of Beersheba, believed the shop owner had cheated him as the bird not only failed to utter a word when he got it home, but was also extremely ill.
>
> The bird—not a Norwegian blue, as in the famed '70s Python sketch, but a galerita cockatoo—proved extremely uninterested in its surroundings, Mr Simkowitz said.

Note that the intro to *The Age* story was 21 words, *The Daily Telegraph* 26 words, and *The Weekend Australian* also 26 words.

There are three steps which will help you master house style. First, buy, read and study an industry-standard style book such as News Limited's *Style*. Second, read and analyse different newspapers and magazines, paying particular attention to how they are written and to differences in house style between publishers. Third, regularly practise writing in news style, using the basics in as much of your writing as possible (even in emails, texting and social networking) so that their use becomes habitual. These tips will help you crack the code that distinguishes professional journalists from other writers. Then, as your career unfolds, learn to adjust and write in different house styles for different publications. Think of yourself as being like a chameleon—it remains the same on the inside but will not survive if it does not change its skin colour to match different environments!

Writing the story

You have done your research, conducted your interviews, gathered the facts, and you understand news writing style. The next steps are to prioritise the information you gathered and write your article. In doing so, use the key questions of *who*, *what*, *when*, *where*, *why* and *how* as signposts. You must also decide what approach you will take to the story. Will it be the inverted pyramid approach explained in Chapter 3? Or maybe a more narrative, story-telling approach? Also think about the news values discussed in Chapter 3. Ask yourself what makes this story interesting. Is it human interest? Is it because it is about something unusual or unexpected? Is it about conflict? Is there an amusing element? How significant is the story and will it have an impact on readers? Answering questions like these will help you develop a strong intro and guide your writing.

The inverted pyramid and effective intros

As discussed in Chapter 3, the inverted pyramid approach to news writing involves getting straight to the point of a story, explaining that point in an intro, following on with the strongest points with the highest news values, incorporating the best quotes, then explaining background information and the least important elements towards the end, or bottom, of the article. The inverted pyramid is a tried-and-tested formula. It is an approach every journalist should learn to use—particularly as it provides a safe fall-back if time is short and other approaches are failing. Stephens dates the inverted pyramid from the second half of the 19th century:

> After the American Civil War, journalists rushing to transmit their most newsworthy information over often unreliable telegraph lines developed the habit of compressing the most crucial facts into short, paragraph-long dispatches, often destined for the top of a column of news... From here it was not a long distance to reserving the first paragraph of their stories, the 'lead', for the most newsworthy facts and then organising supporting material in descending order of newsworthiness (Stephens 1997, p. 246).

Another reason the inverted pyramid model evolved was because print news stories are often cut short to make them fit a particular space on a page. In the days before onscreen computer-based editing, a tradition developed in which sub-editors always cut articles from the bottom up if they were too long. There was tacit agreement between journalists and sub-editors about how the system worked, so journalists prioritised information and put the most important facts first, not only leaving less significant information to taper off towards the end, but also often simply adding a couple of extra paragraphs as 'padding' which could be cut without damaging the main thrust of their stories. Aligned with these traditional influences is the fact that we live in a busy world and there is a twin belief in the newspaper industry that readers want their news in a hurry and that most do not read news items to the end.

A strong intro is a key element of the inverted pyramid approach. To work best it should not be much longer than 25 words. Shorter is often better, but not if it does not make sense or inspire a reader to read on. Rarely, if there is a good reason, an intro can consist of two shorter sentences in one paragraph. With feature stories, and as explained in Chapter 11, introductions may be constructed differently, but they still serve the same purpose: to attract readers. Whatever the approach, care is required because readers are a timid species easily spooked by a deluge of words at the start of an article.

The best intros are catchy and reflect the mood of a story. Also try to focus the intro on the strongest news value—often simply the facts about what happened where. Most journalists write the intro first and the body of the story flows naturally from there. But sometimes, and even after experimenting with several different intros, nothing seems to gel. If that happens it is best to get on and write the rest of your article, then go back and write a new intro. Also be aware that trying to convey too much information in an intro can be worse than not providing enough. It is impossible in one intro to answer all Kipling's questions about what, when, where, why, how and who. Let those answers unfold as the story unfolds. And do not exaggerate by making claims in an intro you do not back up later in the same article. That is what is called a beat-up. It is like the boy who cried wolf and it leaves readers feeling frustrated and cheated. Intros that are too 'clever' have the same effect.

Consider the following intro from a reactive news article in *The Weekend Australian* on February 20, 2010:

> Residents of Katherine Schweitzer's apartment block in the upmarket eastern Sydney suburb of Bellevue Hill were used to surprises in their rubbish (Hohenboken 2010, p. 7).

So? In the third paragraph readers were told no one in the unit block expected to find a body in their rubbish—something that seems like a perfectly reasonable expectation! Then, at the end of the fifth paragraph, readers were let into the secret that, indeed a body had been found in a bin and it was that of Schweitzer, 81. In the seventh paragraph it was revealed she had been 'bound, strangled and discarded like rubbish'. Eight paragraphs into the story readers learnt it was based on a coronial inquest. They were subsequently told the woman who found the body had touched the bin. So had several others and between them they had probably destroyed vital DNA evidence. Three paragraphs from the end of the 17-paragraph article it was revealed the dead woman was a multi-millionaire. How much better for readers if the journalist had come straight to the point and written an intro like this?

> The killer of an 81-year-old female multi-millionaire whose body was found in a bin under her unit might go free because vital DNA evidence was destroyed.

And compare the obscure intro from *The Weekend Australian* with this one from the *Herald Sun* of February 13, 2010, page 28:

> A policeman is to face court for unintentionally firing his weapon inside Australian Federal Police headquarters.

Or this memorable 10-word intro from the 'World' pages of *The Courier-Mail*:

> A US general says it's fun shooting people in Afghanistan (Papps 2005, p. 19).

After the intro, move into the body of the article and explain the basics by working your way through the what, when, where, who, why and how of your story. White advises journalists to follow the intro with 'detail, amplification, quotes, dissenting opinion, background' in descending order of importance (White 1996, p. 177). In doing so, do not get so caught up in the technicalities of writing that you forget to make your story objective, fair and balanced. If you quote one person who is critical of another person, it is your responsibility ethically—as well as legally— to contact the person who is criticised and offer them an opportunity to respond.

Finally, how long should your story be? As long as it needs to be, and no longer. Sometimes it can be hard letting a story go, but once you finish explaining it in a way you would have liked it explained to you, it must end, be filed, and you must move to the next story.

Different news writing models

Alternatives to the inverted pyramid have evolved and fallen in and out of favour at different times. One concern has been that the inverted pyramid approach is event focused, rather than people and reader focused. In the early 1990s, for example, the American Society of Newspaper Editors (ASNE) published a landmark report that said journalists 'should incorporate narrative techniques into stories to lead readers through the whole story' (ASNE 1993, p. 24). The report said narrative story writing encourages readers to read more deeply into news stories. It suggested journalists should be 'actually telling stories, focusing on action, characters and chronology' (ASNE 1993, p. 24). The ASNE report urged journalists to develop alternatives to the inverted pyramid structure.

One example of a different approach explored by the ASNE was the idea of a 'soft' intro—a longer introduction, sometimes in more than one sentence, or in one complex sentence—which does not attempt to explain a story to readers at the start but leads them several paragraphs into an article before focusing on news values and explanations. Other suggested alternatives included structures based on narrative, questions, descriptions and 'teasers'—plays on words or surprise twists.

An effective alternative to the inverted pyramid model which was developed in Australia is an approach known as 'Readers First'. Devised by editorial staff from Australian Regional Media, a division of APN News & Media, the approach has a strong human interest focus. Australian Regional Media group executive editor Peter Owen said company journalists (whom he prefers to refer to as writers rather than reporters) are encouraged to tell stories instead of filing reports. In doing so, they use narrative to flesh out a story. They employ description, detail and context to 'make a story come alive; and use their writing skills to take readers with them and allow them to share the experience' (Owen 2010). He said he did not advocate this approach for all stories, not even most, but 'I think the big news packages—page leads and spreads—will usually benefit from this treatment.'

Owen said part of the reason for declining newspaper readership in many parts of the world was that papers contain too many badly written stories about boring subjects that interest nobody other than journalists themselves. He said:

> We're convinced that this is happening because: (a) it's always happened that way, and (b) because too few editors (and academics) question it. We challenge the notion that news stories must always be written in the inverted pyramid style, and that 'importance' rather than 'interest' is the criterion to determine the contents of page one and page three.

> The inverted pyramid style is, I believe, ideal for news briefs, short reports and news items where the facts themselves are so remarkable that they need just be listed. As we explain these concepts to our staff, we stress that the most powerful way to tell a story is through the experiences and reaction of real people. We point out that the story is hardly ever about the decision and how it's made, but about the effect of that decision on real people (Owen 2010).

Owen said strong and interesting intros are vital. He said the best intros contain elements of mystery which lure readers into wanting to know 'what happens next', and human interest elements of time and character.

> I quote the statistic that nine out of 10 newspaper readers don't get past the first paragraph of a news story. The only logical explanation is that either the intro (usually in an inverted pyramid format) is totally inadequate, or tells all of the story in just the one par, or the subject of the story is dull and uninteresting.

> The inverted pyramid style—where information is arranged in short paragraphs in declining order of importance and interest—has no middle and no end. Readers can stop at any point when they have had enough. In fact, I don't believe readers understand inverted pyramids because the background goes at the bottom. Without context, readers cannot understand the story and can't be bothered trying to find out (Owen 2010).

The Australia Regional Media approach is similar to other non-traditional approaches used across the newspaper industry. But while narrative styles do have a definite place, there can be a fine line between effective story-telling and taking too long to get to the crux of a story. One danger with alternative approaches is that a journalist becomes too trendy, too clever, too superior and too obscure—producing intensely irritating articles that aggravate readers. Pretentious pieces such as these are sometimes referred to disparagingly by more down-to-earth journalists as being the product of 'cappuccino-set journalism'—all froth on top and dubious quality underneath! They particularly tend to appear in trendy magazines and sometimes in 'quality' newspapers.

Another point to bear in mind when considering different approaches to news writing is that, as explained in Chapter 10, the inverted pyramid style is the preferred model for online news. In many organisations this means a journalist must tell the same story in two different ways. As Owen said in relation to his company:

> We encourage our journalists to file their breaking news stories first to their websites, and to produce a different version for their newspapers. In those circumstances I believe it is sound practice to use an inverted pyramid for online, but it seems ludicrous to me that we'd continue to use an inverted pyramid style for the main page lead stories in the print product (Owen 2010).

DISCUSSION POINTS

1   How does news writing differ from academic writing? Is one a better form of communication than the other, or is each ideally suited to its purpose?

2   Would novelists benefit from learning to write like journalists, or could that stifle their creativity?

3   What do you think about the way English is taught in secondary schools? Did the way you were taught English at school help prepare you for a) university, and b) becoming a journalist? Why or why not?

4   Who is the most inarticulate, word-mangling public figure regularly reported in the news at present? Should you feel sorry for her or him and clean up mangled direct quotes, or let she or he fry in their own stew pot like a cooked goose?

5   Would it ever be all right to deviate from house style in a newspaper article? If so, when and how?

6   The inverted pyramid is a tried and true approach. Is it wise to mess with it or abandon it and use a different approach? Why or why not?

7   If you were a freelance journalist who wrote for many different publications, how important would it really be to focus on getting the style right for each? What would be two effective ways you could quickly learn about the style of each?

8   What does the future hold for print editions of newspapers? Why?

NEWS PRACTICE POINTS

1   Go online and conduct research to find out which demographic groups read print editions of newspapers and which read online editions on mobile devices. What, if any, are the differences between the two groups?

2   Having discovered a little about newspaper readership, explain in about 450 words:

a) whether you think you should write for the most dominant group(s) or if you should pitch your writing more widely, and b) the reasons underlying your opinion.

3   List five words that are commonly used inappropriately because people do not understand their true meaning(s).

4   Go online and find a government document that is at least one A4 page in length and which contains complex jargon. Use the style points explained in this chapter to translate the document into plain English written in print news style.

5   Find two reports in two different newspapers—either electronic or print—about the same event. What, if anything, is different about the house style of each report? Is the content different? Has it been prioritised differently in accord with different news values? If there is little or no difference, why do you think that is the case? If there are differences, do they make one story more appealing than the other, and, if so, how and why?

6   Take a sheet of A4 paper and a glue stick. Then collect the following categories of newspaper print edition intros and stick them in groups on the paper:

a) five good intros from inverted pyramid stories

b) five good intros from stories that were clearly not written to the inverted pyramid 'recipe'

c) the five worst intros you can find

d) the best intro you can find, no matter what its style.

e) Now count the words in each intro and calculate the average number of words in the good intros and the average in the bad ones. Which is higher?

7   Find and clip a newspaper or magazine news story that annoys you intensely. In no more than 150 words explain why it is so annoying.

8 Buy a copy of *The Australian* and a copy of your state or territory's most popular tabloid newspaper—the real print editions, not online:

a) Which has the highest number of Australian-sourced news stories in its news pages?

b) Which has the most well written and easily understood news stories?

c) What proportion of news stories in each is written to the inverted pyramid model and what proportion to other models?

d) Which do you prefer? Why?

WRITING BROADCAST NEWS

Why hasn't television killed radio? Because of something television audiences can't do: drive a car while watching.

Mitchell Stephens, *A History of News*, 1997

OBJECTIVES

After reading this chapter you will understand:

» The vital importance of voice in broadcasting

» The basics of broadcast news style

» Broadcast newsroom jargon

» How to script news for radio

» How to script news for television

» Similarities and differences between radio and television news.

Many of television's best news and current affairs presenters and journalists are so familiar, and we are so comfortable with them, we do not think of them as visitors when we turn on a television and invite them into our home. We have similar relationships with radio journalists and presenters. They wake us in the morning, and put some of us to sleep at night. Radio journalists travel with us in our vehicles, accompany us as we walk or jog, and enliven numerous workplaces.

As long as you have access to a radio or television receiver, or another device capable of radio and/or television reception, most broadcast news is free. There are no pay-walls, and no monthly newspaper accounts. Portability, immediacy and the fact that radio signals can carry over long distances also make radio an ideal medium for breaking news and to keep communities informed during times of emergency. And while access fees do apply when accessing data via smartphones, tablets and other mobile devices, radio and television news apps have evolved to sit beside traditional broadcast technologies by allowing downloads of voice- and video-based news.

Challenges of a changing media landscape

Despite the advantages of broadcast news, there has been a clear trend since the early 1990s for an increasing number of people to spend less time accessing news via dedicated radio and television receivers and more time accessing it online or on mobile devices. Results of a major survey of media trends by the US-based Pew Research Centre for the People and the Press released in 2012 reflected the decline in what had once been the absolute supremacy of television news. The survey revealed that despite a growing population base, the regular audience for nightly network news in the US had fallen by 13 per cent between 1991 and 2012 (Pew Research Centre 2012b). This compared with a decline of 27 per cent in regular newspaper readership in the same period and a 21 per cent fall in regular radio news audiences (Pew Research Centre 2012b, p. 1). Interestingly, however, the same survey indicated that the fall in television news audiences had mainly occurred in the early to mid-1990s and audience share had stabilised since the late 1990s, with about 55 per cent of respondents reporting they watched nightly network news 'yesterday'. On the other hand, the decline in radio news audiences and newspaper readership had been a relatively consistent trend between 1991 and 2012, with the percentage of people who read a daily newspaper dropping from 56 per cent in 1991 to 29 per cent in 2012 and radio news audiences declining from 54 per cent to 33 per cent in the same period (Pew Research Centre 2012b, p. 1).

The Pew survey also indicated that audience demographics had changed, with a decline in the proportion of people aged under 30 watching television news (Pew Research Centre 2012b, p. 2). The survey report said:

> Only about a third (34 per cent) of those younger than 30 say they watched TV news yesterday; in 2006, nearly half of young people (49 per cent) said they watched TV news the prior day. Among older age groups, the percentages saying they watched TV yesterday has not changed significantly over this period (Pew Research Centre 2012b, p. 2).

Overall, 39 per cent of respondents across the US said they accessed news online from traditional media organisations in 2012, up from 24 per cent in 2002 (Pew Research Centre 2012b, p. 1). However, the survey revealed that many respondents were relying on emails, podcasts, social networks or Twitter as their main sources of news, with the total percentage accessing news digitally, 50 per cent, only slightly less than the 55 per cent relying on television news (Pew Research Centre 2012b, p. 9).

Despite the popularity of digital news, the Pew survey found that more Americans continued to consume news from traditional news platforms than from digital platforms (Pew Research Centre 2012b, p. 12). It was reported that 71 per cent watched television news, read a print newspaper or listened to radio news compared with the 50 per cent who accessed their news from one or more digital platforms (Pew Research Centre 2012b, p. 12). Notably, close to 40 per cent of those surveyed obtained their news from multiple media platforms. Another interesting finding of the 2012 survey was the continuation of a trend identified in earlier surveys which showed that television news viewers spent much more time accessing news than those who accessed it on radio, in newspapers or online. It was reported that the average time television viewers spent watching news each day was 52 minutes, compared with 45 minutes listening to radio, 36 minutes reading a newspaper, and 40 minutes accessing news online or from a mobile device (Pew Research Centre 2012b, p. 12). Another particularly relevant finding was that the vast majority of those who accessed news on mobile devices and computers did so by accessing the websites of traditional news media organisations, including the sites of broadcast outlets, either by going to such sites directly, via a news app, or through a search engine such as Google or Yahoo! (Pew Research Centre 2012b, p. 12–23).

While there are no comparable surveys in Australia, our media consumption trends, especially in relation to accessing news online and from mobile devices, tend to generally run along the same lines as those in the US.

When interpreting survey data like the Pew results, it is important to understand that major radio and television networks are no longer simply broadcast outlets in the traditional sense of transmitting radio and television signals. Most also 'broadcast' their news online, via mobile apps and/or Internet Protocol television (IPTV). Video news can be viewed on demand, on the web and on mobile devices. There are podcasts and vodcasts of radio and video news and other content. It is also notable that much of the news and many of the news headlines accessed via social media, Twitter and numerous blogs are most likely to have been sourced from traditional broadcast media organisations and/or newspaper websites. In that context, and as discussed in Chapter 8, one of the consequences of the evolution of digital communication technologies since the 1990s was that newspapers found themselves with the means to regain ground lost to radio and television as major sources of breaking news. Radio usurped newspapers as the main source of breaking news in the 1930s and early 1940s—a trend that gained pace during World War II after radio, not newspapers, exclusively conveyed news to the world of the Japanese attack on Pearl Harbor. As news historian Mitchell Stephens said, 'The Second World War gave radio news what the (US) Civil War had given newspapers: a taste of the medium's power to bring news home' (Stephens 1997, p. 246).

Stephens said many early radio news journalists were newspaper journalists who had moved to the new medium. Similarly many of the first television journalists moved to that medium from radio (Stephens 1997, p. 276). Interestingly, Stephens attributed the evolution of contemporary newspaper writing style of short sentences and concise word use to the development of a news writing style suitable for radio (Stephens 1997, p. 272). Closely aligned with that, the inverted pyramid approach which had evolved with the invention of the telegraph as a news writing model for newspapers was found to be ideally suited to radio reporting.

Newspapers took a second battering after television was first broadcast in Australia in 1956. People who had habitually relied on evening papers to tell them what happened while they worked during the day abandoned those papers for a new habit—watching nightly television news. Since the start of the 21st century, however, the wheel has turned and newspapers are once again breaking news, this time by publishing it online and via apps for mobile devices. This changed media landscape has brought increased competition for stories and exclusives as journalists work across multiple media platforms. It means newspaper journalists can again strive to break stories first, while television news journalists try to catch and hold viewers' attention to stop the flick of a remote control button to another channel or medium, and radio journalists do their utmost to get stories on air first to engage listeners so that they do not change stations or turn off. The move to publishing online and via mobile devices such as tablets and smartphones saw journalists who previously only ever wrote for print learning how to shoot still photographs and record video to enhance stories. In short, the lines between print and broadcast news reporting blurred. History repeated itself as print journalists again moved into broadcast, but this time for their own newspaper's website or mobile apps. It is therefore imperative that all journalism students learn at least the basics of each form of reporting: print, radio, television and for online and mobile platforms.

The critical importance of voice

Some years ago veteran journalist and media commentator with *The Australian* Errol Simper described the voice of ABC Radio National music presenter Robyn Johnston thus:

> Johnston has excellent diction and avoids the strident, casual or flippant. She speaks neither too quickly nor too slowly. There are few, if any, irritating voice quirks or mannerisms. She has this calm, well-pitched tone which gives every indication of being natural, as opposed to a modulation especially constructed for the wireless (Simper 2005, p. 22).

Obviously a wellmodulated, clear and pleasant voice is vital when working in radio. And contrary to common belief, an attractive voice is more important than an attractive body if you want to work in television—although possessing both would not be a disadvantage. As accomplished Seven Queensland television journalist, news presenter and journalism educator Rosanna Natoli said:

> The importance of a clear, natural sounding but authoritative voice should never be underestimated. Viewers pay attention to a good voice. Most journalism students don't think it's a must-have quality. They believe if they can speak, then they can voice a story for TV. But they are wrong. It's the one quality that holds graduates back from being readily employed (Natoli 2010).

Leading Australian broadcast voice trainer Melissa Agnew explained that 'newscasting' gives aural form to written, or scripted, text. She believes that broadcast journalists must develop the same highly developed vocal skills as leading actors, and they must combine journalism and performance. As Agnew explained:

> The news of the day is written by journalists and then performed by them on the radio or television, using their voices. The voice is therefore the most important aspect of broadcast news performance... We need switched-on voices that can resonate Australia-wide in our ever-changing news industry. However, the hallmarks of every news network are subtly different... what might sound right on one network might not necessarily fit another's tone; so the voice in news is not as straightforward as some people might think (Agnew 2008, p. ix).

Seven Queensland Director of News Ross Dagan says voice training is especially important (Dagan 2010). 'Viewers know when someone does not sound like they should,' he said. Phillips and Lindgren said voice should be regarded as a tool by radio presenters, and: 'You have to control it absolutely to get the outcome you desire' (Phillips & Lindgren 2013, p. 30).

Voice control can be learnt by anyone. It can tame and refine a voice like a chainsaw, and enrich and embolden the squeakiest mouse-like tones! Every student planning a career in radio or television should make it a priority to find an experienced and well-regarded voice trainer and be prepared to commit to basic voice training. Subsequently, she or he would be well advised to emulate the best radio and television presenters and continue working with a voice coach from time to time. Just as athletics coaches help athletes work on strength, technique and stamina, good voice trainers will not only help presenters become aware of—and overcome—errors that creep into all our speech over time, they will help build strength, modulation and aural dexterity. Phillips and Lindgren emphasised the importance of continuing to work on voice. They said experience, as well as focusing on voice production techniques, helps enrich broadcasters' voices over time.

> The way you present yourself at eighteen will be different from the way you present yourself at twenty-five or thirty-five when you have confidence born of life experience and maturity. Because your voice reflects your persona, it is a question of honing it over time rather than expecting it to emerge fully formed from the start (Phillips & Lindgren 2013, p. 30).

Writing radio news

Radio news stories stand on the strength of spoken words, not words printed on a page. Once spoken they are gone. Unless recorded or archived for later access online they cannot be revisited, mulled over, or read again to extract extra meaning.

The most obvious difference between writing news for print or online and writing it for radio and television is story length. And unlike publication or broadcast platforms such as print, online, mobile device or video news, a radio story must be able to stand alone without a photograph, video images or even a headline. While that can be a disadvantage, it can also be an advantage. As Hilliard said: 'Radio is not limited by what can be presented visually... the writer can develop a picture in the audience's mind that is limited only by the listener's imagination' (Hilliard 2008, pp. 8 & 9). Canadian academic Marshall McLuhan explained the significance of radio's use of words in a paper titled 'Understanding radio' in which he said:

> If we sit and talk in a dark room, words suddenly acquire new meanings and different textures. They become richer... all those gestural qualities that the printed page strips from language come back in the dark, and on the radio (McLuhan, in Crowley & Heyer 2007, p. 237).

Early radio journalists who made the transition from print would have understood what McLuhan meant. Most would have been expert at working with words before they swapped media platforms. Similarly, journalists today who learn to write news for print and learn about the basics of print writing style, word use and the inverted pyramid approach, have an advantage when moving into broadcast news reporting. They have already learnt to gather news, interview, distil information and facts, and use the explanatory guideposts of what, when, where, who, why and how. They understand the importance of finding and using exactly the right word and of writing concise and focused intros. The most difficult issue they encounter is learning to work with many less words than in print. As Phillips and Lindgren said: 'A story that is given a full-page spread in a newspaper can be summed up in three short paragraphs in its radio news equivalent' (Phillips & Lindgren 2013, p. 39).

But once you get a feel for writing radio news, it is not particularly difficult. Think of a radio news story in terms of a newspaper story written to the inverted pyramid format under a headline: you have a radio news item intro (which is equivalent to a newspaper headline and usually read by the newsreader), a lead (equivalent to a print story intro) and one or two extra sentences that add meaning and more information. At least one of the extra sentences can be a 'grab': a recorded quote from an interviewee (known in broadcast as 'the talent').

Most radio news bulletins run from three to five minutes, although extended bulletins broadcast by the ABC several times a day run for between 10 and 15 minutes. A three to five minute bulletin is likely to contain between five and seven stories, with the last few being about sport. Story lengths are measured in terms of the time, or duration, it takes to broadcast them. They vary from about 15 seconds to 50 seconds for a major item. Radio journalists aim to read on air at an average rate of about 180 words per minute, or three words per second. That means a 15-second story will be about 45 words long, a 30-second story 90 words, and a 50-second story 150 words. Average sentence length should generally be between 10 and 20 words, rarely longer, but varying the length is important.

As well as breaking a story up, short sentences can be used to add emphasis, while longer ones can be more explanatory. Agnew also recommends varying your reading pace, using 'a slightly faster pace for greater excitement or joy; a slightly slower pace for heartache, anticipation or suspense' (Agnew 2008, p. 85).

As an aside here, some people naturally read aloud more or less quickly than three words per second. This is an average, so do not worry if your voice sounds better if you read slightly faster or slower. Digital computer editing systems used in both radio and television newsrooms have a capacity to be 'trained' to measure and adapt to different journalists' voices and reading speeds. Once a system is trained, it automatically takes an individual's reading speed into account when timing scripts to be read by that person.

Radio news stories are classified into one of four categories depending on how they are constructed:

— *Copy stories, or word stories,* usually run for between 15 and 30 seconds and contain between 45 and 90 words. They are often reactive stories—text-based and usually straightforward reports—written to be read by a newsreader, and they do not involve grabs.

— *Stand-alone, script with grab, or words and grab stories,* are usually a little longer. Typically they would run from 25 to 45 seconds and contain between 75 and 135 words. They are a copy story, plus a grab from relevant talent. Typically, the grab would be between eight and 20 seconds long and would come after the second or third sentence of the copy story. Grabs add credibility to a story, they break up a news bulletin and give the newsreader a chance to draw breath, cough or sip water.

— *A voice report, or voicer,* is a longer story again in which a journalist other than the newsreader speaks on air. They commonly run for 35 to 55 seconds in total. The news item usually opens with a one or two sentence introduction read by a newsreader and then cuts to a 20 to 40 second report read by the journalist who wrote it. Voice reports can also include one or more grabs. They tend to be used for more complex stories in which the reporting journalist needs to explain background, or if he or she is reporting 'live' from the scene of a breaking story.

— *A wrap* is a package summarising a big story that unfolded over several hours or a day. Typically, it would be about 60 seconds in length and would start with a newsreader's intro followed by a report read by the journalist who wrote it, in the same way as a voice report. But a wrap would also include background information, such as a summary by the reporting journalist of how the story unfolded. Commonly, there would also be two or more grabs. Wraps are most likely to go to air in extended bulletins, such as the 15-minute 7.45am weekday news on ABC radio.

As well as voices, radio news items also sometimes include 'actuality' or natural ambient sound (known as 'nat sound' in television). Examples are sounds such as gunfire in war reports, people screaming or wailing with grief or fear, weather noises such as howling wind from a cyclone, or the crackle of a fire. Actuality adds credibility to stories and helps listeners imagine a news scene.

While some interviews for radio news stories are conducted in the field and some take place in radio studios, a majority of radio stories are based around telephone interviews that can be edited down to grabs. These are then inserted in digitally edited stories. An advantage of this approach is that information telephoned in from the scene of a breaking story can be broadcast almost immediately in a 'newsflash' if a newsworthy event is a big one. The disadvantage is that radio journalists, especially in regional newsrooms where there are only one or two staff, become tied to their desks. They find it difficult to get out of the office to conduct face-to-face interviews or report from the field. Radio journalists also often have hourly deadlines, so they must be able to work the phones quickly, write quickly, edit quickly, and find new angles for stories that develop over time so each bulletin sounds fresh to listeners. A reliance on the telephone means radio journalists depend heavily on credible sources. They must have strong contact lists and build good relationships in the communities they serve.

But not all radio news is locally sourced. Depending to some extent on whether they work in national, state or regional newsrooms, radio journalists also obtain many stories and story leads from wire services such as Australian Associated Press (AAP) which syndicate news. AAP supplies news to many of Australia's 800 newspapers, including 50 dailies; five free-to-air television networks; two pay TV networks; and 550 radio stations (AAP 2012a). The service says it produces about 1200 stories daily, about 300 of which are written in broadcast style. It says its 'broadcast stories are delivered as scripts that are written for the ear, not the eye. The stories are sharp and updated frequently—tailor-made for on-air' (AAP 2012b). As a result, when short of a local story many radio journalists simply 'rip-and-read'. At other times, they build on a syndicated story by developing a local angle and creating proximity by finding relevant people in their broadcast area to interview for grabs and adding regional colour.

Radio news style

While the inverted pyramid model is well suited to radio—in as much as skimming the top layers off the pyramid provides all there is time to report in a radio news story—the *ABC News & Current Affairs Style Guide* (2008) advises the corporation's radio and television journalists that aspects of newspaper writing style are irrelevant for broadcast reporting. The guide says:

> We should write the way we speak. That does not mean we use slang, but we don't use formal, official words and phrases that often obscure meaning or sound inflated... We don't converse with people in long, convoluted sentences, which have several qualifying phrases, and commas, such as this one. So don't write this way (ABC 2008, p. 3).

In a nutshell the basics of radio news writing style are as follows:

— Write in the present tense—it conveys a sense of immediacy.

— Use active voice—it saves words and has more impact than passive voice.

— Do use contractions and abbreviations such as 'don't', 'won't' and 'couldn't', but use them carefully and do not overdo them.

— Do not use more than one word when one will do.

— Do not use a complex, old-fashioned or pompous word when a simple one will do. For example, use 'about', not 'approximately', and 'on', not 'upon'.

— Avoid words such as 'lot', 'got' and 'nice' that do not tell listeners anything.

— As a general rule, avoid adjectives and adverbs.

— Keep your language simple and conversational. Write the way people speak— but Agnew (2008 p. 108) warns against adopting 'bogan' speech patterns.

— Keep your writing tight.

— Capitalise the NAMES of people and places.

— Introduce your talent before a quote or grab.

— Phonetically spell out difficult-to-pronounce or unusual names of people and places immediately after you have spelt the name properly. For example: 'Mr Samten (SAM-TEN) Jones says some people have trouble pronouncing his first name.'

— Depending on the outlet you work for, a transcript of what an interviewee (the talent) said might be included in the script of each story—this is a fall-back in case something goes wrong with a recorded grab, in which case the newsreader can read aloud what the talent said. Transcripts are commonly used for this purpose by ABC radio but rarely by commercial radio.

— Do not use symbols such as '%', '#' or '$'—it is much easier for a newsreader to read the words 'per cent', 'number' and 'dollars' than to interpret symbols.

— Spell out numbers from one to nine, use numerals from 10 to 999, spell out numbers from one thousand to nine thousand, and then use a mix of numerals and words for 10 thousand and above.

— When reporting ages use the format: '27-year-old Florence Fandango was charged with...'

— Do your best to avoid clichés—they are a lazy form of expression that cheapens a story, they can damage credibility, and too many are literally a turn-off. There are, however, some broadcast outlets which actively encourage the use of clichés in the belief that their target audiences are comfortable with deliberately dumbed down language.

— Only use punctuation that makes written words read as if they are spoken.

— Underline words you want emphasised when they are read aloud.

— Avoid pronouns in stories, they tend to be confusing.

— Be aware that unlike print stories, broadcast stories will not be cut. If too long (or too short) they will be sent back for rewriting to exactly the required length.

Radio journalists and newsreaders should always pre-read stories aloud to see how they sound and also to practise pronouncing names. If you make a major factual mistake when live on air, especially if it is one that could have legal consequences, it is best to pause and correct it. But if the error is only minor, it is often better to keep going as if nothing had happened than to go back and attempt a correction. Doing so only draws attention to a mistake and it is likely to affect the timing of a news bulletin.

And timing is everything when a bulletin is assembled. Every story and every grab must be timed to the second, especially when news bulletins are networked to many different stations around the nation and each must slot news into a particular spot in its computer-controlled programming. For that reason, time buffers are usually built into the end of a bulletin. Commonly they are in a weather report, which can either be read in full if there is a need to fill in, or summarised if time is short. Another common ploy when a bulletin falls a few seconds short is for a newsreader to go back and reread the headlines, saying something like 'now to return to the main points in this bulletin...'

Timing is everything when a bulletin is assembled. Every story and every grab must be timed to the second, especially where news bulletins are networked to many different stations around the nation and each must slot news into a particular spot in its computer-controlled programming.

To help familiarise yourself with radio news style, buy a good-quality sound recorder—preferably one with a USB connection that plugs into your computer so you can check timings and edit recordings—and practise writing, then reading stories aloud to set time limits. Also record and then listen to radio news bulletins, and analyse their structure and the ways in which stories were written and constructed. The more you do these things, the more rapidly you will master broadcast news writing.

It will also help if you understand the basics of writing a radio news script. The following are examples of generic script formats used in commercial radio news.

SCRIPT EXAMPLE

A simple copy, or word, story written to be read by a newsreader:

Emergency services are on scene at a serious accident involving a car and a B-double on the JUMPING JOE Highway, near HAPPYVALE. It's still not known how many people have been injured.

Two lanes have been closed, and traffic diverted around the crash site.

A stand-alone story (script with grab, or words with grab) written to be read by a newsreader but with a grab inserted; the 14-second duration (DUR) grab starts with the words 'When we got there' (IN) and ends with 'certainly very fortunate' (ENDS):

A SMITHTOWN family has been left homeless after fire ripped through their timber home early this morning.

Fire fighters couldn't save the two-storey building, but no one was injured. Local Fire Chief MICHAEL JONES says it was lucky no one was home at the time.

MEDIA: Fire Chief 1

DUR: 14 secs

IN: When we got there

ENDS: certainly very fortunate.

A voice report, or voicer, written to be introduced by a newsreader but then narrated by a reporter; in this instance, the reporter is Lucy Smith, the duration (DUR) of her report has been edited to 32 seconds, she starts with the words 'Local residents and' (IN) and finishes with 'Lucy Smith reporting' (ENDS):

Hundreds of people have gathered at the site of the State Government's proposed ROSIE'S CREEK dam.

They're staging a protest against the planned dam which would destroy up to 50 homes. Reporter LUCY SMITH is at the scene.

MEDIA: Lucy Smith—Dam Protest

DUR: 32 secs

IN: Local residents and

ENDS: Lucy Smith reporting.

Radio scripts courtesy Rosanna Natoli

Note that if the foregoing scripts had been used in an ABC radio news bulletin, the word MEDIA would have been replaced by the term CART and in place of the words IN and ENDS there would have been full transcripts of what was said.

Television news

Natoli is passionate about television news reporting:

> For me, television is the most exciting of all the news media, it's intoxicating and addictive. There's a drama that unfolds naturally when you have great vision and sound, and you as the journalist can craft it into a riveting news story (Natoli 2010).

Dagan (2010) has interviewed countless prospective television journalists in his role as a senior television news executive. The key quality he looks for is the kind of passion described by Natoli. In addition to speaking well, he said television journalists must feel comfortable in front of a camera and 'they have to have an exuberance for the profession, for the art of storytelling, using pictures and for communicating with people directly' (Dagan 2010). He said successful television journalists also have a certain indefinable but essential 'it' factor. As Dagan sees it:

> Even with many university degrees now including significant practical elements, most graduates still have some way to go when they present themselves for employment. Work experience or internship programs offer the best way for the academic theory to be married with on-the-road journalism. The weaknesses that emerge don't relate to what they're taught— they relate to what can't be easily taught. A good producer can correct some of the ills of youth and inexperience, but they can't make someone have a presence on air that engages viewers—only time, passion and persistence can do that.
>
> I am often surprised by how ill-prepared would-be journalists are when it comes to their show-reel or an interview situation. Many start by making excuses about why their DVD is not as good as it should be, or present some other reason as to why they are not at their best. They forget that there are any number of others who have also completed a university degree, and have a DVD with some example stories to prove it. If just one of the people projects that indefinable 'it' quality, if they sound like they should, if they have presence like they should, if they write like they should, then it follows that they have a greater chance. There is no room for half measures—there is simply too much choice to accept anyone other than the most promising candidate (Dagan 2010).

TELEVISION NEWS JARGON

Television journalists and news production staff use a specialised jargon journalism students should learn and understand. Basic terms to become familiar with include:

talent	as for radio, an interviewee
grab	much the same as for radio, a snippet of an interview, but in television includes a video image of the talent, also referred to as 'a talking head'
noddy	a shot of a journalist nodding wisely, as if listening to the talent. Noddies are usually recorded at the end of an interview for use in editing.
cutaway	a close-up image of a journalist making notes, asking a question and/or listening to an interviewee. Also often recorded at the end of an interview and used in editing.
close-up, or one-shot	a closely framed image of an interviewee (talent)
two-shot	a closely framed shot of the talent and a journalist talking
intro	different from a newspaper intro, this is the overview of a story read by a newsreader and may be several sentences long
lead	similar in purpose to the intro of a newspaper story, this tells viewers what a story is about and is usually voiced by the journalist who wrote or presents the story
stand-up	a journalist speaking to camera, often from the scene of a breaking story. Also called a 'piece to camera'.
sign off	the end of a package in which a journalists says something like, 'Sarah Jones reporting for National Network News'
throw	a transition from a newsreader or studio-based journalist to another journalist who is commonly in the field—used more often in radio than television because vision can be used as a transition device in television
voiceover, or RVO (reader voice over)	a news script written by a journalist, often to accompany vision, but read by a newsreader, or a journalist or announcer other than the one who wrote the story

SOT	sound on a video (tape) recording—now often digital with no tape
nat sound, or NATSO	the same as actuality in radio—background sound recorded at the scene of a story
worder	a news script read by a newsreader in a story with no video
package	a whole video news item consisting of a journalist interviewing talent, usually a stand-up, and vision voiced by the same journalist. A package is introduced with an intro read by a newsreader.
wrap	two or more video stories packaged together. Often used for different stories written and presented by different journalists but about a common issue or event.
supers	captions which appear at the bottom of the screen when a story is broadcast—usually written by the journalist who wrote the story

Writing television news

The technical aspects of writing television news are similar in many ways to writing radio news, with the most obvious difference being that images replace words in telling at least part of a story. In fact television news has been described as 'radio news with pictures', which is exactly what it was at first (Schechter 1999, p. 182). But therein lies a contradiction. While the actual writing style is not all that different, television news, unlike radio news, is rarely regarded as newsworthy if there is no vision. The need for video images is a blessing and a curse. Images often speak much louder and more eloquently than words, but no matter how strong a news story may be, it is unlikely to be given more than a few seconds in a television news bulletin, if mentioned at all, if there are no strong images. This can frustrate television journalists, and audiences too. So while television news writing is well suited to skimming the top off the inverted pyramid in much the same way as radio news, more often than not it is the news value attached to images that carry more weight than the story itself—thus stories with the strongest vision are more likely to lead a news bulletin than stories that might have better intrinsic news value but are not well supported visually.

The need for video images is a blessing and a curse. Images often speak much louder and more eloquently than words, but no matter how strong a news story may be, it is unlikely to be given more than a few seconds in a television news bulletin, if mentioned at all, if there are no strong images.

Another difference between reporting for radio and for television is that while radio journalists work the telephones for stories, television journalists must spend much more time in the field interviewing face-to-face. Building a television news story, and a television news bulletin, involves many people. It involves effective teamwork—between journalist and camera operator in the field; journalist, editor and camera operator in the newsroom; and journalist, chief-of-staff, producers and newsreaders in preparing a bulletin. These are all things a television journalist becomes adept in dealing with. They are also why a television journalist needs to understand where they fit into the team, and to learn the basic technical requirements and limits that camera operators, editors and producers must contend with.

Because many of the news values associated with television news are related more to eye-catching video images than intrinsic news values, there tends to be a focus on what could be described as 'sub-values' attached to the key top-level news values discussed in Chapter 3. Conflict, proximity, significance, novelty, prominence and human interest are still important in decision making, but within those values, television news tends to focus on particular images such as those of small children, cute animals, sexy-looking talent, raw emotion, and exciting or frightening action. The result, particularly in relation to commercial television news, is that the lines between news and entertainment blur at times. This emphasis on vision is also at least partly why 'tabloid' television current affairs programs lean towards visual sensationalism, shock-horror images and emotive interviews instead of segments resulting from in-depth research.

Television news style

Like radio news items, television news stories must be exactly timed. But because part of the art of television journalism is drawing on vision to help tell a story, the timing for television must include exact timing of vision as well as words. A television script must therefore marry timing, vision and words.

The script should be written in the present tense, and be short and to the point. A transcript of what an interviewee (the talent) said should be included in the script of each story. And just as some radio news items include actuality, many television stories include nat sound.

Another difference between television and radio news is that television news bulletins are longer, so stories run longer. The average duration of a television news stories is about 80 seconds. At a reading rate of three words per second, and if an item does not include nat sound, that amounts to a script of about 240 words.

When writing a news script, work to the vision—do not try to make the vision fit the words. And let vision and sound tell their own parts of stories—do not use your script to explain what the video is showing or what sounds you hear, viewers can work that out for themselves. In nearly all other respects, the actual writing style for television news is the same as that for radio. The following is an example of a generic television news script.

MOUNT ROMAN FIRE (THIS IS THE INTRO)

Three adults, two teenagers and a baby have been choppered to safety after being trapped on top of MOUNT ROMAN, near RUBYVALE.

The walkers were on their way down, when a bushfire began on the side of the mountain, cutting off their only escape route. (*These two paragraphs are the lead.*)

TAKE VTR (*The item now cuts from the newsreader to a recording of the edited sound and vision.*)

///////

RUNS: 1.33 (*The recording's duration is one minute, 33 seconds.*)

ENDS: Nightly News (*The last words of the recording before the newsreader takes over and either introduces the next story or goes to a break.*)

(*The names and information listed in the following part of the script are what will show in captions, or 'supers', inserted into different parts of the story. They are written by the journalist who wrote the story and appear on the bottom of the screen when the story is broadcast.*)

JANE GRACE Reporting	Rescued Bushwalker
Mount Roman	**JAMES ROSE**
MIA JONES	CDE Chopper Rescue
Rescued Bushwalker	**BOB HANSON**
JOHN JONES	Rescued Bushwalker
Rescued Bushwalker	**PETER SMITH**
JOSEPH NASH	Rubyvale Fire Chief

The information in this column relates to vision. The numbers are time codes for the grabs. They represent the location in the original camera operator's footage (known as 'wilds') where each grab is found.	*Information in this column relates to sound and words. The words inside quotation marks are what is said by talent in a grab. The passages outside the quotation marks are either instructions about sound or what the reporting journalist reads aloud.*
	Numbers in this column are time codes for both the 'inwords' (first words) and 'outwords' (final words) of a grab. They are listed by the journalist who wrote the story so an editor can insert the exact grab required. The codes also help in timing a story because they indicate the exact length of each grab.
Aerial shot of the fire and people waving from the top 6:50	As fire raced up the mountain, there were real fears for those trapped at the top.
	(*The journalist reporting*)
	Sound Up (*Journalist's instruction to editor*)
	Fire crackling (*This is nat sound*)
Continue shots of flames	Three years ago, the whole peak went up in less than an hour.
	Grab Mia Jones
	12:45–12:52
	'We kept looking around seeing these flames—I thought, "Oh my God it looks like it's going to overtake us." It really was terrifying.'
Chopper picking up walkers 7:32	Six people, including a baby, were plucked from the top.
	They were trapped by flames below them, the walking trail completely engulfed.
	Grab John Jones
	14:14–14:20
	'The wind was blowing the flames around. If we'd had to go down the other side, it was pretty overgrown, never know what would happen.'
	They'd managed to scramble to a clearing.
	Grab Joseph Nash
	11:45–11:52
	'When I got there—it was really hot. I couldn't stay on the path... had to go through scrub.'

	Grab Chopper Rescue James Rose
	21:20–21:24
	'By the time we flew in, fire was halfway up. With the wind blowing, it could go up real quick.'
Shot of Bob and baby in his arms sleeping 8:43	Local, Bob Hanson, had his eight month old son with him.
	Grab Bob Hanson
	'He's going to have a story to tell when he grows up.'
Chopper with water basket 18:30	After the chopper dropped them to safety, it began water bombing the blaze, to keep it from neighbouring houses.
At the resort 19:05	Sound Up
	Chopper
	…using water from a nearby lake at the Stella Golf Resort.
	Piece To Camera (*Journalist talking to camera*)
	16:20–16:28
	'The fire fighting effort continued as the chopper made countless trips back and forth to the top of the mountain.'
Hoses 15:34	As locals turned their garden hoses on the flames, fire crews back-burned.
	Grab Fire Chief Peter Smith
	20:32–30:41
	'Very difficult, very inaccessible. Flat out getting fire appliances anywhere near where they need to be unfortunately.'
Fire officer running up the hill 13:13	No homes were damaged and no one was injured.
	Jane Grace, Nightly News

Television script courtesy Rosanna Natoli

Finally in relation to broadcast news, the best way to really learn how radio and television news reporting works is to go and do it. An internship or work experience in the final year of a journalism course is invaluable. If you are fortunate enough to find a broadcast outlet and journalist(s) prepared to help you, remember you are a guest and are being offered a privileged insight into people's working lives. Dress appropriately, always arrive at work in plenty of time, take care with personal hygiene, behave professionally, be polite and helpful but not obsequious, and use initiative—especially when it comes to suggesting story ideas. Above all, accept there will be some things you will not understand at first, and do not make the mistake of thinking it is your mission in life to tell your hosts how to do their jobs!

DISCUSSION POINTS

1   It has been said that radio and television reporting suits journalists who do not spell well. Is that a valid proposition today? Why or why not?

2   What factors combine to make broadcast news credible?

3   How credible are commercial radio and television news? Why?

4   How credible are ABC radio and television news? Why?

5   Think of the most significant news story that broke in the past six months. How did you first learn of the story? Is there a best medium for breaking news? If so, is it radio, television, social media, mobile apps or news media websites? Why?

6   Following on from Discussion Point 5, what category of news website is the best at reporting breaking news: sites operated by radio stations, sites operated in conjunction with television stations, newspaper websites, or aggregating sites such as Google News? Why?

NEWS PRACTICE POINTS

1   Select three significant newspaper news stories and script one for broadcast as a 15-second radio story, one for a 30-second radio story, and the other for a 50-second radio story. Explain in a few words how you will time the stories.

2   Think about the point that radio journalists rely heavily on telephone interviews. Make a list of the 10 most significant contacts you would need to build relationships with if you were newly appointed to a radio newsroom.

3   Purchase or borrow a good-quality digital sound recorder (you should have one anyway so you can record interviews). Record yourself reading several news items from a newspaper, then play the recording back. Make a list of five things you like about your voice and five you dislike.

4   Refer to the lists you made in Practice Point 3. Consider each of the things you dislike in your voice. Taking each one at a time, write two sentences explaining positive steps you could take to overcome that particular issue.

5   Returning to the list you made in Practice Point 3 of things you like about your voice, take each one at a time and write two sentences explaining how you could build on and develop that particular strong point.

6   If you are seriously thinking of working in radio or television, find contact details for a voice coach in your region, or if there are none in your region, the nearest person. Contact one or more of those you have identified, ask about cost and the person's experience and clients. Then, if you can afford it, make an initial appointment.

7   Record a radio news broadcast that lasts for at least five minutes. Replay each item and write down whether it is a copy story, stand alone, voicer, or wrap.

8   Watch the 'news' section of a commercial television news bulletin—usually this is about the first 15 minutes. As you view each item, write a brief summary of what the story was about and what the strongest news value was. Then identify if the key news value was in the vision or in the script. At the end of the of news section, go back over your list and consider if, and if so in what order, you would have rearranged the story-list in terms of news values if there had been no vision.

9   Repeat the same exercise as you did for Practice Point 8, but this time for an ABC television news broadcast. Were there differences? If so, what?

10 Identify a significant issue that is likely to have a strong visual component. Then, using the generic television news script in this chapter as a model, write either a real or hypothetical television news script that includes instructions to an editor about vision and sound.

10 WRITING NEWS FOR ONLINE AND PORTABLE DEVICES

The internet is not the enemy of newspapers. It is a medium on which great journalism can reach a larger audience.

John Hartigan, former News Limited chairman and chief executive, 2009

OBJECTIVES

After reading this chapter you will understand:

» Why journalists need to be equipped to work across different media

» That news dissemination is undergoing revolutionary change

» How to write news for online and mobile devices

» Why geographic pointers are crucial in online news

» The importance of linking headings and intros when publishing online

» When to put hyperlinks in articles.

Breaking news from around the globe is reported on mobile devices and online even while it is still happening. Many stories are enhanced with graphics, photographs, video and sound. Radio and television stations were once the first to break reactive news stories, but today they compete with newspaper websites, as well as their own and other broadcasters' online news sites, news apps, and sites such as Google News, which aggregate news stories from many different sources.

One reason for the increased, and fierce, competition is that newspapers have reinvented themselves to combine the formidable news-gathering capacity that once fuelled a cumbersome once-a-day news cycle with the speed, agility and immediacy of electronic publishing on their websites, and via smartphones and other digital devices such as tablets. Veteran television journalist and Sky News newsreader Jim Waley (2010) said the advent of online news had been revolutionary. Sky News is a good example of how news from one organisation is presented across different platforms. In addition to being broadcast via subscription television, it is also presented on YouTube, and as online text with still images on the web. Waley said:

> It's great to be part of a 24-hour news service because it is there available 24/7 for the convenience of our audience. The news is immediate, relevant and limitless; it's accessible in every office, home and mobile phone, anywhere and at any time. We can take viewers to a developing or breaking news story and devote as much time and analysis as necessary. It's a privilege to be part of this news revolution (Waley 2010, p. 6).

An explosion in the number of news websites and related apps since the start of the 21st century dictates that every journalism graduate should be multi-skilled and web savvy—capable of reporting quickly, accurately and ethically for radio, television, or for a newspaper, plus online and for mobile devices. It is also essential to have learnt how to take quality photographs and shoot video. The need for multi-skilling was highlighted in a report of a joint Walkley Foundation and University of New South Wales' research project in 2012, which noted that:

> experienced print journalists are learning audio/video production and other digital journalism skills, either through employer provided on-the-job training or, more likely, through individual initiative. They have to. Across the industry, the trend is toward hiring new staff with digital media skills, to work on the digital platforms (O'Donnell, McKnight & Este 2012, p.41).

An era of change

Addressing the National Press Club in a landmark 2009 speech, former News Limited chairman and chief executive John Hartigan said:

> our newsrooms have completely changed their structures and schedules to embrace multi-platform journalism. The discussions about whether stories should be held for the paper or published immediately are consigned to history... In the digital age, all information is theoretically available to everyone for the first time in history. The journalism that will thrive is journalism that helps people find what they want to know and helps them to do something about it (Hartigan 2009b).

Australian Independent Business Media chief executive Alan Kohler made similar points:

> Before the internet, an exclusive news story lasted 24 hours. When you got a scoop, your competitors could not follow it up until the next day... Now,

with all newspapers online, along with dozens of other websites, exclusive stories are picked up many times within minutes. Scoops now just get you bragging rights... A few publishers don't own the news. It's everywhere all the time. News will never go back to being published once a day (Kohler 2009).

There are three key points here. First, as O'Donnell, McKnight and Este noted in their 2012 report: 'Virtually all of what is misleadingly referred to as "online news" originates in the newsrooms of either newspapers or public broadcasters' (O'Donnell, McKnight, & Este 2012, p. 4). Second, newspaper circulations have been falling dramatically since the mid-1980s. Third, visits to newspaper websites have skyrocketed, particularly since 2008. The majority of newspapers, and newspaper companies, were slow to react at first but after the global financial crisis of 2008, which saw advertising revenue slashed at the same time as circulations were plummeting, newspaper companies finally joined the dots and actively sought to reinvent themselves—shifting their focus from newsprint delivery to online and mobile devices. That transition caused considerable pain and uncertainty, particularly in 2012, a watershed year in the shifting focus from newsprint to online and mobile news delivery. As O'Donnell, McKnight and Este saw it, newspapers were hit with 'a perfect storm of disruption from digital media' in 2012, which combined with the impact of the global financial crisis, 'hit circulation and readership causing a precipitous drop in the advertising revenues on which newspapers have always relied to pay their journalists' (O'Donnell, McKnight & Este 2012, p. 9). As a consequence 'the two major news[paper] groups, Fairfax Media and News Limited, announced major cuts to jobs, internal restructures, centralisation and, in the case of Fairfax, the closure of two printing plants (O'Donnell, McKnight & Este 2012, p. 9). In 2013 the former Fairfax broadsheets *The Age* and *Sydney Morning Herald* moved to tabloid formats in their print editions.

More than 1000 newspaper journalists either lost their jobs or took redundancies in the three years to the start of 2013 (Jackson 2013). But, change is not inherently bad. In many senses Australia's major newspaper publishing companies had been living in the past and resisting change for too long. The writing was certainly on the wall by 2008 when the Australian Press Council reported there had been 'a veritable explosion' in online readership (McKinnon 2008, p. 14). A measure of the growth in the uptake of online news can be seen in the fact that just 33 per cent of Australians had internet access in 2000, 75 per cent had access in 2008 (Internet World Stats, 2008), and close to 90 per cent had access in 2012 (Internet

World Stats, 2012a). In terms of internet penetration—the percentage of a nation's population with internet access—Australia ranked seventh in the world top 10 in 2012, behind Iceland, Norway, Sweden, Falkland Islands, Luxembourg and Greenland, and ahead of the US, the UK, Japan, Germany and Canada (Internet World Stats 2012c).

The implications for journalists and media outlets were obvious—the web and the mobile technologies that feed off it are our main sources of breaking news. Online and mobile devices are ahead of traditional print, radio and television media as the single most accessed medium. Running parallel with the growth in online and mobile news, and the decline in the number of journalists working for newspapers in 2012, there was a marked increase in the number of journalists employed by online news outlets. Jackson (2013) reported that in November 2012 there were 22,000 journalists and writers in Australia (not counting public relations personnel) which was:

> … the highest ever level and an increase of more than 10 per cent on the year before. That is thanks to new media not traditional main media (Jackson 2013).

Writing news for online and mobile devices

There are many similarities between writing news for text-based news websites and mobile apps and writing it for newspapers, but there are significant differences too. This is partly because online and mobile publication offers former print-only news organisations, journalists, editors and news producers a platform for print, sound and vision in a single medium. It is also because there are differences between reading text on a computer screen, tablet or mobile phone and in print, and because of the global nature of online and mobile platforms. But there are few differences between writing radio and television news for traditional broadcast transmission via radio and television signals and writing broadcast news for internet-based online and mobile devices.

Interestingly, and contrary to predictions in the early days of online news publishing, research showed that news articles published on the web tended to be read in more depth than equivalent articles in print. The US-based Poynter

Institute has conducted research into the reading habits of print and online readers since 1990. In 2008 it reported a surprising finding: online participants in its 2007 EyeTrack survey read an average 77 per cent of the story text in articles they chose to read, compared with broadsheet newspaper participants in the same survey who read an average of 62 per cent, and tabloid participants who read an average of 57 per cent (EyeTrack 2007). The findings led Poynter researchers Sara Quinn and Pegie Stark Adam to wonder if the overall length of a story made any difference and if brief stories were read more completely than considerably longer articles. But they found online readers still read more text regardless of story length (EyeTrack 2007).

The Poynter research indicated that print readers were attracted by strong headlines and photos and were particularly drawn by lead stories (those with the strongest headline) on a page. In contrast, online readers were drawn by navigation links such as drop-down menus and navigation bars (EyeTrack 2007). This finding tends to support a view by Kiss (2003), who said there are three main areas to consider when writing for the web: 'use of language, technical considerations and graphic layout' (Kiss 2003).

Key findings of the 2007 EyeTrack survey were reinforced later in the results of a Poynter EyeTrack survey published in 2012, designed to reveal how people read news on tablets. It was reported that when accessing news sites on a tablet:

> as with earlier eyetracking studies, people tended to enter a screen through a dominant element, generally a photograph. Faces in photographs and videos attracted a lot of attention (Dickenson Quinn 2012).

Just as the 2007 EyeTrack survey found that online readers tended to read text stories they had selected in depth, the 2012 survey identified a similar trend among tablet readers (Dickenson Quinn 2012). It was reported that survey respondents viewed an average of 18 separate news items before finally selecting the first one to read. Once that first story was chosen, readers spent an average of slightly more than a minute and a half reading it and 'many text stories were read to completion' (Dickenson Quinn 2012). Findings such as those reinforce the enormous importance of writing intros and headings that attract, then hold, the attention of readers and viewers in online and portable environments. It should also be understood that while there are some differences between writing news for publication on the web and mobile devices compared with writing for print publications and broadcast by traditional media, there is nothing mysterious

There is nothing mysterious about writing online news or news for mobile devices—the key ingredient is journalistic common sense. As with all news writing, the aim is to present relevant and interesting information as effectively as possible, in as few words as possible.

about writing online news or news for mobile devices— the key ingredient is journalistic common sense. As with all news writing, the aim is to present relevant and interesting information as effectively as possible, in as few words as possible, in a bid to hold readers', listeners' and viewers' attention for as long as possible.

The inverted pyramid is an ideal model

All the standard news reporting rules apply to online news writing. Articles must be fair, accurate, objective and balanced. Everything must be attributed and written in proper news writing style. Kipling's what, when, where, who, why and how all apply. The inverted pyramid formula is ideal. It applies as much to 'television-style' online and portable news platforms as it does to audio or text-based news sites.

An advantage of using the inverted pyramid model when writing news for the web and portable devices is that while visitors will only read a full story if they are particularly interested in it (Kiss 2003), eyetracking surveys have shown that they look at the top of a news page first (Outing & Ruel 2004). As noted previously, this makes it important to explain key points in the intro and first few paragraphs, catch readers' attention and lure them into reading the rest of an article in just the same way as a good print journalist attempts to catch and hold readers who scan newspapers. Reporting on the result of the Eyetrack III survey, Outing and Ruel said the research had shown that online news consumers preferred reading short, single-sentence paragraphs. They said: 'stories with short paragraphs received twice as many overall eye fixations as those with longer paragraphs… longer paragraph format seems to discourage viewing' (Outing & Ruel 2004). The Eyetrack III survey also revealed that 95 per cent of visitors to a news web page read some or all of the intro paragraph, but if the intro was not read, neither was the whole article (Outing & Ruel 2004). As Outing and Ruel explained: 'introductory paragraphs are almost a guaranteed "read" for online-news readers. So make them count… realise the power they have to make the news more interesting and accessible to your audience' (Outing & Ruel 2004).

It is also noteworthy that those who consume their news via portable devices and online tend to be less patient than readers of newspapers or viewers of television news. They want news in a hurry—maybe at work while the boss is not around, or during an advertising break in a television program! They scan, swipe and click through web pages. Web design guru Jakob Nielsen said online news consumers are 'ruthless' and 'want sites that get to the point, they have very little patience', they want to 'reach a site quickly, complete a task and leave' (Nielsen 2009).

Another difference that those who have a background as newspaper journalists must take into account when writing for publication on the web or portable devices is that the immediacy of web news dictates it should be written in the present tense. Whereas newspaper reports talk about events that happened 'yesterday', web news—like radio news—is happening 'now' or at least 'today'. This difference is most obvious on news websites run in conjunction with major newspapers, some of which seem to have something of a split personality. The News.com.au website, for example, runs a mix of 'news' stories from around Australia. Some are taken directly from the company's state and territory newspaper pages, most of which are written in the past tense and published online in the same format as they were in print. But the website also carries a continually updated selection of 'breaking news', in which at least the intros tend to be in present tense.

Geographic pointers are essential

Another major difference between publication on portable devices and online compared with traditional media relates to readership, or audience. Real estate agents say the three most important factors to take into account when buying and selling a property are 'location, location and location'. Similarly, readers of web news expect to be told in the first few words where a particular news event or circumstance happened. Online news reports must be written for national and international readers, viewers and listeners, as well as those within a news outlet's traditional circulation or broadcast area. Online reporters and sub-editors cannot take some things for granted which they could assume news consumers would know about in a major metropolitan or regional media market. Geographic and location details must be spelt out so they make sense to people from outside the immediate area because there are no constraints on circulation or broadcast range. This means generalising to some extent by inserting geographic pointers into news articles where possible, for example, referring to 'Altona in Melbourne's western suburbs', 'Chermside on Brisbane's north side', 'Mount Barker in the Adelaide hills' or 'Perth's Scarborough Beach'. Failure to include geographic pointers will frustrate and annoy readers. Take, for example, a news item published in the 'breaking news' section of Sydney-based *The Sunday Telegraph* website, in which the heading and intro said:

Two men bashed in gang attack

TWO men are in hospital, one with severe head injuries and fighting for his life, after being attacked by a gang of up to seven youths armed with baseball bats and other weapons (*The Sunday Telegraph* 7.45am, 2009).

With no geographic pointers in the heading or intro it would have been reasonable for NSW readers to expect the linked article referred to a nasty incident in their own state. But this was not so. Instead, as explained in the body of the article, the bashing happened on the South Gippsland Highway in Victoria.

There was a similar issue with the following heading and intro from the breaking news section of the online edition of the *The West Australian*, thewest.com.au:

Baby survives mum's suicide plunge

A 10-month-old baby survived being plunged from an eight-floor apartment by his suicidal mother by landing on her and bouncing off her body.

It was not until the second paragraph of the linked story that readers were given enough information to work out that the report had nothing to do with Western Australia, or even Australia. In fact the baby survived after his mother hit the footpath in Harlem, New York (thewest.com.au, 7.58am, 2013).

In contrast, the following story published on thewest.com.au the same morning left WA readers with no doubt about location:

Samaritan saves kitten from blowtorch

A lost kitten was rescued from a horrific fate when a Rockingham woman stopped a group of teenage boys from setting it on fire (thewest.com.au 11.22am, 2013).

Now consider the following sequences of stories, an early report then two updates several hours later, all published on the News.com.au website on April 11, 2013:

Mother accused of poisoning daughter, 4

A YOUNG mother will front court this morning accused of poisoning her little girl (News.com.au 10.45am, 2013).

Where did this happen? Was it in Australia? Overseas? It was not until opening the story link that there was finally a geographic clue in the second paragraph, where it emerged that the mother was from the Gold Coast in Queensland. (As an aside, while many readers would interpret the heading and intro as inferring the girl had been murdered, it was noted in the final paragraph that she was actually in a 'dangerous condition' in Brisbane's Royal Children's Hospital.)

Then came the first update. It was considerably more informative:

Qld mum appears in court over poisoning

A YOUNG Gold Coast mum charged with grievous bodily harm after her four-year-old daughter was poisoned has been remanded in custody (News. com.au 1.26pm, 2013).

Subsequently it was reported that the mother was from Arundel, she was 22, and appeared in Brisbane Magistrates Court.

But, strangely, geographic pointers were again missing from the heading and intro, leading into a second update:

Mother accused of poisoning daughter, 4, with alleged chemotherapy drugs bought online

A YOUNG mother has fronted court accused of poisoning her little girl over a 10-month period (News.com.au 2.50pm, 2013).

Contrast those approaches with the following headline and intro on the same day from the often maligned but nearly always interesting *Northern Territory News* website, www.ntnews.com.au. In addition to information in the intro about location, the heading warned of a zone to avoid:

Stay away from the water

A BIG crocodile is terrorising Tiwi islanders (ntnews.com.au 11.41am, 2013).

The story link opened to reveal a map showing Darwin, Melville Island (part of the Tiwi Island group) and the specific location people were warned to avoid. The second and third paragraphs offered highly specific geographic information:

It (the crocodile) is lurking around a beach at Pirlangimpi, on Melville Island, about 130km northwest of Darwin.

Rangers have found tracks of the 3m animal near a picnic table.

In something of an understatement, the story concluded:

Senior Sergeant Debbie Gabolinscy said: 'People should take care' (ntnews. com.au 11.41am, 2013).

The obvious point is that geographic pointers are essential and must come right at the top of a story—in the heading or intro. Also bear in mind that while the absence of geographic pointers in headlines and intros is annoying and counterproductive, blatantly wrong geographic information is even worse because it detracts from the credibility of news and current affairs sites. An embarrassing example of the latter was a report on the ABC's Sydney-based AM current affairs radio program, a transcript of which also appeared on the national broadcaster's website, on April 9, 2013, which said a boat carrying 'more than 60 Sri Lankans turned up in *Gladstone* harbour 400 kilometres north of Perth earlier this week, much to the surprise of local and authorities' (ABC AM 2013). In fact the boat had arrived in Geraldton Western Australia, not Gladstone, which is about 3700km across the continent on the east coast of Queensland! The mistake made the ABC look silly. It was later corrected in the AM transcript and its associated archived radio podcast but the damage had been done.

Cultural, ethnic and language differences

Journalists who write for the web and portable devices also need to become critically aware of cultural and ethnic differences that extend beyond their immediate regions. They must overcome their own ethnocentricity and any ideas about cultural, religious or social superiority. Cultural differences also mean that not everyone will have watched *The Simpsons* or *Home and Away* or will be aware of AFL or Rugby League. Some readers will not own computers, tablets, smartphones or televisions and will only have access to the web at work, school or university. Some will find references to exotic dancers, death or eating certain foods offensive. Others might wonder what it is like to live in houses with running water and a toilet, to travel long distances, or what is meant by fast food. Some will have little idea of what it is like to live in a democratic nation that is a federation as big and diverse as Australia. Others will have little idea about racial and sexual equality. And do not forget time differences—it is the opposite time of year in the northern hemisphere, while some nations to our east are literally a day 'behind' us. Similarly, Australia has three distinct mainland time zones and time differences change seasonally with the start and end of daylight saving.

Language is a significant consideration when writing for the web and mobile devices. English is the most commonly used online language globally, followed by Chinese and Spanish. Together they account for 59 per cent of all internet users, with English being the favoured online language of close to 30 per cent of users (Internet World Stats 2012b)—a figure set to grow as more people learn English as a second language. This growth is especially evident in Asia, with China having become the nation with the highest number of people who speak English (Coonan 2009, p. 31). But it is important to remember that many visitors to news sites do not speak or read English as their first language.

There are also many different varieties of English, with diverse pronunciations, spellings and nuances. It is therefore important to use simple, clear expressions and to avoid jargon, clichés and Australian colloquialisms. Be aware too that some words have different meanings in different cultures—in some cases attaching lewd or offensive connotations to words in one social context that are innocuous in another. Also avoid acronyms and abbreviations—they might be understood by readers in your local area, but may mean nothing to readers in other nations. This does not mean talking down to your audience or dumbing down your stories. But it does mean using simple words where possible, not using two words when one will do, avoiding ambiguous words, and using active but simple sentence constructions. Kiss (2003) said: 'The international platform of the web demands a more careful selection of words, making sure that language bridges both geographic and cultural gaps'.

As discussed in Chapter 8, all good writing is about choosing and using the right words. Finding exactly the right word, or the best word, is especially important when writing for the web, particularly when constructing headings and intros. The web and mobile platforms have also developed languages of their own so journalists should become familiar with, and fully understand terms such as 'portal', 'URL', 'app', 'keyword', 'HTML', and 'hyperlink'. Also be aware that because the language of the web, online and mobile journalism are still evolving, different news organisations sometimes use different terms to mean the same thing. For example, the story headings on the homepages of news websites are variously described as 'headlines', 'heads' and 'headings'. The first paragraph immediately after the 'heading' (the term used in this book) can be labelled as a 'stand-first', 'blurb', 'precede', 'teaser' or 'online intro' (the term used in this book). These appear on the homepages of news websites and are designed to entice readers to open a story. Some news websites repeat the headings and online intros in the actual story pages, while others use different headings and intros once a story is selected and its page is opened via a hyperlink.

In terms of technology, journalists who write for the web encounter a peculiar irony: although web-based news stories and stories written specifically for mobile devices tend to be short and to the point, or the same length as the same story published in associated print editions of newspapers or broadcast on radio or television, those stories could actually be much longer and more explanatory. This is because articles published online and for mobile devices do not have to be slashed to fit a particular 'news hole'. There are no printing or newsprint costs, no broadcast time-slots, and research has shown that if a longer story interests readers they will happily scroll (EyeTrack 2007). That said, it is more difficult to read text on a back-lit computer, tablet or mobile phone screen than it is to read text printed on a piece of paper illuminated by reflected light. Nielsen said that 'reading from computer screens is tiring for the eyes and about 25 percent slower than reading from paper' (Nielsen 2005).

The inverted pyramid: online version

As noted earlier in this chapter, the best approach when writing news for the web and mobile devices is to use the inverted pyramid model. You should also answer as many of the key questions of *what, when, where, who, why* and *how* as you can in ways you would like them explained to you—but, as explained in Chapters 3 and 8, do not try to explain everything in one paragraph!

The online version of the inverted pyramid, as shown in Figure 10.1, is slightly different from the generic version discussed in Chapter 3. Note how the heading and intro must work together and how they must contain a geographic pointer.

As Nielsen said, online readers tend to skip long intros, while short intros increase readership. His advice is: 'Kill the welcome mat and cut to the chase' (Nielsen 2007) and:

> … start the article by telling the reader the conclusion ('After long debate, the Assembly voted to increase state taxes by 10 per cent'), follow by the most important supporting information, and end by giving the background… readers can stop at any time and will still get the most important parts of the article (Nielsen 1996).

Figure 10.1 The online inverted pyramid

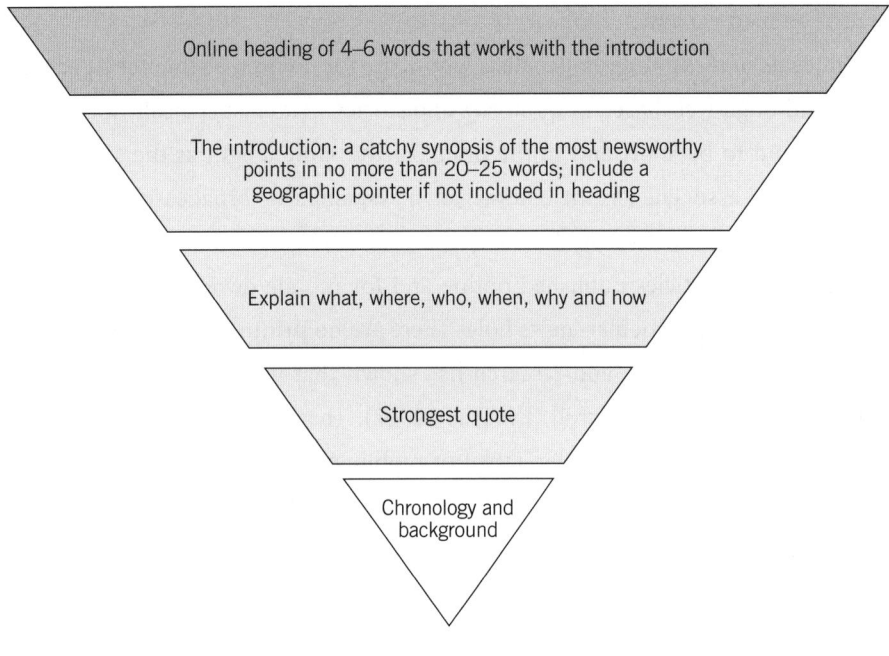

Online heading of 4–6 words that works with the introduction

The introduction: a catchy synopsis of the most newsworthy points in no more than 20–25 words; include a geographic pointer if not included in heading

Explain what, where, who, when, why and how

Strongest quote

Chronology and background

Online headings and intros

Whether writing for print, broadcast, mobile devices or the web, it is a truism that after you find your stories and gather the facts, you must be able to tell the story in a way that will grab your readers' attention and in a way they understand. It helps to know how to attract attention to your work online by being aware of the pathways readers use to find news online. They arrive at news websites via one of three main routes. The most common is by going directly to a news organisation's website or app (Pew Research Centre 2012a). The next most common is via a search engine such as Google. Others follow links from other websites and social media sites such as Facebook and Twitter. But whichever way readers make the journey, the idea is to capture them with a strong heading and intriguing intro on your site's entry page. You must entice them to swipe or click on a link that takes them to your story, then keep them with your work for as long as possible. It is crucial to remember that your story and all the work you have done researching and writing it is only a finger swipe or mouse click from oblivion.

Getting the words right in online story headings and intros is all the more important because there is no—or only a minimal—news hierarchy online. It is relatively rare for there to be enduring headlines or front-page splashes. There is no page three lead, no left-hand or right-hand pages, and no down-page leads. With the exception of significant breaking stories, many of which are reinforced with vision and sound, heading sizes and lengths on many news sites tend to be similar, with trivial stories about cats stuck up trees carrying the same emphasis as articles about major disasters or monumental international events. Without the visual clues newspaper and magazine readers take for granted, and in the absence of strong video or still images, words used in headlines and intros are your primary tool. Those words must work together to advertise your stories, sell them, and compel impatient and unforgiving readers to swipe, click their mouse or tap the touchpad to follow the link to your full story.

Online intros work best when they are active and contain a strong verb. It is essential to capture the key point(s) and arouse curiosity, but to do it without being smart or promising more than you deliver in the body of your article. It will help if you think about the strongest news values discussed in Chapter 3: significance, conflict, human interest, proximity, novelty and prominence. But do not try to introduce too many ideas. An ideal online intro will be a single sentence of no more than 20 to 25 words, which is a little shorter than a newspaper intro. It will be bright, to the point, and encapsulate the main point of the story.

Online headings should also be written in active voice. It is an obvious, but at times overlooked, rule that headings must make sense. They should be from four and six words and should also include a strong verb. Online headings work best in a single line of type. They take time and skill to write, with the templates on some online news sites either refusing to allow more than a set number of letters and spaces in a heading, or automatically rolling it over into a second line if there are too many characters.

When read as one, the heading and intro must complement each other and work together to paint a word picture. There should not be repetition of words or phrases in a heading and intro. Nielsen (2009) ranked the BBC's online news headings the best in the world and said they 'consistently do an awesome job'. He said, for example, he found the following headings in the 'other top stories' section of the BBC website during a single visit:

- Italy buries first quake victims
- Romania blamed over Moldova riots

You must entice readers to swipe their finger or click on a link that takes them to your story, then keep them with your work for as long as possible. It is crucial to remember that your story and all the work you have done researching and writing it is only a finger swipe or mouse click from oblivion.

- Ten arrested in UK anti-terrorism raids
- Villagers hurt in West Bank clash
- Mass Thai protest over leadership
- Iran accuses journalist of spying

Around the world in 38 words. The average headline consumed a mere five words and 34 characters. The amount of meaning they squeezed into this brief space is incredible: every word works hard for its living... each headline conveys the gist of the story on its own (Nielsen 2009).

Nielsen (2009) said people learning to write headings would benefit from making daily visits to the BBC news website and then applying the same standards to their own headings.

In summary:

— Online intros and headings should both be written in active voice—'the dog bit the boy', not 'the boy was bitten by the dog'.

— They must contain a strong verb—'run', not 'go for a run'.

— They must make sense.

— An intro should be no more than 20 to 25 words, and a heading between four and six words.

— Headings and intros must work together, must contain geographic pointers, and should not repeat each other.

This combination is attractive to readers. It is also attractive to the search engines that draw about half your audience, and will help your stories rank highly in search results.

Links in stories

Good hyperlinks enhance online news articles and add depth and value, but unintelligent links are an annoying distraction. Linking helps you take your readers outside their local region, can provide them with relevant expert opinion and help them place a story geographically through the use of maps and other information. As well as linking highlighted words in the text of an article to other stories on your own news organisation's website—potentially to earlier or related articles about the same or a similar topic or issue—links provide a pathway to external websites of interest. In addition to linking on words, you can also insert links into photographs and graphics. When linking, think about the sort of extra information likely to interest your readers, or information that would help them put your story into a wider context.

Providing logical and intuitive links involves thought about the words or images you are going to link on. They should be nouns whenever possible. Avoid linking on verbs. And only make a link if there is a real point to it; there is no value in linking just for the sake of linking. Among other things, there is the risk that a link will sidetrack readers and they will not return to your story or your news site.

Online mistakes

It would be a rare print journalist who has not opened a newspaper or magazine the morning after publication and had a sick feeling in the pit of the stomach when discovering a ghastly mistake in a story she or he had written. If the error was serious, the overwhelming feeling is one of wanting to call the story back and fix it—something impossible in the world of print, a realm in which every embarrassing lapse can be flaunted, mocked and decried by critics or—worse— eagle-eyed lawyers intent on fuelling a defamation action. But make a mistake online, realise quickly enough, and a posted story can be taken down, fixed and republished in minutes. This is one of the advantages of writing for the web.

On the other hand, make an error in print and it will only circulate in a limited area, but make a mistake online and it instantly circulates nationally and globally. That speed of circulation and its global reach also have their own problems—anyone anywhere can print your story, copy it, keep it, or republish it in a bulk email, on YouTube, Facebook, Twitter, or post it on another website. It is also possible that the story will be automatically archived. And, as discussed in Chapter 15, a legally damaging online blunder that does slip through is likely to attract a higher defamation payout than a mistake in print, with the rule of thumb being that the wider the publication, the larger the damages!

DISCUSSION POINTS

1   If you were a journalist working for a regional newspaper, would it really be all that important to include geographic pointers in the headings and intros of stories you loaded on the paper's website when you do not need to include them in the print edition? Why or why not?

2   Some of the most brilliant headlines you see in newspapers involve dry humour and words with more than one meaning. Why then are so many headings on web news stories so boring?

3   List five words that we use as regular and non-offensive figures of speech in Australia which would have a very different meaning if used in another English-speaking nation.

4   What sort of journalism is best suited to the web—variations of text-based, radio or video? Why?

5   Should we agree with Jakob Nielsen's very favourable opinion of the BBC's news website, or is the site boring and old-fashioned? Why?

6   Many online news websites have a listing of 'most popular' articles and 'trending' articles.

   a) Why categorise articles in such ways?

   b) What actually makes the listed articles more popular than others?

   c) Is popularity any guide to quality? Why?

NEWS PRACTICE POINTS

1   Go to the breaking news sections of the websites for *The Age* <www.theage.com.au>, the *Daily Mail* <www.dailymail.co.uk>, *The Washington Post* <www.washingtonpost. com> and *The Courier-Mail* <www.couriermail.com.au>. Explain which sites you consider the best and worst and why.

2   Go to the BBC's Asia news website <www.bbc.co.uk/news/world/asia/>. How many of the stories on the opening page have geographic pointers in the headings and/or intros? How many do not? Also look at the headings and intros on the opening page. What is the average word count for each?

3   *The Mirror* <www.mirror.co.uk> and *The Sun* <www.thesun.co.uk> in the UK have different ways of attracting readers from those commonly seen in Australia.

   a) What are they?

   b) Does it look as though they work?

   c) How would the same recipes work in Australia?

4   Look at the following US newspaper websites: *The New York Times* <www.nytimes. com>, *The Washington Post* <www.washingtonpost.com> and *The Christian Science Monitor* <www.csmonitor.com>. What hints can you see in these websites which could help explain why newspaper circulation in the US is in decline?

5   After looking at the websites listed in Practice Points 1 to 4, what role do you think photos and graphics play in drawing visitors to news websites generally and also to particular stories? Find an Australian news website you think has an appealing balance of images, headings and intros on its opening page. What is it in the mix that makes your chosen site appealing?

6   What was the most recent really big news story to break? When was it covered best: a) in the early stages while it was still breaking? b) later that same day? c) the next day? What conclusions, if any, can you draw from your answers to a, b and c?

7   Get a print copy of *The Australian* newspaper. Find five significant articles from different states or territories and write new headings and intros for each to make them attractive to online readers in accord with the guidelines explained in this chapter.

8   Can you recognise the inverted pyramid when you see it in an online article? Open a Word document and, at the top, copy and paste four online articles you have found which are excellent examples of the use of the inverted pyramid, then do the same for four in which the inverted pyramid was not, but should have been, used.

VIRGINIA TRIOLI _____

Virginia Trioli has been presenting ABC *News Breakfast* since its debut on ABC2 in 2008. She has also been a regular panellist on the ABC's *Insiders* program.

Virginia joined ABC Local Radio in 2001 from *The Bulletin*, Australia's oldest weekly news magazine. For nine years before that she was a news reporter, features writer, assistant news editor and columnist with *The Age* in Melbourne, establishing a reputation as a strong independent voice on politics, social issues and the arts.

Virginia is the author of *Generation F: Sex, Power and the Young Feminist* published in 1996, a riposte to Helen Garner's *First Stone*. She has won two Walkley Awards, one in 1995 for her business reporting, and another in 2001 for her interview with former defence minister Peter Reith over the Children Overboard issue.

1 How did you get your first job as a journalist?

I applied for the cadet intake with *The Age*. I sat the exam and didn't do spectacularly well at it, but a friend of mine had spoken to one of the senior editors and suggested that they take a chance on me, and they did. Oh dear, it really is 'who you know' in this world, isn't it?

2 What advice would you offer a beginning journalist?

Be the most energetic, willing, thoughtful and ACCURATE reporter you can possibly be, and you will find a place. I always want to work with people who have an optimistic attitude, love chasing a good story until they run it into the ground, and who, as my old cadet counsellor used to say, 'Get it right!!'. That's the most essential thing.

3 What is the role of journalism in 21st-century Australian society?

The same as it's ever been: to shine a light in dark places. All that's changed is the technology, and while that poses particular problems for some outlets like papers, it presents phenomenal opportunities for a young reporter.

4 What are the key things a journalism student should learn during their studies?

Accuracy, accuracy, accuracy. And how to get someone to tell you what they really should not: for that you will need to be intelligent, well-read, subtle, and a very good listener. Practise those skills.

5 Is there anything else you would like to say to journalism students and/or about journalism as a profession?

It's the best job in the world: it will require you to work very hard, and complaining will at times seem like a comforting and useful thing to do—but don't. They're paying you to dig out and present issues that are at the cutting edge of what matters to society. So if you get the chance to practise this profession, enjoy every minute of it.

LUCY CARTER

Lucy Carter is currently a bi-media reporter for ABC News and ABC News 24 She has also worked as a sports presenter for ABC News 24 and was the news director at triple j for five years.

1 How did you get your first job as a journalist?

Through my journalism degree at Charles Sturt University in Bathurst, I was lucky enough to win a job as a cadet at National Radio News, an on-campus teaching service that provided the news to numerous community radio stations around Australia. At around the same time, I won a month-long internship with ABC Radio Current Affairs, which in turn led to some paid shifts as an overnight reporter for ABC Radio News in Sydney. After a few months there, I was successful in my application for a full-time position with triple j news.

2 What advice would you offer a beginning journalist?

Don't be afraid to ask stupid or obvious questions in interviews—looking silly to one person is much better than looking silly to many in a published/broadcast piece. Fetch coffees for people willing to give you help or advice. Don't trust Wikipedia as a source. Don't turn your nose up at graveyard shifts—getting ANY paid work is a blessing when you're starting out. Volunteer at as many different places as you can so you can work out what you like. Always check your grammar and spelling, as nothing makes you look more unprofessional than basic errors.

3 What is the role of journalism in 21st-century Australian society?

Though technology may be pushing the industry forwards and in different directions, I think the role of journalism itself remains unchanged as a 'fourth estate', an independent and unbiased watchdog of the legal, political and business events of the world. Journalism may now be delivered to people in a plethora of different formats, but I think readers, listeners and viewers still look to the news media as a body that keeps an eye on, investigates and reports back on the events, people and places of the world.

4 Journalism is being changed and challenged by technology. What are your thoughts about the future of journalism in Australia?

The way journalism and technology is moving forward makes it a really exciting industry to work in at the moment. Social media and especially Twitter mean that news headlines are available instantly, and more and more people are connecting with journalists and their information personally. Twitter also means that finding people who are engaging with an issue you may be researching is easier than ever.

The progression of technology does have its downsides—newspapers in their old format are on the decline, and many digital news outlets are struggling to find ways to make money from their content. Despite this, the future looks bright—young smart people are finding new platforms for news and current affairs, and jobs that couldn't even be conceived of five years ago are now promising options for graduates.

5 What are the key things a journalism student should learn during their studies?

I think the most important thing for a journalist to have is a mind that is engaged and interested in the world's events. No degree can really 'teach' that, but studying a few politics or law subjects is useful in kick-starting it. Learning the basics about the equipment and technology journalists use is also valuable, as is learning to research a given topic quickly and effectively. If you can pick up a good sense of humour and a strong work ethic along the way, it'll help you enormously.

6 Is there anything else you would like to say to journalism students and/or about journalism as a profession?

Take the time to get to know and hear the stories of the senior journalists in whichever newsroom you end up working in. They will be some of the most interesting people you will ever meet, and will have the advice you need to help you find your feet.

GARY KEMBLE _____

Gary Kemble is the social media coordinator for ABC News. He joined the ABC in 2002 and has worked in a range of roles, including producing, sub-editing and reporting. You can follow Gary on Twitter @garykemble and subscribe to his public updates on Facebook <www.facebook.com/gary.kemble>.

1 How did you get your first job as a journalist?

My first job was as a casual reporter with the *Wynnum Herald* (part of the Quest Newspapers group in Queensland). It was one or two days a week, and I started before I had graduated. I got offered the job because another student passed up the opportunity.

2 What advice would you offer a beginning journalist?

Have your goals firmly in mind, but be flexible. When I was offered the casual work with Quest Newspapers, it wasn't my 'dream job' but it lead to a full-time position with Quest Newspapers, which in turn led to work in the UK. When I returned to Australia, I applied for and was offered a job with the *Toowoomba Chronicle*. At the time, moving to Toowoomba wasn't high on my 'to-do' list but I decided to take the job and ended up having a great time

and learning a lot, which helped me find work during my second stint overseas.

3 What is the role of journalism in 21st-century Australian society?

As it always has been—to inform and entertain.

4 What are your thoughts about the impacts on journalism of changing communication technologies?

There's a lot of opportunity but also many challenges in the current media environment. Commercial media outlets are struggling to make money from journalism. The *Global Mail* experience shows it's challenging building an audience for quality journalism in an increasingly fractured environment. And at the ABC, we're facing the challenge of delivering quality content on an ever-increasing range of platforms/services, with the same level of funding.

5 What key things should a journalism student learn?

My background is social media, so I think all journalism students should learn how to use social media as a news-gathering and news-delivery tool. Start building your network on Twitter and Facebook. Instagram is becoming a key source of breaking news photos. Reddit can be a major driver of web traffic, so get to know that one as well. Of course, by the time this is printed there will probably be others. The key is to be across new platforms and try them out, even if it's only for a little while.

6 Is there anything else you would like to say to journalism students and/or about journalism as a profession?

Journalism is an incredibly wide-ranging profession and can take you anywhere—literally as well as metaphorically. I've worked as a sports and general news reporter for a local weekly newspaper, a sports writer and sub-editor for a bi-weekly newspaper in the UK, as a sub-editor for a monthly computer magazine, and pretty much every position going at ABC News Online, during my 10+ years here. My current role—social media coordinator for ABC News—wasn't even a twinkle in anyone's eye when I graduated in 1995. Despite the challenges facing the industry, this is an incredibly exciting time to be a journalist.

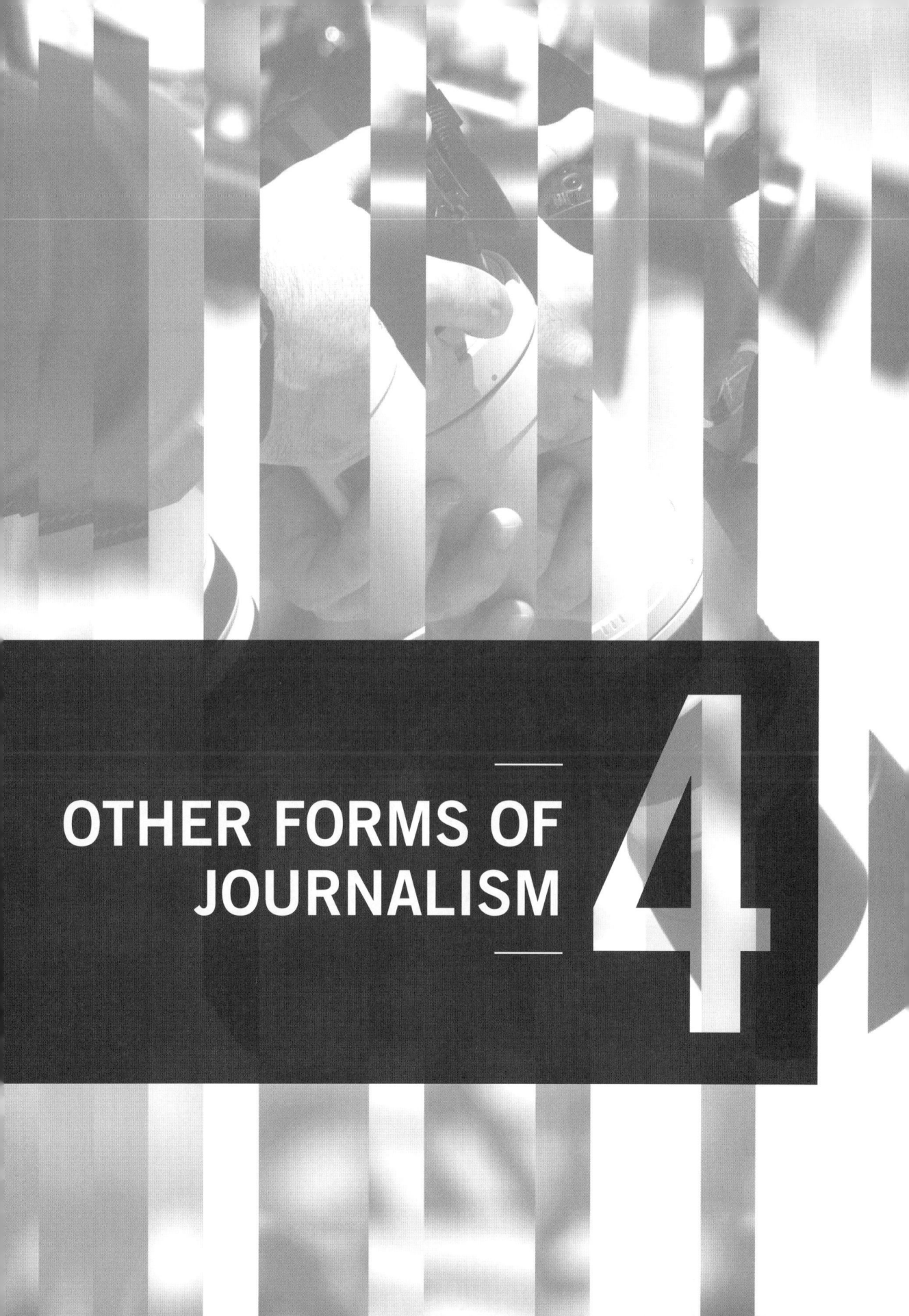

OTHER FORMS OF
JOURNALISM

4

FEATURE WRITING

When something can be read without effort, great effort has gone into its writing.

Enrique Jardiel Poncela, playwright and novelist, 1901–52

OBJECTIVES

After reading this chapter you will understand:

» How feature writing differs from news writing
» That writing creatively involves painting images with words
» Different types of feature articles
» How feature introductions and intros differ from news intros
» How to structure features
» Writing conclusions for features.

If there is a point at which text-based journalism intersects with art, it is in feature writing. Skilled feature writers paint vivid pictures and tell fascinating stories. They work on larger canvases with richer textures and use more words than news writing allows. They draw on imagery, description, insight, observation, analogy, empathy and characterisation to create pictures, smells, sensations and sounds inside readers' heads. They trigger our emotions and inform our decisions.

Little wonder then that feature writing is one of the most satisfying forms of journalism. But as in all professional writing, feature writers must always write for readers, not themselves. Within that imperative, however, there is literally more room for creativity and flair when working on features. Viewed from that perspective, it is easy to see why so many leading journalists over the years have split their professional work between journalism and creative writing. Mark Twain, for example, was an acerbic journalist but a wonderfully descriptive and perceptive novelist. His classics *The Adventures of Tom Sawyer* and *Adventures of Huckleberry*

Finn paint enduring word pictures in the minds of all who read them. Banjo Paterson was another who had an uncanny ability to evoke pictures with words in his news reports, poems and prose. A lawyer, journalist, poet, short story writer and newspaper editor, he reported on the Boer War in South Africa and the aftermath of the Boxer Rebellion in China. In his later years, Paterson was also a freelance sports reporter and feature writer. The powerful imagery he wove into works such as *The Man from Snowy River*, *Mulga Bill's Bicycle*, *Waltzing Matilda* and *Clancy of the Overflow* is legendary. So too are the word pictures created by Daniel Defoe. As noted in Chapter 1, Defoe is regarded as both the first English journalist and the first English novelist. There is a wonderful example of how Defoe triggers readers' imaginations with deceptively simple words in the following passage from his novel *Robinson Crusoe*. It recounts how the castaway hero Crusoe is at first perplexed, then spooked, as he discovers he is no longer alone on the island where he led a solitary existence for the past 15 years:

> It happened one day about noon, going towards my boat, I was exceedingly surprised with the print of a man's naked foot on the shore, which was very plain to be seen in the sand. I stood like one thunder-struck, or as if I had seen an apparition. I listened, I looked around me; I could hear nothing, nor see anything. I went up the rising ground to look farther. I went up the shore and down the shore; but it was all one, I could see no other impression but that one. I went to it again to see if there were any more, and to observe if it might not be my fancy; but there was no room for that, for there was exactly the very print of a foot, toes, heel, and every part of a foot;—how it came thither I knew not, nor could in the least imagine. But after innumerable fluttering thoughts, like a man perfectly confused and out of myself, I came home to my fortification, not feeling, as we say, the ground I went on, but terrified to the last degree, looking behind me at every two or three steps, mistaking every bush and tree, and fancying every stump at a distance, to be a man... (Defoe n.d., p. 88).

Defoe wrote that passage prior to April 1719, when *Robinson Crusoe* was first published. Close to three centuries later the imagery is as powerful, and as relevant to the art of feature writing in the 21st century, as the day it was written. Why? Because Defoe was a master artist whose palette brimmed with words. Noticeably, there are plenty of verbs, few adjectives, and no flowery phrases in his description. His words are ordinary on their own, yet in combination they paint images of a pristine beach, a male footprint, and a castaway gripped in a spiral of fear as his imagination plays havoc with his mind. At different points in the passage you can almost literally hear the waves breaking on the sand, seabirds calling, and Crusoe's heart pounding as he makes his way to his 'fortification'.

Feature writing and news values

The three journalist-cum-creative writers mentioned here—plus others such as Henry Lawson, Charles Dickens, Rudyard Kipling, George Orwell, Ernest Hemingway, CJ Dennis, and Oscar Wilde—each had an interest in common: an abiding and intuitive fascination with other people, something evident in their almost magical ability to make characters come alive. Their work as journalists and creative writers was underpinned by human interest—the news value, more than any other, which informs feature writing. Gifted feature writer, newspaper columnist, sub-editor and journalism educator Jane Fynes-Clinton believes a deep understanding of fellow humans lies at the heart of all good feature writing:

> The underpinning of any good feature, whether it be on a financial matter or social one, is people. People need to read about others' experience or thoughts to connect with the piece. They need to feel and see and hear about what people experience to be moved and feel they are getting into the subject matter. Even the driest topic needs a people component in a feature. I think the idea that 'news tells but features show', is deeply true. If feature writers bear this in mind, they will not fall into the trap of reeling off information rather than colouring in the lines (Fynes-Clinton 2010).

The dominance of human interest as the foremost news value associated with effective feature writing does not mean other values are not important too. What it does mean, though, is that the other news values described in Chapter 3 have most weight when viewed through the lens of human interest. Values particularly relevant to feature writing, and which work symbiotically with human interest, are novelty (or the unusual), proximity (particularly in emotional, cultural and social senses), conflict, significance (especially in relation to things such as diseases or disasters that impact many people) and prominence. Virtually every appealing feature article will reflect a mix of several of those values, as they add depth and colour to a theme with a strong human-interest element. In doing so, features are more likely to lean towards explaining questions about why and how whatever happened to whom, than focus on what, when and where—something of a reversal of the priorities of news writing.

Personal traits of effective feature writers

Feature writers need to be 'street-wise' and to have gained a degree of wisdom as a consequence of life experiences. In addition to being skilled and creative in the selection and use of words and having a deep interest in other people and what makes them tick, good feature writers also need outstanding listening skills, strong imaginations, well-honed powers of observation, an eye for fine detail, a healthy outlook on life, and a genuine ability to empathise with others—as distinct from feeling sorry for them. A wicked sense of humour helps too.

The best feature writers are sensitive, imaginative, intuitive, curious and artistic. In addition to being skilled at explaining things to readers in ways they would want them explained to themselves, feature writers must be honest with readers; being willing to reveal things about themselves and to share insights into how they personally perceive the world. On the other hand, they must be tough and have enough confidence in themselves to withstand the odd nasty barb from readers who dislike what they write.

Different types of feature articles

Many journalists who write feature articles have developed specialised expertise in particular fields over many years. Political journalists, for example, will write features based on their analysis of current issues or political trends; environmental and health specialists write features explaining the latest scientific discoveries and debates; entertainment specialists write about music, art, movies and plays; and investigative journalists write about crime, scams and corruption. As discussed in Chapter 18, specialist writers who have worked in particular news rounds have obviously developed expertise and a strong interest, if not a passion, for the areas they write about. Many also have relevant academic qualifications and/or industry experience. But there are also feature writers who are generalists. They tend to be wonderful writers with broad interests and an ability to understand and explain often-complex stories.

Like all journalists, feature writers variously inform, educate and entertain— often fulfilling two, or all, of those functions in the same article. After all, common sense dictates that a long article which entertains while informing or educating is much more likely to be read by more people, and in more depth, than a dry piece that simply informs or educates.

Within the bounds of these three media functions, features can be broadly categorised into different groups depending on whether they are news features, issues-based, personal profiles, reflect lifestyles and indulgences (including travel) or broad human interest.

NEWS FEATURES

News features ride on the back of a current news story or issue. They explain background, explore different angles and aspects of the story, perhaps speculate on potential outcomes and future events, and examine why things happened as they did. Features may also reveal if people were at fault—who could have prevented some tragic event from happening and who should be called to account. They might explain complex technical concepts and issues in plain English, consider if there were lessons to be learnt from past events, or simply flesh out a story in greater detail.

News features sometimes run beside a news story in the news pages of a paper, or, more commonly, in the middle pages of a paper where there is more room, or in a separate news magazine. Depending on the nature of the news story they relate to, they might be written and appear on the same day the news story breaks, or at a later date. An example of a delayed news feature would be a detailed article about a crime which could not be published when the crime happened or during a subsequent trial because of the limitations of *sub judice* contempt, explained in Chapter 16, but which can be published immediately after a related trial ends.

ISSUES-BASED FEATURES

Issues-based features are closely related to news features. They often deal with trends, broad problems, reactions—or lack of action—by authorities, and social, cultural and legal issues. Examples of topics include the environment, public health and medicine, natural disaster planning and management, town planning, terrorism, flood and bushfire mitigation, sustainability, illegal immigration, energy use and conservation, transport, safety, climate change, interest rates and housing prices. Political analysis, interpretation of political public opinion polls, and detailed opinion and comment pieces are the most common features in this category. Interestingly, issues-based features comprise such a broad category that the work of staff journalists is often supplemented by columns and features written by freelance journalists and guest writers, many of whom are experts in the areas they write about.

PROFILES

Profile features focus on individuals who have done an unusual thing, dealt with a difficult experience, or are inspirational in some way. There is a saying among journalists that everyone has a story to tell, a truism borne out by the fact that subjects of profile features may be of interest because they are prominent, or in many cases because they are not at all prominent—just ordinary people who have done something extraordinary.

Profiles can be some of the most difficult, yet most rewarding, features to write. In effect, the writer becomes a medium through which the subject presents themselves to the world. So when working on a profile, more than in any other type of feature, a writer must unobtrusively slip into the background. The task is to gain the trust of the subject and create a dialogue between the subject and readers, not between the journalist and readers. To do this successfully, a journalist needs to literally 'get inside the head' of the person they are writing about, and to intuitively know when to probe and when to pull back. The key is to be a finely tuned listener who is non-judgmental, open-minded, genuine and empathetic.

LIFESTYLE AND INDULGENCE

Lifestyle and indulgence features are common in print and online editions of weekend newspapers and their colour magazines. Typically they deal with relationships, food and wine, homes and gardens, hobbies, markets, sport and relaxation, motoring, fashion and travel. Most are written by journalists with specialised knowledge and expertise in a field. Many features in this category inspire some sort of action, influence choices, or have other impacts on how people spend money or make lifestyle decisions. Restaurant reviews, for example, may stir interest in a particular type or style of food, not just the restaurant they are written about. Motoring articles influence car buyers; gardening articles serve as reminders of seasonal plantings and other tasks; travel features influence choices of destination and means of travel; features about food that contain recipes affect family menus; and features on diets spark fads.

The stories of ordinary men, women and children—brushes with fame and tragedy, funny experiences and sad, triumphs and disasters, medical miracles and botched surgery, tall tales and true—are the stuff of broad human-interest features because they are stories readers identify with and stories against which we can benchmark our own lives.

Because of their power to influence readers, writers of lifestyle and indulgence features have a major responsibility to respect the trust readers place in them. Information must be reliable, accurate and objective. In accord with the Media Entertainment and Arts Alliance (MEAA)'s *Journalists' Code of Ethics*, feature writers must be upfront about any 'freebies', or 'junkets' as they are known. Readers must be told—usually at least in a disclaimer at the end of an article—if a journalist stayed at such-and-such a resort, visited a named attraction, ate at a specific restaurant, wore brand-name clothes, had use of a vehicle provided by a car company, or flew with an airline because there was some sort of special deal, or if anything else that would normally cost money was free. Readers can then make up their own minds about how objective, or otherwise, they perceive a writer to have been.

As an aside here, travel writing is seen by many as one of journalism's prized rewards. It can be fun and a great way to see at least some of the world while being paid to write interesting and descriptive features. But the realities of travelling and writing are not nearly as idyllic as many people imagine. In fact numerous aspiring travel writers have happily turned to other pastures after a stint of living out of a battered travel bag, waiting for delayed flights, cramming into seats next to stinky fellow travellers, being driven around strange places by suicidal taxi drivers, washing underwear on the run, and suffering the miserable consequences of ingesting unspeakable things disguised as food. Trips are often rushed. Schedules tend to be extremely demanding, and if they involve long flights and moving across time zones, jet lag takes a real toll. In addition, a travel writer must become skilled in dealing with dodgy locals—both official and otherwise—most of whom were obviously trained from birth as thieves. You may also find yourself in places where medical facilities, safety regulations, personal security and transport are at best limited, if not totally absent or downright dangerous.

On the bright side, there is local colour everywhere. And once away from the glitzy tourist traps, you soon learn that most ordinary people the world over are decent and have stories to tell. Describing landscapes, customs and scenery alien to you—and which you know will also be alien to most of your readers but will interest them—can be a rewarding challenge, especially if you match your

The stories of ordinary men, women and children—brushes with fame and tragedy, funny experiences and sad, triumphs and disasters, medical miracles and botched surgery, tall tales and true—are the stuff of broad human-interest features because they are stories readers identify with and stories against which we can benchmark our own lives.

words with your own photographs. It can also be extremely challenging trying to find a new angle and something fresh about the most visited places on earth. How, for example, do you find a fresh angle to write about the Egyptian pyramids, Eiffel Tower, Taj Mahal, Niagara Falls, Uluru or Great Wall of China?

BROAD HUMAN-INTEREST FEATURES

Broad human-interest features differ from profiles. Frequently, the underlying story or theme will draw together several people. Often written for no other reason than they concern interesting identities who have been involved in things that fascinate readers, these features tend to focus on an event, issue or activities rather than a life story. As noted earlier in this chapter, it is a simple fact of human nature that people like reading about other people. Even if they do not want to actually keep up with the Joneses, at least they want to know what the Joneses are up to. While a writer should be careful, human curiosity feeds to some extent on gossip, intrigue and a desire to know if the faces prominent citizens show the world are real or a mask. It also leads us to want to know and understand how others coped with difficult—sometimes life-challenging or life-changing—events and situations.

At the extremes of broad human-interest features are articles touching on the lives of saints and sinners. Think of features about celebrity love, lust and passion—and think of names such as Brangelina, Jennifer Aniston, Tiger Woods and Paris Hilton. At the other extreme, think about devotion to community—and names such as Mary MacKillop, Fred Hollows and Caroline Chisholm. The latter are long dead, but their names live on in the collective national memory and, from time to time, still inform feature articles and inspire readers. Between the extremes are ordinary men, women and children. Their stories—brushes with fame and tragedy, funny experiences and sad, triumphs and disasters, medical miracles and botched surgery, tall tales and true—are the stuff of broad human-interest features because they are stories readers identify with and stories against which we can benchmark our own lives.

Researching for features

Researching for a feature article is similar in most ways to researching a news story, and the approaches discussed in Chapter 6 can guide you. Some features are reactive and others proactive. Those that are reactive deal with current events and issues, and may involve limited research—maybe only interviewing and observation, and nothing more. Proactive features are likely to be based on deeper research. They might require painstaking and persistent investigation, sometimes even the collection of data and information over months and years. As discussed in Chapter 12, investigations can depend on the use of computer-assisted research techniques; finding and analysing primary documents; studying relevant history; checking geographic facts; finding experts willing to talk; tracking down friends, relatives and enemies of a subject; seeking comment from authorities; sifting through archives; fact checking; and much more.

Whether a feature and the research informing it is simple or complex, it will invariably entail interviewing at some point. One good tip is to regard every news story as having the potential to feed a feature. When you interview someone interesting for an immediate news story, listen for a throwaway line that might raise more questions and lead to a feature. Maybe a news story is so interesting and intriguing it demands a feature to help explain it. If it is not possible to ask extra questions at the time you research the news story—possibly because there are journalists from rival media outlets in earshot, or simply because there is not time—follow up later.

Interviewing aside, Ricketson warns against doing so much research that you find yourself running out of time to write your article. He said:

> Most journalists enjoy researching feature stories. They meet interesting and famous people, they learn new things, they get out of the office... True, exceptional journalism relies on making that extra call, but equally true, journalists need to learn when they have enough material and how to give themselves enough time to do it justice (Ricketson 2004, p. 146).

Writing features

You do not have to be a literary genius to write a good feature article. If you can write news in a sound journalistic style, you have a creative streak and some of the other key qualities discussed earlier in this chapter, then you can write features. The best possible preparation for becoming a feature writer is a solid background in news reporting. By reporting on courts, councils and general news, journalists will have learnt the importance of accuracy, attribution, fairness and balance. They will have gained insights into the ways of the world, and human nature. The experience of writing news will also have taught them to use words carefully, discipline their writing, and never try to foist their own opinions on others. As Brendan Hennessy said in his book *Writing Feature Articles*:

> Of course the basic talent has to be there but more people possess it than are conscious of the fact. It is the kind of talent that has to be identified and goaded into action. The difference between successful and unsuccessful writers of non-fiction for newspapers and magazines is mainly a matter of application (Hennessy 1997, p. 1).

Stovall said feature writers must be just as disciplined as news writers, with the major difference between features and news being that features contain greater detail and more description (Stovall 2005, p. 142). Mencher said feature writers should let 'the actions and comments of the personalities' tell the story (Mencher 1997, p. 186). Conveying a sense of how people look, speak, smell, what they were wearing, where they live and why they live there can all be highly relevant. So can describing a landscape and, for example, the sounds of wind, rain, and water gurgling in a stream or crashing on a beach. Do not be afraid to appeal to all the physical senses—sight, sound, smell, touch and taste—as well as to readers' sixth sense: their intuition. But in doing so, be aware that journalists who are new to feature writing commonly make the mistake of thinking creativity and description hinge on the use of adjectives and adverbs. Nothing could be further from the truth. As Fynes-Clinton said:

> The worst thing a feature writer can do is fall into the adjective pot. Ladling on words that describe does not add anything. Instead, often, the strongest verbs can help tell the story more effectively. But having said that, there are times, when used sparingly, adjectives are handy—just not in gross groups (Fynes-Clinton 2010).

One of the fundamental rules of journalism is to do the best job you can in the time you have at your disposal to do it in— then you must let an article go, and move on to the next one.

Also be aware that feature writing is time-consuming. This can be a challenge, especially until you gain experience. But you are writing for publication in a print or online version of a newspaper or magazine, not writing a novel, and they have deadlines. So bear in mind that one of the fundamental rules of journalism is to do the best job you can in the time you have at your disposal to do it in—then you must let an article go, and move on to the next one.

Feature introductions and intros

While the introduction to a feature article serves the same purpose as the intro to a news story—to entice readers and make them want to read on—a feature introduction is often different from a news story intro. While an effective news intro is usually a single stand-alone sentence of no more than 20 to 25 words, the introduction to a feature story is more likely to consist of an intro sentence, which can be up to 30 words, and several other sentences. It can run over one or two paragraphs. Thus a feature can have an intro, and an introduction. An introduction is introduced by an intro sentence, similar to the way in which a news story is led by an intro.

To avoid confusion as you read through the rest of this chapter, the word 'intro' is used to refer to the opening sentence of a feature article, while the word 'introduction' refers to the intro sentence plus the other sentences that open an article.

A good feature story intro sentence is like a tender morsel of bait to a fish—it lures readers, then snares them into at least wanting to read the introduction. Shorter is usually better than longer in an intro sentence. A few well-chosen words can have great impact and be the perfect hook on which to hang a feature. It is then the job of the rest of the introduction to lure readers into wanting to read the main part of your work; to be enchanted by your writing, the research you have done, and story you are telling. If the intro and then the introduction do not entice readers, you have wasted your time. Therefore the intro and introduction must read well and not be obscure, too clever, or so arty that no one except you understands them.

An example of how an intro sentence invites human interest while setting the scene for the remainder of an effective feature article introduction is evident in the following opening lines of a feature published in the print and online editions of *QWeekend* magazine of February 23, 2013:

> It's 9.30am on a Sunday, and the mood inside the school building in Bandung, Indonesia, is festive. Mothers in headscarves and bright lipstick chat and eat coconut cakes. Javanese music thumps from an assembly hall. There are 400 people crammed into the primary school's ground floor. It's hot, noisy and chaotic, and almost everyone is smiling. Twelve-year-old Suminah is not. She looks like she wants to punch somebody (Haworth 2013).

Note that the intro sentence at the start of the foregoing introduction consisted of only 17 words. There were also relatively few words in the intro sentence of the following introduction from *The Weekend Australian Magazine* of March 13–14, 2010:

> The soldier breathes loud and fast as he lays a timed charge on an explosive in a Baghdad street. 'I want these people to know if they are going to leave a bomb on the side of the road for us, we're just going to blow up their f...ing road,' he growls, walking away. Before he can reach safety, an Iraqi punches a code into a mobile phone. The explosion sends the solider flying in a cloud of dust and debris (Lamb 2010, p. 21).

Now consider the following from the Inquirer section of *The Australian* on March 6–7, 2010:

> It is a night of glittering statues, pristine red carpets and gracious speeches. But behind the air-kisses, smiles and displays of magnanimity at the annual Oscars ceremony, dirty, though often expensive battles go on, with competitors more than willing to knife each other if it means taking home a trophy. After all, winning an Oscar means more business at the box office and higher fees in the future. Not to mention the bragging rights and publicity (Ayres 2010, p. 3).

In contrast, think about what readers are likely to make of the following introduction from *The Weekend Australian Magazine* of March 6–7, 2010:

> The fetching pink-and-purple 500-Euro note has many fascinating features. Completing the architectural themes that begin with the classical depictions of the humble €5 note, the €500 sports a window in the modern style on the front, and a stylised version of the Pont de Normandie in France on the reverse. It is also dripping with security measures as befits the world's second-highest denomination note, which is equivalent to $A756 (only the little used 1000 Swiss Franc, worth $1034 [sic], has a higher value); watermarks, hologram strip, reflective glossy stripe, EURion constellation, matted surface, bar-codes, ultraviolet ink, perforations, raised printing, colour-changing ink and a serial number (Graham & Luck 2010, p. 3).

But what is the article about? Why read further? Seven paragraphs after this tedious introduction bereft of even the slightest hint of human interest, brave readers who struggled on—or perhaps just those with a riveting interest in banknotes—were told the €500 note was a favourite of drug smugglers and money launderers.

Structuring a feature

After the introduction comes the body of the feature followed by its conclusion. The fact that there is a conclusion, or 'closer', is another difference between feature writing and news writing, at least if news is written to the inverted pyramid model in which articles simply end and there is no identifiable conclusion. Fynes-Clinton believes that identifying a theme for a feature helps determine its structure because:

> Establishing the reason for the piece from the start of writing makes it easier to order the points that need to be made, and inspires the writer to write around those points. It also makes it easier to discard information that does not tie in with the message or theme, however interesting that information may seem. If it does not help convey the message or illustrate the story, into the delete abyss it must go (Fynes-Clinton 2010).

In addition to establishing a theme, US journalist and journalism educator Carol Rich advises feature writers to set the tone of an article from the start. She said:

> Hard-news stories often have an objective, factual tone, mostly an absence of mood. But in storytelling, you should create a 'tone', or 'mood', such as happiness, sadness, mystery, excitement or some other emotion. You don't need to tell the reader that the mood of the place was festive or mournful. You can show it by the images you select for your story. Another way of creating tone is by your writing style (Rich 2003, p. 22).

Sometimes journalists say a story was so strong it virtually wrote itself. That feeling is not uncommon when writing an interesting feature. After all, the feature is being written because it is about something out of the ordinary, something different—something that elevated a story above a run-of-the-mill news item. The high level of interest helps attract readers. But readers have no obligation to stay with you. It is up to you to offer incentives. Strategically then, once you have drawn readers to your article with a strong introduction, your key mission is to keep them to the end—to grab them by the nose if necessary and draw them through the article to the conclusion, leaving them with a lasting impression.

A good way to achieve this is by burying a string of baits and hooks at strategic points throughout your writing. These are similar to intro sentences. The idea is to keep readers involved by promising, tantalising, reassuring and explaining as you link from idea to idea, or one segment of a story to another. Fynes-Clinton (2010) said linking a series of different ideas with flair can be a challenge for even the most experienced feature writer. But she said it can often be achieved by identifying two points that have a thread of material in common and then easing from one to the other.

Fynes-Clinton also suggests:

> Another strategy is to adopt a kind of loose fact, quote, anecdote model, where each point made is bolstered by a quote and a short story to back it up before moving on with a short linking sentence such as, 'But that is not the whole story', or 'Health Minister Joe Bloggs agrees' (Fynes-Clinton 2010).

As you build a feature, be aware of the words you use as tools. Think in terms of impact and variety and remember how Defoe used simple words. Unlike news writing, do not be afraid to mix longer and shorter words—although avoid those that are pretentious, obscure or complex. Similarly, vary sentence lengths. There are reasons why variations are a good idea. First, varying the words you use helps avoid repetition. Second, a short sentence in a passage in which there are longer sentences can be used for impact to bring a specific point into sharp focus. Third, varying word and sentence length has a visual impact. If all sentences and paragraphs on a page of text are about the same length, the page looks symmetrical, neat—and boring! But a page with long, medium and short sentences and paragraphs is more visually interesting. Variation also helps readers find their place in an article again after being distracted. And just as a short sentence can be used for impact, so can a short paragraph. Fynes-Clinton believes varying length has other benefits too:

> Length of sentence and word choices are very important in a feature article. They provide a rhythm and contribute to tone. Think of it in terms of thinking—you think in long and short thought streams. So it is important that each sentence follows this model. Short sentences add pace and momentum. Longer ones give a feeling of languidity and description (Fynes-Clinton 2010).

Rich agrees sentence length helps contribute to tone. She says 'short, choppy sentences' can reflect fear, excitement and anxiety, while longer sentences can be used to convey 'suffering, thoughtfulness or a quiet mood' (Rich 2003, p. 23).

Direct quotes also have a significant place in feature writing structure and in creating the tone or mood of an article. Used judiciously, they add colour and character and build human interest. In profiles in particular, but also in other features, direct quotes permit interviewees to speak directly to readers in their own 'voice'. That voice helps convey the essence of a person and illustrates thought processes. As psycholinguist Frank Smith said in his book *To Think: In Language, Learning and Education*, 'Stories explain themselves, and they explain the way people think and behave' (Smith 1992, p. 122). And:

> we think as we speak or write, to ourselves or to others. We might occasionally think about what we are going to talk about, but not how we will say it... The flow of conversation—or of thought itself—usually precludes preplanning. Usually we do not know how a sentence will end when we begin it. We talk and our thought progresses (Smith 1992, p. 119).

Thus by quoting interviewees directly, we offer readers similar insights about them as the insights we gleaned ourselves when we interviewed them. For this reason it is particularly important to think twice before 'cleaning up' the quotes of people we interview for features. As noted in Chapter 8, it is acceptable to correct minor grammatical errors in direct quotes, especially in relation to news stories. But be sparing with corrections in features because there is a danger they will work against your ability to convey an interviewee's 'voice', character and thinking. Also beware of over-quoting someone. Too much direct speech becomes boring. It can also result in too much of a good thing in terms of characterisation—perhaps making an interviewee look stupid or boring when all you meant to do was convey a sense of who they are.

Sometimes more than one theme—or a complicated theme with starkly different strands—will emerge as you start writing a feature. Trying to weave all these threads into a single tapestry can be impossible. One solution is to cull the part or parts of the article that do not fit. Another, and often much better, approach is to present the most important information related to, but not a part of, the main theme as one or more breakouts.

A breakout is a separate, stand-alone story or a fact-box or graph inset into the main article or run beside it. One or more breakouts can add great value to a main article and do so in a way that does not confuse readers. As an aside here, a good habit to get into when cutting your own writing is to avoid simply deleting unwanted passages. A much better idea is to open a special cutting file on your computer and to cut and paste your deletions into it. Then, if you change your mind later and regret a cut made in haste, it is simple to copy it from the cutting file and paste it back into the article.

> Beware of over-quoting someone. Too much direct speech becomes boring. It can also result in too much of a good thing in terms of characterisation—perhaps making an interviewee look stupid or boring when all you meant to do was convey a sense of who they are.

As noted earlier in this chapter, feature articles tend to end with a conclusion or 'closer'. Sheridan Burns believes the conclusion is actually the most important part of a feature's structure 'because it is there that the writer reaffirms the themes and draws together the various elements in the narrative' (Sheridan Burns 2002, p. 172). Unlike a news story written to the inverted pyramid format—in which the least important information, or maybe even some padding, is to be found at the end—a feature's closer is likely to bring together the main points of an article and to synthesise them into a summary, closing thought or image presented in the final one or two paragraphs. These paragraphs often tie back to the introduction, perhaps answering a question or reaffirming or contradicting a supposition, proposition or theory. Part of the idea is to reward readers for staying with you, another is to leave them with a lasting impression they can mull over, discuss and perhaps learn something from. But in writing a conclusion, you must remain aware of the technical and logistical constraints on newspaper and magazine design that mean sub-editors still need the latitude to make cuts if they have to. For that reason it is wise to include one or two paragraphs further up a feature, just before the conclusion, which can be safely deleted without ruining the effect at the end. If you do use that technique it obviously becomes important to tell whoever sub-edits your article where those paragraphs are in the text.

DISCUSSION POINTS

1   Feature writing is seen by some as a soft option compared with news writing. How realistic, or unrealistic, is that perception?

2   Read the two longest feature articles in last weekend's edition of *The Weekend Australian Magazine*.

   a) Discuss the introduction, the intro sentence and the writing style.

   b) Was there a conclusion, or 'closer'? If so, was it well done and did it leave a lasting impression?

3   Looking again at the same edition of *The Weekend Australian Magazine* as in Discussion Point 2:

   a) Was there an article that appealed to you more than the two longest? If so, what attracted you?

   b) Was there any article that turned you off? If so, what repelled you?

4   Is it reasonable to assume that the imagery in Defoe's account of finding a footprint in the sand is still as sharp today as it was 300 years ago? Why or why not?

5   Should feature writers also have to write news, if for no other reason than to keep them in touch with the real world and the bread and butter of journalism?

6   What are the main differences between being a feature writer and being a columnist?

NEWS PRACTICE POINTS

1   Reread the quotation from Daniel Defoe's *Robinson Crusoe* discussed in this chapter. Now find another piece of descriptive writing that paints a picture for you. It can be a single phrase, a sentence or a single paragraph.

2   Returning to the passage from *Robinson Crusoe*, consider the fact that it was written close to 300 years ago. Now rewrite it, paying particular attention to updating the words and punctuation.

3   Following on from Practice Point 2, explain in no more than 250 words how effective or otherwise you believe your rewrite was; if it still evokes the same, better or worse imagery; and how difficult it was to write.

4   Go to a public place and find a spot to sit unobtrusively while you take in your surroundings. Imagine you are recreating this scene as it was five minutes before an important but unscheduled news event. Describe the setting in 60 words or less.

5   Was Jane Fynes-Clinton correct when she said human interest is the key to feature writing? Explain your answer in about 250 words.

6   Write a two-paragraph introduction to a feature article on the topic of sex, politics and religion which includes a 20 to 25 word intro sentence.

7   Feature writers are often thought of as having more time to write than news reporters, but that is not always true. Find an example of a feature article that expands on and explains a newly broken news story. Is it written by the same journalist who wrote the news story? How well is it written? How much information and explanation does it add to help you better understand the news story?

8   Write a 2000-word feature article on an interesting and unusual topic. Put it away for a week or so, then revisit your work and polish it. Now be persistent and keep offering it to print and/or online outlets until you get it published. When that happens, keep a copy of the published version with your byline and add it to your portfolio.

12 INVESTIGATIVE JOURNALISM

Sometimes the best breakthroughs that I had weren't as the result of a phone call in the middle of the night, but more giving myself the opportunity to stop and think.
Chris Masters, journalist and author, 2009

OBJECTIVES

After reading this chapter you will understand:

» The social importance of investigative journalism
» How even a simple investigation can break a huge story
» Things to look for and consider in an investigation
» The value of persistence and lateral thinking when investigating
» Freedom of information as a research tool
» The qualities of investigative journalists.

Investigative journalism helps right wrongs, expose cover-ups and rip-offs, shine spotlights on liars and cheats, and warn communities when official systems of accountability fail. It has a vital role in protecting and fostering democracy. Typically it focuses on crime and corruption; exposes incompetence, cant and hypocrisy; and reveals dark secrets. There is practically no aspect of society and culture that is immune from self-seeking, shifty, unscrupulous and lazy individuals. Think about journalistic investigations which have exposed abuse of public trust and the misuse of expense accounts by members of parliament, union officials and other public figures. And what of vision highlighting conditions inside immigration detention centres, sickening animal cruelty in overseas abattoirs, and exploitative Asian sweatshops where clothes are made for trendy Australian brands? Often we would not know about those things if it wasn't for the work of investigative journalists and their sources. From a journalist's perspective, investigative journalism has another plus—it is often highly satisfying, even fun at times, and its outcomes rewarding, especially if you enjoy a mental challenge. On the downside, there can be scary moments and only some journalists are prepared to accept the challenges. Unfortunately is also a fact that too few media outlets are prepared to properly fund investigations.

Two major factors impede investigative journalism in Australia: some of our laws—in particular, but not limited to, sections of our defamation, privacy and discrimination laws (see Chapter 15)—and the financial cost. Investigations can be expensive. Expenses for company searches, legal advice, journalists' wages paid for weeks, maybe months, when researching and not producing easier-to-gather stories, travel and accommodation all add up. On the other hand, some of the most effective investigations in recent years have cost little or nothing. For example, the story that exposed former Federal Court judge Marcus Einfeld, which is discussed in Chapter 4, involved little more than two inquiring minds and a Google search. Much the same can be said of an initial investigation by then *Courier-Mail* journalist Hedley Thomas which revealed that a surgeon who botched operations at Bundaberg Hospital in Queensland, and who was subsequently investigated in relation to the deaths of 17 patients, had previously been banned from practising in the US. The story, which sparked court hearings and appeals which were still being heard in 2013, had its origins in 2005 when Thomas travelled to Bundaberg and spoke with whistleblower nurse Toni Hoffman about Dr Jayant Patel. As Thomas explained later:

> I first became involved as a journalist when the nurse, Toni Hoffman, came to me about Dr Patel and his conduct. After visiting Bundaberg and interviewing patients and nurses, I performed a simple Google search and it showed Dr Patel had been banned from doing surgery in the US because of his appalling record and gross negligence. He had been struck off in New York state, banned and effectively fired in Oregon over the deaths and injuries of his patients. These revelations triggered the furore (Thomas 2007).

Patel subsequently resigned. But the story took another turn when it was revealed that the day after his resignation, the surgeon flew home to the US courtesy of a one-way business-class airfare paid for by the Queensland Government (Morris 2005 p. 95). Patel was subsequently extradited back to Queensland and charged with unlawfully killing three patients and one count of grievous bodily harm. He was jailed and later released on appeal. In early 2013 Patel was found not guilty of unlawfully killing a patient in 2003. He was subsequently ordered to stand trial for grievous bodily harm of another patient, and also faced allegations of fraud (Baskin 2013).

Thomas won a Gold Walkley Award for his work on the story. Toni Hoffman was awarded the 2006 Australian of the Year Local Hero Award and the 2006 Whistleblowers Australia Whistleblower of the Year Award for her role in exposing Patel.

Examples of major investigative stories

There are numerous other examples of investigative stories that have held individuals and organisations accountable for their actions and, just as importantly, inactions. Some of these stories literally changed the world. In many instances, investigative journalism filled a 'fourth estate' function, described in Chapter 14, in which journalists were approached by, and were able to help, individuals whose attempts to solve problems or have wrongs righted through 'official' channels— such as police services or other authorities—were frustrated.

Three landmark examples of research by journalists that had global implications were the Watergate investigation, a series of articles about the Air New Zealand Mount Erebus disaster, and exposés of the CSR and James Hardie asbestos tragedies in Australia.

WATERGATE

Watergate is the classic example of a story about a cover-up. Its genesis was in June 1972, when five men were arrested while trying to hide listening devices in the offices of the Democratic National Committee in the Watergate office complex in Washington. There was a presidential election due in November that year and Republican president Richard Nixon was standing for his second term. The arrests were reported in *The Washington Post* newspaper. The story aroused the curiosity of two young journalists who worked for *The Washington Post*, Bob Woodward and Carl Bernstein. They became even more inquisitive after Woodward learnt from sources that the men wore surgical gloves and were carrying thousands of dollars in cash (*The Washington Post* n.d.). The journalists then discovered that as well as having new dollar notes in their pockets, some of the burglars also had White House phone numbers on scraps of paper. Two days after the burglary, John Mitchell, head of the campaign team to re-elect President Nixon, denied any knowledge of the break-in. Mitchell was a former US attorney-general who had resigned from his role as the nation's top law officer to work on Nixon's campaign. In late September 1972, Bernstein and Woodward reported in *The Washington Post* that Mitchell personally controlled a secret Republican Party slush fund that was used to gather dirt on the rival Democratic Party (Bernstein & Woodward 1972, p. 1).

From then, the story was no longer about a break-in, but about a massive cover-up orchestrated from the president's office. Despite the scandal, Nixon was re-elected in November 1972 with an increased majority. But early in 1973, four of his top staff lost their jobs because of the cover-up. In 1974 it was revealed Nixon himself knew about the Watergate break-in and had played a major role in the cover-up. In August 1974 Nixon became the first US president forced to resign from office.

One of the more interesting facts that emerged later was that Woodward and Bernstein had an inside source whom they protected and only ever referred to by the code name 'Deep Throat'. The source's identity remained a mystery until 2005 when Deep Throat, who by then was an old man, outed himself as a former associate director of the FBI whose real name was Mark Felt (*The Washington Post* n.d.).

The Watergate story had numerous far-reaching outcomes apart from Nixon's resignation. Among them was an overhaul of laws relating to election funds in the US. New ethical guidelines were introduced in the US legislature, limits were placed on the size of donations that could be made to political parties, and new rules were imposed in relation to campaign spending. But the impact of Woodward and Bernstein's work went well beyond the US. There was a global flow-on as politicians around the world realised they could be held accountable via mass media. The story—and its political, social and cultural impacts—also sparked a global revival of investigative journalism and a massive boost in awareness of the important fourth estate role of quality journalism and journalists as investigators. Within the profession of journalism there was also a great lesson about the public benefits that can flow from cultivating and protecting sources.

MT EREBUS DISASTER

The Mt Erebus disaster happened in 1979 when an Air New Zealand McDonnell Douglas DC-10 aircraft carrying 237 passengers and 20 crew smashed into Mt Erebus in Antarctica. The aircraft was on a sightseeing flight. There were no survivors. Early investigations blamed the tragedy on pilot error, but a subsequent royal commission found a navigation computer on the aircraft had been wrongly programmed by maintenance staff and Air New Zealand had tried to cover up the mistake (*The Dominion Post* 2008). While some findings of the royal commission remain controversial, it seems the inquiry would not have been established if the New Zealand Government had not been pressured by media reports. A journalist who did considerable work digging into the background of the crash was then aviation writer with the *Auckland Star* newspaper John McDonald. He wrote a series of investigative articles about the crash and poor safety standards within Air New Zealand.

The inquiry into the accident resulted in improved safety standards in all airlines around the world and new rules about how navigation computers are programmed. Air New Zealand has never again flown sightseeing trips to the remote Antarctic continent.

CSR AND JAMES HARDIE ASBESTOS TRAGEDIES

The asbestos mining tragedies involving CSR and James Hardie are landmark examples of corporate negligence in Australia. The story unfolded gradually over many years and ultimately involved work by many journalists. In 1974 *The Bulletin* magazine led with the first major investigative article on the dangers of asbestos, a cover story headlined 'Is this killer in your home?' (O'Neill & Prince 2005, p. 9). In 1978 a medical writer with *The West Australian* newspaper, Catherine Martin, began asking questions about the high death rate and incidence of illness among workers at CSR's Australian Blue Asbestos Mine at Wittenoom Gorge in the Pilbara region (Australian Women's Register n.d.). Blue asbestos is the most dangerous form of asbestos. In a series of investigative articles, the first of which was headlined 'Blue asbestos: The latent killer', Martin revealed that many of the 6500 workers at the mine, which opened in 1947 and closed in 1967, were becoming ill with a particular form of cancer called mesothelioma. Martin—who later won several Walkley Awards including the inaugural Gold Walkley, and was recognised with a Member of the Order of Australia Award—also revealed that many former workers who were migrants had returned 'home' to other nations, where they, too, were dying.

Subsequent investigations by journalists revealed that James Hardie, the biggest processor of asbestos in Australia, knew of the dangers of asbestos mining and processing as early as the 1930s but did not issue warnings until 1978. It was also revealed that James Hardie operated its own mines, some of which were run by subsidiary companies. Despite the warnings, the company continued manufacturing and selling asbestos products until 1982. It has since been estimated that up to one-third of all houses built in Australia before 1982 probably contain asbestos. The mineral is no longer used as a building product anywhere in the world. Australia has the highest rate of mesothelioma in the world (Leigh et al. 2002).

In 2001 James Hardie moved its corporate headquarters from Australia to the Netherlands. In 2008 an investigative report in *The Weekend Australian*, based on 'secret company documents', suggested James Hardie was planning another move for its headquarters, this time to the US (Higgins 2008). In 2009 Hardie announced it would actually move its headquarters to Ireland because it would pay less tax in that nation (Janda 2009). In 2009 James Hardie also announced that a special fund it had established before leaving Australia to pay compensation to asbestos victims was running out of money. The company said it would be unlikely to contribute to the fund in 2010, and its 2011 contributions would be reduced (Janda 2009). As recently as 2012 the NSW Court of Appeal fined former James Hardie managers over breaches of the Corporations Act when making statements in 2002 about the adequacy of asbestos compensation (ASIC 2012).

Leaders in the field

There are names that stand out in the history of investigative journalism in Australia. While too many to list here, examples include Bob Bottom, an agenda-setting member of Australia's first investigative journalism group, the Insight team at *The Age*; Phil Dickie of *The Courier-Mail*; Chris Masters of *Four Corners*, and *The Australian*'s Hedley Thomas. In their own ways, Dickie and Masters were each responsible for a series of stories that led to the jailing of former Queensland police commissioner Terrence Lewis, the establishment of the Fitzgerald Inquiry, the downfall of the Bjelke-Petersen Government, and the establishment of the Criminal Justice Commission (now Crime and Misconduct Commission) in Queensland. The Commission subsequently paid tribute to the work of Dickie and Masters. It said:

> Anyone living in Queensland in the 1980s would remember the frequent
> rumblings in the media about possible police corruption. There was talk
> of illegal gambling and prostitution, of kickbacks and brown bags, of vice
> at the highest levels. Then came some first-rate investigative journalism

by young *Courier-Mail* reporter Phil Dickie, followed by Chris Masters' now renowned *Four Corners* episode 'Moonlight State' (aired 11 May 1987), and suddenly the rumblings had substance (Crime and Misconduct Commission 2007).

Bob Bottom is another whose name is legendary. Awarded an Order of Australia Medal in 1997 for 'investigating and reporting upon organised crime in Australia', Bottom is credited with writing articles that sparked not only the first royal commission into organised crime in Australia, the Moffitt Royal Commission in 1973, but at least 17 other royal commissions and inquiries. Bottom specialised in investigating organised crime, mainly in NSW and Victoria. He also investigated and wrote on an array of other topics ranging from electoral rorting and branch stacking in the ALP in Queensland to disabled children being locked in cages. The author of numerous books, Bottom has written for *The Age*, *The Bulletin*, *Sydney Morning Herald*, *The Courier-Mail*, *The Australian*, and even small local papers, one of which he owned.

Other investigative journalists of note include David Hellaby, Tony Koch, Marian Wilkinson, David Wilson, Nick Mckenzie, Richard Baker, Sarah Ferguson, Linton Besser, Kate McClymont, Ross Coulthart, Sally Neighbour and Ben Hills, to name a few.

Setting agendas over time

In each example of investigative journalism touched on so far in this chapter, it was journalists who literally made the news. They were proactive, conducted research, discovered information, talked to people, cultivated sources and wrote agenda-setting articles.

The keys to investigative journalism are to be resourceful, thoughtful, persistent, intuitive, and to find the time to devote to investigating. However, unless a story is relatively simple and stems from something like a Google search inspired by a reactive news event (which is what happened in the Einfeld case discussed in Chapter 4), finding time can become a serious issue. For this reason many investigative stories are researched and written over a considerable period. They are something journalists return to in quieter times on slow news days when the demand for more immediate stories and news-gathering eases a little.

But time is not always the enemy. There are many investigative stories that can only be unravelled as events and leads unfold over time. Some investigative stories, which are always proactive, progress a little like a weekly television serial. At first you watch and listen as the scene is set and background information is explained. Then you start learning a little about the characters—the heroes and villains. Over time the plot, and perhaps several subplots, take shape. The plot thickens, there are unexpected twists and turns—some characters you originally thought heroes turn out to be shady, while some who seemed obviously bad reveal a redeeming streak. Then, just as you think you have everything figured out, it turns out the main plot was really only a subplot and there was a hidden agenda you did not suspect.

A different analogy is that investigations can be similar to working on a giant jigsaw puzzle from which pieces are missing. You start assembling pieces and slowly a picture emerges. The image becomes clearer over time, but there are still gaps. Then, maybe with luck, or if you look hard enough, you find a missing piece. It changes the picture slightly. You go off hunting for other missing pieces. You may or may not finally find the last piece, or uncover the final twist in a complex plot, but even if you do not, the picture might still contain enough detail to move forward and publish an article.

Sometimes publishing, or 'floating', an article when you have only part of a picture—especially if there is enough to assemble one or more scenes in a wider tapestry—is enough to bring people forward with vital new information that contributes to the big picture.

While a majority of investigative stories are researched and written over weeks or months, some complex investigations take years of painstaking work. The longest I spent working on the same investigation was six years. The story was extraordinary. There were times when real elements of it seemed more like fiction than fact. It concerned the Victorian Division of the National Safety Council of Australia and its wildly erratic conman boss who went by the name John Friedrich. My first articles were a series published in a regional newspaper in which it was suggested Friedrich appeared to have built a multi-million-dollar paramilitary search-and-rescue operation with former military helicopters, boats, trucks, fixed-wing aircraft and highly trained staff on a shoe-string budget. The story was too big for a regional paper, but I kept working on it and took it with me as my career developed, eventually writing about Friedrich and his organisation when I worked on News Limited papers. One interesting aspect of the story was that it continued

Some investigative stories progress a little like a weekly television serial. At first you watch and listen as the scene is set and background information is explained. Then you start learning a little about the characters—the heroes and villains. Over time the plot, and perhaps several subplots, take shape.

developing and becoming more interesting as I, and later many others, researched it. Over the six years it emerged that Friedrich—who it was claimed later was probably an illegal immigrant whose real name was Friedrich Hohenberger, and who was undoubtedly Australia's leading conman up to that time—had duped and embarrassed the Australian Navy, RAAF, Australian Federal Police, intelligence services, state police, senior state and federal government ministers, foreign governments, and banks. The true figure will never be known, but by the time Friedrich's organisation finally collapsed he had defrauded financial institutions, governments and others of at least $500 million (close to $1.5 billion in 2013 values). Even years later, and despite the fact many other journalists worked on the Friedrich story once it gained momentum, it is unlikely the full extent of his activities or his fraud will ever be known. He supposedly committed suicide in 1991, just days before he was to stand trial in Melbourne on close to 100 fraud charges.

How to investigate

It would seem obvious that the first step in establishing an investigation is to clearly define what will be investigated. But things are rarely so simple. By their nature, investigations can lead anywhere. You can stumble on hidden veins of gold, and you can find yourself in blind alleys. Frequently there is no way to know where you are heading when you start. Therefore it is wise to ease your way into anything other than a simple investigation. Start by doing broad background research in a similar way as you would for a feature article. Talk to people, do a little computer-assisted research, and check your own news organisation's archives. In general, the tools of investigative journalism are exactly the same as the research tools of all journalists that were discussed in Chapter 6. As Waterford said:

> The tools of the investigative reporter do not differ in any significant respect from those available to the ordinary reporter, but the luxury of time may mean more opportunity to gain access to witnesses or experts, to gather and analyse documents, and to develop and test theories about how and why things have occurred (Waterford, in Tanner 2002, p. 38).

Weinberg said in his book *The Reporter's Handbook: An Investigator's Guide to Documents and Techniques*: 'When a reporter is working from the outside in, information already published or broadcast can serve as a starting point for answering basic questions' (Weinberg 1996, p. 5). So when you do basic research, stop and think about what you find. Ask yourself if parts of a picture start to mesh? Do your discoveries lead to more questions? Can secondary source materials you find lead you to primary documents and sources? Seeking primary documents and other resources, including people to interview, should be a major aim. As discussed in Chapter 6, you need to trace your way back to primary sources from secondary sources if you can. That way you should avoid the risk that others who prepared secondary source material made mistakes in their interpretation of primary documents, or missed a vital clue. After all, as noted in Chapter 2, journalists—and particularly investigative journalists—must be able to demonstrate that researched facts supporting a story can be verified and justified, in a law court if necessary, so they must be able to turn back and replicate research outcomes. That process is simpler, and outcomes clearer, when an investigation is based on primary documents. And, as Weinberg noted, 'Primary documents are more readily available than many investigators realise. The best journalists possess the "documents state of mind"... ' (Weinberg 1996, p. 5). Cuillier and Davis (2010) similarly refer to a 'document state of mind'. One approach they recommend is using documents to 'find great stories by identifying what they call a "performance gap"' (Cuillier & Davis 2010, p. 4). They explained:

> The gap between what an agency says it is doing and what it actually does— the performance gap—is a critical engine of accountability for reporters and citizens intent on monitoring government performance. Suppose your local police force says it is intent on stepping up enforcement of speeding violations. That's an invitation for you to measure the performance a few months later (Cuillier & Davis 2010, p. 4).

Legal knowledge and fact checking are important when examining documents. Never make an assumption. Be sure a person mentioned in a document is the right person—is the John Brown you think is a villain really the same John Brown who has just been given an Australia Day good citizenship award by the mayor? Are you 100 per cent certain? Can you prove it? How? Mistakes and sloppy investigations can be expensive. As discussed in Chapter 15, defamation cases not only cost a great deal of money to defend—even if you did have a sound legal excuse for defaming someone—they are also emotionally draining and incredibly time-consuming. One good way to avoid making mistakes is to keep an open mind. Do not fall into the trap of becoming a crusader for a cause or an advocate for a group. Doing so will cloud your objectivity and sense of fairness. Remember, there are always at least two, sometimes many more, sides to a story. As Waterford said:

> Investigative reporting will often disclose that matters are more complex than one originally thought—that some action initially seen as being intrinsically venal, or wicked, was in fact reasonable... or that an event fits into a wider framework or sequence of events (Waterford, in Tanner 2002, p. 39).

Examining how events evolved over time and the sequence in which they occurred can be a powerful tool. It is one Bob Bottom used regularly in his investigations. An advocate of establishing accurate chronologies recording a sequence of events, he said he worked on the theory that 'the past conditions the future' (Bottom 2005). In other words, the way people and organisations behaved at particular points in the past is a likely indicator of how they will behave in the future—hence an old saying among fraud squad police that 'once a white-collar criminal (a corporate crook), always a white-collar criminal'. Chronologies can be built by gathering information from a range of sources including newspaper archives, old and new telephone directories online and in print, company annual reports, company searches, Hansard, online searching via Google and other basic search engines and also the hidden web, and from documents obtained through freedom of information (FoI) searches.

A useful tactic, and one used by police, is to think about and try to imagine how the subject of your investigation would think—do not ever believe anyone else in the world thinks the same way as you do!

Depending on the nature of an investigation, another sound approach is to follow money trails. Ask yourself if the amount of money being spent by an individual or organisation—and particularly the lifestyles of individuals—appears to be supported by his or her income or earning capacity. If things do not seem to add up, or money is being splashed around, ask where it came from. Sometimes searching company records can provide answers. So can speaking with disenchanted investors, business partners and former partners, former employees, and ex-wives and husbands. Face to face is best, but telephone conversations also produce results. But be wary of asking leading questions in writing, especially in emails, or, as explained in Chapter 15, you could invite a defamation writ. Also check with authorities. They may or may not be helpful, but it is possible they will point you in the right direction—particularly if they have information and are aware someone is a villain but they do not have enough evidence to act, or are inhibited in some other way.

Another useful tactic, and one used by police, is to think about and try to imagine how the subject of your investigation would think and react—in doing so imagine yourself as the scoundrel! Do not ever believe anyone else in the world thinks in the same decent and law-abiding way as you do!

A useful tactic, and one used by police, is to think about and try to imagine how the subject of your investigation would think—do not ever believe anyone else in the world thinks the same way as you do!

Freedom of information

The concept of freedom of access to government information originated in China in the seventh century when people with a grievance against the emperor were encouraged to beat a drum outside his palace until their questions were answered and problems resolved. The first 'modern' freedom of information (FoI) legislation as we understand it today was enacted in Sweden in 1766. Since then, the right of Swedish citizens to access government information has been embedded in the Swedish Constitution. In fact Sweden has the most open and accountable system of government, FoI and press freedom in the world. A measure of that is the fact that something like 60 per cent of major news stories in that nation are generated from FoI requests (Lidberg 2001). Not so in Australia. We have some of the worst FoI laws of any democratic nation (Lamble 2004).

In nations such as Sweden, New Zealand, and to a lesser extent the US and Canada, government-generated and held documents and other information are regarded as being owned by the people. Access to information is relatively easy unless it concerns national security or continuing criminal investigations. But Australian governments and public servants have a history of regarding themselves as owners of the information they generate and store. When access is allowed, it tends to be grudging and often with chunks of documents blacked out or missing.

When FoI legislation was first adopted in Australia in 1982 by the Fraser Government, the idea was supposed to be that governments would become transparent and government information would be freely available for the public to access. The only exceptions were documents relating to national security, continuing criminal investigations and information about private matters concerning citizens. But the weak nature of the legislation and its adoption in different forms in different states and territories allowed politicians to tamper with the rules and water down the intent of FoI. Today, and despite overhauls of FoI legislation federally and in some states since mid-2009, government ministers and spin-doctoring ministerial media advisers become paranoid about journalists seeking access to documents. Many do what they can to frustrate requests that might show them or their government in a less than complimentary light.

Part of the problem in Australia is that, as explained in Chapter 14, Australia's political system has no real separation between elected leaders of government in the legislature—the prime minister and cabinet ministers—and the public service. Australian state and federal ministers can, and do, interfere in the workings of the public service (Lamble 2003, pp. 51–5). What happens is that public servants inform spin-doctors in their minister's offices when potentially 'difficult' FoI applications are lodged by journalists. One or more tactics can then be employed to block the application. A favourite is to quote an excessive fee for finding and processing documents. Another is to cause excessive delays so that by the time all the relevant documents have actually been 'found', the issue they related to has lost currency and is dead as a news story. Another trick is to list documents sought by journalists as cabinet documents because documents listed in cabinet agenda papers are exempt from release.

That said, lodging an FoI application is not difficult and sometimes— particularly if public servants and government media minders do not understand the significance of what they are releasing—the process can be used to source valuable information for investigative stories. One tactic journalists can use to gain access to information that might otherwise be blocked is to encourage individuals they are working with (or family members) to lodge personal applications in low-key terms that will not set alarm bells ringing in ministerial offices in the same way an application by a journalist would. Another tactic is to encourage lobby groups to get members to apply individually. Journalists can also exert pressure on reluctant officials and politicians by writing articles saying an application is being blocked.

FoI applications can be lodged with federal, state, territory and local governments. At its best, an application will provide information about a specific topic, issue or government decision. Applications can also be used to confirm whether a specific document actually exists or not, even if it is not released. This is because FoI officers must provide applicants with a list of all documents relevant to a request, even if they deny access. In a quest that tends to infuriate politicians and officials, FoI applications can be lodged by journalists as a 'fishing' exercise—just to see what is out there in relation to a specific topic or issue. Applications can also be used strategically to cover a leak from a confidential source, to confirm leaked information, or by governments that actually want to get sensitive information into the public arena, but wish to distance themselves from the disclosure by making it appear a journalist has asked for it. In relation to the latter tactic, it is not uncommon for a ministerial minder to suggest to a journalist that it might be worthwhile lodging a FoI application on a particular topic.

Most government department and local council websites contain information about how and where to lodge FoI requests. Applications must be specific—the idea is to make it hard for public servants to find reasons for not being able to find information, and being as specific as possible also helps save money because government departments charge by the hour to search for documents (although the federal *Freedom of Information Act 1982* includes a provision that journalists and not-for-profit community groups are not charged for the first five hours). There is no application fee for federal FoI applications but charges apply in some states and territories. Details about application fees are listed on departmental and council websites. There are also charges for 'consulting and decision making' as well as photocopying. In addition there are separate charges for providing supervised access to documents that cannot be photocopied. In the early stages of the process you will be sent a quote estimating how much it will cost to find and copy the information—in some cases the quote will also include a fee for deciding whether or not you will be granted full, part, or no access! There have been instances in the past when a government that did not want to release information quoted an exorbitant amount; in one case more than a million dollars!

In some jurisdictions, for example Queensland, applications must be made by filling in a specific application form. Federally, however, there is no set form and applications may be made in a letter, fax or email sent to the 'specified FOI address' of a particular department. The following is an example of an FoI application letter that could be used by a journalist seeking information from a federal government department. Note how specific it is.

LETTER EXAMPLE

The FOI Contact Officer
Attorney-General's Department
Robert Garran Offices
National Circuit
BARTON ACT 2600

Fred Findout
The Badtown Chronicle
21 Nowhere Street
Badtown
SA 8123
Telephone 08 XXX YYY

April 1, 2016

Dear Sir/Madam,

I hereby request access to information under the terms of the *Freedom of Information Act 1982* concerning the detention of illegal immigrants (asylum seekers) being held in custody on Christmas Island in January and February 2015.

Specifically, I seek details of the names, age and sex of each detainee as well as their nation of origin and details of how they travelled to Australia. I also seek information about how long each detainee has been held in custody.

I seek copies of all letters, notes, memos, attachments, records, annotations, transcripts, files, computer-generated or stored information, tape recordings, images, video recordings, telephone records, emails, facsimiles or other information whether written, typed, computer-generated, stored or recorded in some other way.

Yours faithfully,

Fred Findout

Fred Findout

The following example of a federal FoI application letter could be used by individuals seeking information about themselves. Note that while the personal letter is less threatening than the formal request by a journalist, it still seeks 'everything' in the applicant's file.

LETTER EXAMPLE

Australian Federal Police	**Florence Plod**
Freedom of Information Team	**21 Deadend Street**
PO Box 401	**Noosa Heads**
Canberra City ACT 2601	**QLD 4567**
	Phone 07 XXXX ABCD

April 1, 2018

Dear FoI Officer,

I wish to access information contained in my Australian Federal Police file. I was a member of the AFP from June 1996 until December 2013.

I particularly seek documents relating to my transfer from Darwin Airport to Alice Springs in 2008 and allegations made against me by other officers in 2003 and 2007.

I seek copies of everything in my file related to the above transfer and allegations against me, also all computer records including emails, as well as any other material including tape recordings or memos and even photographs and handwritten notes.

Yours truly,

Florence Plod

Florence Plod

If an FoI application is stonewalled by a federal government department you can appeal to the federal Information Commissioner. Some states have information commissioners or ombudsmen who deal with appeals. There are also alternative ways of obtaining government documents and other information. One is through leaks. Another is to use computer-assisted research methods. In an instance the writer is aware of, a federal government department refused FoI access to a document and even fought an appeal to stop its release, but a journalist using a simple computer-assisted research technique subsequently found a copy of exactly the same document published on a government website! Websites in other nations—particularly in the US, Canada, UK and New Zealand, nations close to Australia politically and socially—can be excellent sources of information about Australia that cannot be accessed from within Australia.

Finally in relation to FoI, note that the laws only relate to government-held and -generated information. They do not relate to corporate or private information—none of which can be accessed through FoI.

Issues that work against investigations

It is uncommon for an investigative story, or more accurately a series of many stories, to take anything like as long to reach a conclusion as the John Friedrich story mentioned earlier in this chapter. But there were many influences working against that investigation. Although rarely encountered to the same degree, there will be factors that inhibit most investigative journalists to at least some extent. Apart from the cost, finding time, and governments blocking FoI requests, examples of inhibiting influences include the following.

LAWYERS AND LEGAL THREATS

Disreputable lawyers who are well paid to protect villainous clients are notorious for threatening journalists. They know that legal threats have a 'chilling effect' on journalism in Australia—something discussed in greater detail in Chapter 15. It is not an uncommon scenario in Australia for journalists to be told by management to back off—particularly if a news outlet is small, family-owned, and does not have the financial resources to cope with a defamation writ. In short, our defamation laws are so restrictive, and legal costs so high, that many stories which would have public benefit are never told.

MISGUIDED SUPPORT OF ACCUSED INDIVIDUALS

The misguided championing of people who have been accused of not acting in the public interest is sometimes a vexed issue. It can result in journalists, whistleblowers, and others who are acting solely for the benefit of the public being vilified. This happened after Bundaberg nurse Toni Hoffman raised questions about patients suffering at the hands of Dr Patel (discussed earlier in this chapter). Hoffman was so concerned about the surgeon, she sought help from her local member of parliament Rob Messenger. He subsequently raised the issue in the

Queensland Parliament and used parliamentary privilege to ask questions about the treatment of 14 patients. Afterwards, Bundaberg Hospital management called on Messenger to apologise, and the Australian Medical Association issued a media release saying he was 'irresponsible'. Hoffman was also vilified (*Australian Story* 2005).

CORPORATE AND GOVERNMENT SPIN-DOCTORS

Corporate and government spin-doctors—many of whom are former journalists who understand how journalists work and media organisations function—have a virtual bagful of tricks to either attempt to stop a story being published or, if they cannot stop publication, divert attention from a story. Tactics vary from attempted sweet-talking and explaining how many innocent people will be damaged for life if a story is published or broadcast, to offering bribes and making outright threats. If all else fails, and if spin-doctors are desperate enough, they will engineer publication or broadcast of a competing story on some other topic that draws attention away from the awkward story. This sort of spin is something governments have become particularly good at. In most Australian jurisdictions, public servants at all levels of government are banned from talking to journalists. The only sources of official information are through ministers' offices, mayoral offices or media departments. Police services are a prime example. Ordinary police officers are usually prohibited from speaking to journalists—at least on the record. All inquiries are handled by police media units. But while staff in police media units are quick to contact media if police want help solving a crime, warning of a danger, or if there is a warm-and-fuzzy story that puts police in a good light, many are also expert at stonewalling awkward inquiries. In some police media units, information is so tightly controlled it is only when it becomes clear a journalist already has all the details of a crime, event or issue that a grudging comment is dragged out of the system.

PERSONAL THREATS AGAINST JOURNALISTS

Personal threats against journalists and/or their families can be especially unsettling. At different times, Bob Bottom and other investigative journalists whose work has upset criminals have had threats made on their lives and against the well-being of members of their families. Fortunately, Australian organised crime bosses seem smart enough to understand that a hit on a journalist would cause them, their crime networks and those who protect them, much more grief than a few irritating stories. They also realise that by the time an uncomfortable story is published, the journalist who wrote it would have a paper trail almost literally leading to the front doors of their criminal empire.

EGOTISTICAL, LAZY AND CORRUPT OFFICIALS

Egotistical, lazy and corrupt officials will sometimes go out of their way to stop stories seeing light of day. Even if they are not actually corrupt, high-paid officials tend to grow used to a comfortable lifestyle and will do much to protect their perks and power bases. And if they are corrupt, they tend to use their power and contact networks to safeguard their positions; at times colluding with others like themselves to shield each other and erect hurdles for journalists.

FINDING PEOPLE PREPARED TO GO ON THE RECORD

Finding people prepared to go on the record can be a big issue. It is not unknown for those who would try to thwart you and your research by hiring lawyers, employing spin-doctors or making direct threats, to employ those same tactics against your sources. As a journalist, you become wise in ways of the world and this makes it difficult for individuals who would try to intimidate you. But sources do not have journalistic training or experience and many are vulnerable.

OBSESSIVE SOURCES

Obsessive sources who can only see their own issues, own point of view and who have something to prove or an axe to grind, can be a menace. Some try to latch on like a limpet—maybe because as a journalist interested in a story, you are literally one of the few people prepared to listen to them. Others actually have a serious mental illness. People like that can become a serious danger to themselves and journalists.

Occasionally their lives become so dominated by their obsession, they bend the truth, tell outright lies or commit criminal acts in mistaken bids to justify themselves. Some harbour festering conspiracy theories in which even the most innocent nuance is seen as 'proof' that someone, or some system, is out to nail them. When dealing with individuals like this, do not get too close. Also bear in

Obsessive sources who can only see their own issues, own point of view and who have something to prove or an axe to grind, can be a menace. Some try to latch on like a limpet—maybe because as a journalist interested in a story, you are literally one of few people prepared to listen to them.

mind the saying that in Australia, if it comes to deciding between something being a conspiracy or a stuff-up, 99 per cent of the time it is a stuff-up!

Other than those with an axe to grind or who are devoured by an issue, there are several other categories of people to be wary of. They are fantasists who dream about and live their own adventures; confidence tricksters who come to believe their own con to the point they live it; and members of religious or other cults. Members of cults might have been brainwashed by others, or have brainwashed themselves into unquestioning belief in the ideals of the group or some supposedly all-powerful guru. While some could be regarded as relatively harmless eccentrics, at least to outsiders, at the extreme are fanatics—potential terrorists prepared to die for their beliefs and quite possibly prepared to kill others.

Qualities of investigative journalists

The best investigative journalists are those whom others trust and talk to. They are people of integrity who have numerous good, credible and reliable contacts from widely diverse backgrounds. Many of the most effective keep a relatively low public profile—they shun the limelight. They could be the woman or man down the street. Despite appearing ordinary, they tend to have a maverick streak, being prepared to buck the system and rarely taking 'no' for answer. They are lateral thinkers, streetwise, have well-developed insight and, like all good journalists, are expert listeners with an eye for detail and an ability to remain focused under pressure. They are probably more curious than most and are drawn to who, how and why questions.

Waterford (2002) said good investigative journalists need specialist skills, including an understanding of how processes of government, agencies and other organisations function; the capacity to read documents and understand them; a lively imagination; an understanding of records and how to access them; and patience and cunning (Waterford, in Tanner 2002, pp. 44–6). Investigative journalists need one other key quality: an ability to learn on the job, to learn what the investigation they are working on dictates they need to learn—whether it is how to read a complex financial report, how drugs interact with each other, or how jet aircraft navigation computers work.

Many investigative journalists have reached the pinnacle of journalism as a profession. They are acknowledged and rewarded in Australia's premier awards for excellence in journalism, the Walkley Awards. They are also recognised in separate media awards in their own states and territories and by their own media organisations. And, as mentioned at the start of this chapter, investigative journalism can be rewarding. Waterford captured the essence of that when he said, 'sometimes it is the chase as much as the capture that makes the process worthwhile' (Waterford, in Tanner 2002, p. 39). That is all the more so if the outcome is of major public benefit, a wrong is righted, lives are saved or changed for the better, and a problem is resolved.

DISCUSSION POINTS

1   What would attract you to investigative journalism as a profession, and what would put you off?

2   Why the fuss about investigative journalism? Is it not the case that all journalism is investigative anyway?

3   Should investigative journalists be permitted to bend, or ignore, the Media Entertainment and Arts Alliance (MEAA)'s *Journalists' Code of Ethics* when pursuing a story if the ends justify the means?

4   Is it reasonable to spend years working on the same story? Who should decide?

5   In the past, investigative journalism has largely been the domain of print and television news organisations.

   a) Is that likely to remain the case with the ever-increasing sophistication of online news sites and portable media?

   b) How suitable are online news sites as a platform for investigative reporting? Why?

6   Who really does own government-held information: the government or the people? Why?

7   What are the two most significant investigative stories that have broken in Australia in the past decade? What is special about them?

8   You are an investigative journalist and someone makes a threat to break your legs with a baseball bat if you do not back off and drop a story. What will you do?

NEWS PRACTICE POINTS

1   Search news archives and online for investigative articles written by some of the journalists named in this chapter. Read the articles carefully and for each article you read, compile a list of the obvious sources of information used by the journalist.

2   Following on from Practice Point 1, compile a list for each story of information that is not fully attributed to a named source. Next to each item on the list, write a brief synopsis of possible sources of that information.

3   Think about issues, people or a phenomenon in your community, state/territory and nationally that you are curious about and that would be worthy of investigating. Then list one potential topic for investigation at each level.

4   Following on from Practice Point 3, select one topic from your list and see what you can discover in a preliminary investigation. Explain the outcome in no more than 500 words.

5   Lodge an FoI request asking for information about a specific public health issue of interest to the community you live in. Once the request is processed (this may take some time), explain its outcome in no more than 750 words.

6   Go to a US government website and see what you can find out about an Australian military defence contract. Now go to the Australian Government's web portal and see if you can find the same or better information.

7   In this chapter there is a discussion about things that can potentially hinder a journalistic investigation. Select two of these and explain in writing how you would react to, and deal with, each if they arose in relation to an investigation you conducted.

8   Find a newspaper, magazine or online article based on information from a whistleblower (you may have to search an online archive) and then try to identify the whistleblower's real motive in speaking out. Explain your conclusions in exactly 250 words.

13 —
PHOTOJOURNALISM

*The still news picture, isolating a moment in time, has an affinity with the way
we remember. It is easier for us, most of the time, to recall an event or
a person by summoning up a single image.*
Harold Evans, editor, *The Sunday Times*, 1978

OBJECTIVES

After reading this chapter you will understand:

» The power of photojournalism and news photography
» How photojournalism evolved
» Different categories of news photos
» How to give editors the photos they need
» How to write informative captions
» Ethical issues related to photography.

Powerful photographs have helped end wars, build support for disaster victims, create fear and loathing of extremists, expose gross wrongs, and add value to news and feature articles. No one who has seen images of the attack on the World Trade Centre in New York on September 11, 2001 will ever forget them. The same can be said of a 1972 photograph of Vietnamese girl Kim Phúc, 9, running down a road naked, screaming and terribly burnt after a napalm bomb explosion during the Vietnam War. Those images were indelible. They captured and froze moments that will never be repeated. They shocked the world. Yet the sources of those images, how they were photographed and their dissemination to the public could hardly have been more different.

First, there were multiple digital and video images of the attack on the World Trade Centre. All were horrifying, and virtually all were captured in colour, something that added to the drama and horror of the mass murder of more than

2700 people in the heart of one of the world's most populous and dynamic cities. In contrast, the photo of Kim Phúc was a single black-and-white image snapped on a rural road outside a bombed village in South Vietnam—something that, in its way, also added to the drama and horror. Third, many of the images of the September 11 attack in New York were not shot by news photographers, but by ordinary people. In contrast, the photo of Kim Phúc was taken by an Associated Press news photographer, Nick Ut. Digital photography had not been invented and Ut used a film camera.

But the differences do not end there. Stunning digital images of the impact of aircraft slamming into the twin towers of the World Trade Centre, subsequent fires, doomed office workers choosing to jump to their deaths rather than burn, and then the collapse and implosion of the towers were flashed around the world via the internet and television literally as those events were happening. In contrast, film from Ut's camera had to be processed in a chemical bath then printed on photographic paper in a darkroom. When the photo dried, it was scanned and eventually transmitted to newspapers via telephone lines, reprocessed so it was suitable for printing, and finally published.

Vietnamese-born Ut was subsequently awarded a Pulitzer prize. Miraculously Kim Phúc survived the burns to more than 60 per cent of her body, and later went to live in Canada.

Ut later told the BBC World Service how his news editors sent the photographs to US news agencies but.

> at first they didn't like the picture because the girl had no clothes. Then I told them about the napalm erupting in the village. The pictures were shown in America, they were shown everywhere. They were shown in all the communist countries—in China and in Vietnam. They still use the photo. Even though pictures (are taken) in every war, they still show the picture of Kim. They don't want it to happen again—not napalm (Ut 2005).

The Washington Post ran the photograph of Kim Phúc on its front page. Afterwards, then US President Richard Nixon reportedly complained the image must have been 'fixed' (Preston 2007). But such was the horror the picture generated in the US that it was credited with hastening the nation's withdrawal from Vietnam and the end of the war (Preston 2007). As former London *Sunday Times* editor Harold Evans (1978) said, 'It is more than a coincidence that the Vietnam war was at once the most unpopular in American history and the most photographed'. Similarly, support for the US-led Iraq War diminished after digital images of Iraqis being tortured and humiliated by US guards at Abu Ghraib Prison near Baghdad in 2004 were published around the globe. Some of those photographs were taken with mobile phone cameras—an invention not imagined in the 1970s, and not yet widely available when the September 11 attack happened.

Other examples of powerful news photo images over the years include:

— photographs of the 1937 explosion of the Hindenburg airship in Lakehurst, New Jersey, with the loss of 36 lives

— horrendous photographs in the aftermath of the 2004 Madrid train bombings in which 10 simultaneous blasts killed 190 people and injured about 1800 (Irby 2004)

— digital photographs from nations around the Indian Ocean of the Boxing Day 2004 tsunami which were flashed around the globe within hours via the internet

— photographs in the aftermath of the 2005 terrorist bombings on the London Underground—one of the first times images of breaking news were taken on mobile phones and sent directly to news outlets by members of the public

— heartbreaking photographs of the 2009 Black Saturday bushfires that claimed 173 lives in Victoria

— on a happier note, an amazing 2009 photograph of 155 people, all of whom were rescued, standing on the wings of a jet airliner that made an emergency landing in the almost-frozen Hudson River in New York

— images of the 2010 earthquakes in Chile and Haiti that killed more than 200,000 people in Haiti alone and left millions homeless in both nations

— graphic photographs of an 'inland tsunami' which devastated the Darling Downs city of Toowoomba and nearby Lockyer Valley in January 2011

— pictures taken with mobile phones during and after the 2013 Boston Marathon bombing.

Whether news photographs are of war, tragedies, lucky escapes or happy events, there is much in the saying attributed to US advertising guru Fred Barnard, who pointed out in a 1927 advertisement for Royal Baking Powder, that one picture really can be 'worth ten thousand words' (quoted in Hepting 2004).

So great was the horror the photo of Kim Phúc generated in the US that it was credited with hastening the nation's withdrawal from Vietnam and the end of the war… Whether news photographs are of war, tragedies, lucky escapes or happy events, there is much in the saying attributed to US advertising guru Fred Barnard, who pointed out in a 1927 advertisement for Royal Baking Powder, that one picture really can be 'worth ten thousand words'.

A brief history of news photography

In 1829, French artist Louis Daguerre invented a system of using light-sensitive salts on metal plates to capture images. The process became known for producing images dubbed 'daguerreotypes' (Stephens 1997, p. 269). Evans said newspaper photographers started working with daguerreotypes in the 1840s (Evans 1978, p. 1). Newspapers and magazines had published images before that, but they were hand-drawn illustrations reproduced with 'woodcuts' and later on zinc plates (Mott 1962, p. 501). In the 1850s and 1860s, newspapers published photographs of the Crimean War and American Civil War. By the 1870s and 1880s, photographs were being published regularly in newspapers and the 'new processes' were resulting in the establishment of new newspapers 'which relied largely on picture appeal' (Mott 1962, p. 502). One of these papers was an eight-page publication described as 'an unsensational forerunner of the modern tabloid' which was launched in 1873 with much fanfare and what turned out to be a sensational, but unsuccessful, promotional stunt to cross the Atlantic by balloon (Mott 1962, p. 502). But while some newspapers had been enthusiastic in embracing the newfangled technology of photography, a majority in the 1880s 'remained unexcited' and 'the toils of invention certainly seem ill-rewarded' (Evans 1978, p. 1).

Although news outlets were generally slow to realise its potential, photography continued evolving. By the mid-1880s photographs were being taken with cameras that recorded images on glass plates. The first Kodak film camera was sold in about 1890. Famous photographs, some of which were later shown to have been faked, were taken on the battlefields of World War I. But it was not until World War II that news photography, like so many other technologies, moved forward in leaps and bounds. Mott reported that during World War II photographers played a greater role than ever before in war reporting and were often able to transmit photographs over telegraph lines and by wireless 'to news desks along with the copy' (Mott 1962, p. 743). What Mott was referring to was the birth of 'photojournalism'. Before World War II, cameras had been so cumbersome and difficult to use that specialist photographers had taken pictures and journalists had written stories. There was little or no crossover. But new, smaller portable cameras were developed during the war. While cumbersome by today's standards, some were waterproof and dustproof and had a built-in flash. They could be used in the field by journalists and a new practice emerged in which 'occasionally a newsman made his report by pictures as well as words' (Mott 1962, p. 744).

Cameras and film continued to advance after World War II. Colour film became widely available and colour printing technology improved. In the late 1940s and through the 1950s, numerous pictorial magazines were published. They posed something of a threat to the advertising revenue of newspapers and the latter responded by publishing more and better photographs—although not in colour because newspaper printing presses were not yet capable of full colour reproduction. In the late 1950s and early 1960s, single-lens reflex (SLR) cameras that allowed users to see images through the lens in the same way the camera saw them—instead of through a separate and not always accurate viewfinder lens—became commercially available. In the 1970s interchangeable lenses for SLR cameras were introduced. This meant the same camera body could be used for a range of photos, with the addition of telephoto lenses for distant shots, and other lenses for mid-range, close-up and wide-angle shots. Autofocus lenses became available in the 1980s. Digital photography was introduced in the latter half of the 1990s, and by the turn of the 21st century it was obvious that the immediacy and convenience of digital image making and storage was going to replace expensive and time-consuming film. In 2005 Kodak—the company that had pioneered the production of film cameras for the masses—closed most of its film-processing plants and four years later, in 2009, it stopped manufacturing colour film.

At the same time as cameras and photography were advancing, newspapers were changing. Prior to the 1990s newspapers had only been able to make limited use of a single colour—known as 'spot colour' and most commonly red—on selected pages. Printing colour photographs on newsprint was difficult, time-consuming to set up, and expensive. But from the late 1990s, advances in photographic image scanning and printing techniques saw newspapers move to full-colour production, and black-and-white photographs were no longer published in anything other than the smallest local papers. In the same period, news photographers started using digital cameras. Aligned with that, the practice of sending news photos over 'the wire' fell by the wayside and was replaced by the much simpler and faster expedient of attaching photos to emails. By the early 21st century, newspapers were often publishing photographs of breaking news events which had been contributed by members of the public.

After 2004, newspapers started routinely publishing breaking news stories and related photographs online—often within minutes of an event or incident happening. Then came smartphones followed by the release of the Apple iPad in 2010. Those advances, and the development of related apps, led to the routine publication of news photographs, sound and video on portable devices.

Digital photojournalism

The combination of rapid technical improvements in photography; the advent of mobile phone cameras, smartphones and tablet computers; unprecedented advances in newspaper production; the evolution of news publication online and for portable devices; and the expectations of news consumers have made it mandatory for every journalist to at least learn the basics of news photography. There is still a role for specialist news photographers, especially when covering major events and for set-up shots. But in addition to their mobile phone and its camera every journalist should at least carry a dedicated lightweight, automatic, self-focusing SLR camera. While often only used for relatively simple photo-stories, just carrying a camera with you means you can capture those rare moments when something unexpected happens. Further, with most SLRs now capable of video recording as well as still photography, you will often be able to capture a still shot and video images. That might be while you are out covering a story—or perhaps even on the way to, or returning from, a story, or on the way to or from work. Then, like the World War II photojournalists, you will be able to file photos, words, and maybe video images as well. As Evans said: 'The writer has a second chance, the photographer rarely' (Evans 1978, p. 21). In other words, a journalist can at least partly make up for a missed question or not being present when a storytelling moment happens by later interviewing witnesses; but the only way to a capture an image of a special moment is to be there and take photographs.

While it would be ideal for every journalism student to undertake a photography course, it is not always possible. Therefore, while the information presented in the rest of this chapter will not turn you into a professional photographer, it does provide a basic photographic survival guide. After all a picture, even if mediocre, will attract a reader's eye, and there is every chance you might fluke the ultimate shot—especially if you take enough photos from different angles and with different camera settings.

As a first step, and to avoid confusion when talking to professional photographers who are not news photographers, it should be noted that there are two different meanings attached to the terms 'photojournalism' and 'photojournalists'. From a journalistic perspective, the terms are taken to mean a journalist who takes photographs and subsequently writes stories related to those images. From a purist photographer's perspective, however, a photojournalist is a person who tells stories without words, or with a bare minimum of words, relying instead on a photograph or series of photographs in what is sometimes referred to as a 'photo-essay'. When the terms are used here, it is in the journalistic sense.

Categories of news photos

There are three main classes of photographs used by newspapers, magazines, news websites and for portable device apps. The first is photographs so powerful they virtually stand alone with nothing more than a headline, or online heading, and a caption. Many of the 9/11 photos and the stark image of Kim Phúc discussed at the start of this chapter fall into this category.

Second, there are photographs that share their impact with words, as the two work together to explain a story. An example of the second category is a photograph of the moment of the 1937 Hindenburg airship explosion in which words were needed to explain that the Zeppelin, which had just arrived at Lakehurst, New Jersey from Germany, was filled with explosive hydrogen gas. After the explosion, which killed 36 people, Associated Press photographer Murray Becker explained how he had been at the right place at the right time and had taken a photograph at the critical newsworthy moment. Unlike a journalist or photographer today armed with a digital camera that can take shot after shot, Becker had to take a single photograph, remove a photographic plate from his camera, then insert a fresh plate before the next shot. He said:

> I had taken several shots as the Hindenburg approached the landing field and had backed away for a general view when the first explosion occurred. I had my camera up to the eye level when the ship burst into flames. Like a hunter, I had my sights on the target and my finger on the trigger. I shot the picture showing the first puff of flames. Changing my plates, I got a second picture of the airship striking the ground with flames shooting the length of the ship, and then started running for it (Becker 1937, p. 1).

The third category of photograph is one that is used to complement words and illustrate a story. Such a photo might be a symbolic image kept on file by a news organisation or one taken specially to illustrate a point. It is unlikely the photograph would be newsworthy in its own right. An example would be a photograph of a person fishing, or skiing, used in conjunction with a travel article.

The mechanics of producing good photos

Start by making a point of always leaving your camera set to autofocus and full general auto exposure mode. Also ensure its batteries are charged regularly and you have spare fully charged replacements. We cannot predict when we will see something which begs for a photo, so it is better to be able to grab the camera, turn it on and shoot, than to miss a shot of a lifetime—even if the resultant image is not perfect. After that initial shot, or series of a few quick shots, you can then do things like swap to a more appropriate lens when using an SLR, and adjust speed and exposure settings. As time passes, you should review the photos you have already taken to ensure the images are good enough and, if they are not, take more.

One of the truisms about photography is that even with the best cameras and lenses, lighting is everything. As Eismann, Duggan and Grey explained:

> The difference between an ordinary picture and a good photograph is the difference between just pointing and shooting and consciously working with composition, light, and camera controls to create a memorable image (Eismann, Duggan & Grey 2004, p. 271).

Generally there is no choice about what time of day or night news photographs are taken, but for portrait shots, images of nature, and landscapes try to avoid harsh midday sunlight. Soft morning light is best. The air is usually as clear as it will be all day, and light from the sun low in the eastern sky is diffused. If you do have to take a photograph in the sun, try to position yourself and, if possible, the subject so that he or she is not facing directly into the sun or the sun is not behind her or him, otherwise the photo will be harsh and there will be strongly contrasting facial shadows. Also try to avoid situations in which there are contrasting patches of bright light and dark areas of low light—a combination that can confuse exposure and focus sensors in cameras. Those points aside, good-quality cameras are remarkably tolerant and will do their best to help you if set to an automatic mode.

COMPOSING A PHOTOGRAPH

One of the most important, and most overlooked, aspects of photography is to look beyond the subject of a photograph to see what is in the background. Many an otherwise perfect shot has been ruined by a cluttered or inappropriate background. Say, for example, you are going to take a portrait shot. Look at the subject through the viewfinder, then look beyond the subject to see what the camera sees. Is there clutter, are there bright colours that will draw the eye away from the subject, is there someone or an animal doing something unfortunate, an advertisement, movement, signs? If so, reposition your subject so she or he is in front of a neutral, uncluttered background. As a general rule, the greater the distance between the subject and the background, the more the subject will stand out and the more blurred the background will become. But if you cannot reposition the subject, one helpful technique is to 'blow the background away' by using a telephoto lens— or telephoto setting, or portrait mode, if the camera has one—and then moving in as close as possible to the subject while maintaining focus on his or her face. If using a camera with autofocus for a portrait, always ensure the focus dot, square, or ring in the viewfinder is centred on the middle of the face—that central point is where most cameras sense focus and light settings. If there is no focus dot or ring, it is safe to assume that the camera will sense its settings from the centre of the lens.

After considering the background, the next most important point is to think about how you will frame your shot. The vital thing here is ensure you provide editors with choices. Page layout, whether for print, online or mobile devices, generally dictates what shape a photograph will need to be before it can be published. There are two basic shapes: vertical—a tall narrow image referred to in computer software as a 'portrait' image; and horizontal—a wide image referred to in computer jargon as 'landscape'. Even if an editor wants to publish a square image, as tends to happen online, she or he will crop it from either a vertical or horizontal shot. Therefore, because you have no idea when out in the field what shape hole on a page a photograph will need to fit into, you should always shoot horizontal and vertical versions of every photo you take—whether of a person, news scene, landscape, building, animal or event. Doing so is simple: hold the camera in its normal position for a horizontal shot, and turn it on its side for a vertical!

If taking portrait-style shots, say, of a character who is the subject of a feature article, always take several close-up head-and-shoulders shots as well as general, often more artistic, portrait images. The reason for doing so is because editors might want to publish a headshot—literally a photo of a head—or head-and-shoulders image as well as a main photograph. Similarly, when taking photographs of landscapes, buildings, news scenes and events, give editors a choice by taking a range of close-up shots and wider, more distant shots.

TIGHT SHOTS

The more tightly an original photograph is framed in the viewfinder, the better it will be when enlarged. This is something many amateurs do not understand. Think of the numerous happy snaps you see in family albums in which there is a wide open foreground, masses of sky in the background and a person in between. Images like these do not work in print, online or for mobile devices. Trying to crop them to get rid of foreground and background rarely works either because enlarging the person in the middle too much is likely to make the focus fuzzy and images pixelate. What does work are tightly framed images virtually cropped in the viewfinder. If you are taking a portrait shot, use the camera's zoom or a telephoto lens and get up close and personal—your aim should be for a warts-and-all image. If you are taking a news photograph, again make the images of the action fill the viewfinder—particularly for your first few shots—then photograph a selection of wider images.

Group photos also need to be tight, not just in the sense of filling the viewfinder, but also in terms of getting people in a group close to each other. Apart from individuals who lack insight, we humans instinctively value our personal space and are generally careful not to invade the personal space around others. While we let those we are close to and care about into our personal space, we literally keep others at arm's length. Thus if you gather together a group of work colleagues, school children, members of a team, or others and ask them to stand or sit together for a group photograph, they will usually come together and stand or sit near each other, but most will instinctively avoid being so close to others they touch them. The resultant photograph will be of a group of individuals, not a group. From a photographer's perspective, you need to get every member of the group so close to those around them that they are touching, even overlapping, each other. The aim should be for a bright and tight photograph. To get it you must put people at their ease—both with you and each other. Aim to make them forget the camera. Talk, joke, get members of the group chatting. Then, because someone will inevitably blink, cough, sneeze, look away or frown, take many more shots than you think you will need. Chances are there will then be at least one that is usable.

As a further tip here, but unfortunately one many wily politicians are aware of, you will occasionally encounter a publicity-seeker whom you do not want in a group shot, but who insists on joining in. If you can arrange the group in such a way that the publicity pest is at either end of the group, she or he can always be cropped out of the image later!

USING FLASH

Options to use 'fill flash' and red eye correction are two of the most useful functions of many cameras. Flash is not just for helping illuminate a scene in low light, it can also be turned on to obtain softer images in bright light. When photographing people and objects in brightly lit surroundings, you can use a camera's built-in flash—or in the case of a professional-level SLR camera, its accessory flash—to eliminate harsh shadows caused by ambient light; this is called fill flash. Check your camera's instruction book for details about how to activate the flash in conditions other than low light. In many SLR cameras with multiple automatic settings there is an option to use the 'P' (program) and/or 'AE' (auto exposure) mode and press a button marked with a lightning bolt symbol (~) to pop up (or turn on) the flash so it can be used to fill in shadows on a subject's face. Many point-and-shoot cameras and smartphone cameras also have a flash that can be turned on—typically by pushing a button marked with a ⚡ symbol or scrolling through a menu until 'fill flash' appears and can be selected.

Using fill flash can make an image that would have been unusable—because parts of it were too light and other parts too dark—usable. But be aware that the average built-in camera flash only works if the subject is within a distance of between one and four or five metres from the camera. If there is less than a metre between the camera and subject, the bottom of the photo might be dark and the top 'blown away', or too bright. If there is too much distance between subject and camera, the flash will not be intense enough to soften or eliminate shadows. These distances will vary if an accessory flash is used.

Another useful tool is red eye correction. If you turn on a flash in a low-light situation, or a camera set to adjust itself automatically decides there is low ambient light and it needs to turn on its own flash, resultant images of human faces are likely to be ruined because the pupils in subjects' eyes will be unnaturally red. There can be similar problems photographing animals, only their eyes can be anything from green to yellow. The problem is caused by the fact that the pupils in human and animal eyes open wide in low light, so that they can see. If a flash photograph is taken when the pupils in a person's eyes are wide open, the burst of light from the flash reflects off the blood-filled retina at the back of each eye and makes the pupils appear red in the photograph.[1] Cameras with red eye compensation work by firing a preliminary flash that makes the pupils contract, then a second burst of flash when the photo is actually taken. Red eye reduction is most effective when a subject is looking at the camera. But sometimes it does not work, so it is wise to take a series of photos and check the images afterwards. If the red eye compensation did not work, try a different approach by turning red eye correction off, then shooting another sequence of photos in which the subject does not look directly at the camera.

If you have an SLR camera with an add-on accessory flash which can be pointed in different directions, an excellent way to avoid red eye problems (and hence any need for red eye correction) and be able to take soft, warm shots in low light is to use what is known as bounce flash. Instead of aiming the flash directly at the subject—something virtually guaranteed to produce a stark image—point the flash at a reflective surface, such as a white ceiling, midway between you and the subject. The burst of light from the flash will then travel from the camera to the reflective surface and be diffused before illuminating the subject. If you do not have an external flash, or a flash that can be pointed in different directions, good results can sometimes be obtained by placing a thin piece of white paper over the flash to diffuse the light.

ACTION PHOTOGRAPHS

There are two basic approaches to taking action photographs. One is to keep the camera as still as possible while you shoot, maybe on a tripod if you are at a sporting event and using a telephoto lens. The other is to move the camera so that it keeps the subject of the photograph—say, a runner or racing car—in focus and

---

1   Many animals, including dogs, have a different eye structure to humans that enables them to see in the dark. A flash reflects off a membrane behind the retina that humans do not have, resulting in a green, blue or yellow pupil.

in the centre of the viewfinder at all times while repeatedly shooting images. This second method is sometimes referred to as 'panning' the camera. If used correctly, it will result in a clear image of the subject against a blurred background, an image that conveys an impression of speed and motion.

Whichever approach you employ, you will get the best results by using the automatic action—or sport—setting on a camera which has that option, or, if a camera has a manual setting, using the highest possible shutter speed for the light conditions. If the camera has autofocus, keep the subject in the centre of the viewfinder. If using manual focus, the best results will be obtained if you can set up the focus prior to taking the shot by finding some point, maybe on the ground or a finish post, where you expect the subject to appear and focusing on that. Then, when the subject moves to that point you know the focus will be sharp. This pre-focusing works especially well with sports such as car racing, or when taking photographs at the finish line of any kind of race.

Another factor that will help get the best possible action shots is to shoot them in as much light as possible. While it is impossible, for example, to control the weather when shooting outdoor sporting events, shots taken when the sun is shining or under thin, high cloud will nearly always turn out better than those taken under heavy cloud or late in the day when light is fading.

Working with photographers

Depending on the size and resources of the publication you work for, and if it employs specialist photographers, it is generally best if you can work with a specialist photographer when covering a breaking news story or interviewing for a feature. While not always possible, and while it is important to be able to take your own photographs, there are major advantages in working as a team. One is that a photographer can get shots while you interview. That way you can each pay full attention to your specific tasks. Among other things, while an interviewee is engrossed in talking to you, she or he is likely to forget about the camera and be less self-conscious, more relaxed and more natural—things that help a photographer who remains in the background capture character-revealing images.

It is also safer when photographers and journalists can work together on difficult or dangerous assignments. They can discuss story ideas and strategies in the same way that television journalists and video camera operators work together. They should look out for each other and warn the other of dangers. Photographers and video camera operators are often vulnerable because they must focus on what they see through the lens and may not have a broad view of a developing situation. The journalists they work with must bear that in mind, warn of dangers and do their best to provide protection.

Caption writing

Many people read a caption under a photograph before they read an accompanying article. This is because it was the image, more than the story's headline or online heading, that drew their eyes. Captions, which are also known as 'block lines', are therefore at least as important as headings and story intros. Yet many journalists and sub-editors do not seem to put the same degree of thought into writing a caption as they would an intro or headline. A former editor of *The Sunday Times* in the 1970s, Evans (1978) had a radical suggestion about how to improve the quality of captions. Complaining that beneath a caption of former US President Jimmy Carter speaking, a caption said 'President Carter speaking' while a photograph of the British Prime Minister getting into a car was captioned 'The Prime Minster enters a car', Evans (who was writing in an era when virtually all editors and nearly all journalists were male) said:

> The tendency of caption writers to treat the reader as a moron is easily corrected by the editor striking his employee a hard blow on the head, twice, with a blunt instrument. When he comes to he should be reminded of the what? where? when? why? questions the picture raises (Evans 1978, p. 257).

Good captions must expand on picture content, not restate it, or describe it. They should add context and make people want to read the accompanying story. The basic rules of caption writing are as follows:

— Do not repeat wording from the headline, online heading, intro or body of an article an image accompanies.

— As a general convention, always identify people in a photo from left to right. The only exception would be if one person in a photograph is more significant to the story the photograph accompanies than all the others, in which case it can be legitimate to name that person first, then name the others from left to right.

— Double-check the spelling of names—are they consistent with spelling in the article?

— Never guess what a subject is thinking or make assumptions about their emotional state—chances are you will be wrong!

— It is a convention of news writing style that captions should always be written in the present tense.

— Keep captions short and to the point. Do not waffle.

— Use active voice and active verbs.

— Ensure information in a caption does not conflict with information in the story a photograph relates to.

Photojournalism ethics

Photographs have been faked and retouched for as long as there has been photography. But the advent of digital cameras and use of computer programs such as Photoshop have made faking and retouching easier. Memorable examples of faked photographs include a 1982 photograph on the front cover of *National Geographic* magazine in which the Egyptian pyramids were moved closer together to make the image fit the page. In 2006 there was an infamous example in which a photographer working for Reuters news agency manipulated a photograph to make it more dramatic by adding heavy plumes of black smoke billowing from buildings in Beirut after an air attack on the Lebanese capital. Reuters subsequently sacked the photographer and issued a 'picture kill' notice while also withdrawing the photograph from its website. The agency apologised and said, 'The image had been digitally altered using the cloning tool in Photoshop so that it showed more smoke' (Reuters 2007).

A few years earlier, there had been what became a famous example of a digital manipulation undertaken by some newspapers for the opposite reason—to sanitise an image to make it less dramatic and less disturbing than it actually was. The photograph was shot by *El Pais* photographer Pablo Torres Guerrero immediately after the 2004 Madrid train bombing. The colour image, which was circulated internationally by Reuters, showed a wrecked train and dead and injured people in a railway yard. In the lower left of the photograph was part of a human thigh and femur. Some newspapers published the photograph as it was. Others manipulated it to either remove the image of the body part; cover it with type; replace it with railway ballast stones; print the photograph in black and white so the thigh was less noticeable; or crop the photograph so tightly the body part was not shown. Poynter Institute visual journalism group leader Kenneth Irby said editors who removed or disguised the thigh and femur believed the photograph was too gruesome, and publishing it without manipulation would have been in bad taste because it would have upset some of the people who viewed it (Irby 2004). He said the manipulation happened despite it being a policy at Reuters that organisations which subscribed to its service should not electronically manipulate a photo to change its content. Newspapers that published the image unchanged included *The Washington Post*, which printed the picture in full colour on its front page, as did Spain's *El Pais*. Irby (2004) said such newspapers felt it was important for readers to see the reality of terror.

Journalists have four sources of news photographs: those taken by their own organisation's professional photographers, images from wire services, photos they take themselves, and contributed photographs. Contributed images are from two main sources: public relations firms and advertisers, and members of the public. If a news organisation and its photographers and photojournalists are ethical and do not manipulate their own photographs in ways that distort truth, the most likely source of faked or (as was highlighted in Chapter 6) misrepresented images are contributed photographs. Problems are exacerbated when photos which have been faked but in which the manipulation has not been detected are subsequently transmitted by news agencies. John Long, then ethics co-chair and a past president of the US National Press Photographers' Association (NPPA), warned more than a decade ago that: 'Our readers and viewers no longer believe everything they see. All images are called into question because the computer has proved that images are malleable, changeable, fluid.' But:

> Once the shutter has been tripped and the moment has been captured on film, in the context of news, we no longer have the right to change the content of the photo in any way. Any change to a news photo—any violation of that moment—is a lie. Big or small, any lie damages your credibility (NPPA 1999).

There is no parallel organisation to the NPPA in Australia, but the Media Entertainment and Arts Alliance (MEAA)'s *Journalists' Code of Ethics* applies equally to photojournalism as it does to all journalism. As explained in detail in Chapter 4, it says respect for truth and the public's right to information are fundamental tenets of journalism, and journalists should report and interpret honestly striving for disclosure of all essential facts (Media Entertainment and Arts Alliance 2013a).

Ethical codes aside, and while there will be scandals from time to time about faked photographs, one of the greatest disincentives to photographic fraud is closely related to the computer technology that makes digital faking possible. While computers, the web and internet make rapid dissemination of photographs possible, they also make it easy for photographs to be digitally examined by experts around the globe. Some of these experts, and certainly many bloggers and websites such as Snopes.com and MuseumofHoaxes.com, delight in exposing fakes—something that should make prospective image manipulators think twice, especially if they value their names and their jobs!

Finally, when should you not take photographs? Details are explained in Chapters 16 and 17, but generally it is illegal to take photographs in courtrooms and even court buildings; to take photographs if trespassing on private land; to photograph subjects engaging in 'private acts' in situations in which they would not generally expect to be photographed; and to publish photographs that identify child victims of crime or victims of sexual offences. As explained in Chapter 16, it can also constitute *sub judice* contempt to publish a photo that identifies a person accused of a crime if there is doubt about whether that person or another person actually committed the crime.

While we do not own our own image and it is generally not a problem taking photographs of people in public places, it can be illegal if a photographer behaves offensively, in a threatening way, causes a public nuisance, or takes indecent photos. Also be careful taking photographs of children. While it is not generally illegal to photograph a child in a public place, community concerns about paedophiles photographing children and publishing pictures via the internet have made child photography a sensitive issue. Unless circumstances of a breaking story dictate otherwise, as they did in relation to the Vietnamese girl Kim Phúc, the common sense approach is to seek parental permission before photographing minors. It should also be borne in mind that large shopping centres are private property and

One of the greatest disincentives to photographic fraud is closely related to the computer technology that makes digital faking possible. While computers, the web and internet make rapid dissemination of photographs possible, they also make it easy for photographs to be digitally examined by experts around the globe.

management can prohibit photographs being taken. Shop and gallery owners can also prohibit photos being taken on their premises. But photographs of the insides of shops and shopping centres can be shot by a photographer who is outside in a public place, such as on a footpath in a public street.

Total packages

One of the biggest advantages in becoming self-sufficient as a photographer and writer is that a photojournalist—and particularly a freelance photojournalist—who can write well and take high-quality photographs can supply total packages of stories and images. Thus a journalist who owns her or his own SLR camera, a portable computer or tablet with a wireless broadband account, and a good mobile phone can become a self-sufficient unit. That journalist has much more to offer than a rival who can only supply words.

And two final tips relating to photojournalism. First, most cameras have plenty of memory, so take many shots of the same subject using a range of different camera settings and different camera angles. Doing so will increase your chances of fluking the ultimate photograph! Second, and this is particularly important if freelancing, find out what file format the organisation(s) you supply photographs to prefers. The most common formats are:

— JPEG, which is the favoured format for images published online, on mobile devices and in newspapers. This is also a near-universal format supported by almost all photographic software and by major camera manufacturers including Nikon and Canon. Eismann, Duggan and Grey recommended setting cameras in which there are file format options to save images at the highest possible quality JPEG format, which is often labelled 'large' (Eismann, Duggan & Grey 2004, p. 27).

— RAW is a generic but brand-specific file format supported by different camera manufacturers. While RAW files are high quality, they can generally only be processed with brand-specific software.

— Photoshop handles different formats but it also supports its own PSD file format.

— TIFF is the other major format, but its files are huge compared with JPEG and they are not readily transmitted as email attachments. However, many publishers of high-quality images use RAW and TIFF files because they produce richer photos than JPEG.

DISCUSSION POINTS

1   Is it reasonable to expect a journalist to conduct interviews and take photographs for the same story? Or is that sort of multi-tasking asking too much?

2   Describe, and if possible obtain a copy of, a recent photograph that literally had the potential to change the way people behave. What makes that image so powerful?

3   Should specialist newspaper and magazine photographers feel threatened by photojournalists who can write and take photographs, or are the two roles so different it does not matter?

4   Is it legitimate, and ethical, for a publication to either crop or digitally manipulate photographs like those of the Madrid train bombings that are so graphic they could disgust and/or disturb readers if published in their original form?

5   What sort of news-related images should never be published? Why? Who should decide?

6   Following on from Discussion Point 5, if you were an editor, would you have published photographs on your newspaper's front page of people literally a fraction of a second from death as they were falling from the World Trade Centre towers in the 9/11 attack? Why or why not?

7   Should a photographer or journalist ever get to a point when they stop being an observer and become a participant in an unfolding event? If so, at what point? If not, why not?

NEWS PRACTICE POINTS

1   In this chapter there is reference to Nick Ut's photograph of Kim Phúc and the impact that image had around the world. There is at least one other starkly horrifying photograph that is also credited with changing US attitudes to the Vietnam War. It was taken by a different photographer almost literally as a person was shot in the head by a Saigon police chief in a street in 1968. Go online and find both photographs. Explain in a few words what made each so compelling.

2   There has been considerable discussion in this chapter about news photographs of tragedy and disaster, but not all news is bad and not all photographs are tragic. Find at least two recent uplifting news photographs from either online or print editions of major news publications. Explain in a few words how you would categorise each image and why—as virtually stand-alone, as one in which picture and words carry equal weight, or as an image that merely adds value to the words in an article.

3   Where could you undertake a good-quality course in photography? Does your university or institution offer one? If not, where is the nearest? Find out how much the course would cost and how long it would take to complete.

4   Conduct an experiment with a group photograph. Get a camera and ask a group of at least five people to stand together for a group shot. Members of the group can be acquainted, but must not be family or partners. Do not ask them to do anything more than stand as a group and look at the camera. Take several photographs. Then tell the members of the group they must bunch up and stand as close as they can—so close their bodies touch each other. Take several more photographs. Compare the images from the first series of photographs with those from the second. Which would you publish?

5   Find three recent captions in a newspaper, magazine or online news site that work well with a photograph and three that the writer should be ashamed of. Briefly explain in writing what is good about each of those you like, and what is bad about each of the others.

6   If you have a camera, read its instruction book and see what it says about using fill flash, or just flash. If you do not own a camera, borrow one (and also its instruction book) and do the same thing. Now take someone outside in bright sunlight and experiment by taking photographs of their face with them facing directly into the sun and also side-on to the sun; first with no flash, then with flash. If there are still shadows on the subject's face after using the flash, move closer and try again. Compare all the shots. Which images are best?

7   Who is the Australian you would most like to write a pictorial feature article about? Explain why in about 250 words.

8   Follow up Practice Point 7 by writing a letter to the person explaining you would like to interview them for a story and take their photo. See if you can get them to agree, then arrange a time and place to conduct the interview and take your photographs. Now write the story, caption your photos, and do your best to have the package published in print, online, or both.

NICK McKENZIE _____

Nick McKenzie is one of Australia's leading investigative journalists. He works for *The Age* and *The Sydney Morning Herald* and occasionally reports for ABC TV's *Four Corners* program. He has won the Walkley Award three times for his work exposing corruption and organised crime. His work has triggered several major inquiries, including Australia's biggest bribery investigation. His latest novel, *The Sting* (2012, Melbourne University Publishing) tells the true story of an Australian law enforcement agency pitted against a tech-savvy, billion-dollar global organised crime empire.

1 How did you get your first job as a journalist?

I began working as a journalist while studying journalism at university. I basically tried to pitch features for newspapers and magazines in order to get my name in print. Having a few stories already published helped when I left university and began to apply for jobs. I applied for at least 10 different jobs in newspapers and journalism and was fortunate enough to get a cadetship at the ABC in Melbourne.

2 What advice would you offer a beginning journalist?

First, get published or broadcast. Editors and bosses are looking for journalists who are fiercely determined; in other words, someone who—despite not having yet established themselves as a working journalist—has dug up stories and got their work published. As a journalist starting out, it is also important not to wait for story ideas to be passed to you. You have to dig things up and constantly come up with ideas. There is no shortage of stories, but the trick is to recognise them and convert them into news or a feature. A good way to do this is to follow topics you are passionate about to ensure you have fun along the way. Passion and determination count for a lot. Remember to always aim high and tell your audience something they don't know.

3 What is the role of journalism in 21st-century Australian society?

Journalism plays a variety of roles, but for me, the most important role remains holding those who hold power—such as politicians, big business, organised crime and the military—to account. The old motto about shining a light into dark places remains as relevant today as it ever was. However, one of the things that has changed in journalism over the last few decades is the way the institutions and people journalists scrutinise interact with the press and vice versa. The internet, television news and cable news have considerably sped up the news cycle, meaning there are more stories with a short shelf life. There are also far more sources of news for consumers. So when working on a story, a journalist must be conscious, even strategic, about how it will feature in today's news cycle.

4 What are your thoughts about the future of journalism in Australia?

Journalism is facing some huge challenges in an era of declining newspaper revenue and new technologies, like the internet. But for a healthy democracy, it must survive. People still want quality news and it is a reality that blogs and other new media mediums are often not best placed to deliver such quality. The newspaper often is.

The key to the future of good investigative journalism is about ensuring it adapts to the new media environment. This might mean newspaper journalists doing their investigations for both print (for a newspaper) and online, with interactive audio-visual elements. A reader may have to pay to access the stories online, or have a subscription. Given the lack of philanthropic support for journalism in Australia (unlike the US), investigative journalism (which costs money and is time-consuming) needs to operate in an environment that can properly sustain its existence.

5 What are the key things a journalism student should learn during their studies?

A student should learn the obvious basics about impartiality, cultivating sources and good, clean writing. They should also be big news consumers while they study. Watch and read everything you can get your hands on. And remember, you should not consider yourself as simply a journalism student. If you want to be a journalist, then be one. While studying, get your work published or aired in the local paper, the *Big Issue* magazine, on local radio... wherever.

6 Is there anything else you would like to say to journalism students and/or about journalism as a profession?

Despite the naysayers and doom predictors about the future of journalism and the difficulty of getting a job, being a journalist is open to anyone with enough determination, passion and the right nose for sniffing out a story. The media will keep on adapting and good journalism will continue to exist, in one way or another. The great thing about the profession is that it can be immensely rewarding and great fun.

ADAM CAREY _____

Adam Carey is transport reporter for *The Age*. Previous roles he has held there include general news reporter, assistant arts editor and sub-editor. Before joining *The Age* he was a freelance journalist, mainly writing on technology, architecture and food.

---

1 How did you get your first job as a journalist?

I applied for a production traineeship at *The Age* and was successful—a case of third time lucky for me! Previously I had applied for the reporting traineeship but never got past the first round of interviews. Prior to the traineeship I worked for a couple of years as a freelance writer and sub-editor. While studying a graduate diploma in journalism at RMIT I had a few stories published in newspapers and magazines, and continued freelancing for a year after I graduated, before getting a full-time job at *The Age*.

2 What advice would you offer a beginning journalist?

Be persistent in your endeavours; never be afraid to keep knocking on the same door. But at the same time, be open-minded about where you start out. And don't shirk lowly, unglamorous work. As a freelancer I made it a policy never to turn down a job, no matter how seemingly uninteresting or outside my fields of interest; a commission for an engineering journal turned into regular writing work that helped pay my rent for two years, and also gave me some knowledge I used to pitch stories to major newspapers.

3 What is the role of journalism in 21st-century Australian society?

The role of journalism remains, or should remain, essentially the same in this society as previous ones. Reporting on powerful people—be they in government, business or whatever—and holding them to account. And telling great stories! Good journalism is never boring.

4 Journalism is being changed and challenged by technology. What are your thoughts about the future of journalism in Australia?

That's a tough one. Journalism is going through an enormous metamorphosis due to innovations in online communication, and I don't think anybody knows yet what it will ultimately look like when it's all over. Newspapers, the medium I work for, are feeling the pressure as much as any. Already there are fewer journalists here than there were three years ago when I arrived. Despite this, I still feel confident newspapers will continue to exist as long as they can give readers a high-quality product. But they may become smaller and more specialised.

5 What are the key things a journalism student should learn during their studies?

Other than the basics of how to gather facts and write a news story, the main lesson I would say is that it's vital to get yourself out there and build a portfolio of work while still studying. This might seem difficult while there are so many assignments due and you have bills to pay, but I think it's still true that in this industry employers attach more weight to work experience than good marks, rightly or wrongly.

6 Is there anything else you would like to say to journalism students and/or about journalism as a profession?

It's rarely as glamorous as it's cracked up to be and it won't make you rich unless you write a series of *Underbelly*-style books and sell the rights, but it can still be an immensely satisfying profession. I love it.

BOB BOTTOM _____

Bob Bottom is one of Australia's most accomplished investigative journalists. He has written for most major newspapers, with many of his major exposés syndicated both in Australia and overseas. He is author of seven best-selling books on organised crime and corruption and was awarded the Order of Australia Medal in 1997 for his work in 'investigating and reporting upon organised crime in Australia'. Throughout a career spanning more than four decades, he has been credited with initiating numerous royal commissions and other inquiries into organised crime and corruption. Likewise, he is credited with being a driving force behind the advent of federal and state crime commissions, asset seizure laws and the legalisation of telephone tapping by law enforcement agencies throughout Australia.

---

1 How did you get your first job as a journalist?

It so happens that my mother spotted an advertisement in the *Barrier Daily Truth* newspaper in Broken Hill where I had grown up and recently left school aged just 15, having completed an intermediate certificate after three years of high school. I applied and was accepted.

Times then were so different from today.

There were no university courses; with a four-year cadetship you had to learn on the job, so to speak. Because of limited staff resources, I had to learn quickly, covering all sorts of duties and assignments. So much so that I was promoted to a D-grade after 12 months.

To teach myself, I used to study metropolitan and overseas newspapers, often retyping good stories to reinforce the art of good writing. It also inspired a will to analyse and investigate matters.

While still only 16 I began writing as a correspondent for *The Bulletin* magazine which provided a stepping stone for my elevation to metropolitan newspapers.

2 What advice would you offer a beginning journalist?

With courses in journalism now available, I would recommend enrolment.

Back in my time, when I joined *The Daily Telegraph* in Sydney in 1968, a move had been introduced to provide an opportunity for university students who had completed an arts degree to be accepted as fourth-year cadets, on the basis that their university course would have taught them at least how to research and assemble fact and opinion. It was successful to a degree, except that a survey in the early 1970s discovered that fellow journalists who had instead had practical country or suburban newspaper experience proved more successful.

In contrast, nowadays modern journalism courses do provide practical lessons and experience.

3 What is the role of journalism in 21st-century Australian society?

There is a diversity to modern journalism that provides a greater variety of opportunities for journalism graduates— that is, apart from covering news for newspapers, television or radio, there is a whole new industry embracing research, advice and public relations.

All may serve the community, but only true journalism serves the public interest.

Without the benefit of any journalism course when I entered the profession, I was much influenced by the writings of John Mansfield. In my first book, *Behind the Barrier*, published four decades ago, I quoted from Mansfield's book, *Complete Journalist, A Study of the Principles and Practice of Newspaper Making* (Pitman, 1962). 'The charge is sometimes made,' wrote Mansfield, 'that journalists live for their work and neglect their citizenship'. In a sense, in some cases, this may be true, but it is contended here that journalism itself is at its best a valuable public service. The press is not merely the eyes and ears of the public; it is sometimes its conscience too. The calling of the journalist is so intimately concerned with the life of the state, the activities of the citizen, that to cultivate it to the full is to enter deeply into the living, being and moving of humanity—to see men, women and children in their homes, their offices, workshops and schools, in their pleasures, arts and crafts, sciences and industries, religions and philosophies, to share their sorrows and tragedies, in fact show them to themselves in the vivid mirror of the front page.

'Beyond this stands the responsibility of leadership, for the Press is rightly a pioneer of progress and a seer of visions,' wrote Mansfield. Thus, I trust that students of journalism aspire not only to pursue true journalism, but to serve the public interest.

4 Journalism is being changed and challenged by technology. What are your thoughts about the future of journalism in Australia?

I am actually optimistic for the future.

In retrospect, I can well remember fears for the continued viability of newspapers with the advent of television in Australia. Just as newspapers capitalised on the earlier introduction of radio, they found themselves in more demand with television, not only through their promotional aspects, but more simply by more people buying newspapers for a television guide.

The mind-boggling scope of the internet certainly makes you wonder. But the very expansion of internet outlets is creating new opportunities for countless journalists. People may like to Twitter, but it is still the principles of journalism behind the best content on the internet that people rely upon.

Likewise, the newspaper industry shall survive to serve those who will continue to prefer the daily or weekly package of news, features and opinion—and occasional exposés—emanating from good journalism in a reliable newspaper.

5 What are the key things a journalism student should learn during their studies?

Of all things, students should give more attention to the practical rather than theoretical aspects of any course.

Those colleges and universities sticking to the basics are finding that more of their students have more success in getting good jobs than those few that have tended to become too theoretical.

As a warning, in 2002, the [then] chief executive officer of News Limited, John Hartigan, himself a successful journalist, warned in a speech to the Pacific Area Newspapers Association that employers were becoming more selective in recruitment from 'the veritable horde of university degree holders knocking at our doors trying to get into journalism... We have to nurture talent through well-crafted training programs and we have to reward excellence.'

'In days gone by,' Hartigan said, 'the most venerated journalists found their news amongst the people. They congregated in pubs, amongst the coppers and crims; they sniffed out their scoops in bars and public places, and they talked to people, face to face, living the truism you don't find news hanging around the office. They were the product of a system which took in copy kids who learned the business from the basement up... '

Thus a course is not only about learning what journalism is all about and how to write a story, but a veritable gold mine of tips, advice and insights into the who, what, when, where, why and how of true journalism.

6 Is there anything else you would like to say to journalism students and/or about journalism as a profession?

Having graduated, so to speak, to investigative journalism, and been credited with initiating or being involved with some 18 royal commissions, judicial and parliamentary inquiries, I can testify to the fact that it can be a satisfying profession. In 1997 I was awarded the Order of Australia Medal for 'investigating and reporting upon organised crime' and an anniversary supplement in *The Sunday Telegraph* of November 22, 2009, noted that after pioneering work for that paper I had become 'a driving force behind the advent of state and federal crime commissions, criminal asset seizure laws and the legalisation of telephone tapping by law enforcement agencies throughout Australia'.

Thus, through journalism, students may aspire to not only serve the public interest, but at times the national interest.

JOURNALISM
LAW

5

HOW WE ARE GOVERNED

14

Power tends to corrupt, and absolute power corrupts absolutely.
First Baron Acton, 1887

OBJECTIVES

After reading this chapter you will understand:

» The structure of Australia's three-tier system of government

» How parliaments make laws

» Who is who in a parliament

» The principle of the separation of powers

» Basics of the Australian legal system

» The concept of journalists as members of the 'fourth estate'.

Politics and political shenanigans underlie so many news stories and have such a big impact on our lives that all journalists must have a solid understanding of how Australia is governed. Journalists must also understand the relationships between members of parliament (legislators), public servants (bureaucrats), the judiciary (judges and magistrates), and the role of mass news media as the 'fourth estate'. Readers and audiences will expect you to be knowledgeable about those things in your role as a professional who provides information to help them make informed decisions about issues affecting the nation and their own lives.

Australia's political and legal system arrived in the then colony of NSW with the First Fleet in 1788 when the first governor, Captain Arthur Phillip, 'disembarked some 1,030 British migrants at Sydney Cove' (Austin 1961, p. 1). Nearly 75 per cent of those migrants were convicts. There were also 36 children, plus guards and government officials (Austin 1961, p. 1). 'Justice' in those days was arbitrary, and government autocratic. The governor, military and naval officers, and, later, magistrates, were all-powerful. It was a time when 'the gallows and triangle cast long shadows' (Pearl, in Pollak 1990, p. 10). Writing in a 1938 supplement of *The Sydney Morning Herald* published to celebrate the 150th anniversary of British settlement in Australia, then president of the Royal Historical Society of Australia KR Cramp explained:

> The character of the inhabitants of the settlement in 1788 was such as necessitated an autocracy. Governor Phillip was consequently invested with the right to life and death over the people he governed. He was the administrative, legislative and judicial head of state. It was his threefold function to make the law, administer the law, and, when circumstances demanded, to construe the law (Cramp 1938, p. 19).

But as the colony's population grew with the arrival of increasing numbers of free settlers as well as convicts, a system of civil and criminal law slowly began to replace military law. Over time, a succession of autocratic, at times despotic, governors gave way to elected colonial governments. Cramp said:

> During the [first] 150 years of British settlement in Australia, the system of government has undergone a complete transformation. It has passed from extreme autocracy to thorough democracy in its internal institutions, and, in external relationships, from the complete dependence of the infant colony on its Motherland to a status of equality and companionship such as exists between the adult daughter and her mother (Cramp 1938, p. 19).

The transformation Cramp described began in 1823 when the *New South Wales Judicature Act 1823* was enacted by the British Parliament. It authorised establishment of Australia's first legislature, the NSW Legislative Council. It originally consisted of 'not more than seven nor fewer than five members' appointed by the governor (Scott 1916, p. 98). Although its powers could be overruled by the governor, the council did have 'power to make laws "for the peace, welfare, and good government" of NSW, provided that they were not repugnant to the laws of England' (Scott 1916, p. 98). The 1823 Act also established Australia's first Supreme Court, which was presided over by our first chief justice Sir Francis Forbes (Scott 1916, p. 98). Trial by jury was introduced in 1830, although former convicts who had been convicted of 'serious offences' were forbidden from jury service (Scott 1916, p. 102).

Between 1855 and 1890 the colonies of Tasmania, Victoria, SA, Queensland and WA all separated from NSW. Each established its own legislative and judicial systems modelled broadly on the British system. Still part of the British Empire, each colony's government evolved into what is known today as a Westminster system of government. The name comes from the fact that the British Parliament—the

House of Commons (which is the lower house) and the House of Lords (the upper house)—are both housed in the Palace of Westminster in London. Canada and New Zealand also have Westminster-style systems of government.

In 1893 principles of 'manhood suffrage and one man one vote were recognised' in NSW (Cramp 1938, p. 19). It was not until 1895 that women were first allowed to vote, and only then in SA—a then radical step towards equality not followed until 1899 in WA, 1902 in NSW, 1903 in Tasmania, 1905 in Queensland, 1908 in Victoria, and 1911 in the Northern Territory and ACT (Australian Electoral Commission 2009).

In 1900 Australia's six states agreed to adopt a federal constitution and move from being separate British colonies, each tied individually to an apron string of the Palace of Westminster, and to form our own federation—the Commonwealth of Australia. The *Commonwealth of Australia Constitution Act* was passed by the British Parliament in 1900 and signed into law by Queen Victoria. On January 1, 1901 the former colonies united into one nation.

The Constitution sets out the rules under which the Federal Government operates. It can only be changed after a referendum in which a majority of voters in a majority of states (four of six) vote 'yes' and a majority of all electors who voted across all states and territories also vote 'yes'—this is known as a 'double majority'. If a proposed change would particularly affect one or more states, a majority of electors in those states must also agree—thus a 'triple majority' would be required (Department of Foreign Affairs and Trade 2008). The NT and ACT are not counted as states in a constitutional referendum, but the votes of electors in those territories count towards the national majority. (The complex voting system is at least part of the reason why at the time of writing in 2013 only eight of 44 proposals to amend the Constitution have succeeded since Federation in 1901.)

As well as ratifying the federal Constitution, the *Commonwealth of Australia Constitution Act* provided for the establishment of the Commonwealth Parliament to make nationally significant laws for the federation. In the Westminster tradition, the Commonwealth Parliament has a lower house—the House of Representatives—and an upper house—the Senate. The former colonies of NSW, Victoria, SA, Queensland, Tasmania and WA became states in the Commonwealth of Australia, with each gaining special recognition in the Senate, or states' house. Women were granted the right to vote in federal elections in 1902, when they were also permitted for the first time to actually stand for election to the Federal

Parliament (Australian Electoral Commission 2009).The NT and ACT were created by the Commonwealth Government in 1911. But it was not until 1986 and the passing of the *Australia Act* by both the Australian and British Parliaments that Australia's constitutional, legislative and judicial ties with Britain were finally severed and Australia became a fully independent nation in its own right. Unlike the US—which is a republic and has a president as its head of state—Australia, the UK, Canada and New Zealand are all monarchies and the Queen is our head of state. She is represented in Australia by the Governor-General.

In a Westminster system, the lower and upper houses of parliament have different roles. For example, the House of Representatives—like the House of Commons in the UK and Legislative Assemblies (or House of Assembly) in each Australian state and territory—is where governments are formed and where the prime minister, state premiers, or chief ministers of territories are based. The Senate—like the House of Lords in the UK and Legislative Councils in NSW, Victoria, Tasmania, SA and WA—is a house of review where decisions made in the lower house are examined and can be accepted, rejected or sent back to the lower house for modification. There are no upper houses in Queensland,[1] the NT or ACT. Parliaments with both an upper and lower house are known as bicameral—two house—parliaments. Those with a single house are referred to as unicameral.

Australia's three tiers of government

Our Federal, or Commonwealth, Parliament, comprising the House of Representatives and Senate, makes laws with national impact and significance. The Commonwealth Constitution specifically empowers the Federal Parliament to make laws relating to a broad range of matters including taxation, defence, foreign affairs, trade between states, telecommunications, postal services, lighthouses, marriage, currency, divorce, industrial disputes that span more than one state, social security benefits, census, intellectual property, 'naturalisation and aliens', bankruptcy, weights and measures, 'the influx of criminals', meteorological 'observations', customs, and numerous other matters (Australian Constitution 1900, Section 51).

---

1   Queensland originally had an upper house but its Legislative Council was abolished by a Labor government in 1922.

It is a generalisation, but state and territory governments commonly have responsibility for any areas not controlled by the Federal Government. Each state has its own constitution, parliament, governor, legal system and public service. States also have rights to impose taxes and charges.

There are many overlaps between state and territory legislation and areas of responsibility and those of the Commonwealth. For example states and territories, and the Commonwealth, each make laws about health, education, transport, water use, mining, police, the environment, disability services, and aged care. Sometimes these shared responsibilities lead to clashes between politicians, public servants and lawyers at different levels. But if a state law conflicts with a Commonwealth law, Section 109 of the Federal Constitution says the Commonwealth law will prevail. The High Court—Australia's top court—has the power to overrule state courts and rule on disputes between states.

Members of state, territory and federal governments either belong to political parties or are independent members of parliament who are not officially aligned with any party—although the vast majority are party members. State, territory and federal governments are all formed in their respective parliament's lower house—the House of Representatives federally, or Houses of Assembly in states and territories—by the party or group of parties (a coalition) with the greatest number of elected members after an election. The beaten party or coalition of parties—the one, or group, with fewer members than the government— becomes the opposition. Rarely, a parliament might be said to be 'hung', in which case two or more opposing political parties have an equal number of elected members. If this happens, one side might be able to scrape together enough support to govern by soliciting support from one or more independent members or from a minor party. This happened in the 2010 state election in Tasmania when the vote was split 10–10–5—Liberal, Labor and the Greens— with the Greens holding the balance of power and deciding to support a Labor government. Similarly, after the 2010 federal election in which Labor and the Coalition each won 72 seats in the 150 seat House of Representatives, Labor leader Julia Gillard was able to form a minority government after gaining the support of the Greens' Andrew Bandt and three independents—Tony Windsor, Rob Oakshott and Andrew Wilkie.

Sometimes a party has enough lower house members to form government but has a minority of members in the upper house. In that case, the upper house is said to be 'hostile' to the government. If there is a hostile upper house, this does not stop a government from governing, but it can make life difficult for a government if the upper house constantly amends or rejects legislation proposed by a government in the lower house. In some circumstances, if a government is repeatedly frustrated by a hostile upper house, it might eventually decide to try to settle the matter by calling an early election, in which case both houses are dissolved and all members go to the polls in what is known as a double dissolution election.

The frequency of elections varies between parliaments. Federally, all members of the House of Representatives must go to the polls at least every three years. Members of the Senate are elected for six years and unless there is a 'double dissolution'—in which case all seats in the lower and upper houses are declared vacant—half the members of the Senate will normally stand for election every three years. For practical reasons, half-Senate elections and House of Representatives elections are normally held at the same time. The majority of state and territory governments serve four-year terms, with members of their upper houses serving anything from four to eight-year terms. Voting is compulsory in all state, territory and federal elections and on average only about 5 per cent of those who are eligible to vote fail to do so (Our Electoral System 2008). All election ballots are secret, with secret ballots having been pioneered in Victoria in 1855 (Department of Foreign Affairs and Trade 2008).

The third tier of government in Australia is local government. Known in some states as regional councils, municipal councils and local authorities, local governments traditionally deal with the 'three Rs'—roads, rates and rubbish. They are also responsible for services such as libraries, sporting grounds, halls and swimming pools. Councils issue a plethora of permits and licences, ranging from cat and dog registration, to planning permits, building permits, and many others covering things such as food vending, building, parking, and vegetation removal. In addition, councils build and maintain facilities such as airports, ports and marinas, cemeteries, and carparks.

Local councils have only one legislative chamber. While state, territory and federal governments enact legislation as acts of parliament, or statutes, local authorities pass bylaws. And while federal government statutes apply nationally, and state and territory legislation applies in the state or territory where an Act was passed, local authority bylaws only apply in the council area where they were made.

There are close to 700 local councils in Australia, with about 450 being in rural and regional areas (LGA 2009). Councils are established and to some extent controlled by state and territory governments. Councillors, or aldermen as they are known in some areas, are usually elected for three- or four-year terms. Mayors chair council meetings and some have executive authority to make limited decisions between meetings. In some states mayors are elected directly by ratepayers, but in others, sitting councillors elect or appoint one of their own to act as mayor.

The day-to-day functions of councils are undertaken by administrative staff under the direction of senior executives such as a town clerk, chief executive officer or manager. Some councils—usually the larger ones—operate on party political lines, while others have members who are not openly politically aligned. Local authorities in larger urbanised areas tend to call themselves city councils, while those in regional areas tend to be known as shire councils. In many areas, councils set their own pay rates for councillors—with the result that some councillors are well paid and regard their positions as full-time jobs, while others—particularly in rural areas—are not well paid and regard their work as councillors as a community service they perform part-time in addition to their normal jobs.

How legislation is made

State, territory and Commonwealth laws are all made in much the same way. The most common approach is for a draft law, or Bill, to be introduced into a lower house of parliament. The vast majority of Bills are introduced by ministers—members of the government who have been appointed to cabinet (a council of ministers) to look after a particular portfolio or area of responsibility; for example, health, foreign affairs, treasury, defence or education. However, Bills can also be introduced by individual members of the parliament, in which case they are referred to as a 'private member's Bill'. Federally, most Bills are introduced in the House of Representatives, but they can be introduced in the Senate—although the Senate actually has less power than the lower house and Bills dealing with money and treasury matters cannot be introduced there (although they can be amended by the Senate).

If a Bill is approved by the parliament it becomes a law, or an 'Act' of parliament, so it must be carefully worded and not be ambiguous. For this reason, Bills are written, or drafted, by specialist staff in an office of parliamentary counsel or similar public service department.

When a minister or member wants to introduce a new Bill, he or she will normally follow this process:

— The Bill is listed on the particular house's notice paper, or agenda, by the clerk of the house.

— After the Bill makes its way to the top of the notice paper, it is introduced and its impact explained by the minister or member who wants it approved.

   • Up to this point the Bill has been confidential, but when it is introduced copies are given to members of the house and also published on the parliamentary website.

   • The process of introducing a Bill is known as its 'first reading'. There is no debate at this stage. Debate does not start until a Bill is 'read for a second time'.

— Commonly the second reading process follows immediately after the first reading, when the person introducing the Bill formally moves that the 'bill be read for a second time' (Making Laws 2008).

— When the introductory speech finishes, discussion is usually deferred to a later date to allow members of the house time to study the Bill and consider its implications.

— After discussion resumes there is often a wide-ranging debate, particularly if a Bill is opposed by the opposition.

— At the end of this debate, the minister or member who introduced the Bill will again formally move 'that this bill be now read a second time' (Making Laws 2008).

— At this point the house will vote on whether to allow the motion. If a majority of members vote in favour, the clerk will read out the title of the Bill and the second reading stage will be complete.

— Following the second reading, a Bill can be considered in detail—clause by clause if deemed necessary. Sometimes the content of a Bill might be amended; at others it will be accepted unopposed, or its content totally opposed. A government might allow extensive debate, or it might decide it wants to cut debate short—in which case a member of the government will move to end discussion and apply what is known the 'guillotine' by declaring the Bill is 'urgent' and there will be no more time for debate.

— Finally, the person who introduced the Bill moves 'that this bill be read a third time' (Making Laws 2008). If the motion is agreed to, the clerk will again read the title of the Bill. The Bill is then regarded as having been passed by the lower house—or in the case of Queensland and the territories where there is no upper house, the parliament.

After a Bill is passed (voted on and agreed to by a majority of members) in the lower house in a bicameral parliament, it is 'sent up' to the upper house—the Senate at the federal level or Legislative Council in the relevant states. In the upper house, a Bill is put through a similar 'three reading' process as in the lower house. At the end of that process it will either be accepted as is, rejected outright, or the upper house will send it back to the lower house with a request that the lower house amend it.

If there is disagreement between the two houses, there can be negotiations about the future of a Bill. If the issues remain unresolved, the Bill can either be 'put aside' and 'not further pursued' or the deadlock can lead to a double dissolution election in which both houses must be adjourned and a simultaneous election called for all members of each house (Making Laws 2008). If—as much more commonly happens—the Bill passes each house, it is sent to the Governor-General who, acting as the Queen's representative, 'assents' to the Bill. At that point the Bill becomes an Act of the parliament.

An Act may contain a clause saying when it will actually become law, but if not it will automatically become a law on the 28th day after the Governor-General assented to it (Making Laws 2008).

It should be noted that during the process of considering a Bill, either house can refer it to a committee. Committees are usually made up of members of a house who have specific interest or expertise in areas related to the content of a Bill. If this happens, a committee can make recommendations about a Bill, but it cannot amend it or approve it in its own right.

If a Bill originates in the upper house—which is very uncommon—the approval process is reversed, with it being read three times in the upper house, then sent to the lower house for three more readings after which, if it is passed, it is sent to the Governor-General for assent.

Voting in a parliament

When a Bill or a motion about some particular issue is put to a house for a vote, there are two ways a decision can be made. First, at a less formal level, a resolution can be accepted or refused 'on the voices'. The speaker of a lower house, president of the Senate, or chair of a committee (if a matter has been debated by a committee) puts forward the question that is to be decided to those members present in the house at the time, asking those who agree to say 'aye' and those who disagree 'no'. The speaker, president or chair then makes a judgment saying either 'I think the ayes have it' or 'I think the noes have it' (Making Laws 2008). If the call is disputed by more than one member, there must be a formal vote.

A formal vote in a parliament is known as a 'division' for the simple reason that the house literally divides—with members who agree with a motion moving to the side of the chamber on the right of the speaker's or president's chair, and those who disagree to the left. When a division is called, the clerk of the house activates a system of bells that ring throughout the relevant area of parliament house for a particular chamber for four minutes. The bells alert members who were not in the chamber when the motion—known as a question—was put. At the end of the four minutes, doors to the chamber are locked, meaning that only those inside at that time can participate in the division.

A formal vote in a parliament is known as a 'division' for the simple reason that the house literally divides—with members who agree with a motion moving to the side of the chamber on the right of the speaker's or president's chair, and those who disagree to the left.

If the vote is tied in a lower house, the speaker—who is not permitted to vote otherwise—has a casting vote (Making Laws 2008). In the Senate, the president has a deliberative vote only and no casting vote. Chairs of House of Representative committees only have a casting vote and no deliberative vote, but chairs of Senate committees have a deliberative vote and casting vote. Most divisions are voted for or against in accord with party policy, with all the members of a party moving as a block to one side of a house or another. Occasionally, however, individual members might disagree with the policy of her or his party and decide to vote with another party which has moved to the opposite side of the house. This is known as 'crossing the floor' and it is generally frowned on by party bosses. Rarely, and usually only in relation to highly controversial issues, parties allow a 'conscience' or 'free' vote in which members do not have to toe the party line and can vote as they see fit.

Votes in local councils are usually made by a simple show of hands, with councillors putting up a hand to vote for a motion proposed by another councillor or the mayor. In most local authorities, the mayor has a deliberative vote and a casting vote.

In all parliaments and local councils, only elected members may vote. Staff members are often called on to give advice in local councils but are not permitted to vote.

Who's who in a parliament?

Each lower house of parliament in Australia is chaired by a member of parliament whom members have elected as 'speaker'. Upper houses are chaired by an elected 'president'. The speaker or president is the most powerful person in each house and, although elected from the ranks of the majority party in each house, is expected to be fair and impartial. They are responsible for enforcing the rules, or 'standing orders', of a house, controlling debate, disciplining members who step out of line, and the smooth functioning of a parliament and all its services.

Speakers and presidents are assisted by a 'clerk' of each respective house. Clerks are senior public servants and not elected. They are the only non-elected people to have a speaking role in a house, being responsible for reading aloud the names of Bills when they are discussed by a house and also having roles in ringing the bells and counting votes in divisions (The Clerk and Other Officials 2008). Clerks also provide advice to individual members about procedural matters including interpretation of standing orders, constitutional matters and precedent in relation to parliamentary practice.

The other main non-elected official in each house is the forbidding-sounding 'sergeant-at-arms' in a lower house, or quaintly titled 'usher of the black rod' in an upper house—both of whom draw their titles, not from the pages of a *Monty Python* script, but from their archaic namesakes in the UK Parliament. The sergeant or usher, or a deputy, must be present at all times when a house sits (The Clerk and Other Officials 2008). Their main responsibilities are for the security of the house and parliament generally, including physical removal of members of parliament or members of the public who misbehave.

As noted previously, political leadership in a lower house is provided by the prime minister, premier, or chief minister, plus leader of an opposition. Leaders in upper houses are known simply as the leader of the government or leader of the opposition.

Ministers are senior members of a government appointed by the prime minister, state premier or chief minister to provide leadership in particular fields—or 'portfolios'—such as treasury, health and education. Federally, there are also ministers for national interest areas such as defence, trade and foreign affairs.

Senior ministers become members of cabinet. Cabinets are basically a committee of senior members of parliament chaired by the prime minister, premier or chief minister. They meet in private and discussions are kept secret. Cabinet ministers have more or less power depending on how different prime ministers, premiers or chief ministers run their governments and how much they are prepared to delegate responsibilities. Ministers are commonly 'shadowed' in their portfolios by senior members of the opposition in a 'shadow cabinet'—this reflects the tradition that an opposition is regarded as an alternative government if for any reason a government loses its majority in a lower house.

The leader of the house is a minister who is responsible for the management of government business in that house. He or she has control of the order in which Bills will be debated and other procedural matters.

The leader is assisted by the government whip. There is also an opposition whip. The whips decide the order in which members of the government and opposition will speak during debates, and are responsible for ensuring members attend a house to vote in divisions, functioning of committees, and matters introduced into a house by members acting on their own behalf in 'private members' business' (The House, Government and Opposition 2008).

In parliament, the prime minister, premier or chief minister, and cabinet ministers, sit in the front row of seats on the side of the house occupied by the government—the side to the right of the speaker's chair—hence the terms 'member of the front bench' or 'front bencher'. Similarly, members of the 'shadow cabinet' sit with the leader of the opposition on the front bench of the opposition's side of the house to the left of the speaker's chair. Other members, including the whips, sit behind the front row—hence the terms 'member of the back bench' or 'back bencher'.

There are no formal cabinets in local government and no ministers, although some councils have committee structures in which groups of councillors deal with specific issues such as planning. In some cases, the councillors who chair these committees are delegated a degree of authority by the full council—especially when dealing with staff—and there is a basic portfolio system.

Parliamentary privilege

As explained in detail in Chapter 16, members of parliament have privileges not available to the public. One of these is a guarantee of freedom of speech known as absolute privilege. It means members are protected from the laws of defamation in relation to anything said in a house while that house is in session, or 'sitting'. Similarly, members speaking in a house cannot be prosecuted for breaking a law by making statements that would 'otherwise be a criminal offence' (Parliamentary Privilege 2008). Transcripts of all speeches made in a house are published daily in Hansard—a record of proceedings that is also protected by absolute parliamentary privilege and therefore a document journalists can quote freely without fear of being sued for defamation.

The idea underlying parliamentary freedom of speech is that members should be able to debate issues honestly and openly without fear or favour or threats of reprisal. Parliamentary privilege also extends to members of the public called on to speak in a house, for example as witnesses in an inquiry being conducted by a properly constituted parliamentary committee. Members have other privileges too. For example, members may not be required to attend courts or tribunals as witnesses, or be arrested or detained in civil matters on sitting days and for five days before and after sitting days. Such immunities also apply when a parliamentarian is a member of a committee that is meeting. These immunities are justified on the ground that the first duty of members, and others involved, is to Parliament and this overrides other obligations (Parliamentary Privilege 2008).

There is no equivalent of parliamentary privilege for members of local councils. As explained in Chapter 15, although Australia's uniform defamation laws allow publication of fair reports of proceedings of public concern, including reports of proceedings of local council meetings, there is no absolute protection.

> The idea underlying parliamentary freedom of speech is that members should be able to debate issues honestly and openly without fear or favour or threats of reprisal.

The separation of powers

Theoretically at least, there are three arms of federal, state and territory governments in a democratic political system—the legislature (or parliament), executive (public service) and judiciary (courts and legal system). This supposed separation is at the heart of a concept referred to as the doctrine of the separation of powers. The doctrine is meant to provide a safeguard against potential abuse of power and to stop a dictator seizing control of a government. It applies in varying degrees in Westminster system nations, and also in the US. A graphic example of a breakdown in the separation of powers occurred in Fiji, a former British colony, when military chief Frank Bainimarama seized control from the elected prime minister and government in a 2006 coup, and then also took control of the public service and judicial system.

In Australia all members of parliament (the first arm of government) are elected by the people. Parliamentarians are meant to represent all the people in their electorate, their constituents, whether they actually voted for them or not. (In addition, members of the Senate have a constitutional requirement to represent the interests of the states in which they were elected.) The second arm of government is the executive, or public service. Its job is to implement legislation enacted by the parliament and do the day-to-day work of delivering government services. In the process, public servants and the government departments they work for become a major interface between the legislature and citizens. The third arm of government—the judiciary—administers, interprets and enforces the laws, or statutes, made by parliament, as well as administering, interpreting, enforcing and actually making the common law.[2]

While a key concept underlying the doctrine of the separation of powers is that each of the three arms of government is separate and accountable, in Australia

Figure 14.1
The separation of powers

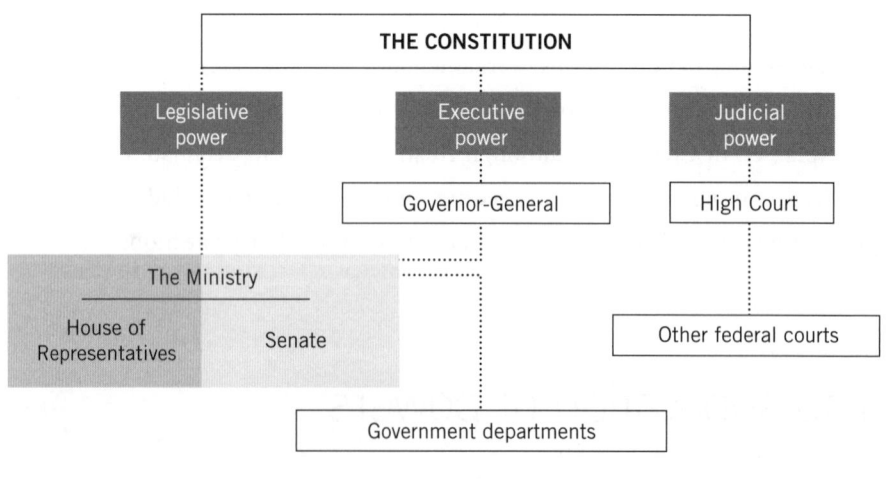

Source: Parliament of Australia http://www.aph.gov.au/parl.htm/

2   As explained later in this chapter, common law is court- and judge-made law based on legal precedent.

there is little if any real separation between the legislature and the executive. This is largely because the public service is controlled by cabinet. As noted earlier in this chapter, cabinets are chaired by the prime minister, state premiers or chief ministers. Members of cabinet are ministers drawn from the legislature, or parliament, who were appointed to the cabinet by the prime minister, premier or chief minister. During their time in cabinet, each minister becomes the de facto head of the public service department which serves his or her portfolio. Thus there is no effective separation between the top levels of parliaments and top levels of the public service—a breakdown in the doctrine of the separation of powers between the legislature and executive. The doctrine is further undermined by governments and ministers who appoint public service department heads sympathetic to their own political leanings. This commonly happens after a change of government in a general election when department heads appointed by a defeated government are replaced by appointees sympathetic to the victor.

On the other hand there is a jealously guarded separation between the judiciary, judges and courts in Australia on the one side, and the parliament and public service on the other—even though, like public service heads, judges are also appointed by the government of the day (Spry 2000). Once a judge has been appointed, woe betide any politician who sticks his or her nose into the court system   to do so is to invite a stinging rebuke from judges.

As an aside here, it is important to note that the separation of powers is different in the US. In that nation there is a clear separation between the legislature (the two houses of Congress) and the executive. This is largely because the US president, although elected, is not a member of Congress. He or she is a public servant who is elected in a totally separate poll as the head of the public service or executive. The president then hires his or her own 'cabinet ministers', public servants, as heads of different public service departments. Thus there is full separation between legislature and executive in the US.

Two sources of law

Laws in Westminster-system nations such as Australia come from two sources— common law and statute law. In essence, statute law is law made by parliaments when a Bill is passed and becomes an Act. Common law is made by courts and judges when they interpret existing laws, or make rulings in cases in which no statute laws apply.

Under a principle known as the doctrine of precedent, each court is bound by the decisions of all courts higher than it in the court hierarchy (see below). The doctrine of precedent provides that judges should stand by previous decisions in similar cases and in higher courts. The idea underlying precedent is consistency—so that judgments and penalties in similar cases are treated in similar ways.

As well as having two different types of law—statute and common—we also have two different categories of law. They are criminal law, where the state, usually through police or other law enforcement agencies, takes action on behalf of the whole community; and civil law, which applies if there is a dispute between individuals. Murder, rape and theft are examples of criminal law. Disputes over property, defamation and arguments between neighbours are usually civil law issues.

The court hierarchy

Each type of law is administered by the courts. As mentioned previously, there is a hierarchical structure to the courts. In simple terms we have courts presided over by magistrates at the bottom of the pecking order, and the High Court at the top.

Magistrates' Courts (known as Local Courts in NSW) are state and territory courts. They are where most criminal cases first appear in the system. Generally, cases involving drunks, driving offences, things like shoplifting and drug offences, as well as civil law arguments between feuding neighbours are dealt with in these courts.

Magistrates' and Local Courts are presided over by a sole magistrate who makes all the decisions—there are no juries. 'Justice' tends to be quick and arbitrary. In some cases an offender can ask to have her or his case 'sent up' to a higher court to be dealt with by a judge and/or jury.

Magistrates also conduct what are known as committal hearings in criminal cases. Committal hearings are held in nearly all occasions when a person is charged with a serious crime. In a committal hearing, a magistrate is asked to consider the police evidence and decide if that evidence is convincing enough for an alleged offender to be sent to trial, or committed for trial, before a judge and jury in a higher court. But if the evidence is not strong enough, the case is dismissed and the accused goes free. Alternatively, if an accused person enters a guilty plea in a committal hearing, the magistrate will refer her or him to an appropriate higher court for sentencing. In the NT, ACT and Tasmania, matters that are too serious to be dealt with by magistrates go to the Supreme Court of the relevant territory or state. But in Queensland, WA, NSW, SA and Victoria there are mid-level courts between Magistrates' Courts and Supreme Courts. They are known as County Courts in Victoria, and as District Courts in the other jurisdictions. District and County Courts are presided over by a judge. Many cases are also heard in front of juries, with jurors deciding if a person is guilty or not guilty, and judges handing down sentences when guilty verdicts are returned.

The District and County Courts deal with more serious criminal offences like armed robbery, assault causing grievous bodily harm, and dangerous driving—all crimes that can attract lengthy jail sentences. They also deal with civil disputes involving claims for damages, injunctions and arguments over large sums of money.

Supreme Courts are the highest state and territory courts. They are presided over by a single judge (or a panel of judges if the court is hearing an appeal against a previous court decision). Nearly all Supreme Court cases involve juries. Supreme Courts deal with the most serious criminal cases—offences such as murder, manslaughter and rape, as well as major civil disputes.

There are other specialist state and territory courts, including courts dealing with children, planning and environment, coronial matters, land, drugs and small debts.

Finally, there are the federal courts. They are the Federal Magistrates' Court, which deals with less complex cases than would normally be heard by the Federal or Family Court; Federal Court, which mainly deals with federal laws; Family Court, which deals with divorce, custody, maintenance and property settlements; and the High Court.

The most powerful court in the nation, the High Court deals with constitutional issues and disputes between states. It may also hear appeals from any other court, including state and territory courts. It is the highest court of appeal, with appeal cases heard before a panel—or 'bench'—of judges, who are called 'justices'. There are branches of the Federal Magistrates' Court, Federal Court and Family Court in each state and territory. The High Court usually sits in its own special building in Canberra but it does also conduct short hearings in Sydney and Melbourne and will sit in other state and territory capital cities at least once a year if there is sufficient demand.

In addition to the courts, there are also many state and federal tribunals, as well as royal commissions and commissions of inquiry.

Journalists and the fourth estate

Journalists fulfil a fourth estate role every time they shine a spotlight on official corruption or, sometimes, official laziness. On other occasions they step in when officials themselves have fallen victim to a fabric of lies and deceit.

Every so often an Australian journalist writes an article or scripts a broadcast that ultimately leads to a crooked judge, bent police officer or shifty politician being jailed. When that happens, the journalist has acted in the public interest in what is sometimes described as a 'fourth estate' role. What that means is that a journalist has stepped in and investigated an issue and/or exposed a wrong when authorities who should normally be expected to have dealt with a problem, failed to act properly.

Journalists fulfil a fourth estate role every time they shine a spotlight on official corruption or, sometimes, official laziness. On other occasions they step in when officials themselves have fallen victim to a fabric of lies and deceit. A good example of the latter was discussed in Chapter 4, where it was explained how former judge Marcus Einfeld came to be caught out by a journalist and was subsequently jailed for perjury. Court officials, a magistrate and lawyers were duped by Einfeld's lies and hypocrisy. But a simple check by a nosy journalist with a healthy sense of scepticism was his undoing.

Other examples of journalists acting in fourth estate roles abound. Several significant examples are discussed in Chapter 12. One of the most notable was the Watergate cover-up in the US, in which a 1972 investigation by journalists resulted in the resignation of President Richard Nixon. Another classic instance of fourth estate investigative journalism which had major repercussions was the work of Chris Masters (ABC's *Four Corners*) and Phil Dickie (*The Courier-Mail*), which led to the Fitzgerald Inquiry into police protection rackets and deep-seated political corruption in Queensland in the 1980s.

It is a truism that one of news media's most important roles is to help keep governments, powerful corporations, and those in authority honest and accountable.

However, the actual concept of the 'fourth estate' is somewhat ambiguous. For example, UK academic Mark Wheeler said in his book *Politics and the Mass Media*:

> In traditional liberal thought the press has been advanced as a 'public watchdog' over the state. It occupies a fourth estate which is separate from the Crown, Parliament and the Judiciary. Therefore, it may reveal the authorities' abuses and maintain a mature democracy (Wheeler 1997, p. 6).

But it seems Wheeler might have muddled a variation of the principle of the separation of powers with the original 18th-century derivation of the term 'the fourth estate'. In 1997, then chief justice of the High Court of Australia Sir Gerard Brennan explained that:

> In 1840, Thomas Carlyle attributed the term to Edmund Burke. 'Burke' he wrote—'said there were three estates in [the English] Parliament; but, in the reporters' gallery yonder, there sat a *Fourth Estate* more important far than they all. It is not a figure of speech, or a witty saying; it is a literal fact,—very momentous to us in these times... Whoever can speak, speaking now to the whole nation, becomes a power, a branch of government, with inalienable weight in law-making, in all acts of authority' (Brennan 1997).

Edmund Burke's reference to the three estates related to the fact that in the medieval evolution of parliamentary systems in England, and also some European nations, three categories of people were represented: the church or clergy, nobility, and common people (Pollard 1920, p. 61). Brennan said members of the fourth estate were originally 'men of letters', but the term had broadened over time to include radio, television and online journalists, and:

> They present the three branches of Government to the people. The fourth estate is not a fourth branch of government but, in the life of a free and democratic society, it has great power and influence. Its power and influence will be expanded by new technology (Brennan 1997).

Schultz offered a similar explanation. She said the fourth estate was an 'ideal' that at its most basic sees news media as:

> a conduit for information, ideas and opinions to assist in the good governance of society; to act as a check on the powerful, by reporting, analysing and criticising their actions on behalf of the public, which lacks direct access to information or power. The ideal casts the media as the handmaiden of democracy (Schultz 1998, pp. 51 & 52).

Most, although not all, fourth estate journalism is proactive and involves investigation of some sort. These approaches were discussed in Chapter 12.

DISCUSSION POINTS

1   Is politics boring or is it exciting? Should the Australian public take much greater interest in how they are governed?

2   Every Australian aged 18 and above must vote in every state and federal election. What are the pros and cons of compulsory voting?

3   Australia's political system is a Westminster system and the British monarch is still our head of state. But the British Empire is long gone. Is our model of government still relevant, or should we change it? Why or why not?

4   Should we do away with states and territories in Australia and just have a federal government and local councils? Why or why not?

5   Australian governments are employing increasing numbers of spin-doctor media managers. Does this trend make the principle of the separation of powers obsolete because governments now control everything anyway, or does it make the principle even more relevant and important?

6   What, if any, are the links between journalists being regarded as members of a fourth estate and the *Journalists' Code of Ethics*?

NEWS PRACTICE POINTS

1   What state electorate do you live in? Who is your state member of parliament? What party does he or she represent? What is your federal electorate, who is the sitting member, and what party does she or he represent? Who is your local councillor and is he or she affiliated with a political party? How much is each of the three paid annually?

2   Go online, find a full copy of the Australian Federal Constitution—in the *Commonwealth of Australia Constitution Act 1900*—and read through the entire document. List five points you think are out of date or need changing. Beside each point, briefly describe how it could be improved.

3   Taking the five suggestions you made in relation to Practice Point 2, draft a formal letter to the Prime Minister outlining the changes, explaining why they are needed, how they could be made, and ask the Prime Minister to conduct a referendum so they can be adopted. What, if any, was the reply?

4   It is sometimes said that Australia is over-governed and Australian society is over-regulated. Are we? Explain your thoughts and cite credible sources to support your argument in a 750-word comment article.

5   Although Australia and the US share a common political heritage, to the extent
    that we were both British colonies, there are major differences between the way the
    doctrine of the separation of powers is applied in the US and Australia. List those
    differences and briefly explain why each exists.

6   Occasionally we hear a parliament described as 'cowards' castle' because members
    of parliament can say outrageous—and even totally untrue—things about other
    people while speaking in a house under the protection of parliamentary privilege.
    Do a little investigating and find three instances where what has been said in such
    a situation has been totally justified and three in which there has been an obvious
    abuse of the system.

7   Citing the examples you discovered in relation to Practice Point 5, write an article
    about the pros and cons of parliamentary privilege and also about what recourse
    is available to people whose reputations have been damaged under parliamentary
    privilege.

8   Find a news story that broke in the past year which you would classify as a story
    with strong 'fourth estate' values. In exactly 1000 words, explain how the story
    originated, describe its fourth estate values, and discuss its immediate social and/
    or political impact and its likely impact over time.

15

DEFAMATION

The greater the truth, the greater the libel.
Lord Mansfield, former Lord Chief Justice of England, about 1789

OBJECTIVES

After reading this chapter you will understand:

» The basics of Australian defamation law

» Why journalists must understand defamation law

» The nature of online defamation risks

» The key defences to allegations of defamation

» The 'chilling effects' of defamation law

» How to protect yourself as a journalist.

Journalists should develop a sound working knowledge of defamation law for three important reasons. First, so they can keep themselves and their employers out of trouble. Second, so they are not intimidated and 'chilled' by the law. Third, because a sound understanding of defamation law makes it harder for shifty lawyers, dodgy politicians, spin-doctors, and others to mislead them about legal matters.

Australia has stringent defamation laws—in fact they are some of the harshest in the world, and certainly much stricter than those in the US. One reason for this is because the US has a Bill of Rights—the first 10 amendments to its Constitution— which, among its many provisions, says legislators cannot pass laws that would inhibit free speech or freedom of the press (or media). There is no Bill of Rights in Australia, and no explicit constitutional guarantee of freedom of speech or media freedom. This can be a challenge for Australian journalists because it is literally impossible to report news without defaming individuals and organisations.

In Australia, defamation is controlled by state and territory laws. Before 2006, that meant we had eight separate—and different—defamation laws. The system was a shambles. It caused major problems, especially for news outlets that publish and broadcast nationally or online. Fortunately, all states and territories now have 'uniform' defamation statutes that mirror each other in most respects.[1] The relevant statute in each state is known as the *Defamation Act 2005*. In the Northern Territory it is the *Defamation Act 2006*, and in the ACT defamation is covered by Chapter 9 of the *Civil Law (Wrongs) Act 2002*.

Defamation is generally a civil matter (between individuals), although in rare cases it can be treated as a crime (against the state). The purpose of defamation law is to attempt to balance freedom of expression against the rights of individuals to their good name and to provide a remedy for a person whose reputation has been unfairly damaged. These 'rights' are extinguished when a person dies. In all states and territories except Tasmania, the uniform defamation statutes specifically exclude defamation of the dead. But even in Tasmania, where the relevant clause was omitted from the statute, the exclusion means the common law[2] applies, and it is not possible to defame a dead person at common law (Rolph 2008).

As discussed in Chapter 2, an overriding aim of journalism is to discover truth and report it. Yet there is an old saying among lawyers and journalists that the greater the truth, the bigger the defamation. This is partly because a statement does not have to be false to be defamatory—although truth can be a defence to defamation. Journalists and others regularly defame people and organisations by making totally true statements. It is also important to understand that it is very easy to defame another person by accident—in fact you can do it without realising you have done it! Add to that the fact that one of the inherently nasty aspects of Australia's defamation laws is that a person who appears in court accused of defamation (the 'defendant') must convince a court that either: (a) he or she did not defame the person who has brought the action against them (the 'plaintiff'), or (b) she or he had an acceptable legal excuse for the defamation. This is in contrast to criminal cases in which a person is presumed innocent until found guilty.

Note also that most defamation judgments are based on a lesser 'standard of proof' than criminal cases. This is because the standard of proof in civil cases is 'on the balance of probabilities', a lesser test than that applied in criminal courts, where a case must be proved 'beyond reasonable doubt'.

---

1   Note that while defamation is controlled by the uniform Defamation Acts, the provisions of these Acts—like all Acts—are subject to interpretation by the courts: see Chapter 14.
2   As explained in Chapter 14, common law is made in courts. It is based on principles of precedent in which lower court judgments should reflect previous judgments of higher courts in similar cases.

The remedy for defamation is usually financial—with a court ordering the person who did the defaming to pay money, known as 'damages', to the person whose reputation was sullied. In rare cases in which the state steps into a defamation case and it becomes a criminal matter, a convicted defamer can be jailed.

Defamation defined

So what is this thing called defamation? If you boil it down to basics, defamation is saying something nasty about another person. It is saying, writing, or in other ways depicting something that damages or ruins another's reputation by exposing that person to hatred, contempt or ridicule or making others want to shun or avoid that person (Australian Press Council 2007). Obviously if you wrote an article saying someone was a child molester, mass murderer, rapist or drug addict you would have defamed that person because those who read your article would be likely to shun and avoid them. Defamation law applies not only to journalists and writers, but to everyone.

None of Australia's defamation statutes actually define defamation. Instead, they rely on common law definitions that imply a publication could be defamatory if it contains '[words that] tend to lower the plaintiff in the estimation of right-thinking members of society generally' (Atkin 1936). Note the use of the word 'tend'. The law does not say the plaintiff actually has to have her or his reputation damaged.

One problem with the definition lies with having to decide what 'right-thinking members of society' might think at any given time. What, for example, happens if one 'right-thinking' member of society thinks a particular statement or implication is defamatory and another 'right-thinking' member of society thinks it is not?

Further, it is not only words which can be defamatory. Photographs, drawings, cartoons, video images, and even works of art can all damage reputations. Butler and Rodrick proposed a good plain-English definition. They said: 'Defamation occurs where one person communicates, by words, photographs, video, illustrations or other means, material which has the effect or tendency of damaging the reputation of another' (Butler & Rodrick 2007, p. 27). Tellingly for journalists, they added: 'Protection of reputation has an obvious conflict with the promotion of freedom of speech' (Butler & Rodrick 2007, p. 27).

A statement or visual representation is considered to be defamatory if it satisfies three specific conditions:

— It must contain a defamatory imputation.

— The defamatory imputation must be understood to refer to a specific person who complains she or he has been defamed.

— The imputation must have been published.

DEFAMATORY IMPUTATION

A defamatory imputation is a statement, visual representation or meaning that makes others think less of, or ridicule, the person the offending words or images referred to, or that injures them in their trade or profession. It is not defamatory if what is said, written or depicted merely hurts someone's pride or results in them feeling indignant or offended. The imputation must be perceived to impact negatively on how a person is thought of by others. Examples of imputations that could injure someone in their profession or trade would be to describe a surgeon as a butcher, accuse an author of plagiarising, or say a real estate agent was shifty.

Imputations can be direct statements clearly saying, for example, that Mr Jones or Ms Smith is a crook, a drunk, a child molester, adulterer, scoundrel, conniving cheat, bully, or liar. This is called a direct imputation. It comes from what the law refers to as 'the natural and ordinary meaning' of words—words taken at face value. But other imputations can be indirect—expressed as an innuendo, or what the law calls 'popular innuendo'; that is, words that gain meaning when people read between the lines. An example of a defamatory innuendo would be to say that Mr Jones likes the company of young boys, something that could be seen to imply he is a homosexual paedophile. Similarly, writing that Ms Smith was being investigated by the police fraud squad could be seen to imply she was dishonest and had been involved in a financial scam. One of the problems with innuendo is that people might read much more into what was said than was actually meant by the person responsible for the imputation.

It is not defamatory if what is said, written or depicted merely hurts someone's pride or results in them feeling indignant or offended. The imputation must be perceived to impact negatively on how a person is thought of by others.

ABOUT A PERSON

The second condition that has to be met for something to be considered defamatory is that the defamatory imputation must be understood to refer to a specific person who complains she or he has been defamed (or, to use common law jargon, the imputation must be 'of and concerning' a particular person). Thus it would not be defamatory to say all doctors are quacks because that statement refers to a big and diverse group and does not single out any individual doctor. But it would be different if you said a particular doctor was a quack. In that case, the statement would be considered to be an imputation 'of and concerning' that individual. Similarly, if you said the doctors in one specific medical practice were quacks, that would be defamatory of each doctor in the practice because the group is small enough for each to be identifiable as a target of the imputation.

PUBLICATION

The third condition—and this is something that puts journalists inherently at risk because of what we do—is that the imputation must have been published. Now publication in a legal sense can be something very much less than you might expect. At its simplest, publication is deemed to have taken place when a defamatory imputation is communicated to a third person; that is, to someone other than the person who created the imputation and the person the imputation was about. If something is printed in a newspaper, broadcast on radio or television, printed in a book, or uploaded onto a website, it has obviously been published. Less obviously, however, publication can be in a letter, postcard, email, fax or note, a comment on Facebook or Twitter which is read by a third person, or even spoken to a third person in the case of verbal imputations.

One common law interpretation of what is meant by publication in a legal sense is drawn from the 1891 British defamation case *Pullman v Hill & Co.*, in which there was debate about whether a letter given to a clerk to type on a typewriter could be considered to have been published. Explaining his judgment in the case, Lord Esher said:

> The first question is, whether, assuming the letter to contain defamatory matter, there has been a publication of it. What is the meaning of 'publication'? The making known the defamatory matter after it has been written to some person other than the person of whom it is written. If the writer of a letter shews [sic] it to his own clerk in order that the clerk may copy it for him, is that a publication of the letter? Certainly it is shewing it to a third person; the writer cannot say to the person to whom the letter is addressed, 'I have shewn it to you and to no one else'. I cannot, therefore, feel any doubt that, if the writer of a letter shews it to any person other than the person to whom

it is written, he publishes it. If he wishes not to publish it, he must, so far as he possibly can, keep it to himself, or he must send it himself straight to the person to whom it is written. There was therefore, in this case a publication to the type-writer [clerk] (*Pullman v Hill & Co.* 1891, p. 527).

However, in the same case Lord Esher also made the point that if an imputation is published to a third person even though the originator of the material took reasonable precautions to keep it confidential, then there would be no publication in a legal sense. He said: 'if the writer of a letter locks it up in his own desk, and a thief comes and breaks open the desk and takes the letter and makes its content known, I should say that would not be publication' (*Pullman v Hill & Co.* 1891, p. 527).

Thus if someone wrote something nasty about you that had a tendency to make other people want to avoid you, ridicule you and/or hate you, or harmed you in the pursuit of your profession or trade, and they sent the offending imputation to you in a letter marked 'private and confidential', they would not have defamed you—even if someone else who was not authorised to do so wrongly opened the letter and read it. But if the person who sent you the letter made a copy which he or she subsequently left lying around where one or more others saw it and read it, you would have been defamed because the letter contained an imputation, that imputation was about you, and it was published to a third person. Similarly, if you pinned a note on a person's office door that said she was a cheat, a liar and a drug dealer who would sell her own mother to raise a dollar, and that note was read by someone else, the imputations would have been published. The person whose office door the note was pinned to would have been defamed and she or he could seek damages from you. Likewise, if you spoke too loudly when making defamatory comments to another person and were overheard by a third person, that would be publication. The same would apply if you sent a defamatory fax and it was read by a third person while it was sitting on a fax machine waiting to be picked up by the person you sent it to. In the same way, printing and distributing a defamatory email or text message, or simply just forwarding it to a third person (or more), or even accidentally sending an email to the wrong person (or people) constitutes publication—as could accidentally putting a defamatory letter in a wrong envelope addressed to a third person. The same can be said of social media and posting comments on sites such as Facebook or via Twitter which can be accessed by more than one person other than the individual who made the comment and the person the comment was about.

The narrow legal definition of publication means journalists should be especially careful when, as sometimes happens, a prospective interviewee asks them to put questions in writing. If any of those written questions carry a defamatory imputation about either the person they are sent to or another person, and if that letter, fax or email is read by a third person, there could be grounds for a defamation action. Emails and text messages pose a particular danger in this context because they are so easily forwarded and circulated.

A related danger is the republication of a defamatory statement made by someone else. If for example, you receive a funny but defamatory email and decide to forward it, you can become a party to the original defamation because you have republished the imputation. Similarly, if you write a story that includes a defamatory quote from another journalist's or media outlet's story, you could be joined to any defamation action stemming from the original story because you had republished the original imputation. The same applies to letters to the editor. If a letter writer defamed someone and the letter was published, the editor and letter writer could both be sued. There is a similar danger with blogs—the owner or publisher of a blog could be sued if a contributor posted a defamatory comment.

Publication also has the effect of determining who is liable for defamation and who a court will determine has to pay damages. This is because any person who takes part in the publication—including the people who edited the words—not just the writer, can be sued for defamation. Technically, the list can also include printers, webmasters, blog owners, and media organisations.

Within Australia, a defamation action can be launched in any state or territory in which a statement was published—although an action is most likely to be launched, and most likely to succeed, in a plaintiff's home state or territory because that is where they would be best known and could be expected to have suffered most damage. Internationally, there is potential for a person involved in an online or social media defamation to be sued in any nation in which the defamatory material can be downloaded if the material is in breach of that nation's particular defamation laws.

Libel and slander

Defamation can be either written, in which case it is called libel; or verbal, when it is known as slander. Australia's uniform defamation laws do not distinguish between libel and slander. However, it is still useful to understand that libel is defined as defamation in a written or other permanent form, such as an effigy, a photograph, drawing, video, cartoon or graffiti. It covers things such as newspaper and magazine articles, web publications, faxes, emails, social media, blogs and (somewhat strangely) radio or television broadcasts. Slander is regarded as defamation in a more transitory verbal form, such as in a personal conversation.

These differences aside, and while defamatory radio and television broadcasts are generally categorised as libel, print and web journalists are potentially more likely to encounter problems with defamation than broadcast journalists for the simple reason that once something is printed in a newspaper or magazine, uploaded to the web, accessed via an app on a portable device, or posted on Facebook or Twitter, it is in a form in which it can be read over and over again—not to mention scrutinised by pedantic lawyers searching for every nuance, real or imagined. Broadcast words, however, are generally gone as soon as they are uttered. This does not mean broadcast journalism is safer than print or online journalism, simply that print and web publications tend to be perceived by the public as being more permanent than broadcast—a perception that should be tempered by the fact that some of the largest damages awards in Australian legal history have been paid by broadcast outlets that have lost defamation cases.

Defamation is a tort

Defaming someone involves what is called a 'tort'. A tort is a common law principle that dates from medieval times. A good definition of a tort is 'a wrongful act other than a breach of contract that injures another and for which the law imposes civil liability: a violation of a duty (as to exercise due care) imposed by law...' (FindLaw 2008). The Irish Law Reform Commission explained the concept well when it said:

> The law of tort seeks to redress two types of injury, namely, injury to the person and injury to property. Injuries to the person may be physical or non-physical. The core of the defamation action is one type of non-physical injury to the person, that is, injury to reputation (The Law Reform Commission 1991 p. 3).

One notion underpinning tort law is that we each owe a 'duty of care' to other people. This includes a tradition that unless we have done something bad, such as committed a crime, each of us has a right to our good name and we have a duty of

Does a journalist or publisher owe a duty of care to an individual who is defamed in the process of reporting a news story, or is there is a greater duty of care to the community as a whole in reporting the story?

care not to damage the good names of others. In essence, the law says that if we do damage a person's reputation without having a legally recognised excuse for doing so, then we have to make amends by paying damages to the person whose name we smeared. But this raises questions about whether a journalist or publisher owes a duty of care to an individual who is defamed in the process of reporting a news story, or if there is a greater duty of care to the community as a whole in reporting the story?

Examples of other areas of law that draw on torts include actions involving personal injury compensation, negligence, trespass and medical malpractice.

Who can sue?

Any living person can sue for damages in any Australian jurisdiction. The dead, however, cannot sue. That means that even if person has taken defamation action and the action is still before a court at the time they die, the case automatically ends. In essence, what the law says is that once a person is dead, no matter how badly their reputation is sullied, they are beyond harm. Similarly, an action ceases if a defendant dies—meaning his or her estate cannot be ordered to pay damages. In all states and territories except Tasmania, the defamation statutes specifically say that a person acting on behalf of a dead person cannot institute or continue a defamation action if a plaintiff or defendant dies. For example, Section 10 of the NSW *Defamation Act 2005* says:

> A person (including a personal representative of a deceased person) cannot assert, continue or enforce a cause of action for defamation in relation to:
>
> (a) the publication of defamatory matter about a deceased person (whether published before or after his or her death), or
>
> (b) the publication of defamatory matter by a person who has died since publishing the matter (NSW *Defamation Act 2005*, Section 10).

If you defame a dead person you do, however, need to be careful not to also defame living relatives or business acquaintances by association, because they could sue you in their own right.

While the dead are not litigious, some other groups in society are renowned for taking legal action. One particularly interesting landmark study of defamation cases was conducted some years ago by Minter Ellison law firm partner Patrick George who researched defamation verdicts around Australia between 1977 and 2002. He concluded that Sydney was the 'defamation capital of the world' and the number of defamation actions per head of population seemed out of all proportion to the number of actions in other Australian states (*PANPA Bulletin* 2003, p. 9). Of the 290 verdicts George examined, 46 were in NSW, SA had 13, the ACT 11, Victoria nine, Queensland and WA eight each, the NT three, and Tasmania two. George particularly looked at who took action. He concluded that: 'Businessmen and companies dominated, making up 26 per cent of the total. By comparison, lawyers represented 10 per cent and politicians 9 per cent' (*PANPA Bulletin* 2003, p. 9). The survey found that a 'substantial majority' of verdicts were awarded against newspapers, less against television, and relatively few against magazines and radio. George also categorised the defamatory imputations cases were based on. He found that the most common imputations, in descending order, were suggestions of criminality, dishonesty and misuse of position. Together they accounted for about 80 per cent of actions. Allegations of incompetence, immorality and other uncomplimentary insinuations made up the other 20 per cent (*PANPA Bulletin* 2003, p. 9).

As well as individuals, it is also possible for some small companies to sue, although large ones cannot. Companies that can sue must have fewer than 10 staff (or the part-time equivalent of 10) or be not for profit organisations such as incorporated clubs or charities. Local councils, government departments and other public authorities cannot bring an action. However, even though neither large corporations nor government authorities can sue, individual staff who work for those organisations may take action if they can demonstrate that a defamatory comment about their organisation also defamed them personally—even if only by implication.

Time limits and penalties

As a general rule, defamation actions must be launched within one year of the publication of a defamatory imputation, although this can be extended to three years if a court accepts it was not reasonable in the circumstances for a plaintiff to have commenced an action inside 12 months.

Courts can order a defendant who is found to have defamed a plaintiff to pay compensatory damages and legal costs. The uniform legislation initially limited such damages to $250,000, but this amount was only a starting point. It is indexed through a link to changes in average weekly earnings and subject to annual review by state and territory governments, and may also be increased by courts in some circumstances. In NSW, for example, the cap on damages had risen in line with indexation to $339,000 in 2012, an amount likely to continue increasing annually roughly in line with increases in the consumer price index (CPI). Courts can award additional damages for economic loss—an amount that is not capped but which can sometimes be high, particularly if a plaintiff's business or professional life was damaged by a defamatory imputation.

When determining the amount of compensatory damages, a court can take account of mitigating circumstances such as publication of an apology by a defendant and the correction of any wrong information relevant to a case. The amount awarded is supposed to relate to the damage caused by the defendant. For example, Section 34 of the NSW *Defamation Act 2005* says:

> In determining the amount of damages to be awarded in any defamation proceedings, the court is to ensure that there is an appropriate and rational relationship between the harm sustained by the plaintiff and the amount of damages awarded (NSW *Defamation Act 2005*).

On top of a base damages award, courts can also award what are known as 'aggravated damages'. These are likely to be awarded if a defendant's behaviour was particularly reckless; for example, by publishing an imputation even though he or she knew it was false, if the defendant was malicious, if the plaintiff was not offered an opportunity to comment on allegations against her or him, or if the defendant continued to publish defamatory material even though a complaint had been lodged by the plaintiff.

There was a good example of the latter in 2012 when Google lost a defamation action after ignoring a request by Melbourne show-business manager Milorad Trkulja (also known as Michael Trkulja) to remove material from the internet which Mr Trkulja said defamed him. A respected member of the Serbian community who had a top-rating television show in the 1990s, Mr Trkulja was shot in the back of the head by an unknown gunman as he dined with his mother in a St Albans restaurant in 2004 (Merhab 2012). Google subsequently published photos of Mr Trkulja beside images of notorious gangland figure Tony Mokbel and another man who had been accused of murder. Google search results also linked Mr Trkulja to a page on a website headed 'Melbourne Crime', which published photographs of others but which were captioned with his name. During the defamation hearing the jury of six heard that on one page there was an article headed 'Shooting probe urged November 20, 2007' with a large photograph of Mr Trkulja and nine photographs of individuals either known to have committed serious criminal offences or against whom serious criminal allegations had been made (*Trkulja v Google Inc. LLC & Anor*).

Mr Trkulja said his reputation had been severely tarnished because the publication implied he 'was so involved with crime in Melbourne that his rivals had hired a hit man to murder him'. He said: 'my life is my reputation, and you know, if a person loses his reputation, he has nothing' (*Trkulja v Google Inc. LLC & Anor*).

The jury subsequently found in favour of Mr Trkulja. He was awarded $200,000 in damages. Commenting on the award Justice David Beach said: 'the amount of the damages to be awarded must be sufficient (in the words of some of the authorities) to "nail the lie" in respect of the imputation upon which the plaintiff has succeeded' (*Trkulja v Google Inc. LLC & Anor*). Commenting on the fact that Google had not heeded Mr Trkulja's request to remove the defamatory material from the internet, Justice Beach said:

> the failure of an entity with the power to stop publication and which fails to stop publication after a reasonable time, is capable of leading to an inference that that entity consents to the publication. Such an inference is clearly capable of being drawn in the right circumstances (including the circumstances of this case) (*Trkulja v Google Inc. LLC & Anor*).

In addition to winning his case against Google, Mr Trkulja was also awarded damages of $250,000 in a separate but similar action against Yahoo!. Commenting after the judgment against Google he said he had not initially intended to sue Google but took the action when his request for the defamatory material to be removed from the search engine was ignored (Oakes 2012).

Often, damages awards are only part of the story—sometimes just a small part—with exorbitant legal costs adding at least to the total cost of losing a defamation case. There is no set formula relating to costs, but it was reported in the NSW Parliament back in 2003 that for a defamation action involving $10,000 in damages, legal costs for one party to the action could be expected to range from about \$80,000 to \$100,000 (NSW Legislative Assembly *Hansard* 2004, p. 7134). Costs in high-profile cases can be much higher. Obviously the sums of money involved in settlements and costs have increased since 2003 but it would not be unreasonable to conclude that proportionately the legal costs in high profile cases can still be up to 10 times the actual amounts awarded in damages. In 2008, for example, the Seven Network was estimated to have paid several million dollars in legal costs incurred in defending defamation actions brought against it by the mother and sister of convicted drug smuggler Schapelle Corby over an exclusive interview with former Corby family friend Jodie Power (Jackson 2008 p. 3). As well as its costs, the network also reached out-of-court settlements with each plaintiff.

One common way of saving costs, especially if a media organisation knows it is in the wrong, is to apologise early, arrange mediation between the parties and settle a case out of court. In fact one of the stated aims of the uniform Defamation Acts is 'to promote speedy and non-litigious methods of resolving disputes' (NSW *Defamation Act 2005*, Section 3(d)).

Stress and chilling effects

Worry about legal costs and potential damages can place a strain on individual journalists. Becoming embroiled in a defamation case can be incredibly time-consuming and emotionally draining. Journalists are likely to spend hours with lawyers, in drafting court documents, waiting outside courtrooms to be called to give evidence, giving that evidence, and then being cross-examined—sometimes by sneering barristers who make no secret of their disdain for media. Before a case finally gets into court, and even when it is in court, journalists will still be expected to go about their normal duties of finding stories and writing articles. The strain gets worse if a case is not going well, or if questions are asked in court about confidential sources.

The personal stress, the threat of a potential damages award, fears about the impact of a bad outcome on their career and family finances, worrying about what might happen to sources quoted in a story that sparked an action, and high legal costs have a cumulative impact on journalists. There can also be serious tension created within news organisations—especially in small ones which can be financially ruined by the cost of a defamation action.

The cumulative impact can have a 'chilling effect' on journalists and news organisations. What this means in practice is that when individual journalists and/or the organisations they work for fear becoming ensnared by Australia's defamation laws, there is a tendency to self-censor. Journalists who face a potentially difficult story in terms of defamation have two alternatives—either work and write to the defamation defences outlined later in this chapter, or drop the story. If they decide to work to the defences and they are supported by management, this is likely to involve their chief-of-staff and/or editor consulting lawyers and having the story 'legalled' before publication. Sometimes, no matter how much it is in the best interests of the community that a particular story should be published, if company lawyers advise the risk is too great, the story will never see the light of day. Journalists should also understand that any sources they quote who are subsequently sued will generally have to mount, and pay for, their own defences. News organisations do not, as a general rule, indemnify sources. But neither do they sue sources who provide wrong information.

Journalists whose knowledge of the law is shaky, or who are meek, mild, and want a quiet life, are particularly likely to self-censor and let issues drop. This tendency, in combination with a lack of preparedness by media organisations to invest in research by journalists, has had the effect of dumbing down investigative journalism in Australia in the past three decades.

Journalists whose knowledge of the law is shaky, or who are meek, mild, and want a quiet life are particularly likely to self-censor and let issues drop. This tendency has had the effect of dumbing down investigative journalism in Australia.

State of mind is irrelevant

But even those journalists who self-censor in a bid to avoid troublesome and expensive defamation actions can find themselves defending a defamation writ. This is because it is often not those cases in which someone is defamed deliberately that cause the most angst. Major cases can result from a plaintiff being defamed by accident. Unfortunately, and as many journalists have found to their cost, breaking a law by accident is no excuse, and neither is ignorance of the law. Worse, Australia's defamation laws specifically say that the state of mind of a defendant is generally not relevant in awarding damages. What that means is that the law does not care whether a defendant actually meant to damage a plaintiff's reputation or if it happened by accident. The main concern is the damage that was done.

You can defame a person accidentally by doing something silly such as putting a wrong caption on a photo or misspelling a name. Factual mistakes are also dangerous, as are rumours, gossip, making even the smallest assumption, inaccurate quotes, and reporting defamatory comments made by sources. Inaccurate headlines and errors introduced by sub-editors can also cause trouble. So too can the use of words naturally heavy with innuendo—words such as killer, bankrupt, immoral, terrorist, sacked, drug user, affair and cover-up. Ironically, therefore, while journalists deal with issues surrounding such words every day, they must be careful how they write about those issues.

It is also possible to defame someone without naming them, or even when using a fictitious name. For example, in a precedent set in a 1974 defamation action in NSW, the owner of a trucking business, who was not named, took action over a newspaper article about the suspected theft of millions of dollars' worth of wheat from silos in Armatree, Merriwa, Nevertire, Geuri and Narromine. The newspaper report said police investigations indicated big trucks were being used to transport stolen wheat which was being sold to pig and chicken farmers in outer Sydney. The plaintiff, who had previous criminal convictions, had been running a large-scale wheat-carting business in the area. She won the case after the court was satisfied that although she was not named in the article, it referred to her and implied she was a police suspect (*Steele v Mirror Newspapers Ltd* 1974).

Another landmark case centred on a made-up name which was found to actually refer to a real person, who, as bad luck would have it, was a barrister. The case went to court in the UK in 1909 after the barrister—whose real name was Thomas Jones, but who used the name Artemus Jones because it distinguished him from other men called Thomas (or Tom) Jones—sued over an article published in the *Sunday Chronicle* newspaper. The article was about a factual event, but the journalist had invented a character he called 'Artemus Jones' to add human interest, writing that Artemus Jones had behaved 'disgracefully' at a car race in France. The fictitious Artemus Jones was described as a church warden who had been at the race with 'a woman who is not his wife, who must be, you know—the other thing!' (*Jones v Hulton & Co.* 1909). The article went on:

> Here, in the atmosphere of Dieppe on the French side of the Channel, he is the life and soul of the gay little band that haunts the casino and turns night into day, besides betraying a most unholy delight in the society of female butterflies (*Jones v Hulton & Co.* 1909).

The court heard that the real Artemus Jones had not been in France during the car race. But unknown to the writer of the offending article and his then editor, the real Mr Jones had contributed articles to the *Sunday Chronicle* in the past. Evidence was given that five people who remembered those articles believed the fictitious Artemus Jones was actually one and the same as the real Artemus Jones. The newspaper printed an apology but still lost the case. It subsequently appealed the decision to the House of Lords but also lost the appeal (*E Hulton & Co. v Jones* 1910). During the appeal, one of the three judges, Lord Loreburn LC, said:

> A person charged with libel cannot defend himself by shewing (sic) that he intended in his own breast not to defame, or that he intended not to defame the plaintiff, if in fact he did both. He has none-the-less imputed something disgraceful and has none-the-less injured the plaintiff (*E Hulton & Co v Jones* 1910).

Despite the foregoing case and the common law precedent it set, it does appear that a lack of malice or recklessness on the part of a defendant may be taken into account at least to some extent in cases based on Australia's uniform defamation statutes. For example, Butler and Rodrick suggest that while:

> the intention or motive of the publisher is irrelevant to the question of whether the published material is defamatory or not... the intention or motive of the publisher may be relevant in relation to certain defences, such as qualified privilege and honest opinion, and to the assessment of damages (Butler & Rodrick 2007, p. 41).

Online defamation

One factor courts take into account when deciding how much to award in damages is how widely defamatory imputations were published and how many people became aware of them. Logically, a defamatory statement printed in a local newspaper with a small circulation—while still potentially extremely damaging to a citizen living in that particular circulation area—is unlikely to have as much impact as if the same imputation was published state-wide, nationally or internationally. This is because fewer people would have an opportunity to read the imputation in a local paper than if it was printed in a publication with a much larger and wider circulation. Similarly, as happened in the cases involving Google and Yahoo mentioned earlier in this chapter, if an imputation is published on the web—either on a news website, in a blog, on YouTube, Facebook, Twitter, via a search engine, or any other publicly accessible site, including those accessed via portable devices—it will have been published even more widely than if it was printed in a national newspaper or broadcast in a regional area because it was published to the world.

Obviously therefore, journalists must be particularly careful when writing articles for publication online and for mobile devices. But this is only part of the story when it comes to defamation and the web. Journalists must also be especially wary when dealing with information others have published online. One dangerous legal trap associated with online news reporting is to assume that material published on the web in one nation is safe to quote in a different nation. Nothing could be further from the truth. The problem is that different nations have different legal systems and totally different defamation laws. Thus an article that can be safely published in one nation might attract a writ in another. A good example can be found in the legal differences between Australia and the US because, as noted earlier in this chapter, journalists in the US operate in a much more tolerant legal environment compared with their Australian counterparts. This is something Australian journalists must understand very clearly when researching on the web and using computer-assisted research methods. But while there is greater freedom of speech in the US, and while journalists in that nation are not 'chilled' by defamation law to the same extent as Australian journalists, the downside from the perspective of Australian journalists is that, ironically, information on US-based news websites in particular (but also on US websites generally) is not necessarily constrained by the same standards of truth, accuracy or balance as information published on Australian-based websites.

> One dangerous legal trap associated with online news reporting is to assume that material published on the web in one nation is safe to quote in a different nation. Nothing could be further from the truth. The problem is that different nations have different legal systems and totally different defamation laws. Thus an article that can be safely published in one nation might attract a writ in another.

In a reversal of the situation in Australia, a defamation plaintiff in the US must prove that what was said or written was false, that the publisher was at fault at the level of 'actual malice', and that the plaintiff had suffered harm (Drechsel 1998, p. 394). In a landmark 1964 US case, *New York Times v Sullivan*, the US Supreme Court said news media in that nation could avoid being punished for libel for reporting false information about public officials if journalists had not acted out of malice. Reddick and King said:

> The court reasoned that American democracy depended in part on a vigorous press, but a vigorous press was bound to make mistakes from time to time. Therefore, the press needed 'breathing room' in which it could make mistakes without being punished (Reddick & King 1997, p. 206).

The *New York Times v Sullivan* judgment came to be known as the '*Times doctrine*' (Mencher 1997, p. 586). When read in conjunction with the outcomes of some other US cases, the decision actually extended First Amendment protections of free speech and press freedom (Mencher 1997, p. 583). There is no equivalent doctrine in Australia. It is therefore imperative that Australian journalists do not think that simply because they find something on a US website, it would automatically be all right to publish anything similar in Australia. Also be aware that US journalists can afford to take bigger risks in treating information more directly at face value than journalists in Australia because there is not the same emphasis on truth. In addition, US journalists have significantly more latitude when gathering and reporting information about public officials.

Problems arising from fundamental differences in defamation law between Australia and the US, and the potential global impact of these differences on web publishers, were highlighted in a precedent-setting legal action involving Melbourne businessman Joseph Gutnick and US corporation Dow Jones. The corporation publishes the online journal *Barron's*. In 2000, *Barron's* carried an article that alleged Gutnick had connections with a convicted money launderer and fraudster, Nachum Goldberg. Gutnick denied the allegation and launched a defamation action in the Victorian Supreme Court. His legal team argued Gutnick could bring the action in Victoria because that was where he had downloaded the *Barron's* article, and it was where he lived and therefore suffered most damage. Dow Jones said the case should be heard under US law in the US—where defamation cases are a great deal harder to win than in Australia—because the story had actually been posted online in the US.

The matter went the Australian High Court. It upheld Gutnick's right to sue in Victoria. In 2004 the case was settled out of court with Dow Jones reportedly agreeing to pay Gutnick $A180,000 in damages and $A400,000 in legal costs (O'Neill 2004). The case shocked web publishers around the globe because of its implication that a citizen of one nation, with its own peculiar laws, can take action against a citizen or legal entity of another nation, where the laws are totally different. In that sense, the case raised more questions than it answered. What, for example, would have happened if Dow Jones had simply refused to take notice of Australian courts? What if it had refused to settle or pay? What if a US citizen sued an Australian web publisher for something they downloaded in the US? One thing the case made crystal clear, however, is that the internet and online publication pose idiosyncratic legal challenges that journalists and publishers cannot afford to ignore—in particular, never assume that something you found online which appears to damage someone's reputation or business is safe to republish just because you found it on the web or via an app.

Defamation defences

As noted earlier in this chapter, one of the most important things to remember about defamation is that it is impossible to be a news-reporting journalist without defaming people and organisations. In fact—and this is something many people, including some journalists and authors, find very hard to understand—it is perfectly legitimate, even highly desirable and in some circumstances in the public interest, to do so. Despite the fact that unlike defamation laws in the US which value free speech and media freedom over individual rights, Australian defamation laws lean towards protecting individual reputations over free speech, there are situations in which Australian law accepts someone's reputation might have to be damaged for the overall good of society. That is another good reason why every journalist should understand, and always work to, the legal defences to defamation.

JUSTIFICATION (TRUTH)

This is the best and strongest defence, but while proving something is true might sound simple, it can be difficult. As the Ancient Greek philosopher Protagoras saw it, absolute truth does not exist and all truth is relative—or, as New Zealand professor of philosophy Ray Bradley explained: 'What tastes sweet to one person may taste bitter to another. What sounds melodious to me may sound cacophonous to you. And so on' (Bradley 2004).

One problem with the defence is that it puts the onus on a defendant journalist or publisher to prove the truth of what was written or broadcast. It is not up to a plaintiff to prove something was untrue. Another problem is that if innuendos can be attached to imputations, they could result in untrue meanings a writer did not intend being read into a published story or report. Further, second-hand accounts of events from sources, particularly protected sources, are considered to be 'hearsay'—something a person learns or 'hears' from another, but of which the first person has no direct experience—and therefore cannot be taken into account when attempting to prove truth.

Truth and credibility go hand in hand. This means stories must be accurate, names and facts must be correct, and so must quotes. Journalists must be able to produce original documents, notes and witnesses who can speak for themselves under cross-examination. It is not good enough to argue that 'everyone knows' a particular 'fact' is true, or that a trusted source said it was. As News Limited says in its *Style* guide for journalists:

> Journalists must check and double-check all facts, canvas all sides of a story, and elicit responses from those who may be upset by what is being said about them. Journalists will need to demonstrate that they have taken all possible steps to establish truth (McLeod & Lockwood 2009, p. 234).

It is therefore wise to be pedantic when news writing. For example, unless a person pleads guilty to a crime, they should not be referred to as a rapist, killer or stalker. If a person has been convicted after a trial in which she or he pleaded not guilty, it is much safer to refer to that person as a 'convicted murderer', 'convicted rapist' or 'convicted thief'. The reason is simple: if for some reason a murder conviction is overturned, perhaps on appeal, the person described as a 'killer' could sue for defamation and truth could not be invoked as a defence. If, however, the same person was described as a 'convicted murderer' truth could be called on later as a defence because the individual was convicted before his or her appeal.

Overall, while truth can be the best defence, it is unwise to rely on it as the only defence—it is much better to avoid putting all your eggs in one basket and to build a secure foundation for your articles by working to several strong defences at the same time.

CONTEXTUAL TRUTH

In essence, contextual truth has been taken to mean that a journalist who makes a *minor* mistake in an article might be protected provided the main thrust of the article is true. In an article written for the Australian Press Council, Ryan explained the defence thus:

> Where untrue imputations are published they may fall within the defence of contextual truth if they are published together with other imputations that are substantially true and the damage to reputation caused by the untrue imputations is no greater than that which is caused by the true imputations (Ryan 2006).

Ryan cited an example in which an article accurately stated that an individual was a murderer, but then incorrectly said he had been charged with murder. If the murderer subsequently sued for defamation because the imputation that he had been charged with murder was false and defamatory, the defence of contextual truth could be relied on because the main defamatory imputation, which was that he was a murderer, was correct. Therefore, even though it had been wrongly stated in the article that he had been charged, this was not likely to do any more damage to his reputation than the fact of him actually being a murderer.

ABSOLUTE PRIVILEGE

Absolute privilege is not a defence for journalists. It only protects members of parliament speaking in a chamber while they are formally in session during a parliamentary sitting (see Chapter 14), or judges, lawyers, witnesses and others giving evidence in a court or before a royal commission or inquiry. In these circumstances, absolute privilege protects everything said, no matter how defamatory and damaging it is.

QUALIFIED PRIVILEGE

This defence is potentially strong, but to invoke it a journalist must be able to demonstrate to a court that the publication of the imputation was 'reasonable'. This can be difficult, because a judge's interpretation of what is reasonable (which is supposed to be objective) can be quite different from a journalist's (subjective) view. The uniform defamation laws say that for the defence to succeed a defendant must prove:

(a) the recipient (of defamatory information) has an interest or apparent interest in having information on some subject, and

(b) the matter is published to the recipient in the course of giving to the recipient information on that subject, and

(c) the conduct of the defendant in publishing that matter is reasonable in the circumstances (NSW *Defamation Act 2005*, Section 30(1)).

The law also says that when considering if the conduct of a defendant in publishing matter about a person was reasonable, a court may take into account:

(a) the extent to which the matter published is of public interest, and

(b) the extent to which the matter published relates to the performance of the public functions or activities of the person, and

(c) the seriousness of any defamatory imputation carried by the matter published, and

(d) the extent to which the matter published distinguishes between suspicions, allegations and proven facts, and

(e) whether it was in the public interest in the circumstances for the matter published to be published expeditiously, and

(f) the nature of the business environment in which the defendant operates, and

(g) the sources of the information in the matter published and the integrity of those sources, and

(h) whether the matter published contained the substance of the person's side of the story and, if not, whether a reasonable attempt was made by the defendant to obtain and publish a response from the person, and

(i) any other steps taken to verify the information in the matter published, and

(j) any other circumstances that the court considers relevant (NSW *Defamation Act 2005*, Section 30(3)).

For the defence to succeed, a report must be not only about a matter of public interest, but published for the benefit of the public. In that context it is important to understand the difference between a report being *in* the public interest, as opposed to a report being interesting to the public. For something to be published *in* the public interest, it must be true and must *concern* a matter of public interest, not merely be something to amuse or titillate. Examples of issues that would meet this test include matters related to corruption, public health and safety, national defence, a hazard of some kind, and political debate.

Part of the idea of a public benefit or public interest requirement is that it provides a degree of privacy protection for people in the public eye. A key point here is to refrain from being judgmental—to remember that no matter how bad a villain seems to be, or how open and shut an argument, there is always another side. Therefore a defamed person must always be offered a genuine opportunity to explain her or his side. Whether the offer is accepted or not is up to the defamed person.

As well as being subject to a test of what was 'reasonable', the defence of qualified privilege will be defeated if a report is judged to have been motivated by malice. Evidence of 'malice' in a legal sense can be drawn not just from the motivation of a journalist who wrote a particular story but also from the words used, especially if the language is 'grossly exaggerated or disproportionate to the facts' (Butler & Rodrick 2007, p. 71).

In addition to the statutory defence of qualified privilege there is also a related, but largely untested, common law precedent relating to what has become known as political qualified privilege. In 1997 the Australian High Court dealt with an appeal in a defamation case brought by former New Zealand prime minister David Lange against the ABC. In essence, the *Lange* judgment found there was a constitutional 'implication' of freedom to discuss political matters in Australia. In the judgment the court ruled that journalists had a defence to defamation if they acted reasonably in reporting on or writing about government and political matters. The conditions of the defence are that the writer/publisher must have:

- had reasonable grounds for believing a defamatory imputation was true
- taken reasonable steps to verify the accuracy of their information
- believed the information was true and was not untrue
- sought a response from the defamed person, and published it if provided (Conley & Lamble, 2006, p. 420).

PUBLICATION OF PUBLIC DOCUMENTS

This defence applies to publication of information contained in official documents that are in the public domain, or should be in the public domain, provided that the publication aims to honestly convey information to the public or is for 'the advancement of education'. In addition to covering publication of documents, the defence covers publication of a fair summary or fair extract from such documents. For the purpose of this defence, public documents include court or tribunal transcripts, court orders and judgments; reports and papers published by parliaments and local councils; and documents published officially in other nations or recognised by international organisations such as the UN.

FAIR REPORT OF PROCEEDINGS OF PUBLIC CONCERN

This defence applies to fair and accurate reports of the proceedings of a broad range of formally constituted bodies. The information must be 'published honestly for the information of the public or the advancement of education' (NSW *Defamation Act 2005*, Section 29). Examples of organisations that conduct 'proceedings of public concern' include parliaments, both in Australia and overseas; local council meetings; courts, including courts in other nations and international courts of justice; public inquiries and standing commissions of inquiry such as the Independent Commission Against Corruption (ICAC) in NSW; international organisations such as the UN; sporting tribunals; public meetings about matters of public concern; reports by ombudsmen, law reform bodies and learned societies; and meetings of shareholders of public companies.

HONEST OPINION

This is an important defence, especially in relation to political and social comment; movie, book, theatre and food reviews; opinion pieces and blogs. It is similar to and partly supersedes an earlier common law defence known as 'fair comment'.

It is one instance in which Australian law makes allowance for freedom of speech, but to benefit from the defence a defendant must prove the defamatory material was presented as an expression of opinion, as distinct from a statement of fact. The opinion must be 'honestly held by the defendant', must relate to a matter of public interest, and be based on 'proper material' (NSW *Defamation Act 2005*, Section 31). 'Proper material' is defined in the uniform statutes as material that is substantially true, or was published on 'an occasion' of absolute or qualified privilege, or was based on 'an occasion' that attracted defamation defences relating to the publication of public documents or fair reporting of proceedings of public concern (NSW *Defamation Act 2005*, Section 31). To benefit from the defence any person criticised in a comment or analysis must have been offered a right of reply, or right to put their side of the story.

The defence is particularly relevant to comment on parliamentary proceedings, court cases (although be careful of contempt—see Chapter 16), and reports of local council meetings and public meetings. However, Ryan (2006) specifically warns that: 'If an expression of opinion can be interpreted by the reader as being a statement of fact, the court may reject the fair comment defence.' Commentary and analysis must therefore be clearly labelled as such.

INNOCENT DISSEMINATION

This defence protects people who disseminate material which is later found to be defamatory but who had no reason to know it was defamatory and whose lack of such knowledge was not a result of negligence. It can apply to booksellers, newsagents and librarians, as well as broadcasters if they have no effective control over what is said on air.

TRIVIALITY

To benefit from this defence a journalist must prove the defamatory matter a plaintiff complains of is so trivial it is unlikely to have caused harm (NSW *Defamation Act 2005*, Section 33). Note that it is also impossible for a person to defame himself or herself.

Criminal defamation

Defamation is rarely treated as a crime against the state in Australian jurisdictions, although criminal defamation is a statutory offence in most jurisdictions. With a few notable exceptions, such as the eventually unsuccessful pursuit of author Frank Hardy in 1951,[3] criminal defamation has usually been reserved for the most serious cases, or cases in which a person with no assets (who is therefore immune from the threat of having to pay damages) does the defaming.

It differs from civil defamation in several significant ways. First, the defamation must be published in a permanent form such as print (slander is not included). Second, in most jurisdictions a defendant's intent can become relevant. Third, criminal standards of proof apply and a defamer must be proved guilty beyond reasonable doubt.

Because criminal defamation is a matter of state and territory law, the legislation differs slightly between jurisdictions. However, the NSW law, which is spelt out in Section 529 of that state's *Crimes Act 1900*, is broadly representative of the intent of such laws in Australia. It says:

> A person who, without lawful excuse, publishes matter defamatory of another living person (the 'victim'):
>
> (a) knowing the matter to be false, and
>
> (b) with intent to cause serious harm to the victim or any other person or being reckless as to whether such harm is caused, is guilty of an offence (NSW *Crimes Act 1900*).

---

3   Hardy was pursued by the wife of Melbourne businessman and political power broker John Wren after publication of the book *Power Without Glory*.

Penalties include jail sentences and fines, and are likely to result in a conviction being recorded—something that could prevent a journalist from gaining a visa to visit other nations.

How to minimise defamation risks

Apart from always working to the defences, one of the most obvious protections is to consider how you would feel about what you had written if it was written about you. If it would make you uncomfortable, angry and upset, that is how the person you have written about is likely to feel. While this is not a reason to refrain from publishing a story—especially if the person you have written about is an unsavoury character who has hurt others—such feelings should sound a warning bell to be careful.

Overall, always strive for balance, ensure you are accurate at all times, never assume anything, and never leave yourself open to allegations of malice—if for no other reason than the fact that malice on the part of a defamer negates all legal defences. Specifically:

— Never make even a single assumption, and never guess anything. Near enough can never be good enough when it comes to legal matters.

— Trust your sixth sense. If something does not feel right, it probably is not.

— Always present all sides of an argument and at least attempt to give each protagonist a say—preferably in the presence of a witness or in some other way you can prove later.

— Do not write things that are outrageous.

— Use moderate language and think about the words you use—some are loaded with defamatory meanings.

— Take care with headlines and captions.

— Be careful when sub-editing that you do not introduce legal problems into the work of others.

— Avoid making comment when writing news.

— Clearly distinguish between fact and opinion, but base opinion pieces on fact.

— Date and label all interview notes and keep your notebooks for at least three years in case you ever need to refer back to them in a defamation case.

— Use a digital voice recorder when conducting potentially difficult interviews and keep a copy of the recording as a file on your computer, tablet or a memory stick. Then, so long as the relevant parts of the recording are transcribed accurately, it should be impossible for a person to show you have misquoted them.

— Never argue with a person you interview—that could be construed in a court as malice on your part.

— Never ignore a complaint—the sooner it is dealt with the better.

— Do not make admissions and do not apologise without consulting your editor or news producer.

— Be careful of emails, text messages, information you find on the web, blogs, letters to the editor, and anonymous 'news tips'.

— Take extra care with social media sites such as Twitter, Facebook and YouTube—as many journalists and others have found to their cost, social media sites are a minefield because comments made in the heat of a moment can rarely, if ever, be retracted.

Finally, if you suspect a story you are working carries a risk of defamation, or if you are accused of defaming someone, pass the buck to your chief-of-staff, news producer or editor as soon as you possibly can. Those people are the ones to decide if a story should be sent to a specialist defamation lawyer before publication, or if a lawyer should be consulted over allegations of defamation. Managers will also have considerably more faith in a journalist who alerts them to potential legal problems than one who invites trouble by putting her or his head in the sand.

DISCUSSION POINTS

1   Would it be reasonable for a journalist to argue that defamation law will not concern them because they are working in a specialised area such as travel or book reviews and will never write articles that defame anyone?

2   In 1824 the Duke of Wellington, who was married, famously told a former mistress who threatened to release intimate details of her relationship with him to 'publish and be damned'. In doing so, he threatened to sue the woman for defamation. She

subsequently published, he was mocked by the public, but he never did sue. What is the most likely reason why he did not?

3   Every so often an Australian parliament has been described as a 'cowards' castle' because politicians have used parliamentary privilege to defame members of the public and destroy reputations. Should politicians speaking in parliament therefore be subject to the same defamation laws as everyone else?

4   What are the main problems with relying on justification (truth) as a defence to defamation? What are the advantages?

5   You write a defamatory email to a trusted source. Without your permission and unknown to you, the source forwards the email to other people. One of these other people then publishes your email on a website. Who could be sued? Why?

6   What is the difference between an imputation and an innuendo?

7   Why is a defamatory innuendo potentially more damaging than a direct imputation?

NEWS PRACTICE POINTS

1   Find an example of a recent defamation case in which truth has been successfully argued as the major defence.

2   Explain the differences between the way the onus of proof applies in civil defamation cases compared with how the onus of proof is applied in criminal cases.

3   If you were a court reporter, why should you seek as much personal information as you could about an accused person appearing in court (for example, full name, age, occupation and full address)?

4   Search the web and find details of an Australian defamation hearing and its outcome, and the details of a US defamation hearing and its outcome. Write a short article highlighting differences in the way the cases were handled that reflect the basic difference in defamation law in each nation.

5   What are the most significant implications for Google and Yahoo! of the successful defamation actions against them by Milorad (Michael) Trkulja? Explain in no more than 750 words.

6   See what you can find about the Gutnick case and its impact on defamation law in nations other than Australia and the US. Has it made a difference to web publishing in those other nations? If so, how?

7   As a general rule, in order to be able to defend defamation you must have given the defamed person a right of reply. What are the most common defences that are underpinned by that rule?

8   You have defamed someone by accident. Is it wise to publish an apology immediately or would it be better to just ignore their complaints and wait for the matter to go to court? Why?

9   Go online and find a copy of your state or territory's *Defamation Act*. Check the statute carefully to see if it contains a clause that says it is a defence to defamation to say a comment was made in fun, by accident, or as a joke? What are the implications of your finding?

10 What is 'libel tourism'? What impact has it had, particularly in the US and UK?

CONTEMPT 16

The matter must be judged by contemporary Australian standards. It may be offensive, but it is not contempt of court, for a person to describe a judge as a wanker.

Justice Philip Cummins, Supreme Court of Victoria, 1999

OBJECTIVES

After reading this chapter you will understand:

» Why journalists should understand Australia's contempt laws
» Different types of contempt of court
» How to work within *sub judice* laws
» Contempt of commissions and standing commissions of inquiry
» Contempt of parliament
» Restrictions on identifying individuals.

Australia's wide-ranging laws of contempt are seen by many as draconian and arbitrary. They apply to everyone, not just journalists. Among other things, the laws are designed to uphold the dignity of courts and parliaments, ensure fair trials for individuals accused of crimes, protect children and victims of crime, shield litigants in the Family Court from publicity, and punish those who obstruct the pursuit of justice. While the intent of those laws is generally laudable, they present particular hazards for journalists, publishers and broadcasters.

The areas of contempt most likely to affect the work of journalists are those relating to contempt of court, contempt of parliament and contempt of commissions and inquiries. Specific contempt laws apply in relation to the Family Court, coroners' courts, children's courts, parliaments, and commissions of inquiry, including standing commissions such the Independent Commission Against Corruption (ICAC) in NSW, Crime and Misconduct Commission in Queensland,

and federally the Australian Crime Commission. Journalists also need to become familiar with contempt-related laws concerning reporting on matters involving children and sexual offences.

Contempt is most commonly a criminal matter and a person found guilty of contempt is likely to have a conviction recorded against his or her name. It is therefore imperative that just as journalists should understand and work to defamation law, they understand and work within the laws of contempt.

Contempt laws differ from most other criminal laws in several significant ways:

— First, there is no right to a jury trial and the person who brings a charge of contempt—often a judge or magistrate who has been offended—can be the same person who arbitrarily decides guilt or innocence and also imposes the penalty. Punishments can range from community service to fines and jail sentences.

— Second, a jail sentence can be open-ended with an offender held in custody until she or he agrees to abide by a court order, to answer questions, or produce documents.

— Third, a person can be charged with contempt, found guilty and convicted on the spot, without being given time to seek legal representation or prepare a defence.

Contempt of court

Broadly, there are three different categories of contempt of court:

1 contempt in the face of a court—when a person does or does not do something in a courtroom or court building that offends a court or shows contempt for its processes, staff or the law

2 scandalising a court—commonly when a person does something outside a court, such as writing a derisive newspaper article, that could be seen to unreasonably denigrate a court, its staff or a particular decision

3 *sub judice* contempt—laws designed to ensure an accused person has a trial free of outside influences such as 'trial by media'; one major aim is to prevent jurors from being swayed by media reports.

Contempt in the face of a court

Contempt in the face of a court would be what you could be found guilty of if, for example, you were disrespectful to a judge or magistrate, swore at them, made an obscene gesture, or called out during a hearing. Eating, chewing gum, or audibly whispering while a court is in session could also be construed as contemptuous. Laughing could invite trouble, as could reading a newspaper or book, or texting on a mobile phone. Even perching sunglasses on the top of the head instead of removing them has been known to draw the ire of a grumpy magistrate. It would also be considered contempt in the face of the court to use a voice recorder in court without permission, to take photos or record video. Protesting in a court building or immediately outside if a protest disrupts a hearing is also illegal.

For those who become involved in a case, it is an offence to disobey orders to appear in court, produce papers or answer questions during a hearing—something of particular concern to journalists because every so often one is jailed or fined for refusing to reveal the identity of a protected source. This is one reason why the Media Entertainment and Arts Alliance (MEAA)'s *Journalists' Code of Ethics* indirectly cautions against offering to protect the identity of sources. At point three, the code says:

> aim to attribute information to its source. Where a source seeks anonymity, do not agree without first considering the source's motives and any alternative attributable source. Where confidences are accepted, respect them in all circumstances (Media Entertainment and Arts Alliance 2013a).

What the code implies is that it would be most unwise to offer to protect the identity of a source unless you are prepared to go to jail for it because once you make that commitment there is no turning back, not even if a magistrate or judge orders you to reveal the person's identity.

To understand the seriousness of that ethical commitment, you need to think about how it would destroy your reputation and your career as a journalist if you did promise to protect a source but later changed your mind. Your word and your reputation would be in tatters—as could be the life and career of the person you let down. So there is enormous moral pressure to honour your pledge. The trouble is that the courts do not recognise the *Journalists' Code of Ethics*. It has no legal standing—something some self-righteous judges or magistrates who already despise journalists and media would be only too happy to point out! That said, a shield law of sorts was introduced in NSW in 1997 which offered limited protection for journalists from having to reveal their sources if a judge decided a source would be harmed if they were identified. The laws were strengthened in 2011 when NSW became the first state to enact shield laws specifically for journalists by amending its *Evidence Act 1995* (Samford et al. 2012, p.ii).

In 2007, the Federal Government adopted the early NSW model when it introduced a limited form of protection for journalists. It meant judges could decide, at their discretion, whether or not it was in the public interest to force a journalist to reveal her or his sources. But this 'protection' was criticised by journalists, the Australian Press Council, media company executives and the MEAA as being weak. New Commonwealth laws were introduced in 2011 which provided greater protection but still left it up to judges to decide if 'public interest in disclosure of the informant's identity outweighs any likely adverse effect of the disclosure' (Samford et al. 2012, p.ii).

Shield laws were adopted in the ACT in 2011 and Victoria and WA in 2012. They supposedly protect journalists, professionals and whistleblowers from having to reveal the identities of sources but still leave final discretion with judges. Despite improvements in legislative protection in some jurisdictions, journalists Steve Pennells, Adele Ferguson, Richard Baker, Nick McKenzie, Philip Dorling and Paddy Manning all faced legal actions in relation the protection of sources in 2013 (Media Entertainment and Arts Alliance 2013b).

Shield laws are much stronger in the US. In 26 states in that nation there are statutes similar to a Swedish law that says journalists cannot be compelled by courts to reveal the identity of a person who has supplied information (Rowat 1981, pp. 127 & 128). In some US states the shield laws also safeguard actual information obtained by journalists. This not only fosters investigative journalism, it also helps protect the identities of whistleblowers and shields them against allegations of defamation. As noted in Chapter 15, understanding these international differences becomes crucial when you consider information published on the web. While you might see stories online that mention journalists being protected by shield laws in the US or Sweden, do not be fooled into thinking the same rules apply in Australia.

Examples of Australian journalists who have been jailed for contempt in the face of the court after refusing to reveal sources include Tony Barrass, who was imprisoned for five days and ultimately fined $10,000 in a WA case in 1989–90

(*Director of Public Prosecutions v Luders* 1989). Also in 1989, *Courier-Mail* journalist Joe Budd was sentenced to 14 days' jail for contempt of court after failing to answer questions in court about his sources. He was released after a week. In SA, former ABC journalist Christopher Nichols was jailed for four months in 1993. There were other cases in 1993: also in SA, *Advertiser* journalist David Hellaby was fined; while in NSW, Deborah Cornwall—then with *The Sydney Morning Herald*— was ordered to perform 90 hours' community service after being found guilty of contempt of the ICAC. In Queensland in 1994, Madonna King, then of *The Australian*, and Paul Whittaker, then of *The Courier-Mail*, were threatened with contempt charges after their newspapers printed material arising from Criminal Justice Commission (now Crime and Misconduct Commission) investigations, although the matter was later dropped. In 2007 *Herald Sun* journalists Michael Harvey and Gerard McManus were each convicted of contempt of court and fined $7000 for refusing to reveal the identity of a source who leaked information about a federal government plan to save hundreds of millions of dollars by cutting benefits paid to war veterans.

Scandalising a court

Another type of contempt is what is known as 'scandalising' a court. You could be accused of doing this if you wrote or said something that was published and had the effect of undermining public faith in the administration of justice. The fact that scandalising a court is a particular form of contempt involving publication makes it of concern to journalists.

The usual interpretation of scandalising a court is publishing something that is excessively critical of a judge, court official or judgment, or asserting that a judge is corrupt, has been unduly influenced, or is grossly incompetent. It is not contemptuous, however, to make a reasoned comment about a trial, verdict, or behaviour of a judge or court official. Journalists encounter few problems when they make fair and temperate criticism of court decisions and the judiciary. Provided a matter is no longer before the courts (*sub judice*), they are free to be critical of judgments—even say they are wrong—and to discuss their implications. The courts and judges regard that freedom to make reasoned criticism as an essential part of the democratic process.

Journalists encounter few problems when they make fair and temperate criticism of court decisions and the judiciary. Provided a matter is no longer before the courts (*sub judice*), they are free to be critical of judgments—even say they are wrong—and to discuss their implications.

The distinction between what is acceptable criticism and what is not, was well explained in a UK case in 1900, in which Lord Russell of Killowen described scandalising the court as:

> Any act done or writing published calculated to bring a court or a judge of the court into contempt, or to lower his authority... That description of that class of contempt is to be taken subject to one and an important qualification. Judges and courts are alike open to criticism, and if reasonable argument or expostulation is offered against any judicial act as contrary to law or the public good, no court could or would treat that as contempt of court (*R v Gray* 1900).

In 2003, Melbourne barrister Colin Lovitt was found to have offered less than reasonable criticism when he referred to Brisbane magistrate Bruce Zahner as a 'complete cretin'. Lovitt was fined $10,000 in the Brisbane Supreme Court in a hearing in which Justice Richard Chesterman said the barrister was lucky to escape a jail sentence. Reporting on the case, *The Courier-Mail* said:

> Justice Chesterman heard evidence Lovitt referred to Mr Zahner as a cretin to a group of journalists covering a court hearing over allegations Melbourne couple John and Alessandra Gabriel assisted their son, Claude, to abscond from Queensland authorities. Several journalists testified Lovitt said: 'This bloke's a complete cretin. Surely they can't all be like this.' The court was later told that after a favourable ruling, he added: 'I take it back. He's not a complete cretin' (*The Courier-Mail* 2003, p. 12).

In an earlier landmark case, then president of the Builders' Labourers Federation Norm Gallagher was jailed for three months in 1983 after being found guilty of scandalising a court. Gallagher had told a television journalist in a recorded interview that a court case he was involved in had been won because the court was influenced by the actions of union members 'in demonstrating in walking off jobs' (*Gallagher v Durack* 1983).

Yet courts can be unpredictable. While Gallagher was sent to jail, a solicitor who was charged with scandalising the court in a 1999 case in which he said in front of police that a Victorian supreme court judge 'had his hand on his dick' escaped a conviction. The case, *Anissa Pty Ltd v Parsons*, arose after a family property dispute in which one of the parties was Simon Harry Parsons, a solicitor. The court heard that after a bizarre chain of events—which culminated in a bulldozer hired by Parsons being used to disrupt an auction on a rural property and to then knock down fences and trees, dig up an access road and cut an underground telephone cable—Justice Beach of the Supreme Court issued an urgent injunction to the effect that the bulldozer must stop causing damage.

By this time, two police were at the property, as were a second solicitor, a Mr Efklides, and a liquidator. Efklides subsequently served the injunction on Parsons by reading it aloud to him. The court transcript describes what happened next:

> At the conclusion of the reading of the Orders, the defendant said 'Is that all?' and Mr Efklides said 'Yes and when Justice Beach signs the Orders I will fax you a copy'. The defendant then said: 'And Justice Beach has got his hand on his dick'. Mr Efklides replied: 'I'll have to remember to tell him you said that'. The defendant said: 'Tell him, because if you don't I will'. The defendant then put his wrists out to the police officers and said: 'Guys, please arrest me if you like but this has been the funniest day of my life' (*Anissa Pty Ltd v Parsons* 1999).

Parsons was subsequently charged with scandalising the court. In acquitting Parsons, Justice Cummins explained:

> Finally I turn to whether, in the context I have defined, the words uttered by the defendant constitute contempt of court. The matter must be judged by contemporary Australian standards. It may be offensive, but it is not contempt of court, for a person to describe a judge as a wanker. The words uttered by the defendant, albeit particularised, say just that. The words spoken by the defendant do not undermine confidence in the administration of justice. They undermine confidence in the persona of the solicitor who spoke them. The words 'Tell him, because if you don't I will' are arrogant but not literal. The defendant interrupted but did not prevent oral service upon him of the court process. He then complied with it. His words were gratuitous and offensive but they fall short of contempt of court (*Anissa Pty Ltd v Parsons* 1999).

While not nearly so entertaining, there was an excellent example of reasoned and legitimate criticism of a judge some years ago when *The Weekend Australian* cited unnamed 'victims' of a Family Court judge in a February 2005 story headlined 'High price of snail's pace justice'. The article alleged that Justice Michael Hannon had taken 'up to four years to deliver his judgments, making him perhaps the slowest judge in Australia' (Denholm 2005, p. 1). Justice Hannon retired from the bench several months later.

Journalists also need to be aware that there can be a fine line between scandalising a court and defaming participants in a court case. One entertaining case that resulted in a defamation action rather than a contempt case occurred in Victoria in 1854 after the *Geelong Advertiser* newspaper published a wonderful article that said in part: 'With a drunken crown prosecutor and a selfish judge, the administration of justice is sinking into contempt...'. While the article might reasonably have been expected to attract a contempt action for scandalising the court, the crown prosecutor, one George Mackay, sued for defamation. By coincidence or otherwise, the case was heard before Mr Justice Williams, a judge the newspaper had accused in an earlier article of being selfish. After being found guilty of defamation, the paper's editor was ordered to pay £800—the equivalent of more than $130,000 today—to Mackay (Cryle 1997, pp. 59, 60 & 61). Obviously the outcome was far more rewarding for Mackay than if there had been action for contempt because the penalty in that case would not have been a monetary one.

Sub judice contempt

The Latin term *sub judice* literally means 'under a judge' (or magistrate) and/or 'before the courts'. The main aim of *sub judice* contempt law is to ensure a fair trial for an accused person in a criminal case. In essence, the law says no one, including individuals, media and people posting to social media websites, should publish anything that would interfere with the process of justice, or report anything that might be construed to indicate a charged person was innocent or guilty. This means the court becomes the only forum in which the case can be discussed. Comment articles, or the use of emotive words in a news report, can be particularly dangerous in this regard. So can comments and opinion posted on social media sites such as Twitter, Facebook and YouTube. One of the overriding aims is to protect jurors from reading, seeing or hearing anything that might colour their thinking and interfere with them making a proper decision.

Similarly, the law also aims to prevent publication of information that has the potential to contaminate witnesses' memories of events, or in extreme cases influence a judge or magistrate. In general, journalists must not:

— reveal or discuss any crime details after an alleged offender is arrested that might influence a jury or any potential jury

— reveal details of any past criminal record of an accused or details of any confession

— publish a photograph of an accused if there is any chance the accused's identity might become an issue during a trial

— comment on a case.

An example of the way Australian courts view *sub judice* contempt occurred in 1998 when *The Australian* newspaper was fined $75,000 and one of its business writers, Mark Westfield, fined $10,000 for what Victorian Supreme Court Justice Bill Gillard said was a 'nasty, spiteful' and 'absolutely appalling' article commenting on the unfinished trial of former Coles Myer chief Brian Quinn, who was defending charges of defrauding the company of $4.5 million (*R v Nationwide News* 1997). In the same year, then Sydney talkback radio host John Laws went on air and described a person currently on trial as 'absolute scum' and guilty of murder. The trial was aborted as a result. Laws was subsequently fined $50,000 and his radio station, 2UE, was fined $200,000 (*Attorney-General for the State of NSW v Radio 2UE Sydney Pty Ltd and John Laws* 1998). Outspoken journalist Derryn Hinch was sentenced to five month's home detention in 2011 after being convicted of contempt of court for publicly naming two sex offenders on his website and at a rally outside the Victorian parliament. Hinch was charged again with contempt in 2013 after allegedly breaching suppression orders in an article and link published on his website, relating to Adrian Ernest Bayley, the man who later pleaded guilty to raping and murdering ABC employee Jill Meagher (Akerman 2013).

To work safely within the law of *sub judice* contempt you need to develop a sound understanding of what are known as the six *sub judice* time zones. Officially, the *sub judice* process starts the instant a person is formally charged with a crime, but for a range of reasons—including the fact that it is not always possible for a journalist to know when an individual who has been taken in by police for questioning is actually charged—it is safest to regard the period as starting from the time a suspect is arrested. From then until the end of a trial, or subsequent appeal if there is one, all a journalist can report are the 'bare facts' of a case, such as the fact a murder had happened, where the body was found, its condition, who found it and when, that an arrest had been made and, maybe, who the dead person was. You are strictly limited to reporting only what the courts have defined as 'extrinsic ascertained facts to which any eyewitness could bear testimony' (*Packer v Peacock* 1912).

Once a matter has gone to court and an accused has appeared and been formally charged, it is generally safe to name her or him. Exceptions would be if the person was a juvenile, if a court issued a suppression order prohibiting publication of an accused's name, or if identifying an alleged offender would identify a child victim of crime or a victim of a sexual offence. From there on it is quite safe to fairly and accurately report anything said in open court. In a trial involving a jury, this means everything said in the presence of the jury, but nothing said in its absence. But journalists must not comment on proceedings, not even by describing how an accused or witness looked, or his or her demeanour.

The *sub judice* period ends once an accused has been found guilty or acquitted—unless there is an appeal, when the period is extended until the end of the appeal. Note here the words 'guilty' or 'acquitted'. 'Acquitted', or 'not guilty', does not necessarily equate with 'innocent'. The fact that an accused was not found to be guilty 'beyond reasonable doubt', does not mean she or he did not commit the crime—it may simply mean there was insufficient evidence, too much doubt, or the jury was bamboozled by a slick lawyer!

Journalists also need to be aware that they must not attempt to interview witnesses during the *sub judice* period, although they can generally be interviewed after the period ends. Neither can journalists approach jurors, nor identify them. In some jurisdictions jurors can never be interviewed—not even years after a trial—and doing so would be a criminal offence that could result in a jail sentence.

The six *sub judice* time zones are as follows:

1 *After a crime is committed but before an arrest.* The *sub judice* period has not yet started and there is no restriction on what can be reported. It is safe to interview victims, witnesses and police, and to describe a suspect. But you must be careful of defamation. What could happen if, for example, a person police said was the prime suspect was later found not guilty? You might find yourself faced with a difficult-to-defend defamation writ!

2 *After an arrest but before an accused is formally charged.* This can be a tricky period because it is often very difficult to know when police have moved from interviewing someone 'helping with inquiries' to formally charging that person. It is also possible an accused will be charged between the time she or he was arrested and/or taken in for interview (in which case it could perhaps be reported that an unnamed person was helping police with their inquiries) and when the next day's newspaper is published. It is legally dangerous to

name someone at this stage if that person's identity could become an issue in a subsequent trial. Reporting is therefore limited to the bare facts.

3   *After being charged but before trial.* The guidelines for the second time zone apply, except that you can usually also report on an accused's name, occupation and address. You can also report fairly and accurately on anything said in any open court appearances such as committal hearings. If you are reporting on a bail hearing, however, be careful not to report on things said during the hearing if they relate to previous convictions or alleged confessions, neither of which can be mentioned until a trial is over.

4   *During the trial.* You can report anything said in open court. Your reports must be fair and accurate. Reports of prosecution and defence cases should be balanced—something that can present a challenge when a case runs over many days or weeks.

5   *After the trial but before the expiry date for lodging an appeal, which is usually 28 days.* If there has been no notice of intention to appeal it is generally fairly safe to interview witnesses and other people involved in a case, but be careful not to sensationalise. Do not forget that in some states and territories you cannot interview, or even approach, former jurors.

6   *After appeal, expiry of the time for lodging an appeal, or after an acquittal, or guilty verdict and sentencing.* There are no longer any restrictions but beware of defamation.

Sub judice laws are not generally as strict in relation to appeals or civil cases, particularly those that do not involve juries, but you must still be careful. In civil cases, the *sub judice* period starts with the issue of a writ, statement of claim or summons. It ends when a court has made a decision. There are three main reasons why the law is not as rigid in civil cases:

1   the standard of proof is lower in civil cases

2   a person's liberty is not at stake

3   in cases heard by judges and magistrates sitting alone there is no concern that juries might be influenced. In addition, judges and magistrates are legally trained professionals and therefore consider themselves as being less easily influenced by media reports than members of the public who form juries.

SUB JUDICE CONTEMPT AND ONLINE PUBLICATION

The continuing evolution of the internet, web, social media and mobile communication has challenged concepts of *sub judice* contempt. What happens, for example, when the time-honoured Westminster *sub judice* contempt principle—which is generally respected by media in the Westminster-style systems of government found in many former British colonies—clash head-to-head with US cultural expectations about freedom of speech that underlie much of the publication found online? Take, for example, the furore which erupted in Melbourne in 2000 when the Supreme Court of Victoria decided *sub judice* rules had been so compromised by information posted on a WA–based internet site known as CrimeNet that a murder trial was aborted. Interestingly, publication of the offending material on the private CrimeNet database—which contained details drawn from previously published reports about the alleged criminal background of a person on trial—would have been legally safe in the US because it would have been protected by the First Amendment. In all probability, publication would also have been regarded as acceptable in Australia if the information had been printed in a newspaper or even broadcast on radio and television in WA, because publication within that specific jurisdiction would not have been considered likely to prejudice jurors sitting in a trial in Melbourne, several thousand kilometres to the east. However, although no claims were made that any juror had actually accessed the CrimeNet site, publication on the web was considered a serious breach by the court because it was publication to the whole world.

Similarly, while the law is clear in relation to *sub judice* contempt, journalistic reporting and media publication, it is less able to regulate and control publication by individuals of comments about court cases on social networking sites such as Facebook, YouTube and Twitter—so again journalists need to be careful. Repeating comments about a crime or suspect found, for example, on the Facebook site of a victim, could invite a contempt action against the journalist and her or his media outlet, even if the Facebook publisher was not charged.

Part of the problem faced by Australian legal authorities when dealing with *sub judice* contempt on social media sites is that unlike journalists, who are, or should be, sufficiently aware of the rules of *sub judice* to refrain from publishing information which could jeopardise a trial, is that users of social media sites generally lack legal training and have little or no understanding of the potential

> Unlike journalists, who are, or should be, sufficiently aware of the rules of *sub judice* to refrain from publishing information which could jeopardise a trial, users of social media sites generally lack legal training and have little or no understanding of the potential legal consequences of their posts.

legal consequences of their posts. The issue was highlighted in relation to two high profile murder cases in 2012–13. In October 2012 Victorian Deputy Chief Magistrate Felicity Broughton attempted to ban publication of comments about the accused killer of Melbourne woman Jill Meagher because social media sites had been 'flooded with potentially prejudicial material about the case' (Starke 2013). News.com.au reported that:

> At the time, Victoria Police Chief Commissioner Ken Lay criticised Facebook for hosting web pages that were inciting hatred and undermining the legal system, describing them as 'offensive garbage'... Days later the family of Sunshine Coast 13-year-old Daniel Morcombe, whose body was discovered in August [2011] after he went missing in 2003, made a plea to the public not to publish information on social media that could interfere with the trial of his accused killer (Starke 2013).

A second issue relating to comments on social media in Australia which breach our *sub judice* laws is that many of the postings which invite prosecution here could be published without breaking the law in some overseas nations—for example the US and France—where there are different legal systems and different approaches to laws of contempt.

Interestingly too in this context, one of the reasons we have strict *sub judice* laws in Australia is because we have an adversarial legal system—a system in which an accused person is regarded as innocent until proved guilty beyond reasonable doubt. In contrast, there is no *sub judice* law in nations such as Indonesia or France that have inquisitorial legal systems, in which a person is regarded as guilty until, or unless, they are proved not guilty. Hence much of the reporting we saw in Australia during the pre-trial period and trials of high-profile drug cases such as those of Schapelle Corby or the 'Bali Nine', as well as much of the online reporting and commentary on these cases, could not have happened if those involved had been charged and tried in Australian courts.

SUB JUDICE DEFENCES

There are recognised defences to *sub judice* contempt. One of the most commonly cited is what is known as the *Bread Manufacturers* principle (Pearson 2007, p. 96). It derives from a 1937 court case which itself resulted from moves by a group of bakers in Sydney to artificially inflate the price of bread. The case was launched by a man who said he had been defamed in a letter written by a company called Bread

Manufacturers Ltd. While the defamation case was running, *Truth* newspaper published a series of articles that was critical of a group of master bakers who were part of Bread Manufacturers Ltd. The articles alleged the bakers had conspired to keep bread prices artificially high and they had pressured other bakers who were not members of the company to do the same thing. Bread Manufacturers Ltd claimed the articles were in contempt because they prejudiced its defence in the defamation case. *Truth* said the articles were about matters that had been on the public agenda and were discussed before the defamation action started. The resulting case, *Bread Manufacturers Ltd; Re Truth and Sportsman Ltd*, set a precedent to the effect that if a matter had been an issue of public concern before the *sub judice* period started, discussion could continue as long as any prejudice that stemmed from the discussion was unintended and incidental. In its judgment, a ruling later confirmed by the High Court, the court said:

> It is of extreme public interest that no conduct should be permitted which is likely to prevent a litigant in a court of justice from having his case tried free from all matter of prejudice. But the administration of justice, important though it undoubtedly is, is not the only matter in which the public is vitally interested; and if in the course of the ventilation of a question of public concern matter is published which may prejudice a party in the conduct of a law suit, it does not follow that a contempt has been committed. The case may be one in which as between competing matters of public interest the possibility of prejudice to a litigant may be required to yield to other and superior considerations. The discussion of public affairs and the denunciation of public abuses, actual or supposed, cannot be required to be suspended merely because the discussion or the denunciation may, as an incidental but not intended by-product, cause some likelihood of prejudice to a person who happens at the time to be a litigant (*Bread Manufacturers Ltd* 1937, pp. 249–50).

More specifically the court ruled that:

> It is well settled that a person cannot be prevented by process of contempt from continuing to discuss publicly a matter which may fairly be regarded as one of public interest, by reason merely of the fact that the matter in question has become the subject of litigation, or that a person whose conduct is being publicly criticised has become a party to litigation either as plaintiff or as defendant, and whether in relation to the matter which is under discussion or with respect to some other matter... (*Bread Manufacturers Ltd* 1937, pp. 249–50).

It should be noted, however, that the *Bread Manufacturers* precedent was set in a civil case. It is less likely to protect journalists and media outlets accused of prejudicing a criminal trial (Butler & Rodrick 2007, p. 274).

A second potential defence to *sub judice* contempt has been suggested in cases where proceedings drag on for an excessively long time. In such cases, and where there is a stifling of debate that could reasonably be expected to take place in the public interest, the courts may take a lenient approach.

A third potential defence concerns what are known as 'stop writs'. A stop writ, or 'gagging writ' as it is sometimes called, is a writ issued by a plaintiff for defamation or some other action purely for the purpose of stifling discussion or publication by intentionally bringing on the *sub judice* period. The courts take a dim view of such a practice and such writs generally do not prevent further discussion; although there would be a risk of damages being increased if a publication continued to publish but later lost the case brought on by the writ.

Restrictions on court reporting

The idea that justice must not only be done, but must be seen to be done, is recognised internationally in Article 10 of the *Universal Declaration of Human Rights*. It says criminal charges must be heard in a 'fair and public' hearing (*Universal Declaration of Human Rights* 1948). The concept is also embedded in our common law by a precedent set in a 1913 British divorce case known as *Scott v Scott*. This was a landmark case that eventually went to the House of Lords and Privy Council on appeal. In that final appeal it was ruled that the judge in the original hearing had erred by allowing the case to be held *in camera* (in private). A member of the House of Lords, Lord Atkinson, said in that case:

> The hearing of a case in public may be, and often is, no doubt, painful, humiliating, or deterrent to both parties and witnesses, and in many cases, especially those of a criminal nature, the details may be so indecent as to tend to injure public morals, but all this is tolerated and endured, because it is felt that in public trial is to be found, on the whole, the best security for the pure, impartial, and efficient administration of justice, the best means for winning for it public confidence and respect (Atkinson 1913).

In the same case, another member of the House of Lords, Lord Shaw, quoted philosopher Jeremy Bentham, who had said:

> Publicity is the very soul of justice. It is the keenest spur to exertion, and the surest of all guards against improbity. It keeps the judge himself, while trying, under trial (Bentham 1844, p. 115).

The precedent set in *Scott v Scott* is an important one for journalists. It has been upheld many times. In one legal action in Victoria in 1999, in which a magistrate sought to stop the *Herald Sun* reporting on a case in his court, a higher court upheld the decision in *Scott v Scott* with an appeal judge later commenting that:

> Since not everyone can visit [courts], citizens in a democracy depend to a substantial extent upon accurate and published reporting of what takes place. Restrictions on access to the courts or on the dissemination of events which take place in court ought, it seems to be generally thought, only be imposed if it is necessary to do so for the proper administration of justice… In an open and truly democratic society, the right of various forms of the media (that is, the media as a means of communication of the issues, parties and the hearing) to be present and publish is generally regarded as being in the public interest, so long as the reports are accurate and do not misrepresent, by omission or unbalanced selection, the evidence and its effect. The right to report is seen as an adjunct of the right to attend (Justice Hedigan, in Bhojani 2001, pp. 5 & 6).

As a result of *Scott v Scott* and some other cases, media are free to report fairly and accurately on most cases. The main exceptions are in cases of sexual assault, cases involving juveniles under the age of 18 (or 17 in Queensland), when there is legal discussion in the absence of a jury (a *voir dire*), or cases when a court rules it must be closed 'in the interests of justice'. The restrictions can be grouped into two broad categories:

— limits on the public's right, including a journalist's right, to be present in a court room

— limits on what might be reported by journalists and media.

The restrictions aim to protect victims of crime, protect some witnesses, protect jurors, and also shield the public from the gory and depraved details of some cases.

ISSUES OF IDENTIFICATION

It is illegal in all Australian jurisdictions to identify victims of sexual offences, participants in Family Court cases, juveniles, ASIO officers and, in some jurisdictions, jurors. In addition, in Queensland it is illegal to identify a person who has been charged with a sexual offence until that person has actually been committed to stand trial for that offence. If you fail to observe these restrictions you could face specific penalties and also be found in contempt of court.

When dealing with identification issues, it is important to understand that it is not only illegal to identify specific individuals, it is also illegal to publish other details that could lead to their identification. This would include things like their school, address, place of employment, or any other information that might indirectly identify them. Be particularly careful not to publish photos, sketches or video that could pinpoint a protected individual.

Family Court cases warrant a special mention. The court is open and you can sit in on cases, but there is a strict ban on identifying any party or witness without specific permission from the court—something that is generally only granted if one parent absconds with a child of marriage and the court believes publicity might aid the child's return.

Coronial courts can also be tricky. As a general rule the law says you cannot identify anyone or report any of the evidence where the finding is, or it appears it could be, suicide.

Also be careful with photos and video—including the use of mobile phone and tablet cameras—because it is an offence to take a photo in or near a courtroom, even an empty courtroom or a passage leading to a court. As well as being illegal to take such a photo, it is a separate offence to publish it.

Be especially careful about identification issues if court reporting in small towns and regional areas where everyone tends to know everyone else and even a seemingly innocuous clue could identify an individual.

> When dealing with identification issues, it is important to understand that it is not only illegal to identify specific individuals, it is also illegal to publish other details that could lead to their identification.

Contempt of parliament

The concept of contempt of parliament has been handed down to Australian parliaments from the House of Commons in the UK. Contempt of parliament is broadly defined as 'any act or omission which directly or indirectly impedes the performance of the functions of a House of Parliament or a member or officer of parliament…' (Walker 1989, p. 105). The relevant laws were designed to ensure parliaments and its individual members are treated respectfully and are free to engage in debate and undertake the business of governing without interference or threats of interference. As noted by Armstrong and others:

> Freedom of speech in the federal and state parliaments is absolute, controlled by the parliaments and not by the courts. This freedom of speech is particularly important in a country such as Australia, the defamation laws of which often make it dangerous to expose corruption in any other forum (Armstrong et al. 1995, p. 134).

To understand what is involved in contempt of parliament, it is first necessary to understand that there is also an offence known as 'breach of parliamentary privilege', which was discussed briefly in Chapter 14. Contempt of parliament and breach of parliamentary privilege are related, although they are not exactly the same. Breach of parliamentary privilege refers to an infringement, or alleged infringement, of the rights and privileges of members of a parliament. Anything interfering with the right to free speech by a member of parliament speaking in the house would be regarded as a breach of parliamentary privilege. So would any attempt to improperly influence a member with, say, a bribe or threat. Each Australian parliament has its own special privileges committee to protect the rights of its elected members, conduct hearings and rule on matters of privilege.

One of the greatest risks for journalists in this regard relates to the publication of information based on leaked documents, particularly documents emanating from parliamentary committees which have not been tabled in the full house. Committees often meet *in camera*, or behind closed doors, and it is an offence to report on their confidential deliberations.

Despite the antics of some of our less-than-well-mannered politicians, contempt of parliament can also include such things as disorderly conduct within parliamentary precincts and refusal to obey orders of a speaker or president. An example of contempt of parliament would be for a person who was not an elected member to walk on to the floor of a house and start making a speech. Similarly, a person who called out from a public gallery, or who actually did something to damage a parliament building, or who made threats against a member, would be in contempt. It is also an offence to insult or discredit a parliament as a whole, as could happen, for example, through publication of a false or perverted account of parliamentary proceedings. In addition, refusing to answer a question posed by a parliamentary committee can constitute contempt. Walker said contempt of parliament could include a comment that 'reflects' adversely on a house, such as an article headlined 'political bludgers' (Walker 1989, p. 111). Offenders can be charged with contempt of parliament and summoned to appear before a house. If found guilty, they can be fined or jailed.

A person charged with contempt of parliament can be ordered to appear in parliament before 'the bar of the house' to answer the charge. The 'trial' would be conducted by the parliament or its privileges committee, not by a court. A little like contempt of court, the parliament acts as the prosecutor, jury and judge. There are no legal excuses or recognised defences. A person convicted of contempt of Federal Parliament could be jailed for up to six months or fined. Most other parliaments can also impose a jail sentence.

Further, a parliament can ask police to investigate a leak and to charge suspected offenders. That is what happened in 2007 when the Federal Government asked police to investigate the leaking of cabinet documents, which revealed cabinet intended short-changing war veterans by spending only about $108 million of the $650 million in extra entitlements that had been recommended by an independent review (Robinson 2007, p. 3). Melbourne *Herald Sun* journalists Michael Harvey and Gerard McManus were each convicted and fined $7000 because they refused to give evidence at a pre-trial hearing that had resulted from the police investigation. Public servant Desmond Kelly was also convicted but eventually acquitted after an appeal. When sentencing the two journalists, Judge Michael Rozenes criticised the government, saying 'the Commonwealth was suffering from a serious case of schizophrenia' (Merritt 2007, p. 3).

Contempt of commissions, inquiries and other related offences

In addition to contempt of court and contempt of parliament, it is also possible to be held in contempt of a royal commission, a commission of inquiry, and a tribunal or standing commission of inquiry such as the Crime and Misconduct Commission in Queensland, Victoria's Independent Broad-based Anti-corruption Commission (IBAC), and the Independent Commission Against Crime (ICAC) in NSW. Most restrictions invoked by specific commissions, inquiries and tribunals are set out in the legislation establishing them.

As a general rule, contempt would include insulting, disruptive or disobedient behaviour, including a refusal to give evidence or answer questions. As an aside, it is interesting to note that an inquiry itself could be held to be in contempt of court if its activities interfered with the course of justice.

Finally, there are several offences that while not actually constituting contempt, are closely related to it. One is what is known as the criminal offence of perverting the course of justice. Actually perverting the course of justice, or conspiring or attempting to do it, are all offences under both common law and specific statutes. Note that the offence applies from the time a crime is committed, not just when someone is charged. While the offence is fairly self-explanatory, it is well explained in the NSW *Crimes Act 1900*. It defines perverting the course of justice as 'obstructing, preventing, perverting or defeating the course of justice or the administration of the law' (NSW *Crimes Act 1900*, Section 312). The offence includes such things as making false allegations, hindering an investigation, threatening or intimidating victims or witnesses, tampering with evidence, concealing a serious indictable offence, and interference with court officers, witnesses or jurors. Anyone convicted of the crime can face up to 14 years in jail.

Some other contempt-related offences include perjury (lying under oath), fabricating evidence, bribery, and pressuring parties to start, stop or compromise a court action.

DISCUSSION POINTS

1   If you were to argue that Australia's contempt of court laws are draconian and in desperate need of reform, what would you put forward as the two areas of those laws most in need of updating?

2   Is it reasonable for Australian journalists to be heavily restricted by *sub judice* laws when journalists and users of social media sites in other nations are not?

3   High-profile Victorian journalist Derryn Hinch has been convicted multiple times for breaching contempt laws—especially those of *sub judice*. Is Hinch to be admired or has he set a bad example? Why?

4   Is it fair and reasonable that *sub judice* laws prevent journalists from warning the public that a well-known serial paedophile, who is on bail after facing fresh charges of molesting children, is living in their neighbourhood? Why or why not?

5   Should all courts, including the Family Court and children's courts, be opened up to journalists so that we can truly say that justice is not only done, it is seen to be done in every Australian court?

6   Does it make sense that parliaments and courts have separate systems of contempt? Should both systems be rationalised and updated? If so, why and how?

NEWS PRACTICE POINTS

1   Go online and find an example of an Australian court case that was conducted *in camera*. What reason can you find for the court being closed?

2   You are a journalist and you interviewed a 16-year-old girl who was convicted of the (hypothetical) new crime of cyber-terrorism. She was convicted, fined and released. You photograph her with her parents. Can your story and the photographs be published? Why or why not?

3   Find an example of a recent contempt of court case involving a prosecution for contempt in the face of the court. Explain the key points of the case in 500 words.

4   Find the most recent case you can involving a charge of scandalising a court. Who was involved and what was the outcome?

5   What are two of the most significant differences between *sub judice* laws in Australia and the US?

6   Go online and find details of a contempt case in which a person refused to give evidence—or gave false or perjured evidence—to a hearing conducted by a standing inquiry with the powers of a royal commission.

7   You are a journalist who has agreed to protect the identity of a source who works in a sensitive position inside a security agency. You subsequently research and write a story about corruption at the highest levels of government and include information provided by the source. The Australian Federal Police then launch an inquiry, not into the corruption allegations, but into where you obtained the information. During a subsequent court case you are ordered by a judge to hand over your contact book so the police can use it in their attempt to find your source. What will you do? Why?

8   Can you ever report on an accused person's prior criminal convictions? If so, when?

17

OTHER LEGAL PERILS

The law is a ass—a idiot
Mr Bumble in Charles Dickens, *Oliver Twist*, Chapter 51

OBJECTIVES

After reading this chapter you will understand:

» How to work within the laws of trespass and nuisance

» Legal obligations to respect confidences

» Laws relating to hidden cameras and voice recorders

» The basics of Australia's tangled web of privacy laws

» Concepts of intellectual property, copyright law, and dangers of plagiarism

» Laws and regulations relating to discrimination, censorship, sedition and 'spent' convictions.

Defamation and contempt tend to be the areas of law that cause the most common potential problems for journalists, and most expensive legal bills, but some other lesser known and sometimes quirky legal traps have a nasty sting in the tail too and can also prove costly. This chapter is therefore a potpourri—we start with trespass and then examine an assortment of laws ranging from breach of confidence to sedition, nuisance, privacy and copyright.

Trespass and nuisance

Trespass laws are straightforward from a journalist's perspective. Basically, they mean that if you are told to leave private property, you must leave and do so immediately. As a general rule it is legally safe to enter a property by an obvious route, such as a front gate or marked pathway, and make your way to the front door to seek an interview or ask for information. This is because the presence of a gate or pathway indicates what is known as an implied invitation to enter. It is not all right, though, to take a detour, walk around a property and look in windows or explore the backyard. Similarly, there is an implied invitation to enter a shopping centre or shop if the entrance is open or there is an 'open' or 'enter' sign.

If, however, a person answers a knock on the front door of their home, or even calls out without opening the door, and tells you to go away, you must leave the property immediately without arguing. The same applies if you are told to leave a shop, shopping centre or other property or premises. A person who has been told to leave private property (including a shop, shopping centre or private carpark) and who does not, may be ejected by force if she or he does not go within a reasonable time. A person whose land has been trespassed on may sue the trespasser for damages because, among other things, trespass is a tort,[1] which means we all have a duty not to trespass. Trespass laws also have teeth, something the Nine Network learnt to its cost in 2006 when it was ordered to pay damages of $230,000 for trespass plus $80,000 for false and misleading conduct after *A Current Affair* reporter Ben Fordham and a camera crew refused to leave a builder's home when told to go (*Craftsman Homes v TCN* 2006). Fordham had used a false name and a deceptive story to gain entry to the home on four separate occasions. After an appeal, the amount was reduced to a total of $170,000 (*TCN Channel Nine v Ilvariy Pty Ltd* 2008), but the legal costs of six years of litigation would have been hefty.

As well as being a civil matter, trespass can also invite criminal charges, with a variety of statutes dealing with trespass in different jurisdictions. In Queensland, for example, the *Invasion of Privacy Act* has a special section about invading the privacy of others by entering a 'dwelling house' or 'the yard of a dwelling house'. It sets the maximum penalty at one year's jail for anyone who enters a house without the consent of the lawful occupier. The Act also makes it an offence punishable by up to 18 months' jail to gain entry by force, 'threats or intimidation of any kind', deceit or 'fraudulent trick'. It says a person found in a dwelling or yard must be able to prove they had a lawful excuse to be there (*Invasion of Privacy Act 1971*, Section 48A).

---

1   A tort is a civil wrong, as opposed to a crime. See Chapter 15.

PHOTOS AND TRESPASS

In Australia there are no laws that say we own our own image. So while it is obvious that journalists, photographers and video camera operators are free to take photographs or film people if they have permission, it is less well known that images can be shot without permission providing the camera and person using it are outside the relevant person's property, or the individual being photographed is in a public place. But to enter private property and record video or take photographs without permission is to invite legal action for trespass. The Nine Network was reminded of that in 2002 when it was ordered by a court to pay $100,000 damages plus interest to a man renting a rural property because a camera crew for *A Current Affair* entered the property with cameras rolling and recorded video without permission. The court ruled that while the camera crew had an implied right to enter the property to ask permission to record video, there was no implied right to actually record without consent (*TCN Channel Nine v Anning* 2002). The damages were subsequently reduced to $25,000 on appeal but that amount was probably trivial compared with the legal costs.

To enter private property and record video or take photographs without permission is to invite legal action for trespass. But it is legal to video someone in his or her own backyard as long as the camera operator is on public land or is on private land, such as the block next door, with the permission of the owner.

On the other hand a photographer may use a telephoto lens to take photos or record video from the footpath or road outside a property because the footpath and road are public land accessible to everyone. She or he may also take photos or record video from a neighbouring property if the neighbour has given permission to do so. Neither is it an offence to take aerial photographs, although a helicopter or drone hovering over a backyard for more than a short time might be regarded legally as a 'nuisance'—something discussed later in this chapter. In other words, it is legal to video someone having a barbecue or swimming in a pool (or even staggering around drunk and dishevelled) in his or her own backyard as long as the camera operator is on public land or is on private land, such as the block next door, with the permission of the owner. But be aware that publication of unflattering images could invite a defamation action. It should also be noted that it is an offence, and can constitute an assault, for journalists or photographers to actually touch, shove or hold someone they are trying to photograph.

Trespass laws aside, and as noted in Chapter 13, it is not generally an offence to take photographs or record video of people in public places, such as on beaches or in crowds, even if they do not want you to—although photographers who make a nuisance of themselves by taking photos in some situations, such as of women sun-baking topless or children playing on beaches or in other public places, can be charged under public nuisance and offensive behaviour laws. In most jurisdictions it is also illegal to photograph 'private acts', 'indecent acts' and 'private activities' that happen in places where people normally expect privacy. Also beware that any photo that could be construed to depict a juvenile in a sexual context could result in paedophilia-related charges. In addition, there are specific laws that prohibit taking photographs on some government-controlled land such as military bases, power stations, airports and railway property. Overall, journalists, video camera operators or news photographers going about their normal business of reporting are unlikely to encounter legal problems if they do not infringe trespass laws and do not take photographs on prohibited government sites.

NUISANCE

Nuisance is primarily a common law[2] tort, although specific statutes have been adopted in some jurisdictions. The fundamental aim of nuisance laws is to protect a person's use and enjoyment of her or his property. Nuisance can include interference caused by things such as bad smells, smoke, animals and noise. It must involve a real 'detraction from the rights of enjoyment of the occupier' (Armstrong et al. 1995, p. 184).

Journalists are most likely to find themselves in trouble over nuisance if they constantly telephone someone in a bid to get an interview, or if they 'stake out' a property or conduct surveillance of a person on it (Pearson 2007, p. 385). The nuisance laws mean you should not continue to harass an individual if they have made it clear they do not want to talk to you. Legal remedies include the granting of injunctions to make a journalist stay away and/or to prevent publication of material obtained as a result of the nuisance.

Breach of confidence

In Charles Dickens' novel *Oliver Twist*, Mr Bumble tells us 'the law is a ass—a idiot'. Nowhere could there be a better demonstration of that than in the law surrounding breach of confidence.

---

2   As explained in Chapter 14, common law is law made in the courts (as opposed to statute law, which is made by Acts of Parliament).

In essence, it is a law that is the reverse of another area of law. In Chapter 16 it was explained that a journalist who refuses to reveal the identity of a confidential source faces the possibility of being jailed for contempt in the face of the court. But when it comes to breach of confidence, a journalist could be breaking the law by doing the opposite—revealing the identity of a source! Briefly, under common law it is illegal to 'divulge to the world information received in confidence' (Lord Denning, quoted in Jones & Benson 2002, p. 3). Thus a journalist who breaches an agreement with a source not to name that source, or publish particular information, could be in trouble. Breach of confidence also relates to information that people are obliged to keep confidential by virtue of their profession, for example doctor–patient or lawyer–client information, personal diaries and letters or emails clearly marked at the top as being 'private and confidential'. Additionally, breach of confidence can relate to matters of national security and disclosure of some other categories of government information.

A plaintiff seeking to sue you for breach of confidence must prove:

— The published information really was confidential.

— The information was used without authority and to the plaintiff's detriment.

— The information had been communicated in such a way as to indicate there was an obligation to keep it confidential—for example, a document was headed 'private and confidential', or the information was originally disclosed or provided in such a way that confidentiality was implied.

A problem media outlets face in attempting to defend allegations of breach of confidence is that the law in this area is fuzzy. For example, publication of confidential material in the broad public interest is not a defence in Australia. It is only when the confidential information relates to an 'iniquity' (meaning 'a crime, civil wrong or serious misdeed of public importance') and that what is disclosed is of 'public importance' (in the sense that it affects a whole community or 'affects the public welfare') that there may be a defence (Ligertwood & Jackson 2007, p. 22). Another issue is that individuals can sue for damages if they are 'distressed'— as opposed to actually suffering a psychological or psychiatric injury—by the publication of material created in confidence (Merritt 2008b). In addition, media outlets can be found liable 'even if unaware the material in question is covered by the relationship of confidence' (Merritt 2008a).

Defences are available if information was already public knowledge before it was published, if it was disclosed with consent of the source, or if the disclosure was the result of a court order. Interestingly, if government secrets are involved, the onus of proof is on the government to prove there was a public interest (meaning a public benefit) in the information being kept confidential. There was a landmark case in 2007 when the ABC was ordered to pay $234,000 compensation to a woman who had been raped after her name and the suburb she lived in were broadcast in news bulletins on the day her attacker, who was her estranged husband, was jailed (*Jane Doe v ABC* 2007). During the damages hearing, the court was told that 'Ms Doe' had an expectation her name and other private details would not be revealed because it was an offence to publish information identifying a victim of a sexual offence (*Jane Doe v ABC* 2007). The court awarded damages not only for breach of confidence, but also for psychiatric injury caused by the breach of confidence, plus an amount for the hurt, distress, embarrassment, humiliation, shame and guilt experienced as a result of the news broadcasts (*Jane Doe v ABC* 2007).

Hidden cameras and voice recorders

It is illegal to conceal cameras, sound recorders, mobile phones or other devices in order to spy on people without their knowledge. But as a general rule it is not illegal to photograph or video a person as long as the camera is not hidden, the person using it has not trespassed, and the subject of the photo or video was not in a situation in which a person would normally expect privacy. It is not generally an offence to make a sound or video recording in situations in which a person should reasonably expect what was said or done would be overheard or seen by others, for example in a public place.

In the past it has also been broadly regarded as safe to record a conversation or make a video recording using an unseen recorder or camera as long as the person making the recording is a party to whatever is being recorded and there is a public benefit in the recording being made; or if the person making the recording does so to protect their own interests. But in some jurisdictions there is a distinction between making a sound and video recording in such circumstances and in publishing the resultant material, with the law allowing recording but prohibiting publication.

Overall, though, this is a complex area of law with different rules in different states, territories and federally. It is also an area of law in which legislation is being outpaced by rapidly developing technology, while there is also ever-increasing pressure for new privacy rules. We can therefore expect new and more restrictive laws to be introduced over time as legislators and the judicial system attempt to catch up and keep pace with change. Consequently the best advice is to check the current legal situation in your jurisdiction before attempting to surreptitiously record or video anyone.

Privacy

Despite what many people believe, and others would have you believe when trying desperately to stop you pursing a story about themselves or their client, there is no general right to privacy in Australia. Similarly, there is no single law relating to privacy, or which prevents publication of information people might find embarrassing or distressing. Privacy is instead covered by a range of different and complex laws. The Australian Press Council says the nation has 'a myriad of federal, state and territory laws that regulate privacy protection, in areas such as telecommunications, surveillance, listening devices, health records, data matching, trespass, matters affecting children, adoption, sexual offences, juries, prisoners, security, and family law'(Australian Press Council 2008a). However, while there was no all-embracing privacy law in Australia at the time this book was written, privacy is a controversial area that is regularly debated, especially among politicians. For example, the Australian Law Reform Commission has twice recommended the introduction of a new statute that would introduce a tort of privacy and allow individuals to take action for invasion of privacy (Merrit 2013). The Gillard Labor Government considered the matter in 2011 after pressure from then Greens leader Bob Brown. It subsequently outlined a broad plan to introduce new laws which would have allowed people to sue each other for breaches of privacy. However, in early 2013 then Attorney-General Mark Dreyfus dropped the proposal because he said experience in other nations which had introduced similar laws indicated that litigation was limiting freedom of speech (Merrit 2013).

Among the quirks in Australian privacy law is the fact that, despite its name, the federal *Privacy Act 1988* only deals with limited aspects of privacy. Its main focus has been on health and financial information, although it also protects some information regarding old criminal convictions, telecommunications and data-matching. Within these areas, the Act covers the way information is collected, used and disclosed, and allows individuals to access and correct errors in data about themselves. In terms of financial information, the Act gives some protection to tax file numbers and credit records. It allows you to refuse to give your tax file number and prevents the number being used as a form of personal identification.

The Act covers information collected by both the Federal Government and the private sector. Generally speaking, however, while the Act relates to all health service providers, it does not apply as broadly to the business sector. This is because the Act only pertains to businesses with an annual turnover exceeding $3 million. In this area, its main provisions are directed towards regulating credit providers such as banks and other financial institutions.

In many senses the Act is confusing, difficult to understand, and something of a toothless tiger when viewed from the perspective of the ordinary person. Interestingly, however, Section 66(1A) of the Act appears to offer something of rare shield for journalists by allowing them to refuse to disclose their sources if requested to do so within the terms of the Act (*Privacy Act 1988*, Section 66). But the exemption is so confusing and its wording so circular that it is virtually meaningless. Similarly, while the Act lists 11 guiding privacy principles, they are such complex gobbledegook that not even a 'plain English' summary of them published by the Office of the Privacy Commissioner makes much sense (Office of the Privacy Commissioner 2010).

Stalking

Most states and territories have statutes dealing with stalking. They are broader than nuisance laws because they were designed to prevent unwanted contact not only on a person's own property, but anywhere and everywhere. The statutes most commonly relate to a person who has been involved in—or who wants to become involved in—a personal relationship with another person, and where the first person repeatedly makes some form of unwelcome contact with the other. This unwelcome contact can take the form of telephone calls, emails, unwanted approaches, spying, letters and/or following.

It has been argued that stalking laws inhibit journalists, especially if they are trying to 'stake-out' a person of interest in a bid to obtain an interview or photograph. However, in reality the offence of stalking generally does not apply to journalists because it most commonly requires intimidation leading to fear of harm, or actual violence or unwanted physical contact—things no journalist should engage in.

Spent convictions

It can sometimes be a crime to publish information about past criminal convictions. There are laws that aim to protect people who are genuinely rehabilitated after making one silly mistake so they can make a fresh start in life. But every so often, individuals who are not genuinely rehabilitated hide behind the rehabilitation laws. This can be particularly frustrating for a journalist who must abide by the law even though she or he knows that an individual has continued to offend but has avoided detection by authorities since the original conviction was spent. In the past, the laws have prevented publication of details of past criminal convictions of some people with unsavoury backgrounds who were elected to parliament. They have also protected school teachers who molested children, allowing them to return to teaching once their convictions were spent. Federally, Part VIIC of the *Crimes Act 1914* prohibits disclosure of information about criminal convictions 10 years after sentencing if an offender was jailed for less than 30 months. People who were juveniles when convicted are protected from having convictions disclosed after five years. It is also illegal to publicly identify people who have been pardoned or had convictions quashed.

There are similar laws in most states and territories. In those jurisdictions it is a criminal offence punishable by a fine or jail term to reveal a spent conviction—in Queensland, for example, the penalty for disclosing a spent conviction is up to two years' jail (*Criminal Law (Rehabilitation of Offenders) Act 1986*, Section 12).

Blasphemy

'Blasphemous libel' is an offence in Tasmania, where it is proscribed in Section 119 of the *Criminal Code Act 1924*. In that state, it is also an offence to interfere with an officiating minister of religion, or to disturb religious worship. Technically, blasphemy is also an offence in NSW, where it is covered by Section 574 of the *Crimes Act 1900*. In addition there are federal regulations prohibiting the importation of blasphemous films.

Despite these laws there has never been a prosecution for blasphemy in Australia. This might be at least partly because Section 116 of our Federal Constitution specifically prohibits laws that would purport to establish any religion or inhibit freedom of religion. Interestingly, blasphemy used to be a crime in the UK but was abolished as an offence in that nation in 2008.

Obscenity

Concepts of obscenity date from early British laws that aimed to stop people challenging each other to duels after one made insulting, degrading or provocative comments about another. Today, laws about 'obscene' or 'indecent' material vary in different Australian jurisdictions. Ideas about what is perceived as obscene or pornographic depend to a large extent on the context in which material is presented and the likely audience. Standards also change over time, although it is an offence in all jurisdictions to use or publish obscene language. Generally there is greater tolerance of vulgarity where there is an adult audience or where readership is restricted—for example in novels, art and theatre—than in mainstream newspapers, online, or radio and television news and current affairs. That point is reflected in the News Limited *Style* guide for journalists which, under the heading 'Obscenity, profanity, vulgarity' advises journalists writing for its company's publications: 'do not use without a compelling reason. If an obscene word has to be used always use the form *f---* or *sh--* and so on. Never write the word out in full' (McLeod & Lockwood 2009, p. 183). Overall, however, as Pearson said, most news media reportage is done within the bounds of normal community standards, the yardstick courts use to determine whether material is obscene or indecent (Pearson 2007, p. 388).

Censorship

Australia has a plethora of censorship laws and laws classifying printed material, films and websites. The Australian Press Council says a uniform classification system applies to printed material in NSW, SA, Victoria and the ACT and NT.

But Queensland, Tasmania and WA have their own classification schemes (Australian Press Council 2009b). In addition to censorship statutes, the Press Council warns there is also a common law offence of 'obscene libel'. The council says most prosecutions for the common law offence relate to depictions of sexual matters, violence, cruelty and harmful drug taking (Australian Press Council 2009b).

Australia also has a vague and sometimes secretive system of online censorship. In 2007 the first Rudd Labor Government announced its intention to introduce an 'internet filter' to block access to websites rated by the Australian Communications and Media Authority (ACMA) as containing excessive violence or sexual violence, detailed instruction in crime, violence or drug use, and/or material that advocates the doing of a terrorist act. Plans for the filter were backed by church groups but, because the web is global, the ACMA had an impossible task—to some extent it could police Australian ISPs and computer users but not those in other nations, and particularly not in rogue states such as the Seychelles, Mauritius and Virgin Islands, in which there is little control over ISPs; money laundering and tax evasion are rife; and where the majority of illegal material that circulates globally via the internet is published and stored online. After five years of trying to develop a suitable system and in the face of growing protests by civil libertarians, technology organisations and individuals concerned about threats to freedom of access to information, then Communications Minister Stephen Conroy dumped the proposed filter in late-2012. In its place Senator Conroy said the government would force internet service providers to block 'worst of the worst' sites on a child-abuse list maintained by Interpol (Packham 2012).

Despite the backdown there was a furore in 2013 when it was revealed that in the process of trying to block access to a website suspected of fraudulent financial activities the Australian Securities and Investment Commission (ASIC) accidentally blocked more than 1200 legitimate websites including the Melbourne Free University site, which could not be accessed for six weeks! (Porter 2013). Melbourne Free University co-founder Jasmine Westendorf said her organisation had approached the Attorney-General's office, Australian Communications and Media Authority, and Australian Federal Police but 'all said they weren't involved but they still couldn't or wouldn't give us any information about why we were blocked' (Porter 2013).

Broad issues of government web censorship aside, it is a serious offence punishable by a jail term to store hard-core pornography, paedophilia material, and 'seditious' or terrorism-related information on a computer. Thus, if you were a journalist working on an investigative story about porn on the web, for example, or terrorist websites, you could be committing criminal offences if you downloaded sample data or images onto a computer, even if that downloading was ultimately for the public benefit. Just publishing the URL web addresses of banned sites can also be a criminal offence. This became clear in 2009 when the Wikileaks whistleblower and freedom of information website published a secret 'blacklist' of 2395 URLs which the ACMA claimed contained illegal and highly offensive material that should be banned. The ACMA responded to the online publication by warning that Australians caught distributing the list, linking to any of the blacklisted sites, or accessing sites on the list could face criminal charges with potential fines of up to $11,000 a day, and up to 10 years' jail (Lake 2009).

Discrimination and vilification

Australia has relatively strict, if fragmented, laws dealing with racial discrimination and vilification. There are federal, and state and territory laws as well as regulations about what can and cannot be published or broadcast. The Australian Human Rights Commission is the peak body dealing with discrimination issues.

The federal *Racial Hatred Act 1995* prohibits conduct based on a person's race, skin colour, nationality or ethnic origin if that conduct is likely to offend, insult, humiliate or intimidate. There are exemptions for debate and fair comment on matters of public interest, and for fair and accurate reports of a racist act. Similarly, there are laws that aim to prevent discrimination on grounds of sex or sexual preference, religion, disability and age.

Breaches of the relevant legislation can be resolved through civil action and tort law applies. At a federal level the Australian Human Rights Commission is empowered to resolve complaints of discrimination or breaches of human rights under federal laws and to give legal advice to those pursuing action through the courts. Section 46PO(4) of the *Australian Human Rights Commission Act 1986* empowers the Federal Court to issue orders forbidding a person to repeat or continue 'unlawful discrimination'. It also empowers the Federal Court to make 'an order requiring a respondent to pay to an applicant damages by way of compensation for any loss or damage suffered because of the conduct of the respondent' (*Australian Human Rights Commission Act 1986*).

Sedition

Sedition is a relic of an English law that saw offenders sentenced to seven years' jail and fortnightly whippings for criticising corruption in Queen Anne's Government during the early part of the 18th century. In Australia, Section 30A(3) of the federal *Crimes Act 1914* makes it an offence to have a 'seditious intention' to 'urge another person to attempt to procure a change, otherwise than by lawful means, to any matter established by law of the Commonwealth', or 'to promote feelings of ill-will or hostility between different groups so as to threaten the peace, order and good government of the Commonwealth' (*Crimes Act 1914*). Penalties no longer include whippings, but can be up to seven years' jail (Lamb 2006, p. 22).

Section 30AB of the Act makes it a crime to refuse to answer questions asked by the federal Attorney-General or to 'furnish information' or 'allow the inspection of documents' relating to an 'unlawful association' (*Crimes Act 1914*). 'Unlawful associations' are defined as 'any body of persons' which advocate or encourage overthrow of the Constitution by revolution or sabotage, damage to government property or which supports or encourages 'seditious intention'. The penalty for failing to comply is six months' jail (*Crimes Act 1914*).

The Section 30 provisions were enacted as amendments to the *Crimes Act* in 2006 as part of a package of anti-terrorism laws. Another part of the package involved the introduction of laws that allow ASIO to detain people without charge for blocks of seven days, with the start of a new period of detention being permitted after the previous seven-day period expires. Further, it is an offence, punishable by up to five years' jail, to reveal that a person is being held or questioned by ASIO. The Media Entertainment and Arts Alliance has severely criticised the laws relating to ASIO. Among other things, the alliance said the laws severely limit press freedom and erode civil liberties and it is 'entirely inappropriate for journalists to face the prospect of jail for reporting matters in the public interest' (Media Entertainment and Arts Alliance 2013b).[3]

---

3   Prior to the 2006 changes to the *Crimes Act*, no sedition charge had been laid in Australia since 1953, and even that charge was ultimately dismissed (Lamb 2006, p. 22).

Intellectual property, copyright and plagiarism

In broad terms, intellectual property can be described as the *expression* of a person's original thoughts and ideas—not the ideas themselves. Unlike concrete physical property such as houses, cars, land or personal possessions, intellectual property is usually described as being intangible, although its physical expression—as in such things as books, papers, new products and machines, paintings, computer software, music and new plant varieties—is often presented in a tangible form. While intellectual property is intangible, its tangible expression often has a monetary value and can be sold or traded.

Intellectual property is generally regulated by statute law. There are specific laws relating to patents, trademarks, designs, circuit layouts, plant breeders' rights, trade secrets and copyright—which are all forms of intellectual property. The main area journalists need to be aware of is copyright.

The greatest threats to copyright are plagiarism and/or unauthorised copying—but there is a significant difference between plagiarism and breach of copyright. Put simply, plagiarism—which is the use of another person's intellectual property without attributing the material to its source—is theft and misrepresentation. It is also cheating, and something that will cost you your job as a journalist if you are ever caught doing it. Note that plagiarism relates not only to theft of another person's work, but also their ideas. Therefore, taking what someone else has written or said and putting it in your own words without attribution to the source is still plagiarism because you would be actually taking another's ideas and presenting them as your own.

The big difference between plagiarism and breach of copyright is that ideas cannot be copyright—only the expression of those ideas in a tangible form such as writing, music or art. The Australian Copyright Agency, which collects copyright fees for many Australian writers, defines copyright in the following terms:

> Copyright is a form of intellectual property that protects a variety of literary, artistic, musical and dramatic endeavours as well as other things such as sound recordings and films. It is not ideas but their expression that are protected by copyright law... Copyright is intended to protect creative works from being used without the agreement of the owner and to provide an incentive for creators to continue to create new material (Copyright Agency Ltd 2012).

In Australia copyright is controlled by the Federal Government through the *Copyright Act 1968* and its subsequent amendments. The same laws apply to online publishing and for mobile devices as to print and broadcast. Australia is also a party to international treaties in relation to copyright and our legislation must comply with those treaties. The main treaties are controlled by a section of the UN known as the World Intellectual Property Organisation, which is based in Geneva.

One major treaty we belong to is the Berne Convention. Dating from 1886, it is the oldest and most significant copyright treaty. It sets out the basic categories of what can be protected under copyright; these categories are generally regarded as written expression, visual arts, music and films. The convention also sets out rights of reproduction, broadcasting and adaptation, as well as describing exceptions to rights and the duration of copyright protection.

Copyright comes into effect the moment a work is created. It is free and automatic—it does not have to be registered and it does not matter if a work has been published or not. It is, as the word suggests, recognised as a right.

Under Australian law, a creator is generally the first owner of copyright and copyright protection usually continues for 70 years after the creator dies. The creator can bequeath his or her copyright to another person in a will, and if there is no will it passes to the next of kin. Because copyright is automatic, a creator does not have to specifically mark work with a little © as being protected. The symbol is a reminder, not a legal requirement. If, however, a copyright notice and copyright symbol are used, they should identify the copyright owner by name and show the year of first publication or, if the material has not been published, the year it was created.

Infringement of copyright is a criminal offence, and the Australian Copyright Council warns that penalties range from $1320 for a minimal breach, to close to $100,000, five years' jail or both for a serious offence. A company can be fined up to five times that amount (Australian Copyright Council 2012, p. 4). There are also steep penalties for people who import items that breach copyright into Australia and advertise them for sale. In some instances, instead of the matter going to court, police can issue an infringement notice, which enables an alleged offender to avoid prosecution if they pay a fine.

A copyright owner can also seek civil remedies for breach of copyright, such as damages, payment of any profits an infringer has made from using a work, and/or an injunction prohibiting an infringer from continuing to infringe copyright (Australian Copyright Council 2012, p. 4). There was an example of such as case in 2013 when the family of convicted drug smuggler Schapelle Corby was awarded more than $50,000 damages after Allen & Unwin published five family-owned photos without permission in a book titled *Sins of the Father* (AAP 2013). During the hearing a representative of the publisher said the organisation did not know who owned copyright of the photographs and had not tried to find out. In addition to the damages Allen & Unwin was ordered to destroy undistributed copies of the book (AAP 2013).

Copyright can be assigned to another person or organisation, usually by an agreement in writing. Journalists and news organisations often come to an arrangement about who owns the copyright in journalists' work. The Copyright Agency (2009) says different rules often apply to staff journalists and freelancers, and rules also vary depending on what type of organisation you work for. For example, copyright is commonly split between staff journalists (who are being paid a wage or salary by newspapers and magazines) and their employers, whereby the journalist owns copyright for photocopying work directly from a hardcopy original or for inclusion in a book; but the employer owns the copyright for all other purposes, including online and magazine publishing, digital copying and facsimile transmission (Copyright Agency 2009). Different rules apply to freelance journalists, who are not actually employed by a newspaper or magazine. If, for example, a journalist is commissioned to produce a particular story and/or photographs, the employer would usually own copyright (including digital rights). But if a freelancer writes an article and then offers to sell it to a publisher, the journalist would usually be the first owner of copyright unless a written agreement is made to the contrary. It is also worth noting that when articles are written or created 'under the direction or control of' of a state or territory government, copyright is vested in the government (Copyright Agency 2009).

So what do you do if you are desperate to reproduce someone else's work? That depends to some extent on why you want to use the material—in a general sense for entertainment, or in the course of reporting or commenting on news. If it is for entertainment or general interest you *must* seek permission in writing from the copyright owner—even if she or he is overseas and/or hard to find. In doing so, you need to understand that the copyright owner is not under any obligation to give you permission. Normally, however, most people will be reasonable. Their response might also depend on why you want to reproduce the work. If it is for a good cause, say a charity or publication in the public interest, the owner might allow you to use material free or for a nominal cost. If it is for a money-making venture, such as your latest potentially best-selling novel, she or he would probably want a substantial fee. These details can all be negotiated.

Different rules apply if you want to use copyright material in the course of reporting news or commenting on news. Sections 42 and 103B of the *Copyright Act* permit 'fair dealing' for news reporting provided you acknowledge the author and title of the work (*Copyright Act 1968*). But the Australian Copyright Council says using music in news reports is not permitted unless playing the music is part of the news story being reported. The council says the Federal Court has ruled 'news' is not restricted to current events and old material may be reproduced provided it is relevant to a current story. Similarly, investigative journalists may be able to use copyright material they have discovered that relates to past events (Australian Copyright Council 2009). But the council is cautious about the use of copyright material in reporting humorous news stories. It says:

> The crucial element in determining whether the (fair dealing) exception applies seems to be whether the primary purpose is to report or comment on news. Although courts have held that reporting news may involve the use of humour, it seems that where a court considers the purpose of using the material is primarily to entertain, the presence of newsworthy issues is not sufficient to make the use a fair dealing (Australian Copyright Council 2009).

Finally in relation to copyright: what cannot be copyright? Newspaper headlines are not, neither are single words, nor advertising slogans. There is no copyright on news, facts or data. Also, material in which copyright has expired is regarded as being in the public domain and can be freely reproduced – thus the music of many classical composers, such as Mozart, Bach and Tchaikovsky, and works by authors such as Daniel Defoe, 'Banjo' Patterson and Mark Twain, can be freely download from the internet because they died more than 70 years ago, but you must pay to download recent works.

DISCUSSION POINTS

1   If you think about it, shopping centres are really public places even if they are privately owned. Is it reasonable then that journalists and photographers can be told to leave shopping centres and shopping centre carparks because they are trespassing?

2   If you were working on a complex investigative article about high-level abuse of public trust and a lack of accountability, would it be morally acceptable to trespass

on private property or government land because you believed you might find valuable information? What if you were caught? Would the end justify the means?

3   When could the camera in your smartphone or tablet computer be used legally as a hidden camera?

4   It is said that we do not own our image, especially when in a public place. Should the law be changed to allow members of the public to stop media outlets publishing photographs or video of them which was shot in or from a public place?

5   A source gives you a copy of a diary belonging to a public figure. The diary contains minute details about how its owner has misused her position for personal gain. An article is published based on information you found in the dairy and later verified by other means. Would you be liable if the owner of the diary took action against you for breach of confidence?

6   Australia's privacy laws mainly focus on financial and medical matters. Should they be widened? And should the Federal Government have pushed ahead with plans for a wide-ranging internet filter? Why?

7   A breach of copyright is a serious matter if you are a professional writer because it means you are cheated of royalty payments which you rely on for income to support you and your family. Is it any less serious if you download pirated music or movies via the internet? Why?

NEWS PRACTICE POINTS

1   Go online and find the case *TCN Channel Nine Pty Limited v Henry Alfred Anning* [2002] NSWCA 82 (25 March 2002) at www.austlii.edu.au/au/cases/nsw/NSWCA/2002/82.html. Read all the case details including the three appeal judges' reasoning. The case provides an excellent summary of the laws of trespass. Taking those details into account, explain in no more than 750 words why you agree or disagree with the judges' decision to reduce damages to $25,000.

2   Use a recent example to demonstrate when it would be appropriate and in the public interest for a journalist to report details about the private life of a politician.

3   It is not illegal to photograph a person against her or his will provided the photographer is in a public place, so why do paparazzi have such a bad name? Explain your thoughts on the issue in exactly 450 words.

4   Give one example of each to demonstrate when it would be appropriate to report on a person's (a) race, (b) skin colour, (c) nationality (d) religious affiliation and (e) ethnic origin.

5   What, if anything, has eventuated in relation to privacy law in Australia since this book was published? If there have been changes, what are the implications for journalists and freedom of speech?

6   Find out what the Australian Press Council and the Media Entertainment and Arts Alliance think about Australia's sedition laws. Do you think the laws are too tough because they stifle reporting on some issues, or are they warranted as a means of helping defeat terrorism?

7   Does a person who plagiarises the work of another by using the work without attribution or permission also automatically breach the copyright of the person whose work they have stolen? Explain.

8   Does the state or territory you live in have laws about spent criminal convictions? If so what do they say about penalties for revealing information about an old conviction? Are there any loopholes a journalist could use to get around the law to write a report if doing so would be in the public interest?

9   What, if anything, do your state or territory's stalking laws say that is of relevance to journalists' work practices?

10 As a future professional writer, investigate joining the Copyright Agency Limited.

PETER GREGORY _____

Peter Gregory teaches university courses in journalism and law and is enrolled in a PhD. With a former court reporting colleague, he runs presentations about media law for the Media Entertainment and Arts Alliance. He was a journalist for 28 years, specialising in court reporting for *The Age*. He has also covered stories as a police and industrial reporter, been a bureau chief on the Gold Coast, and a sport and general reporter. He was a Walkley Award finalist in 2003, and has won numerous legal reporting awards in Victoria.

---

1 How did you get your first job as a journalist?

I finished my journalism course at university, and was working at the Department of Social Security in Brisbane, Queensland. My then girlfriend (now my wife) and my family also lived there, so I started my search in that state. Aside from contacting the Brisbane papers, I started writing letters to country papers in the state, starting with those about 100km from my home, and moving outwards. I was lucky to get work as a cadet at the *Toowoomba Chronicle*, a daily newspaper in a decent-sized town about 120km inland from Brisbane. I spent about a year there, and got a wide experience in reporting and sub-editing.

2 What advice would you offer a beginning journalist?

Be prepared to travel for your work. Listen to others and evaluate their advice. Read, listen to and watch as many news bulletins and other journalistic productions as you can. Be flexible. Dress up, not down, when in the office. You never know when you might be the person asked to go to a function because you were one of the few people in the newsroom relatively formally dressed. Read your stories after they have been subbed so you can see how they have been changed. Don't be afraid to ask questions, but understand when deadline pressures are greatest at your organisation, so you don't hassle people under immediate pressure.

3 What is the role of journalism in 21st-century Australian society?

You could write a thesis on this topic. Traditional views range from seeing journalism as a way of describing society to itself, to regarding it as a vehicle for marrying advertisers and consumers. Whatever it is, journalism in many Western countries is struggling to provide even basic coverage of daily events. Some theorists think this is fine, because journalism should be more interpretive and go further than just 'reporting the facts'. Frankly, I think that view suits those who believe in running smaller-staffed newsrooms. You don't need to attend events or cover stories as comprehensively. You hire a bank of (hopefully controversial) columnists who can analyse topics and events whether or not they have specific knowledge about them. The best mainstream journalism—that is, news reporting—and sometimes the best writing and analysis seems to occur when media outlets have to pour resources into big stories. Look at the coverage of the September 11 aftermath and the Black Saturday bushfires as examples.

4 Journalism is being changed and challenged by technology. What are your thoughts about the future of journalism in Australia?

Aside from technological changes, we should remember two things. We are a country with a relatively small and ageing population. When we consider whether newspapers, for example, will disappear, we should ask what will replace them. Will they be broad-based, or will they serve narrow markets? And how will they make money? The current trend in the big organisations is to keep cutting the numbers of 'doers' and increasing the numbers of managers, who spend their time having meetings to work out how to do more with less. Whatever form journalism takes, young participants will be asked to do everything and have wide multimedia knowledge. Australian media proprietors might need to examine markets where journalism is growing, such as Asia, and see if opportunities exist there.

5 What are the key things a journalism student should learn during their studies?

It might sound silly, but learning how to listen is a key skill. As is how to get on with people. Students should realise that their reputation for honesty and thoroughness will follow them in a positive way during their career. They should pay attention to detail, know how to spell, and be unafraid to ask questions, even if they sound silly. It is a truism that you can find a smart answer by asking a very basic question. Public surveys seem to tell us that journalists are not trusted. In my experience, you become trusted if you are accurate. Lawyers, for example, can be tolerant if journalists need

information about the law and the way it works. They will be very unhappy if their names are misspelt.

6 Is there anything else you would like to say to journalism students and/or about journalism as a profession?

Despite the financial cuts and current hard times, it [journalism] is still a worthwhile craft. I don't describe journalism as a profession, because members of the public do not need a licence to practise it. I think journalism works best when it tells consumers what is happening in their community. It works poorly when journalists have closed minds, and write selfishly and narrowly for those who support their viewpoints. Also, there is no shame in being sad about the stories you write. Don't be afraid to talk to others about that. You should understand that your reports can affect the lives of others. If you are writing a tough story about someone, make sure it is correct.

A journalist who refuses to reveal the identity of a confidential source could be jailed for contempt in the face of the court. But when it comes to breach of confidence, a journalist could be breaking the law by doing the opposite—revealing the identity of a source!

HEDLEY THOMAS ——————————

Hedley Thomas is *The Australian*'s Brisbane-based national chief correspondent. He specialises in investigations of legal, medical, public administration, crime and corruption issues. He has won five Walkley Awards, including a Gold Walkley Award for his investigative and news reporting, and features writing.

1 How did you get your first job as a journalist?

In my impatience to be a journalist I decided to grab any opportunity to join a newspaper, doing any task, because I believed that it was vital to just get my foot in the door. While in my final year of high school in Southport, Queensland, I discovered a potential path into the local newspaper— the *Gold Coast Bulletin*—as a copyboy. I was 16 when I first wrote to the then editor of the newspaper, John

Burton, who agreed to interview me. I told Mr Burton that I wanted a journalism cadetship, but that if he employed me I would work hard as a copyboy until such an opportunity arose. I landed the job and started within a week of finishing Year 12 at the end of 1984. I did the most menial work—making tea and coffee several times a day for the sub-editors, fetching their lunch, managing the cartoons-and-crossword page, running photographs, advertising material and sub-edited copy-paper around the building, even submitting the expenses and collecting the cash for the reporters. It was busy and challenging and I would not change anything—it gave me a valuable insight into how each section of a daily newspaper worked, just before the transition from typewriters to video display units (VDUs). I got my cadetship and first bylines within a year.

2 What advice would you offer a beginning journalist?

Be hungry, hard-working and open-minded. Some things are fundamental and should be obvious—you must know what your media outlet is producing each day or even hour. In newspapers, for example, keen reporters have read the print version of their own paper from back to front as well as rival papers before they have begun work that day. There are few things more disappointing than the discovery that junior reporters do not know what is in their own paper. Identify external contacts—they might be friends of your friends who work in the local hospital, emergency services, or council—and develop professional relationships. At social events, be alert to the possibility of a throwaway line in conversation becoming the basis of an interesting human interest story, news yarn or even the start of an investigation. Ideas for stories are only limited by your imagination.

3 What is the role of journalism in 21st-century Australian society?

The role of journalism should be little different to its role at any time, notwithstanding changes in the pace of delivery and richness of content. The most important journalism in any society, in my opinion, breaks stories that reveal surprising truths about matters that would otherwise have been covered up, against the public interest. Journalism is not a popularity contest, and journalists wouldn't win one anyway. They will often be outsiders opposed by powerful interests. This is how it should be.

4 What are your thoughts about the impacts on journalism of changing communication technologies?

There is increasing impatience and demand among online readers and viewers for up-to-the-minute news.

One news event, a serious car accident for example, might be updated online half a dozen times until the facts and curiosity have been exhausted. In these situations, accuracy and fairness can be sacrificed for speed. The allocation of newsroom resources to reporting and updating such stories must mean that the capacity of media outlets to also 'break' unique stories is more limited. We need to guard against the real risk that dedicating too much effort to the immediacy of news online will have a corresponding adverse impact on the arguably more important work of digging-out and exposing news that has deeper, more serious implications.

5 What key things should a journalism student learn?

Never take anything at face value. Question why a certain line or being message is being peddled in media-releases or press conferences, irrespective of whether it is from the premier or prime minister or police commissioner. You are gatekeepers for the message and your report may be the first draft of history. If the message, which has often been crafted by strategists before you hear it by people with a particular objective, is disingenuous or worse, part of your job is to prick that balloon of spin.

6 Is there anything else you would like to say to journalism students and/or about journalism as a profession?

Be brave and bold. Do not go with the flow, or herd. Do not try to be politically correct, or a captive of any particular interest group. Beware of becoming a mouthpiece for your contacts. Respect for your professionalism as a journalist will not come from swallowing the official line and staying on a steady, easy drip-feed of self-serving leaks. By challenging this orthodoxy and highlighting the spin, you will attract sources and information of much greater value.

Some journalism students come to the profession under the misapprehension that they are already well-versed in the craft. This is dangerous trap to fall into. Journalism in practice is vastly different to journalism in academia; or journalism taught by academics.

NEWS
ROUNDS

6

COURTS, CRIME, COUNCILS AND SPORTS

18

Contacts are a key. It's a bit like police; the key to a good detective is his (or her) informants
Bob Bottom 2005

OBJECTIVES

After reading this chapter you will understand:

» How being assigned to a round can help your career
» How to set up a news round and the importance of reliable contacts
» What is involved in court reporting
» Different approaches to crime reporting
» How reporting on local councils can be a stepping stone to state and federal political reporting
» That specialist sport reporting is a complex and rewarding area of journalism.

Being appointed to cover a specific round in which you become responsible for news-gathering in a specialised field is a significant feather in your cap and a sign your career is moving forward. Such an appointment usually follows a period as a general reporter during which you demonstrated your work was accurate, fair, objective and ethical, that you had a strong news sense, a good understanding of media law, and had developed broad contacts.

Assignment to a round usually means management has faith in you and your work and you are trusted. In a sense it is little like being given your own territory to govern—there is freedom, but also responsibility. If you perform well, you will become king or queen of your own castle, but if you underperform, you will fall from grace and be deposed!

The key to successfully managing a round is to be a self-starter who quickly acquires knowledgeable and trustworthy contacts in the field covered by the round. A journalist who takes ownership of a round (known as a 'beat' in the US) is expected to be, or quickly become, an expert in that field. Depending on the size of the media outlet she or he works for, it is possible that one journalist might be assigned more than one round, or at least one regular round plus some general reporting. In addition to reporting news or sport as the case may be, rounds journalists with newspapers and online are also called on at times to write feature articles or write commentary and analysis relevant to their areas of expertise. Television and radio journalists who report on specific rounds, for example state politics, may also be expected to work on documentaries, or research and report on current affairs in that field.

Over time, a journalist working a particular round has an opportunity to build his or her name with the public and earn a formidable reputation as a trusted expert. As explained in Quinn and Lamble:

> Sometimes one beat (round), such as court reporting, might be a stepping-stone to another more highly prized beat higher up the scale. In many organisations a reporter who has earned the respect of the public, their own editors and other journalists may work the same beat for decades—perhaps the bulk of their career—eventually holding positions akin to a knowledgeable tribal elder or guru in the eyes of the public (Quinn & Lamble 2008, p. 105).

Think of names such as Paul Kelly from *The Australian*, Michelle Grattan formerly of *The Age* and more recently an academic and chief political correspondent with *The Conversation*, and Nine Network political commentator Laurie Oakes. Each worked a political round, and each used that round as the foundation for a career that took them to the top of Australian journalism.

A brief look at their career paths is informative. Kelly graduated with a Bachelor of Arts degree and Diploma of Education from the University of Sydney before joining the Prime Minister's Department in Canberra in 1969. He moved to journalism in 1971. Three years later he was appointed chief political correspondent with *The Australian*. He became deputy editor of the long-defunct *The National Times* in 1978, and chief political correspondent with the *Sydney Morning Herald* in 1981. Moving back to *The Australian*, he was national affairs editor from 1985 to 1991, became editor-in-chief in 1991, and was appointed editor-at-large in 1996 (Kelly 2007). Grattan graduated from the University of Melbourne with a Bachelor of Arts Honours degree in politics. She joined *The Age* in 1970 and moved to the newspaper's Canberra bureau in 1971 to report on federal politics. She was later a specialist political writer for the *Australian Financial Review* and *The Sydney Morning Herald* before returning to *The Age*, being appointed political editor in 2004 (Grattan 2007). In 2013 she left *The Age* and took up an academic position at the University of Canberra and as associate editor (politics) and chief political correspondent with *The Conversation*. Oakes graduated from The University of Sydney with a Bachelor of Arts degree in 1963. In 1964, he joined *The Daily Mirror* newspaper in Sydney and in 1965 was appointed to the state political round. In 1979 he moved from print to television and became a reporter for Channel 10. After five years in that role he went to the Nine Network, where he became political editor (Oakes 2010).

Working your way into a new round

Sometimes journalists are assigned a particular round because they have specialised knowledge and have shown interest in a field, but on other occasions being assigned a round comes as a surprise. As Rich said:

> You don't have to be a doctor to cover medicine or a scientist to cover the environment, but you do need to acquire knowledge of the subject... The challenge for writers of specialised subjects is to make the stories clear and to define the jargon so the average reader can understand the story (Rich 2003, pp. 362 & 363).

In addition to learning as much as you can as quickly as you can about the specialised fields of knowledge relevant to your round, you must discover who the main players are, and then build good working relationships with them. If you had a medical round, for example, you would need to introduce yourself to, and build rapport with, such people as members of the local division of general practice, the president of the regional branch of the Australian Medical Association, leaders of patient support groups, university experts, heads of the relevant branch of the nursing union, key staff in the health department, the ambulance service and individual ambulance officers, health inspectors, helicopter rescue organisations, infectious diseases experts, chemists, pathologists, veterinarians and the local coroner. Be strategic—get out of the office and visit these significant people. Take them for a coffee, shout them lunch, chat. Ensure you leave potential sources with your business card so they have your name and contact details. Also collect their cards and contact details. You will not establish a contact network overnight, but

As you build your knowledge and understanding of the field covered by your round and develop your contact network, you should also learn the language of the round. Every occupation, sport, professional group, field of study, club, hobby group, even social and cultural group, has its own jargon. Insiders understand and speak that jargon. You should learn how to translate what the jargon tells you into simple plain English so it can inform your stories.

it should be built as quickly as possible. One excellent tip when developing key contacts and sources for a round is to ask people you interview or seek information from if they know of other key people in the field whom you should also interview or speak with. This has a multiplier effect, with the additional people and their networks becoming contacts who refer you to even more contacts.

As you build your knowledge and understanding of the field covered by your round and develop your contact network, you should also learn the language of the round. Every occupation, sport, professional group, field of study, club, hobby group, even social and cultural group, has its own jargon. Insiders understand and speak that jargon. Those who do not are clearly not part of the group. They might not only fail to understand significant information, they could be ostracised, ignored or treated like a well-meaning but silly outsider. You must identify the jargon, learn what it means, learn when to use it yourself and, most importantly, learn how to translate what the jargon tells you into simple plain English so it can inform your stories.

Learning as much as you can about trends in the field covered by your round(s) is also important. If, for example, you have a police round, the police you have contact with and the public would expect you to be knowledgeable about such things as crime rates, trouble spots in the area, how crime in your region compares with crime in other similar regions, global crime trends, 'good' and 'bad' lawyers and judges, juvenile crime and relevant laws. Similarly, if you are covering a sport you would be expected to know what teams are near the top of the ladder, which ones are headed for the wooden spoon, how each team performed over the past few seasons, and to have similar knowledge about star players. Using the research tools discussed in Chapter 6 will help you build background knowledge specific to your round, and help you interpret jargon, understand trends, and keep abreast of new developments.

To successfully manage any round, a journalist must also have a genuine interest in, and broad knowledge of, current affairs—not just in her or his area of interest, although that is essential, but also generally. How, for example, will a proposed change in the federal budget, or the appointment of a new minister for sport and leisure, impact on hockey clubs in your region, or the annual basket-weaving competition? Building awareness of current affairs is an essential element of the sort of broad liberal arts education mentioned in the Introduction to this book. It involves reading newspapers and online news stories, watching television news and current affairs, and listening to radio news and current affairs—not just writing and reporting it! Journalists must draw on all media—radio, television, print, and online via computers and mobile devices   to build and maintain a deep understanding of local, national and international events.

If a journalist is a self-starter, has strong news sense, common sense, and understands how to write news, setting up a round is not as difficult as perhaps it might appear. As well as considering the points in Chapter 6 about how to research, also read the section of Chapter 5 headed 'Finding stories'—there are good tips there that will help. Also be prepared to co-operate and collaborate with other journalists within your news organisation. They will hear things and discover information in the course of their news-gathering which relate to your round. It is in your own interest to get on well with all of them, to treat them at least as well as you would your external sources, and be prepared to trade information. Newsrooms can be highly competitive and work politics can occasionally be toxic, but newsrooms are also vibrant information exchanges and if you want others to help you, then you must play the game and help them.

There will also be times, particularly in larger newsrooms, when journalists from different rounds collaborate on stories—or will do a better job if they do. For instance, a health and medical rounds journalist working on a story about abuse of prescription drugs might develop a much stronger story than she or he would otherwise by collaborating with a police and crime rounds journalist, and maybe also whoever is responsible for the education round. Or a journalist with an environment round might add value to a story by talking to the person who has the political round, local council round, real estate writers and business reporter. There will also be times when a big news story demands that input from general reporters must be backed up with stories, comment and analysis provided by specialist rounds reporters in order to cover as many angles as possible.

Tread carefully with sources and think outside the square

While there are many pluses in being assigned to a round, there can also be disadvantages and traps. One trap relates to the ethical and practical difficulties of regularly relying on specific sources. A police rounds journalist, for example, will build relationships with particular police officers. He or she will come to depend on those officers for information to inform stories. But what if one of those officers does something wrong? What if you had previously offered to protect that officer as a protected source? In addition to the ethical issues associated with protecting sources that were discussed in Chapter 4 and potential legal risks explained in Chapter 16, there are the dangers mentioned in Chapter 5 of conflict of interest arising because a journalist has failed to remain professional in dealing with a source and become too close. Weinberg warned of the risk of rounds reporters taking an easy option and failing to follow up and dig for information that might offend sources 'because they have become too used to the official version from sources they have no wish to alienate' (Weinberg 1996, p. 4). And as White said of police rounds: 'Corruption stories are notoriously hard to write and can destroy your contact network overnight' (White 1996, p. 132).

Another danger is becoming too inward looking—so focused on your round, you do not see the big picture. Part of being successful in working a round is being able to look beyond immediate stories. A court reporter, for example, might report on a case in which a homeless youth was convicted and ordered to complete community service after being caught shoplifting. There might be several similar cases in the next few weeks involving different young homeless people stealing from the same shopping centre, but the court reporter does not bother to report them because of their similarity with the first story and the repetitive nature of the cases. The journalist has focused on what happened in court, but there might be a much bigger story and a wider picture. Why was there an upsurge in shoplifting by homeless youths? Did it relate to the closure of the local youth hostel because of a government funding cut? What items were the youths stealing, and why those items? As Waterford said:

> All journalists, certainly those involved in particular rounds, should regard themselves as potential investigative reporters on issues and subjects arising from their work... A rounds journalist should always be alert for a theme... (Waterford, in Tanner 2002, p. 42).

There is also pressure when working a news round or in a specialised area such as sport not to be scooped, or miss a story related to your round. Conversely, there is an expectation that as the resident expert, you will scoop other news outlets and beat them to stories. Stephens said rounds were initially set up by newspapers with the idea of journalists keeping 'a systematic watch on the world' (Stephens

1997, p. 232). In doing so newspapers made a commitment to not just *find* news but also not to *miss* news (Stephens 1997, p. 232). A journalist who has a round is expected to file stories regularly, to be up to date with news from his or her specialised field, find and write exclusive, proactive agenda-setting stories and feature articles, or contribute to broadcast current affairs and documentaries. Those pressures increased dramatically after reporting moved to a 24-hour news cycle and news consumers moved from accessing their news via traditional media to seeking it on-demand via portable devices. As noted in Quinn and Lamble, a rounds journalist is expected to become a bridge between one specialist minority group and the general community so:

> Missing a story, or failing to zoom in on the best angle, is likely to result in a 'please explain' from your editor or news producer. And while we are all human and make the occasional lapse, a reporter who does not perform well in a particular beat (round) is likely to find themselves transferred back to general reporting and facing a limited future (Quinn & Lamble 2008, p. 106).

Overall, though, working in a specific round is positive and rewarding. And, as noted earlier, it can be the doorway to a long and rewarding career in a specialised field.

There are four specialised rounds every journalist should be capable of working effectively. They are court, crime, council and sport reporting. Each can be an end in its own right, or become a stepping stone to other rounds. There is also something of a tradition among editors and news producers of throwing new recruits in their newsrooms into the 'deep end' by sending them off to report on one or more of those rounds as a means of assessing how capable, or otherwise, that recruit is.

Court reporting

It has been said that court reporters deal with the sad, the mad and the bad. Court reporters are uniquely placed to observe a passing parade of those who either by accident or intent breach society's norms and rules. Cases they report on range from drunks and public nuisance offenders picked up by police every weekend and paraded through Magistrates' or Local Courts around the nation on Monday mornings, to white-collar fraud, serious assault, rape and murder, to coronial inquests, planning appeals, family feuds, and arguments over barking dogs. Some cases are mind-boggling in their complexity, others trivial, many sad or tragic, some strange and, occasionally, hilarious.

Court reporting was a staple of newspapers from their earliest days. Mott said reports about 'crime, disasters and monstrosities' were the stuff of 17th- and 18th-century news, as were stories about 'pirates, fires, counterfeiting, murders, robberies and suicides' (Mott 1962, p. 520). Many of those stories were based on court reports and court documents. Stories of crime, trials and punishment were often combined in a single report. That was the case when, in 1704, a special news 'extra' was printed between the usual weekly editions of the Boston *News-letter* 'telling of the trial of Quelch the pirate and his hanging' (Mott 1962, p. 51). The report was fascinating. Things were not going well for the prosecution and at one point it seemed Quelch the pirate captain—who was on trial for mass murder, as were all his crew—might be set free. That was until:

> The judges went into a whispered huddle. When they came out of it the Governor-General announced that 'this court will consider granting full pardon to any man who will give evidence for the Queen and tell in truth and detail of the events that took place aboard the commissioned brigantine Charles from...' His voice was drowned by the eager shouts of three men... it was all over. Quelch and five others were sentenced to death by hanging... the six pirates stood beneath a gibbet erected on the banks of the River Charles while a large crowd waited expectantly (Bartum 1960, p. 15).

While governors-general no longer interfere in court cases, and crowds no longer gather and wait in expectation of a good hanging, the public is still fascinated with details of crimes as they emerge in court. And from the perspective of news media, reporting court cases is relatively safe because, as explained in Chapters 15 and 16, what is said in court is privileged and legally protected so it can be repeated without fear of an adverse defamation judgment. As one of Australia's most experienced former court reporters Peter Gregory said:

> Courts contain conflict and drama, two staples of newsgathering. They appeal to the voyeur in ordinary citizens; they show the way laws and decisions by business and government impact on the community through the examples of a few (Gregory 2005, p. 12).

Being a court reporter calls for a sound knowledge of criminal and civil law, a good understanding of the court system and court hierarchy, knowledge of the bail process, understanding of laws of contempt, and a knowledge of how juries are selected and the respective roles of jurors and judges. Many of these matters are considered in Chapters 15, 16 and 17, but a court reporter needs to read more widely and develop a deep understanding of law and legal processes. In terms of sources, a court reporter must have good working relationships with court officials, police, prosecutors and lawyers generally. He or she must be a fast and accurate note-taker, be tactful in dealing with members of the public in what are often strained circumstances, and have a strong and non-judgmental interest in people. It is also important to understand that while many who appear in court are outright villains, others are vulnerable, perhaps suffering from mental illnesses, having learning disabilities, or being past victims of crime themselves.

Court reporters must have a strong commitment to the *Journalists' Code of Ethics* (Media Entertainment and Arts Alliance 2013a) and understand the utmost importance of being accurate, objective, balanced and fair in their reporting. If they are not accurate and balanced—reporting each side of a case equally—they risk incurring the ire of judges and magistrates and, in extreme cases, charges of contempt. In a simple case which ends after a few minutes, hours or a day, writing a fair and balanced report involves little more than summarising what the prosecution and defence sides of a case said, and perhaps peppering the story with a few relevant direct quotes. But when reporting on a bigger case—especially if it runs for days, weeks or longer—fair and balanced reporting is more complex. At a basic level it usually involves reporting one side of a case early in a trial—usually the prosecution case in a criminal trial, and a plaintiff's case in a civil trial—followed later, maybe days or weeks later, with reporting the defence case. It is often also important to report on a judge's summing-up and, in a criminal trial in which an alleged offender is found guilty, reporting on the sentencing hearing and what the judge said then.

Ideally, court reporters should be trained in shorthand. There are official court reporters whose job is to prepare transcripts of cases in higher courts. Their transcripts must be accurate and can be compared later with quotes and versions of events written by journalists—something that can leave a journalist who made mistakes in note-taking red-faced. To avoid mistakes, it is sometimes possible to obtain official transcripts and use them as the basis of a story, but not for day-to-day reporting. This is because transcripts are not generally available until late in a hearing day; usually after deadlines for evening television news bulletins and too late for tomorrow's newspaper. As an aid to journalists, and as a means of helping

Court reporters must have a strong commitment to the *Journalists' Code of Ethics* and understand the utmost importance of being accurate, objective, balanced and fair in their reporting. If they are not accurate and balanced—reporting each side of a case equally—they risk incurring the ire of judges and magistrates and, in extreme cases, charges of contempt.

ensure the accuracy of court reports, some courts allow journalists working for recognised news outlets to record court proceedings with a voice recorder. In jurisdictions in which journalists are permitted to use recorders, they must first obtain permission from the court and agree to abide by strict conditions. For example, a practice note issued by Local Courts in NSW says journalists can apply through court registrars to use recorders for the purpose of making 'fair and accurate reports' of proceedings (Practice Note 2 of 2008). In that state, a journalist given permission to use a recorder must promise not to allow the recordings to be broadcast on radio, television or the internet, to delete the recording within 24 hours, not to record private conversations before or after a hearing, and to use the recordings 'to provide reasonable assistance to other journalists seeking to prepare a fair and accurate report of the proceedings' (Practice Note 2 of 2008).

One of the most important parts of working in a court round is to decide which cases to cover. Obviously, a journalist needs to report on the most newsworthy hearings. In all jurisdictions it is possible to have a reasonable idea in advance of when significant cases will be heard because hearing dates have been set during preliminary hearings, such as bail and committal hearings. Case lists for District/County, Supreme and other higher courts are published on the web by justice departments and courts in each state and territory. In many instances, especially in relation to high-profile cases, there is plenty of background information available in the form of archived news stories dating from when a crime was committed, action started, or suspect arrested. But there is often little or no formal notice of the nature of cases conducted in Magistrates' or Local Courts. In those courts, the names of alleged offenders or parties to cases are called out by a bailiff or other court official and hearings commence as soon as those involved enter the court. Sometimes, a person who has been held in custody is brought into a court from a holding cell and enters the dock with little or no fanfare. On other occasions a person—such as someone who has failed to attend court when directed—can be tried in her or his absence. In a region in which there is only a single courtroom in a town, all a journalist needs to do is attend the court as hearing follows hearing. But problems arise in larger centres and cities where there are multiple courts in the one building. In those situations, where several cases are being heard at the same time in different courtrooms, it can be difficult to know which cases will be of interest to the public and which will be trivial. Often the only real way to find out is to move from one courtroom to another, sit in for a while, listen, and learn what a case is about. While this is a useful strategy, it can also be risky. The problem is that while a journalist is observing one case that seems interesting, there might be an even more interesting hearing starting or in progress in another court.

Building good relationships with court staff, prosecutors, police and lawyers is the best way for journalists to keep themselves informed about which cases are most likely to be worth reporting. Sometimes it is possible to view court documents, or documents lawyers plan to present in court, as a way of building background to a case—although be extremely careful never to publish details of a document that has not actually been tendered in court because it will not be legally privileged until officially entered into the court record. When a case ends and the rules of *sub judice* (see the following section) no longer apply, a court reporter can sometimes broaden a story by interviewing witnesses and others involved in a hearing, and, in the case of an acquittal, the person who had been charged. In instances such as these, however, be careful of defamation. Also be careful in dealings with jurors and former jurors—check the rules in your state or territory because in some jurisdictions, such as Queensland, it is a criminal offence punishable by a jail term to publish anything said by a juror.

As a final tip related to court reporting, be wary of trusting other journalists! In some areas where there are multiple courts in session at once, journalists from different—often competing—news organisations will sometimes come to an arrangement in which they literally swap notes of hearings. The practice happens because journalists working for rival outlets do not want to appear to have missed details of a case that might be more newsworthy than the hearing they are covering. Reporting on a case of lesser interest while a rival outlet carries reports of a more newsworthy one can result in a 'please explain', or worse, from an irritated editor or news producer. Swapping notes is therefore seen by some as insurance, with the idea among the journalists who co-operate with each other being that what one misses one time, the other will pick up on, so the scales are balanced and their respective news editors or producers are kept happy. While such co-operation might sound sensible, there are risks—a lesser one being that if one journalist makes a genuine mistake in his or her notes, that mistake will be repeated by the person the first journalist swaps notes with. Among the more extreme dangers are a risk that one journalist working for one outlet might deliberately provide misleading information, withhold key details, or have taken notes when they should not have, for example during a discussion in the absence of a jury, or when a person who should not be identified was giving evidence. To be safe, journalists should only report on things they have actually seen and heard in a court, what is in an official court transcript, or if another journalist provides a sound recording of what was said in a court if that recording was made with permission from the court.

Crime reporting

There are similarities and overlaps between crime and court reporting, but there are many differences too. Like court reporting, crime reporting demands a solid knowledge of law. It also relies heavily on building contacts with police, lawyers and others involved in crime prevention, detection and prosecution.

The most important areas of law for a crime round journalist to understand are those relating to *sub judice* contempt and the non-identification of victims and alleged offenders. Those laws are discussed in Chapters 15, 16 and 17. In essence, *sub judice* laws mean that most crime reporting happens before and after an alleged offender appears in court. There are no restrictions—other than those inherent in avoiding a defamation writ—in what can be reported in the time between a crime being committed and an alleged offender being arrested and charged. Similarly, once a trial is over—if there is no immediate notice of an appeal—crime details can be discussed in depth and explained.

In addition to having a good working knowledge of the law, crime reporters also need to develop understandings of criminology. This means learning about crime detection and prevention, policing, human rights, psychology, sociology, cycles of disadvantage and crime, and forensic sciences. Effective crime reporters have both a big-picture macro perspective of crime and society, and small-picture micro understandings of specific crimes. While the vast majority of reporting is taken up with accounts of specific crimes and those involved, it helps add value to crime stories when a journalist writes about those specific crimes in a wider context.

Obviously, the more serious a crime, the more likely it is to be reported and the wider that reporting. This means violent crimes such as murder, manslaughter, grievous bodily harm, rape and serious assault are the most widely publicised. Among the other crimes that are the focus of crime reporting are sexual assault,

Good crime reporters have both a big-picture macro perspective of crime and society, and small-picture micro understandings of specific crimes.

crimes against children and the elderly, armed robbery, major fraud, drug offences, financial scams, organised crime and official corruption.

Much crime reporting is reactive—a crime happens and it is reported on. This is particularly so in relation to violent crime and offences that breach standards of human decency and people's duty of care to others. Proactive crime stories are more likely to be feature stories and documentary or current affairs reports resulting from investigations into organised crime, trends in relation to particular crimes, and exposés of corruption.

Whether crime reporting is reactive or proactive, it relies heavily on building networks of contacts. Individuals in that network range from police, to criminals and/or those with criminal connections, lawyers, members of victims' groups, private security providers, insurance industry representatives, firearms dealers, prison guards, victims and their families, and families of convicted criminals. Sources are also likely to include federal police, private investigators, customs officers, maybe staff from national security agencies, and investigators attached to organisations such as state offices of fair trading.

Obviously, individual police officers are the most important sources. While official police media units are supposedly the only point of contact between police and journalists in most states and territories, as noted in Chapter 12 many of those units fail because as well as supposedly providing details of crimes to journalists, they have a dual function as spin-doctors who are instructed by their bosses to paint police in the best possible light. The latter function sometimes results in police media units filtering information, stonewalling questions from journalists, or becoming hostile—especially when police have made mistakes or acted badly. There are also times when police on the ground do not pass on information to their own media units. It is therefore vitally important for crime reporting journalists to supplement official lines of communication by building their own contacts with individual police. It is also important to actually go to crime scenes to make your own observations, interview your own witnesses, and talk to police and other officials such as ambulance officers and fire-fighters when appropriate. Often different individuals will make off-the-record comments. Sometimes, and particularly at the scene of a major crime, a senior police officer or other official will be designated as a person authorised to comment to media. Also, as you repeatedly visit different crime scenes over time you are likely to encounter some of the same emergency services staff and will develop working relationships with them.

A journalist who successfully builds useful contacts with police and others in relation to a crime round will have demonstrated over time that she or he can be trusted. It is essential not to link off-the-record comments back to individuals who made them, to protect officials who become sources, co-operate at times with those sources, act responsibly at crime scenes and not do anything that could contaminate a scene or damage evidence, not do anything that could endanger yourself or anyone else, and not make stupid or tactless comments. A successful crime reporter's stories will be accurate and will not beat up or over-dramatise events.

In addition to visiting crime scenes, a crime round journalist will also become expert in working the phones. In those areas where police do not yet use digital radios, which cannot be monitored, the journalist will develop a good ear for picking up police radio transmissions monitored on radio scanners. Listening to a scanner is often the best way of learning a crime has happened. Without a scanner, journalists rely on members of the public who might or might not think to telephone a news organisation with a news tip; on official police sources to tell them—which often does not happen until long after an event, if at all; and on information from other emergency services. Often, while a journalist might have good unofficial police sources, those sources will not directly contact a journalist because details of phone calls they make can be accessed later if there is ever an inquiry into how information was leaked. Issues like these, when combined with being unable to use a radio scanner to monitor digital police radio, mean journalists must have alternative ways of discovering when crimes happen. One approach that works reasonably well is to monitor other emergency services such as ambulance, fire brigade, tow trucks, state emergency service and other volunteer organisations like marine and helicopter rescue services. One or all of those services will often be called to a crime scene, especially if a crime has been serious. Another good idea is to encourage anonymous online tips via email, text messages or comments on news organisation websites.

Apart from official sources, the most informative people to interview about crime are those most closely affected. They include victims and their families, neighbours, friends and locals generally. Frequently, people who live nearby can provide good background. Some might have heard or seen something, such as a car driving off, a gunshot, screams, an explosion, argument or a window breaking. They might know a victim or perpetrator and be able to provide information about them. Also think about photographs and video at a crime scene. Can you, or a photographer, take photos of the scene or shoot video? Is it possible to obtain, or re-photograph, a photo of a victim or an accused or both? Is there visual damage to buildings or equipment? Can you photograph or record video of a weapon? Also ask about descriptions of alleged perpetrators, especially if on the run and being sought by police. Maybe police will assemble an artist's Comfit image in time for it to be published or broadcast in conjunction with your story.

Finally in relation to crime, there will nearly always be follow-up stories. Watch the progress of any subsequent trial. If the crime was significant and newsworthy, be prepared for—maybe even pre-write—a follow-up story after the verdict is delivered.

Council reporting

A local council news round can be a stepping stone on the pathway to becoming a state or federal political reporter. As explained in Chapter 14, councils are the level of government considered closest to the people. They have multi-million-dollar budgets and deal with the 'three Rs' of basic services: roads, rates and rubbish.

There are two main aspects to council reporting. The first is direct reactive reporting of debates and decisions that happen during council meetings and, in some councils, portfolio committee meetings. Many councils are driven by personalities as much as—or in numerous councils in place of—political party loyalties. Debates can be fiery and personal. To some extent the level of debate depends on how well, or otherwise, a mayor chairs meetings. It can also depend on whether or not there are dominant groups or alignments of councillors and how well they behave. Councillors are vulnerable to lobbying by land developers, environmental and residents' groups, as well as chambers of commerce, individuals, and state and federal politicians. In some councils the mayor represents one party or group, while councillors are dominated by an opposing, even hostile, party or group. There are also councillors whose theatrics could win Oscars—especially if trying to impress residents from divisions, wards, or ridings in a city or shire they represent.

Issues discussed, debated and decided by local councils can also be highly emotive. Among the more potentially divisive are topics like land clearing, pet control and registration, heritage listing of buildings and features, residential zonings, environmental and conservation issues such as habitat protection, pest control and pesticides, noise control, parking near hospitals and sports grounds, conditions imposed on land developers, and covenants on what can and cannot be done in new estates. Many debates are newsworthy and colourful because they centre around the strong news values of conflict, novelty, proximity and human interest. When covering these debates it is important to keep reports as well balanced as possible by reporting main points argued by proponents of diverse, even extreme, points of view. When councillors vote on emotive or significant issues, you should list who voted for, and who was against. In many municipalities mayors have a normal procedural vote in the same way as other councillors, and also a second—casting—vote if a decision is tied. In such instances it is important to report which side the mayor voted for or against.

At a second level, a journalist with a council round needs to look well beyond actual council meetings and to proactively investigate and report on council-related issues that affect ratepayers. This might mean reporting on matters before, after or during consideration by councillors and council staff. It might involve a close examination of potential implications of council decisions. Investigative reporting and a local government news round often go hand in hand. It can be useful for council and crime round reporters to collaborate and swap notes. It can also be rewarding from a journalistic perspective to follow money trails and attempt to discover who is financing big-ticket items such as land development and large building projects. As with other news rounds discussed in this chapter, apply the research tools described in Chapters 6 and 12. It is also important to cultivate contacts, the best of whom tend to be specific councillors and council staff. Former councillors can also be fountains of information because they know how the system works, while some will have axes to grind after being dumped in elections—beaten by more politically savvy or better funded opponents. Although a word of warning here, too. Some former councillors, like other rejected politicians or hopeful but unsuccessful candidates, become obsessive and jaundiced, with a few viewing almost everything in terms of conspiracy theories.

A local government round journalist needs to obtain and learn to understand relevant documents. These include meeting agendas and minutes, briefing notes, background papers, plans, maps, reports, discussion papers, correspondence and memos. Many are freely available and are provided by council staff either online or as hard copies. Some are less accessible and can only be provided by councillors or staff who are prepared to leak them to you. In the latter instance, you may need to be prepared to protect sources, respect confidences, and not use documents in such a way that would point to where they came from.

As with all levels of politics, council stories tend to heat up in the lead into and following elections. Unusual or offbeat candidates commonly add colour that contrasts with profiles of lacklustre sitting councillors and more conservative challengers. Human interest is a significant news value in election periods. A little investigative journalism can also be rewarding. In the writer's experience of council reporting, investigations that focused on the backgrounds of candidates revealed criminal pasts, family associations with dodgy land developers, gross hypocrisy, candidates who professed to be environmentalists but who were backed by land developers, candidates who had blackmailed other candidates, and a few who were wildly eccentric!

As with all rounds, there is a need to accept that you will not please all your contacts all the time. There will also be times when you create enemies simply by balanced reporting and putting both sides of arguments. But even with those who would shoot the messenger, the best defence is open, objective and fair reporting in the interests of the public. Also be wary of council media managers and public relations officers. They can be helpful and provide access to staff and information, but remember their job is to make a council, and often its mayor, councillors and staff, look good to ratepayers.

There will be times when you create enemies simply by balanced reporting and putting both sides of arguments. But even with those who would shoot the messenger, the best defence is open, objective and fair reporting in the interests of the public.

Sport reporting

In many media organisations in Australia and the UK, sport sections are dubbed 'the toy department' because all they deal with is games! The reality is that sport reporting is a form of entertainment reporting. Like performers and musicians, many leading sporting figures lap up publicity when things are going well, but do all they can to avoid or negate it if caught doing the wrong thing. And, like prominent entertainers, high-profile sporting identities are often surrounded by a bevy of managers, public relations minders, advertising representatives, and promoters—all part of the baggage associated with lucrative sponsorship contracts. Senior sport is big business. It is an arm of business that thrives in

Australia because we are a nation obsessed with sport. As Jobling said, sport has been described as a national 'religion' in Australia and is an important institution in our society (Jobling, in Henningham 1999, p. 251). Perhaps one reason for the popularity of sport is because it attracts mass television coverage; and maybe that is because it is cheaper to produce and broadcast sport than drama and many other programs, while sport attracts strong ratings which appeal to advertisers (Jobling, in Henningham 1999, p. 269).

Most journalists will report on at least some sport during their career—often at the start when as junior staff members they are sent to fill in if an experienced sportswriter is ill, or if there is a major sporting event and as many journalists as possible are needed to cover it. Those who go on to focus on sport and are assigned to it as a round are usually people with a strong interest in sport generally, or who have special interest in a particular area of sport.

Basic sport reporting is much like basic news reporting. Its focus is on providing answers to questions of who, what, when, where, why and how. Reports can be as simple as listing results and briefly describing a game, or the most significant part of a game. Similarly, the basic news values discussed in Chapter 3 apply—especially conflict, prominence and human interest. Specialised sport reporting, however, involves much more than the basics. It operates at three levels: commentary, listing results, and analysis or interpretation:

— Commentary involves directly describing a game as it happens for broadcast on radio, television and, increasingly, online. In addition to the description of what is happening, commentators flavour their narration with facts, figures, background and analysis—particularly if the game is slow or dull.

— Listing results frequently involves more than simply transcribing a long list. It often entails updating related statistics, such as league tables and data relating to a sport generally, a series, or an individual player or competitor.

— Analysis and interpretation are commonly what most interest readers and audiences, aside from results. Analysis can take the form of previews, explanations as a game unfolds, and reflection afterwards.

The mix of different approaches allows sportswriters to be more creative and to inject more comment and opinion into their work than journalists who report news. Rich (2003) said sportswriters not only witness a game and report on it, they must also focus on 'how' and 'why' questions, and interviews with players and coaches, to interpret what they witnessed and the final result. She said the challenge is to provide more than basic facts, so sportswriters for newspapers must 'rely on feature techniques of descriptive and interpretive writing' and 'some of the best writing—as well as some of the worst' appears in sport reports (Rich 2003, pp. 369 & 370). Hohenberg (1983) said one difficulty in writing sport for a newspaper is that many readers will know the result of a game before their papers are delivered. He said followers of particular sports 'invariably pride themselves on being experts' who thirst for inside knowledge about things such as strategy (Hohenberg 1983, p. 245). He also said feature writing techniques are ideal for sport, and writers should focus on:

> the bright anecdote, the sharp quote, the interview with all concerned in a disputed play or a disputed decision, the description of a part of the contest that television downplayed (Hohenberg 1983, p. 247).

Obviously anyone who reports on sport must have an excellent knowledge of games and rules. She or he must know who the key players are and have access to background information and data about each of them. Like any journalist working a specific round, a sport reporter must also develop a wide contact network and get on well with people. Developing a broad knowledge of the rules, culture and jargon associated with different games ranging from golf to netball, ping-pong to lawn bowls, Australian Rules football, soccer, rugby, cycling, rugby league, tennis, basketball, squash, gymnastics, swimming, croquet, athletics, rowing and triathlon, to name a few, makes a sport round complex and demanding. As Hohenberg said:

> Anyone who undertakes to write about sports must have an intimate knowledge of the assignment. The three great necessities are accuracy, restraint and a decent respect for the English language (Hohenberg 1983, p. 247).

In addition to reporting on a game or sporting event in a broad overall sense, a sport journalist must be also constantly looking for a big story—maybe the back page 'splash', or lead, in a newspaper; top story on a website; or lead sport story in a radio or television news broadcast. Working to deadlines is also a major issue, especially for online journalists and broadcast sports reporters who must provide almost instant gratification to fanatical fans glued to their tablets, smartphones, radios and televisions. The problem they have is that the vast majority of major sporting events are held during afternoons and evenings. Games often do not end until late in the day. Therefore, unlike spectators who go and watch a game to relax, sportswriters must be analysing a game or match as it unfolds. They make notes and write their stories as events progress so they can be ready to file a finished story almost literally as soon as a final result is known. Leading Australian online sporting writer and cricket specialist Peter English said many people who do not understand sport reporting are surprised to learn how little of a game a journalist actually sees because she or he must focus on writing as well as watching, and:

> Because of the deadlines, if you are doing the match report you usually need to file within five minutes of the end of a game—and often sooner. So when you factor in the writing time, especially with sports such as rugby league, union, and soccer, you may not have seen half the play. 'You're there to work, not to watch,' is a saying I've heard a few times (English 2010).

Again, like all journalists who work a particular round, sport journalists must also be careful about how they deal with sources and contacts. Good contacts are extremely important. But those contacts are likely to cut a journalist off, or at least threaten to do so, if he or she writes reports critical of the source's team or sport. For this reason there is a tendency for sport journalists and sources to become too cosy in their relationships. Related to that is the influence of managers and public relations practitioners. As noted earlier, there are close associations between sport and business. Corporations invest millions of dollars in sponsoring individuals, teams and events. They do not want the clean, healthy image of a sport they support damaged by adverse publicity. Therefore many leading sporting identities are carefully groomed and coached in how to deal with media. To even get an interview with them involves working through managers and public relations firms. Then, when an interview is arranged, the manager or a public relations operative will sit in and try to head off awkward questions. Resultant quotes from sporting stars are often so scripted they are at best bland and at worst incomprehensible. Things get worse if a sporting identity becomes embroiled in a controversy, especially if it involves his or her personal life. In those instances managers, coaches and public relations minders almost literally form a human chain of protection around the fallen star, who goes into virtual hiding for weeks, even months.

From the perspective of competitors themselves, especially those at or near the top of their sport, reputation can be everything. There is a need for reassurance that the journalists they speak with will be fair, accurate and balanced. The cult of celebrity means sporting stars are sometimes harassed by a hero-worshipping public, lunatics, well-meaning but irritating fans, paparazzi photographers, and journalists wanting interviews. Being misquoted can be worse than embarrassing;

it might damage a sport itself, damage the star or the star's family, ruin a sponsorship arrangement, or upset other players. A sporting celebrity is therefore likely to want to check the backgrounds of those who seek to interview them to see if they can be trusted. Once trust builds, it tends to deepen and often mutual respect develops. As Nine Network sport journalist Roz Kelly said:

> In a way, building contacts as a sports journalist is much harder than when working as a news journalist because sportsmen and women, unlike politicians, generally don't need the media to push an agenda. They are often private people thrust into the spotlight just because they are good athletes (Kelly 2010).

But what if a journalist who has developed a good relationship with a sporting heroine or hero discovers a dark side to that person, some sort of dirty deal, or becomes aware he or she is using performance enhancing drugs? If the journalist writes about what has been discovered, the price could be being cut off—maybe not just by the offended individual, but perhaps even from a whole sport. But if the matter is not reported, the public would be let down. Some news organisations attempt to get around the problem by passing the difficult story to another journalist who reports news, not sport. Sometimes this approach works, other times it does not—particularly when the sporting identity blames a whole publication or news outlet for an exposé, not just the journalists who broke the story.

Another issue sportswriters must contend with relates to fanatical supporters and fans. Supporters of many team games—think AFL and NRL—tend to have a tribal loyalty and can see no wrong in the team they support, while viewing competing teams as pure evil. The same people regularly accuse sportswriters, no matter how objective they are, of being either 'cheerleaders' for their team or inordinately biased in favour of the opposition. In that sense sport journalists share the middle ground with umpires. Occasionally they make mistakes, but generally they get it right! As Mencher said, sport reporters should be loyal to a sport, not a team (1997, p. 487).

All journalists who become specialists face similar issues and dilemmas. There is great wisdom in advice offered by respected finance reporter and commentator Alan Kohler when he was interviewed on ABC Radio National some years ago:

> One of the, if not *the*, main problems or issue with being a specialist journalist is that you do have to keep seeing the same people all the time... you have to be independent and you can't become friends with these people, because it just doesn't work out; you're not then representing your audience

or your readers in the way that you should represent them. So it's prickly and sometimes difficult... the only way one can deal with the situation is to be straight and to be honest about it and to not be deceitful (Kohler 2002).

DISCUSSION POINTS

1   What would be the best two news rounds to be assigned to cover? What would be the least attractive? Why?

2   Is it best to focus on a particular round—say education, crime, sport or business— and to develop specialised knowledge and understandings of the field, or would it really be better and more interesting to remain a generalist who does a bit of everything?

3   You are a court reporter. A witness in a case you are covering tells you she was in contact with a member of the jury via her Facebook page and the jury member asked if she thought the man on trial was guilty or not. The jury member says she wants to be a protected source and you cannot tell anyone. What will you do? Why?

4   You are a crime reporter and one of your contacts tells you a known criminal with a history of violence is going to have your legs broken with a baseball bat if you write a story about her. You are working on the story, you believe the threat is real, and you know the woman who made it was associated with the Melbourne gangland killings. How will you handle the situation?

5   In the course of working your local council round you learn that the leader of a local environmental and conservation group, who is also close to the mayor, is on the payroll of a land development company which has an application for a development before council. If approved, the application will result in the mass destruction of flora and fauna as land is cleared for a huge, upmarket housing estate. How are you going to verify the facts and get the story published without being sued for defamation?

6   You are a sport reporter and you discover one of your best sources once took performance-enhancing drugs. What will you do—write the story yourself, pass it over to another journalist, or ignore what you discovered and do nothing? Why?

NEWS PRACTICE POINTS

1   Identify four leading journalists, other than those named in this chapter, who cover specific news rounds. In each case find out what qualifications the journalist has and if any of those qualifications relate directly to the round she or he covers.

2   Write a 400-word application explaining why you would like to take up one of the rounds described in this chapter, explain what attracts you to that round, and what special attributes you would bring to the role.

3   Go to your nearest courthouse while courts are in session. Quietly go in and out of different courtrooms until you find a case being covered by a journalist—he or she will usually be sitting at a special desk or table at the back of the court. Sit in the public gallery at the back of the court and take your own notes on the case. When the journalist leaves the court follow her or him out and introduce yourself as a journalism student. Find out what media outlet the journalist works for. Go and write your own 250- to 300-word court report story relating to the case. Then follow up and obtain a copy of the story written by the court reporter—either by buying the relevant newspaper, finding the story online, or as it was broadcast. How does it compare with your story? Which was the most accurate?

4   Attend a local council meeting. Ask for a copy of the agenda and follow the meeting. Take particular note of how it is chaired by the mayor, how decisions are made and votes cast. See if you can identify the different roles of council staff who attend the meeting.

5   Watch a major sporting event such as a football game, tennis match or cricket match on television. Take your own notes during the broadcast. Buy tomorrow's newspaper and see how the event was reported. In about 300 words write a critique of the newspaper report highlighting what you believe were its strengths and weaknesses.

6   Go online and find reports of a major crime, preferably a crime that resulted in a series of reports over several days or longer. Read the reports carefully, then make a list of information in them that was fully attributed to named sources, and another list of information that just seemed to be there without attribution. Beside each item on the list of information that was not attributed, make another list of occupational groups (such as police, prison guards or lawyers) from whom you suspect the journalist obtained the information.

7   Find a news story or feature article online, in a magazine or newspaper in which journalists who normally work different rounds have come together and co-operated. Identify each journalist and her or his specific round. Then see if you can deconstruct the story and identify which journalist was likely to have written which sections.

8   What would you do if an important source threatened to cut you off if you reported on a story the source was not happy about? Explain in no more than 600 words how you would handle the situation and why you would deal with it that way.

DINA ROSENDORFF

Dina Rosendorff currently lives in Boston and works for National Public Radio as a senior producer. Previously, she has worked at the ABC as a radio and television journalist, and before that at the *Herald Sun* newspaper. In 2007 she won a Quill Award for Young Journalist of the Year. Judges praised her versatile portfolio of work, which included a fashion video blog and coverage of bushfires. Judges said Dina had the ability to 'file accurate, descriptive copy under deadline pressure, even in situations of danger'.

1 How did you get your first job as a journalist?

My first job was at the *Herald Sun* as an editorial assistant (which is basically just a fancy term for copy-kid). I started work at the paper while I was studying postgraduate journalism at RMIT, so I'd go to uni during the day, and work in the newsroom in the evenings. It was an excellent foot in the door and I was able to start getting stories published and put together a portfolio.

2 What advice would you offer a beginning journalist?

Do as much work experience as you can and take whatever job you can get. All you need is that foot in the door. When you're starting out, no job is beneath you—you never know where it may lead or who you may meet, and the more experience under your belt, the better!

3 What is the role of journalism in 21st-century Australian society?

Journalists are just as vital to the gathering and dissemination of news as they ever were. Yes, the media landscape is certainly changing, and citizen journalists play more of a role than ever before by contributing to issues with blogs, photos and tweets. But people still turn to established mastheads when big news breaks. Reporters are still the most trustworthy source for accurate, reliable information.

4 What are your thoughts about the future of journalism in Australia?

Journalism in Australia has gone through a rough patch in the last number of years. Most media outlets have shed jobs, making it even tougher for journalism graduates to find work. But organisations have emerged more streamlined and ready to adopt new technology (and with it, tech-savvy, multimedia reporters) to take reporting well into the 21st century and beyond.

5 What are the key things a journalism student should learn during their studies?

One of the first things a lecturer told me when I started studying journalism is that it's not a profession for people who think they're good writers. That can be taught. Journalism is for people who like asking questions, and are keen to get their hands dirty and delve into issues, not just coast on their surface. I think if you can come out at the end of your studies not afraid to ask potentially embarrassing or sensitive questions, you've got a successful future ahead of you.

6 Is there anything else you would like to say to journalism students and/or about journalism as a profession?

It's the most fabulous profession. You have the opportunity to meet all sorts of interesting people from all walks of life—and you're paid to ask them whatever questions you want! Not a day goes by where I don't learn something new. It's the perfect profession for the curious and the easily bored!

DANIEL ZIFFER

Shaking hands with Barack Obama, Daniel Ziffer realised his career was a fortunate mess: he had written for *The Age*, *New York Post*, *The Gippsland Times* and the official magazine of Victoria Bitter beer. Daniel edited his first magazine at 20 before working on more established titles, writing a Masters thesis and hosting breakfast radio. *The Age* hired him and he strolled the red carpet as their entertainment reporter. Fascinated by politics, he quit to cover the 2008 US election for Australian radio and newspapers, and is now senior producer of *Mornings with Jon Faine*, 774 ABC Mebourne.

1 How did you get your first job as a journalist?

I fell into working on magazines, starting at free 'street press' titles and moving up to editorships at glossy 'newsstand' titles. I'd read newspapers since I could string words together but thought that I was too old—at 26—to get a cadetship. I completely fluffed both final interviews at the *Herald Sun* and *The Age*, and felt like throwing myself under a bus after the latter. Somehow I was selected and then I started to really work. Our group had an intensive year of training and a confronting range of jobs across the newspaper. The buzz was addictive, the grind was manageable and I can't see myself doing anything else.

2 What advice would you offer a beginning journalist?

Work. Journalism degrees are useful, but I don't think they'll bring you a job. At most, they 'tick some boxes' in the mind of an interviewer, but that's it. Your extra-curricular activities are key. Community radio, university papers and the infinite world of the internet are the best places to develop your skills and build a substantial and convincing body of work.

3 What is the role of journalism in 21st-century Australian society?

The public is always going to need people to filter information for their consumption. The fact that more information than ever is available—to anyone—is fantastic. It changes journalists' role and increases their value. Blogs, tweets and commentary are great, but I don't see many bloggers sitting in court, observing at bushfires, challenging government ministers at doorstop interviews or even making a phone call to check a fact. Talking isn't doing.

4 Journalism is being changed and challenged by technology. What are your thoughts about the future of journalism in Australia?

We've got one, but there's going to be a lot of pain this decade until we work out how to make it work financially. People want to know about the world around them and the issues that affect their lives, and the ability to receive news in different ways on various devices doesn't change the fact that someone has to create it. Informed, experienced and trained journalists do that job well. Advertising pays for Australian journalism, with the exception of the government-funded ABC, and as long as there is an audience for news there will be companies who will pay to give them a commercial message at the same time.

5 What are the key things a journalism student should learn during their studies?

Be proficient in new technology, but don't be overwhelmed by its abilities. Being able to send messages to thousands of people is amazing, but if you don't say anything worth knowing... who cares? If you can talk to a wide range of people and are diligent, you're halfway there. Curiosity is a key element in journalism, but if you're reading this you're probably already one of those people who drove their parents nuts asking the most compelling question: 'Why?'

6 Is there anything else you would like to say to journalism students and/or about journalism as a profession?

Thank you. There are a lot easier and more financially rewarding things you could be doing than journalism, and your intent to make it your career is a shot of confidence for a profession that gets way too down on itself.

Citizens in countries that don't have a free press dream about one. Go to a couple and see what you think of their public life. You'll realise journalism helps keep us free. You probably won't think that as you're writing your tenth article on rising petrol prices, but there are many places in the world where the papers will 'report' that skyrocketing prices are actually stable, thanks to the intervention of the General. Journalism does help keep us free.

KATHLEEN SKENE _____

Kathleen Skene began her career as a cadet at North Queensland's *Herbert River Express* in 2002. She has won awards for her work in business, political, community and investigative journalism on regional and state levels. In 2011 she received the Walkley Award for Coverage of Indigenous Affairs for a series of investigative articles she completed as chief reporter at the *Townsville Bulletin*. She is currently day editor at the *Gold Coast Bulletin*.

1 How did you get your first job as a journalist?

I was completing an internship at the *Townsville Bulletin* as part of my university degree when a position came up at the *Herbert River Express*, then a tri-weekly paper at Ingham, a sugar-farming community 110km north of Townsville. Knowing how scarce journalists' positions were, I took the role, despite some reservations about working in such a small town. Turns out it was the best thing I ever did—I spent more than five years there and gained experience working just about every round possible. I was able to cover court, police, sports, community and political news stories which I may ever have been able to pursue at a larger masthead. The skills I learnt there also proved invaluable—as well as researching, interviewing and writing articles, I was also responsible for taking the photos, sub-editing, building and sending the pages. It was the strongest career foundation I could have asked for.

2 What advice would you offer a beginning journalist?

Be prepared to cover the less interesting stories while you're still gaining experience, and expect to work for free until you make a name for yourself. This is an increasingly competitive and changing industry. Making a brand out of your name will become more important as the way journalism is done continues to shift. Figure out early what principles you stand for and stick to them—credibility is gold in the growing sea of information available to people.

3 What is the role of journalism in 21st-century Australian society?

I don't think the key roles of journalism have changed—it is mostly in the way content is delivered and digested by the audience. Journalism has been and remains an integral part of a fair and democratic world. It must always be fair and interesting, and journalists must balance the requirement to give people the information they need as well as the information they want. It is not always the same thing.

4 What are your thoughts about the impacts on journalism of changing communication technologies?

I think it's incredibly exciting that good journalism is reaching more people than ever before. The ways we tell stories now are diverse and rich—it is no longer the case that media organisations can simply broadcast news while people consume it. Social media, and the expansion of the online world generally, means that many more people are able to set the agenda and participate in creating and evolving the news. It is an incredibly exciting time to be a journalist.

5 What key things should a journalism student learn?

As well as the obvious skills you're getting from your uni course, there are other things which will help you. Be curious. Listen to people and ask them the questions that you as a person want to know about their story. Learn to accept criticism—fair and unfair—and grow from it. People will 'shoot the messenger', and that's ok. Be persistent—never accept a response that doesn't answer your question. Don't be afraid to ask questions yourself if you don't fully understand something you're writing about—it's your name on the story.

6 Is there anything else you would like to say to journalism students and/or about journalism as a profession?

Good on you for choosing it—it's wonderful, challenging, important work. Don't listen to the doom and gloom—change is hard and necessary, but there will always be a basic human need to know about the world around us. True, good quality journalism will not go away simply because technology changes. Listen to your teachers and experienced journalists, but bear in mind that the 'rules' of the industry are not static—and probably never will be. If you have a great idea—pitch it, and never stop thinking about how things could be done better.

EPILOGUE

If you would not be forgotten as soon as you are dead and rotten, either write something worth reading or do things worth the writing.
Benjamin Franklin 1706–90

The years from 2010 to 2013 were one of the most tumultuous and challenging periods in the history of Australian journalism and news production. As noted elsewhere in this book, at least 1000 jobs were lost in traditional newspaper and television newsrooms (Jackson 2013) as a result of still-evolving structural reforms. *The Age* and *The Sydney Morning Herald* morphed from broadsheets to tabloid, there was a massive shift by newspaper companies to publish news for portable devices such as smartphones and tablets, news media were threatened with what many regarded as draconian new government regulations, and previously popular news websites operated by News Limited and Fairfax went behind pay-walls.

Yet media and journalists are resilient and inventive, and the sky did not fall in. In fact by the start of 2013 it was reported that there were about 22,000 journalists and writers in Australia—the highest number ever (Jackson 2013). Much of the increase was due to a re-alignment of priorities as media companies adapted to changing economic circumstances and consumer priorities by redirecting jobs from traditional platforms such as newspapers towards publication online and for mobile devices. On the downside, however, the shift in focus from traditional newsprint publication was accompanied by a greater reliance on reactive journalism and a decline in quality proactive investigative reporting. There was also a growth in the influence of public relations and marketing, with Jackson (2013) reporting that 'growth in the PR industry was far outpacing journalism'.

Overall, however, there can be no doubt that journalism will adapt structurally as it continues to be shaped by new technology—it always has been. Over time it will regain its balance in an information hungry world. But journalists must remain vigilant to protect free speech and media freedom. The Gillard Labor government's attempted regulation of news media, journalists and free speech in 2013 highlighted the vulnerability of Australian news media to political interference. Potential threats arose in three areas: proposals for a new tort of privacy which did not include a public interest or fair comment defence (Bartlett 2012), proposed new anti-discrimination legislation which would have made it illegal to offend or insult an individual, and appointment of a government-funded 'public interest media advocate' with power to oversee print and online media and remove journalists' protection under the *Privacy Act* if their employers did not co-operate with the advocate (Crowe 2013). As noted elsewhere, Australia does have not have a 'Bill of Rights' to protect free-speech and media freedom. Consequently, while each of those proposals would have been rejected outright in the US on constitutional grounds, they would have become law in Australia if they had been accepted by the Federal Parliament. Fortunately, after often heated debate and fierce lobbying of crossbenchers who held the balance of power in the minority government, each proposed restriction was eventually abandoned.

Paradoxically, however, it too often seems to take a threat or crisis in Australia before we become concerned about issues such as freedom of speech and media freedom, things we tend to take for granted but the rights to which are not secure. As touched on in Chapter 1, one of those who literally fought against governments to establish a right for media freedom was US statesman Benjamin Franklin. He left many priceless legacies—not the least being the ideal that a free press and freedom of speech are essential elements in a healthy democracy.

But Franklin was not alone. Another remarkable 18th century statesman was Finnish/Swedish scholar Anders Chydenius, also mentioned in Chapter 1. As well as reminding us there was a free press in China from the 7th century, and for hundreds of years after that, Chydenius was instrumental in the development of press freedom in Europe. A medical doctor, clergyman, politician, economist and writer, as well as a learned scholar, Chydenius was at least as extraordinary in his own way as Franklin. In 1766 Chydenius convinced the Swedish Parliament to pass the *Freedom-of-Press and the Right-of-Access to Public Records Act*, a statute that enshrined concepts of freedom of information and press freedom in the Swedish Constitution, where they remain to this day. In fact Sweden remains the ultimate model of media and journalistic freedom in the modern world. Its journalists are freer than journalists in any other nation. They are highly responsible professionals who observe strict ethical standards and professional principles, not because they are intimidated into doing so by a government that frets about controlling its public image, but because they are self-regulated and that is their culture.

It is hard to imagine that Franklin—an accomplished diplomat who spent time in France and England during and after the 1760s—would not have at least heard of Sweden's *Freedom-of-Press and the Right-of-Access to Public Records Act*; a statute adopted 23 years before the US Constitution was approved and 25 years before ratification of the First Amendment to the US Constitution, a clause that also guarantees media freedom and freedom of speech. But notions of media freedom aside for the moment, Franklin was also credited with discovering that quality newspapers built around good journalism could be financed by selling space on their pages to advertisers—something that eventually earned him sufficient money as a newspaper proprietor to support his political career. There is therefore a deep irony in the fact that the two greatest threats to quality journalism in Australia today stem from the actions and lack of actions of governments, and financial restructuring by media companies.

The first threat is that (as noted previously) unlike Sweden and the US, Australia lacks any constitutional guarantee of free speech or free media. Neither are we like Canada and New Zealand, which each has statutes guaranteeing those rights and freedoms. In that sense Australia is an exception (Australian Press Council 2009a). Instead, our journalists are 'chilled' by laws of defamation and contempt that are harsh and restrictive, particularly in comparison with the US. Our state and federal governments, no matter what their persuasions, tend to be paternalistic, secretive, manipulative and dishonest. There is a history of governments doing their utmost to evade accountability and hide decision-making processes while armies of spin-doctors go forth and multiply.

Interestingly—in view of how freedom of speech and media freedom evolved and were enshrined in law in Europe and the US but have never been constitutionally embedded in Australia—the 2008 Global Press Freedom survey ranked the Scandinavian nations of Finland, Sweden, Iceland, Denmark and Norway, as well as Belgium, as the top five nations in the world for media freedom. New Zealand was eighth, the US 21st. Australia was ranked 35th, behind nations such as Taiwan, Barbados, Costa Rica, the Bahamas and Czech Republic! China was ranked 181st, with Burma and North Korea listed last at 194th and 195th respectively (Global Press Freedom 2008).

The second threat to quality journalism in Australia today comes from within the industry. In some cases, journalism has been damaged by greedy and/or incompetent media organisations that make an art form out of squeezing newsroom budgets. As mentioned earlier, there has also been mounting pressure on the bottom line because of greater competition sparked by online news publication (some of which is by new players in the market) and the need for structural reform. That said, there are times when news media shines, when it goes through an active phase in which there is a flurry of proactive agenda-setting, as journalists expose abuses of power, criminality, hypocrisy and lack of accountability.

From a big-picture perspective, everyone—with the obvious exceptions of those who have things to hide, who are lazy, or hope to escape accountability—has much to gain from encouraging journalists to do their jobs as effectively and ethically as they can. If news outlets are to be credible, to attract readers, listeners and viewers, they must be free to offend and defame those who should be offended and defamed, to commend those who should be commended, and be empowered to expose slimy politicians, incompetent governments, dodgy spin-doctors, corporate crooks and others who fear them. To that end, society and governments have to understand—as do journalists themselves—that it is impossible, and ultimately bad for society, for journalists to even try to be all things to all people, or to please all people. That is not their role. Their task is to seek truth and report it accurately, objectively, fairly and without fear or favour.

This book began with Benjamin Franklin. Although we live in a very different time and place, it is fitting to close with him too, and an 'old fable' he published at the end of his 'An Apology for Printers' in the *Pennsylvania Gazette* in 1731. Franklin wrote the 'apology' after being attacked for printing an advertisement some found offensive. The following should be read with an awareness that at the time it appeared, printers and journalists were often one and the same, and that printers' 'letters' were made of lead.

> A certain well-meaning Man and his Son, were travelling towards a Market Town, with an Ass which they had to sell. The Road was bad; and the old Man therefore rid, but the Son went a-foot. The first Passenger they met, asked the Father if he was not ashamed to ride by himself, and suffer the poor Lad to wade along thro' the Mire; this induced him to take up his Son behind him: He had not travelled far when he met other, who said, they were two unmerciful Lubbers to get both on the Back of that poor Ass, in such a deep Road. Upon this the old Man gets off, and let his Son ride alone. The next they met called the Lad a graceless, rascally young Jackanapes, to ride in that Manner thro' the Dirt, while his aged Father trudged along on Foot; and they said the old Man was a Fool, for suffering it. He then bid his Son come down, and walk with him, and they travell'd on leading the Ass by the Halter; 'till they met another Company, who called them a Couple of

senseless Blockheads, for going both on Foot in such a dirty Way, when they had an empty Ass with them, which they might ride upon. The old Man could bear no longer; My Son, said he, it grieves me much that we cannot please all these People: Let us throw the Ass over the next Bridge, and be no farther troubled with him.

Had the old Man been seen acting this last Resolution, he would probably have been call'd a Fool for troubling himself about the different Opinions of all that were pleas'd to find Fault with him: Therefore, tho' I have a Temper almost as complying as his, I intend not to imitate him in this last Particular. I consider the Variety of Humours among Men, and despair of pleasing every Body; yet I shall not therefore leave off Printing. I shall continue my Business. I shall not burn my Press and melt my Letters (Franklin 1731).

Finally, do not make the mistake of thinking that because news media is less than perfect, because journalists are constrained in some ways, and because paranoid governments sporadically attempt to limit media freedom and free speech, that all is doom and gloom. It is not. Whether you are reporting news or working in other fields, journalism is a marvellous, satisfying and essential profession. Yes, it can be stressful, but it is also stimulating and great fun, even exhilarating at times. To make your mark, and make a difference for the better, you must value your good name and your individuality above all else. Never run with the pack. Resist pressure to be unethical. Be responsible in how you exercise the power vested in you as a journalist. Be true to yourself and accountable to your public. Within reason, and while whoever pays you has rights and expectations too, remember that ultimately as a journalist you have only two masters: yourself and the public you serve. If you find yourself working in a media environment you do not feel comfortable in, think back to what happened at the *News of the World* in the UK and do what you can to change that culture. If you cannot change it, bide your time and as soon as possible move to a fresh environment. Above all, no matter how much you are criticised for doing your job, continue your Business—never burn your press nor melt your letters!

APPENDIX 1

Media Entertainment and Arts Alliance
Journalists' Code of Ethics

Respect for truth and the public's right to information are fundamental principles of journalism. Journalists describe society to itself. They convey information, ideas and opinions, a privileged role. They search, disclose, record, question, entertain, suggest and remember. They inform citizens and animate democracy. They give a practical form to freedom of expression. Many journalists work in private enterprise, but all have these public responsibilities. They scrutinise power, but also exercise it, and should be accountable. Accountability engenders trust. Without trust, journalists do not fulfil their public responsibilities. Alliance members engaged in journalism commit themselves to:

- *Honesty*
- *Fairness*
- *Independence*
- *Respect for the rights of others*

Journalists will educate themselves about ethics and apply the following standards:

1 Report and interpret honestly, striving for accuracy, fairness and disclosure of all essential facts. Do not suppress relevant available facts, or give distorting emphasis. Do your utmost to give a fair opportunity for reply.

2 Do not place unnecessary emphasis on personal characteristics, including race, ethnicity, nationality, gender, age, sexual orientation, family relationships, religious belief, or physical or intellectual disability.

3 Aim to attribute information to its source. Where a source seeks anonymity, do not agree without first considering the source's motives and any alternative attributable source. Where confidences are accepted, respect them in all circumstances.

4 Do not allow personal interest, or any belief, commitment, payment, gift or benefit, to undermine your accuracy, fairness or independence.

5 Disclose conflicts of interest that affect, or could be seen to affect, the accuracy, fairness or independence of your journalism. Do not improperly use a journalistic position for personal gain.

6 Do not allow advertising or other commercial considerations to undermine accuracy, fairness or independence.

7 Do your utmost to ensure disclosure of any direct or indirect payment made for interviews, pictures, information or stories.

8 Use fair, responsible and honest means to obtain material. Identify yourself and your employer before obtaining any interview for publication or broadcast. Never exploit a person's vulnerability or ignorance of media practice.

9   Present pictures and sound which are true and accurate. Any manipulation likely to mislead should be disclosed.

10   Do not plagiarise.

11   Respect private grief and personal privacy. Journalists have the right to resist compulsion to intrude.

12   Do your utmost to achieve fair correction of errors.

Guidance Clause

Basic values often need interpretation and sometimes come into conflict. Ethical journalism requires conscientious decision-making in context. Only substantial advancement of the public interest or risk of substantial harm to people allows any standard to be overridden.

APPENDIX 2

Australian Press Council *General Statement of Principles*

The Council has published the following General Statement of Principles. Along with the Statement of Privacy Principles, the General Statement is applied by the Council when providing advice or adjudicating on individual complaints.

General Principle 1: Accurate, fair and balanced reporting
Publications should take reasonable steps to ensure reports are accurate, fair and balanced. They should not deliberately mislead or misinform readers either by omission or commission.

General Principle 2: Correction of inaccuracy
Where it is established that a serious inaccuracy has been published, a publication should promptly correct the error, giving the correction due prominence.

General Principle 3: Publishing responses.
Where individuals or groups are a major focus of news reports or commentary, the publication should ensure fairness and balance in the original article. Failing that, it should provide a reasonable and swift opportunity for a balancing response in an appropriate section of the publication.

General Principle 4: Respect for privacy and sensibilities
News and comment should be presented honestly and fairly, and with respect for the privacy and sensibilities of individuals. However, the right to privacy is not to be interpreted as preventing publication of matters of public record or obvious or significant public interest. Rumour and unconfirmed reports should be identified as such.

General Principle 5: Honest and fair investigation; preservation of confidences
Information obtained by dishonest or unfair means, or the publication of which would involve a breach of confidence, should not be published unless there is an over-riding public interest.

General Principle 6: Transparent and fair presentation
Publications are free to advocate their own views and publish the bylined opinions of others, as long as readers can recognise what is fact and what is opinion. Relevant facts should not be misrepresented or suppressed, headlines and captions should fairly reflect the tenor of an article and readers should be advised of any manipulation of images and potential conflicts of interest.

General Principle 7: Discretion and causing offence
Publications have a wide discretion in publishing material, but they should balance the public interest with the sensibilities of their readers, particularly when the material, such as photographs, could reasonably be expected to cause offence.

General Principle 8: Gratuitous emphasis on characteristics
Publications should not place any gratuitous emphasis on the race, religion, nationality, colour, country of origin, gender, sexual orientation, marital status, disability, illness, or age of an individual

or group. Where it is relevant and in the public interest, publications may report and express opinions in these areas.

General Principle 9: Publication of Council adjudications

Where the Council issues an adjudication, the publication concerned should publish the adjudication, promptly and with due prominence.

Note 1 'Public interest'

For the purposes of these principles, 'public interest' is defined as involving a matter capable of affecting the people at large so they might be legitimately interested in, or concerned about, what is going on, or what may happen to them or to others.

Note 2 'Due prominence'

The Council interprets 'due prominence' as requiring the publication to ensure the retraction, clarification, correction, explanation or apology has the effect, as far as possible, of neutralising any damage arising from the original publication, and that any published adjudication is likely to be seen by those who saw the material on which the complaint was based.

APPENDIX 3

Links to Industry Codes of Practice and Complaints-handling Organisations

Australian Broadcasting Corporation (ABC) Code of Practice (Revised 2013)

www.acma.gov.au/webwr/_assets/main/lib100060/abc-2011_code_of_practice-revised_2013.pdf

Commercial Radio Australia Codes of Practice and Guidelines

www.acma.gov.au/webwr/aba/contentreg/codes/radio/documents/commercial_radio-codes_and_guidelines_5sept2011.pdf

Community broadcasting codes of practice, and guidelines

www.acma.gov.au/~/media/Community%20Broadcasting/Regulation/pdf/Community%20Radio%20Broadcasting%20Codes%20of%20Practice.PDF

Free TV Australia's Commercial Television Industry Code of Practice

www.freetv.com.au/media/Code_of_Practice/2010_Commercial_Television_Industry_Code_of_Practice.pdf

Independent Media Council Code of Conduct

www.independentmediacouncil.com.au/code-of-conduct.html

Special Broadcasting Service (SBS) Codes of Practice (Amended 2012)

http://media.sbs.com.au/home/upload_media/site_20_rand_744214925_sbs_codes_of_practice_2006_12_december_2012_.pdf

General information about media regulation by the Australian Communications and Media Authority (ACMA)

www.acma.gov.au/theACMA/About/The-ACMA-story/Regulating

GLOSSARY OF JOURNALISM TERMS

ACTUALITY
Sounds and/or video images recorded in the field when a story is being reported.

ADVERTORIAL
Advertising presented as editorial. Ethically, it should be labelled as advertising or an advertising feature or section, but often it is not. Sometimes it is advertising disguised as news.

ANGLE
The approach taken in a news story. Usually emphasised in the first sentence—or intro—whether in print, online, or broadcast.

BACKBENCH
Senior newspaper and online editorial production staff such as the night editor or a senior sub-editor.

BACKGROUNDER
An article—often a feature—that literally backgrounds a news story in a separate explanation which focuses on interpretation and analysis.

BLOCK-LINE
Another name for a caption for a photograph. Called a block-line because newspaper photographs were originally printed from etched metal plates attached to wooden blocks.

BROADSHEET
A large-format newspaper such as *The Australian* with pages double the size of a tabloid such as *The Age*.

BYLINE
A journalist's name attached to the start or end of a story, or for a photographer under a photograph.

COLUMN CENTIMETRES
A measure of the length of a print story calculated to a formula based on the actual physical length the story would be if printed in a set font and point size in a single column of a set width. Length and word count obviously vary depending on column width, font, and font size.

CLIP
A cutting or 'tear sheet' of a newspaper or magazine story.

CONFERENCE
Also known as an editor's conference, or news conference. A meeting attended by senior editorial staff, or in some organisations all editorial staff including journalists, to plan the news coverage for a day or part of a day.

COPY
Any material written for publication.

CROP
To trim unwanted parts of an image from a photograph.

CROSS PROMOTION
A technique used by one media company which has an interest in different media—for example, a television network and a magazine publisher—to advertise and/or promote each medium in the other.

CUE
To prepare material, in sequence, for broadcast. Also means a signal to begin or finish.

CUT
To reduce the length of a story.

DEADLINE
The absolute latest time a journalist can submit a story for editing, or when a sub-editor must submit a page for production, or a story can be edited for broadcast.

DECK
The number of lines or rows in a headline: for example, a three-deck head above a newspaper, magazine or online article means three rows of type.

DUMMY
Layout or diagram of newspaper or magazine pages showing the size and position of advertising, and the spaces remaining to be filled by news articles or features.

EDITION
A newspaper issue targeted for a specific area or region or printed at a particular time. Metropolitan newspapers may print several updated editions, or press runs. Usually the day's first edition is the state/territory edition and is transported out to regional areas where delivery takes longer.

EMBARGO
Information released on the strict condition it will not be published or broadcast before a date and time set by the person who releases it.

FOLLOW-UP
Either an update of a story already broadcast or published, or a separate story on the same topic written when new information becomes available.

GRAB
Recorded sound, or video images plus sound, to be included in a broadcast report.

HOOK
A particular fact, event or angle which an article, or part of an article or broadcast story, is built around.

HOUSE STYLE
A set of internal rules adopted by a media outlet with the aim of ensuring consistency of grammar, spelling, word use, punctuation, etc.

INTRO
Sometimes also called the lead. It is a news story's first sentence. Normally intros are one short sentence in a single stand-alone paragraph. Also known as a teaser, standfirst, precede or blurb when used to summarise and introduce an online story.

INTRODUCTION
The same as an intro in a print news story, but in a radio news story or a print feature article it may take in two or more sentences after an intro sentence.

KILL A STORY
Delete or not use it. Similar to spiking, but more final.

LEAD
See intro. Can also refer to the main story on a page, in which case it is often called the page lead. In broadcast refers to the main, or first, story of a news bulletin.

LIFT, LIFTING
A dubious and unprofessional practice—which carries the danger of becoming outright plagiarism—of news outlets adopting stories, story lines, and/or quotes published by other news outlets.

MAKE-UP
Designing or laying out a page.

NAT SOUND
Similar to actuality but sound only, recorded in the field when a story is being reported. Often used to add atmosphere to a broadcast news report.

OMNI-DIRECTIONAL MICROPHONE
One that picks up sounds equally from any direction.

PACKAGE
A complete television news report. Usually includes a scripted report by the news presenter, a stand-up by a journalist reporting the story, and interviews with talent. Also used in radio when referring to a composite news report.

PIC
Photograph.

ROUNDS
Specific coverage of areas such as health, police, courts and sport, by journalists who specialise in reporting on those areas. Known as 'beats' in the US.

SLUG, OR SLUG-LINE
A word or two used by a journalist to 'tag' a story so it can be easily found in a news list by sub-editors.

SPIKE A STORY
Not publish it. But sometimes the story might be revived for another edition or at a later time.

SPILL
When a story begins on one page and continues on another. Also called a roll-over.

SPLASH
Front page lead story, often with a large headline and photograph.

STANDFIRST
A broad introduction to a print story which sits between the headline and intro. Commonly written by a sub-editor. Can have a slightly different meaning online, when it can also refer to a story's intro.

STAND-UP
A television journalist speaking directly to a video camera, usually from the site of a news event.

STRINGER
A regular correspondent for a newspaper, online news site or broadcast outlet, who is not a staff member.

TABLOID
A newspaper with A3 size pages—half the size of pages in a broadsheet such as *The Australian*. 'Tabloid' can also be a derogatory term used to refer to sensational journalism published or broadcast on any platform.

TALENT
A person or people interviewed for a radio or television news story.

THROW
A transition device, usually scripted, that involves a broadcast presenter introducing a journalist or a journalist introducing talent (an interviewee) in a report.

VOICER
Audio from a radio journalist. Can sometimes be from the site of a news event, but usually just refers to a news story read by a news presenter.

VOX POP
A technique used to obtain a snapshot of public opinion on an issue by randomly asking people in a public place what they think. From the Latin *vox populi*, meaning 'voice of the people'.

WIDOW
A term used in print or online publications to refer to a word, or a few words, from the end of a sentence that began in a previous column sitting awkwardly at the top of the next column.

WILDS
Raw, unedited video shot by a television news camera operator for a news story.

WRAP
Includes a voicer from a radio reporter combined with interviews and a studio introduction. Also used as a television term to mean the bundling together of two or more stories. Can also mean the end.

WRITE-OFF
A very short item on the front page of a newspaper or cover of a magazine which points to a larger story inside, or a brief summary on the home page of a website which links to a story on another page.

GLOSSARY OF ONLINE TERMS

ANDROID
A computer operating system developed by Google. Commonly runs many smartphones and tablet computers which do not use Apple or Microsoft software.

APP
An application, or small computer program, designed to perform a specific task on a mobile phone or tablet computer.

BANDWIDTH
A measurement of how much data can be transmitted over a network in a set time, usually seconds. The higher the bandwidth, the faster a connection.

BLOG
A 'web log' of an individual's thoughts, ideas and opinions. Often self-opinionated, sometimes expert comment, and commonly in the style of a diary or journal.

BLUETOOTH
A wireless computer protocol used to exchange information between linked computers, mobile phones and other devices in the immediate vicinity.

BROWSER
Software that draws data to a computer via the internet and presents it as text, images and sounds. Internet Explorer is the most popular web browser. Others include Chrome, Firefox, Opera and Safari.

BROADBAND
A high speed 'always on' internet connection.

COOKIE
A small file installed on a computer when particular websites are visited. Can be used to provide information about a user's browsing activity and to allow users to personalise how they interact with sites.

DOMAIN IDENTIFIER CODES
Abbreviations in a web address or URL. For example '.gov' stands for government, '.edu' for educational.

EMAIL
A message system that lets users communicate with individuals and groups via the internet.

FIREWALL
A security system designed to stop unauthorised access to a computer's files.

FTP
File Transfer Protocol. Software that allows the transfer of files between computers.

HTML
Hypertext Markup Language. An online language that provides the coding that makes web pages look the way they do.

HTTP
Hypertext Transfer Protocol. A computer 'language' that communicates instructions for sending and receiving data via the internet.

HYPERLINK
A highlighted word or phrase, often within text, that links users who click on it to related websites.

INTERNET
A multitude of interlinked global computer networks that can be accessed through a modem and fixed telephone lines, wireless, mobile telephones, or other network protocols. It makes possible the transmission of text, images, files, sound and video.

INTERNET BULLETIN BOARDS
Specialist sites, usually provided by a group or company, that provide information to users; also discussion forums.

INTERNET DIRECTORY
An internet database of files that researchers have structured in subjects or categories.

META SEARCH ENGINES
Search engines that search other search engines. They permit multiple searches and subject directories to be used simultaneously from one search platform.

NEWSGROUPS
Forums for people interested in particular topics, in which documents can be sought and messages left to be answered.

SEARCH ENGINES
Services such as, but not restricted to, Google, that allow users to access information from many websites, through keyword searches.

TABLET
A small, thin, highly portable touch-screen computer designed to be hand-held and run on battery power for extended periods.

TROJANS AND VIRUSES
Destructive code designed to take control of or damage computers and/or networks.

URL
Universal Resource Locator. The address of a website.

USENET
A network of newsgroups.

WORLD WIDE WEB
Otherwise known as the web. The umbrella system that delivers 'web pages', which contain text, audio and pictures.

RECOMMENDED READING

Australian journals and periodicals

Asia Pacific Media Educator, University of Wollongong, NSW.

Australian Journalism Review, Journalism Education Association of Australia, University of South Australia.

Australian Press Council Annual Report, Australian Press Council, Sydney.

Media International Australia, University of Queensland.

PANPA Bulletin, Newspaper Publishers' Association and Pacific Area Newspaper Publishers' Association, Pyrmont, NSW.

Overseas journals and periodicals

American Journalism Review, College of Journalism of the University of Maryland, College Park, MD

British Journalism Review, SAGE Publications, London

Columbia Journalism Review, Columbia University, New York

Pacific Journalism Review, Auckland University of Technology

Books

Adams, Sally with Hicks, Wynford. (2009) *Interviewing for Journalists*, second edition, Routledge, London.

Butler, Des & Rodrick, Sharon. (2011) *Australian Media Law*, fourth edition, Thomson Reuters Australia, Pyrmont NSW.

Hicks, Wynford. (2008) *Writing for Journalists*, third edition, Routledge, New York.

McLeod, Chris & Lockwood, Kim. (2009) *Style: The Essential Guide for Journalists and Professional Writers*, fourth edition, News Custom Publishing, Southbank, Vic.

Mencher, Melvin. (2008) *News Reporting and Writing*, twelfth edition, McGraw-Hill Companies, Columbus, OH.

Pearson, Mark & Polden, Mark. (2010) *The Journalist's Guide to Media Law*, fourth edition, Allen & Unwin, Crows Nest, NSW.

Phillips, Gail, Lindgren, Mia & Bishop, Russell. (2013) *Australian Broadcast Journalism*, third edition, Oxford University Press, South Melbourne.

Quinn, Stephen & Lamble, Stephen. (2008) *Online Newsgathering: Research and Reporting for Journalism*, Focal Press, Burlington, MA.

Ricketson, Matthew. (2012) *Australian Journalism Today*, Palgrave Macmillan, Yarra, Vic.

White, Sally 1996, *Reporting in Australia*, Macmillan, Melbourne.

Website

http://JournalismAustralia.com

BIBLIOGRAPHY

AAP (2002) 'Kernot "had affair with Gareth Evans"', *The Sydney Morning Herald*, July 3, accessed October 23, 2009 from www.smh.com.au/articles/2002/07/03/1025667005180.html

—— (2012a) 'About AAP Newswire', December 20, accessed July 7, 2013 from www.aapnewswire.com.au/About

—— (2012b) 'Broadcast news: Fast, furious and accurate when time matters most', December 20, accessed July 7, 2013 from www.aapnewswire.com.au/News/Broadcast

—— (2013) 'Corbys win $50,000 damages', *The Australian*, April 12, p. 3.

ABC (2008) *News & Current Affairs Style Guide*, Australian Broadcasting Corporation, Sydney.

—— (2012) 'About Media Watch', June 13, accessed July 7, 2013 from www.abc.net.au/mediawatch/more.htm

ABC AM (2013) 'Gladstone harbour arrivals could motivate more asylum seekers', 2013, accessed July 7, 2013 from www.abc.net.au/news/2013-04-11/gladstone-harbour-arrivals-could-motivate-more/4621920

ABC News—Offbeat. (2009) 'Headlines that will make you smile, laugh or just scratch your head', September 23, www.abc.net.au/news/offbeat/

Adams, Sally with Wynford Hicks,(2001) *Interviewing for Journalists*, Routledge, London & New York.

Adegoke, Yinka. (2012) 'Twitter embarrassed by fake Wendi Murdoch account', Reuters, January 4, accessed 28 June 2012 from www.reuters.com/article/2012/01/04/us-wendimurdoch-twitter-idUSTRE80305620120104

Adrian, Paul. (1999) 'Put your career in the fast lane with CAR' in Paul Nora (ed.) *When Nerds and Worlds Collide: Reflections on the Development of Computer Assisted Reporting*, The Poynter Institute for Media Studies, St Petersburg, Florida.

The Age. (2009). '*The Age* Code of Conduct', October 16, accessed July 7, 2013 from www.theage.com.au/ethicsconduct.html

Agnew, Melissa. (2008) *Here is the [Australian] News: A Voice Training Handbook for the Australian Newscaster*, Wenga Books, Qld.

Akerman, P. (2013) 'Derryn Hinch to fight contempt charges over the Jill Meagher case', *The Australian*, April 10, accessed June 29, 2013 from www.theaustralian.com.au/news/nation/derryn-hinch-to-fight-contempt-charges-over-the-jill-meagher

American Society of Newspaper Editors. (1993) 'Ways with Words', American Society of Newspaper Editors in cooperation with The Poynter Institute for Media Studies, the *St Petersburg Times* and the University of Wisconsin-Madison.

Anissa Pty Ltd v Simon Harry Parsons (on application of the Prothonotary of the Supreme Court of Victoria). (1999) VSC 430, November 8, 1999.

Annan, Kofi. (1997) Address to World Bank 'Global Knowledge '97', accessed May 27, 2012 from www.un.org/News/Press/docs/1997/19970623.sgsm6268.html

Apology. (2002) 'Apology to Mater Hospital', *The Courier-Mail*, January 19, p. 3.

Armstrong, Mark, Blakeney, Michael & Watterson, Ray. (1995) *Media Law in Australia*, third edition, Oxford University Press, Melbourne.

ASIC. (2012) '12-275MR Decision in James Hardie penalty proceedings', November 13, accessed May 12, 2013 from www.asic.gov.au/asic/asic.nsf/byheadline/12-275MR+Decision+in+James+Hardie+penalty+proceedings?openDocument

Atkin [Lord Atkin]. (1936) In *Sim v Stretch* [1936] 2 All ER 1237 at 1240.

Atkinson [Lord Atkinson]. (1913). In *Scott v Scott*, AC 417, accessed May 31, 2009 from www.lawlink.nsw.gov.au/lrc.nsf/pages/R39CHP2.

Attorney-General for the State of New South Wales v Radio 2UE Sydney Pty Ltd and John Laws. (1998) Matter No 40236/96 [1998] NSWSC 28, March 11, 1998.

Austin, A. (1961) *Australian Education 1788–1900*, Sir Isaac Pitman & Sons, Ltd, Melbourne.

Australian Communications and Media Authority. (2013) 'About communications & media regulation', May 24, www.acma.gov.au/WEB/STANDARD/pc=PUB_REG_ABOUT

Australian Constitution. (1900) *Commonwealth of Australia Constitution Act 1900*, an Act of the Parliament of the United Kingdom at Westminster.

Australian Copyright Council. (2009) 'Using copyright material for reporting news', accessed January 17, 2010 from www.copyright.org.au/information/cit028/wp0062

—— (2012) 'Infringement: Actions, Remedies, Offences and Penalties', Information Sheet, January 2012, p. 4.

Australian Human Rights Commission Act 1986, Commonwealth of Australia, Canberra.

Australian Press Council. (2007) 'Defamation', Press Law in Australia, accessed December 10, 2009 from www.presscouncil.org.au/pcsite/fop/auspres.html#defam

—— (2008a) 'Report on free speech issues 2007–2008', accessed June 11, 2009 from www.presscouncil.org.au/pcsite/fop/fop_ar/ar08.html#privacy

—— (2008b) 'State of the news print media in Australia 2008', accessed February 5, 2009 from www.presscouncil.org.au/snpma/snpma2008/index_snpma2008.html

—— (2009a) 'Press law in Australia', accessed June 11, 2009 from www.presscouncil.org.au/pcsite/fop/auspres.html#blasp

—— (2009b) 'How to make a complaint', accessed October 18, 2009 from www.presscouncil.org.au/pcsite/complain.html

—— (2013) 'Handling of complaints', accessed May 24, 2013 from www.presscouncil.org.au/handling-of-complaints

Australian Story. (2005) 'At Death's Door— Transcript', June 27, accessed March 21, 2010 from www.abc.net.au/austory/content/2005/s1402495.htm

Ayres, Chris. (2010) 'Oscar puts his foot down', *The Weekend Australian*, Inquirer section, March 6–7, p. 3.

Bainton, George. (1890) *The Art of Authorship: Literary reminiscences, methods of work, and advice to young beginners, personally contributed by leading authors of the day*, D. Appleton and Company, New York, pp. 87 & 88.

Bartlett, Peter. (2012) 'Risks far greater than rewards in push on privacy', *The Australian*, May 4, p. 30.

Bartum, SW. (1960) 'Mr Quelch, a pirate on the Spanish Main', *The Age*, October 17, 1960, p. 15.

Baskin, Brooke. (2013) 'Former Bundaberg surgeon Jayant Patel will stand trial for grievous bodily harm of patient Ian Vowels later this year', *The Courier-Mail*, April 26, accessed May 12, 2013 from www.couriermail.com.au/news/queensland/former-bundaberg-surgeon-jayant-patel-will-stand-trial-for-grievous-bodily-harm-of-patient-ian-vowels-later-this-year/story-e6freoof-1226629848057

BBC. (2009) 'The "misunderestimated" president?', accessed February 14, 2010 from http://news.bbc.co.uk/2/hi/7809160.stm

—— (2012) 'Q&A: News of the World phone-hacking scandal', August 4, accessed May 23, 2013, www.bbc.co.uk/news/uk-11195407

—— (2013) 'David Cameron halts press regulation talks', March 14, accessed May 24, 2013 from www.bbc.co.uk/news/uk-21785611

BBC NewsWatch. (2004) 'We'll learn from hoax says BBC', December 6, accessed June 21, 2009 from http://news.bbc.co.uk/newswatch/ukfs/hi/newsid_4070000/newsid_4072400/4072491.stm

Becker, Murray. (1937) 'Photographer got "shot" of Zeppelin blast', *The Ellensburg Evening Record*, Washington, p. 1.

Beggs Sunter, Anne. (2005) 'Seekamp, Henry (1829?–1864)', *Australian Dictionary of Biography*, Supplementary Volume, Melbourne University Press.

Bentham, Jeremy. (1825) *A Treatise on Judicial Evidence*, Baldwin, Cradock & Joy, London.

—— (1844) *Benthamiana, or Select Extracts from the Works of Jeremy Bentham*, Lea and Blanchard, Philadelphia.

Bernstein, Carl & Woodward, Bob. (1972) 'Mitchell controlled secret GOP fund', *The Washington Post*, September 29, p. 1.

Bhojani, Sitesch. (2001) *Principles of Fairness and Accountability*, Penalties: Policy, Principles & Practice in Government Regulation—Conference, June 8, Australian Law Reform Commission.

Blainey, Geoffrey. (1980) *A Land Half Won*, Macmillan Company of Australia Pty Ltd, South Melbourne.

—— (1982) *The Tyranny of Distance—How Distance Shaped Australia's History*, revised edition, Sun Books, Melbourne.

—— (2000) *A Short History of the World*, Viking, an imprint of Penguin Books Australia Ltd, Ringwood, Victoria.

Boorstin, Daniel. (1961) 'From news gathering to news making: A flood of pseudo events' in *The Image: A Guide to Pseudo Events in America*, Athenaeum, New York, p. 7.

Bottom, Bob. (2005) personal interview.

Bradley, Ray. (2004) 'Is everything relative, including truth?', accessed April 26, 2009 from www.sciencechatforum.com/viewtopic.php?f=10&t=3085

Bread Manufacturers Ltd.; Re Truth and Sportsman Ltd. (1937) 37 SR (NSW) 242, pp. 249–250.

Breen, M. [ed.] (1998). *Journalism theory and practice*, Macleay Press, Paddington, NSW.

Breen, Neil. (2009) 'Pauline: we're sorry, they weren't you', *The Sunday Telegraph*, March 22, p. 35.

Brennan, Gerard. (1997) 'The Third Branch and the Fourth Estate', second lecture in the series 'Broadcasting, Society And The Law', delivered to the Faculty of Law, University College Dublin by Hon Sir Gerard Brennan, Chief Justice of Australia, April 22, accessed November 29, 2009 from www.hcourt.gov.au/speeches/brennanj/brennanj_irish.htm

Brinkman, W (Bill) & Lang, D. (1999) 'Physics and the communications industry', *Reviews of Modern Physics*, Bell Laboratories, Lucent Technologies, Murray Hill, New Jersey, accessed February 6 2009 from www.bell-labs.com/history/physicscomm/Physics_Com_wFig.pdf

Brooks, Brian, Kennedy, George, Moen, Daryl & Ranly, Don (1996) *News Reporting and Writing*, fifth edition, St Martin's Press, School of Journalism University of Missouri, Columbia.

'Bushfire Authority Reports on Progress 100 Days On' (2009) Victorian Bushfire Reconstruction and Recovery Authority, May 17, accessed September 20 2009 from www.wewillrebuild.vic.gov.au/publications/305-vbrra-100-day-report.html

Butler, Des & Rodrick, Sharon. (2007) *Australian Media Law*, third edition, Lawbook Co., Pyrmont, NSW.

Byrnes, J. (1966) 'Howe, George (1769–1821)', *Australian Dictionary of Biography*, vol. 1, Melbourne University Press.

Cameron, Michael. (2007) *Australian Media Law*, News Custom Publishing, Southbank, Victoria.

Chadwick, Paul. (1999) 'Media and accountability', AN Smith Lecture in Journalism, Melbourne University, November 17.

Chydenius, Anders. (1765) *Memorandum on the Freedom of the Press*, accessed January 15, 2009, from www.chydenius.net/historia/mita_sanoi/e_ilmaisunvapaudesta.asp

Clark, CMH. (1962) *Select Documents in Australian History*, Angus and Robertson Ltd, Sydney.

The Clerk and Other Officials. (2008) Infosheet, House of Representatives, No. 21, March.

College of Letters and Science. (2009) 'A Liberal Arts Education', University of California, Berkeley, accessed April 5 2010 from http://ls.berkeley.edu/?q=about-college/liberal-arts-education

Conley, David & Lamble, Stephen. (2006) *The Daily Miracle: An Introduction to Journalism*, third edition, Oxford University Press, South Melbourne.

Conroy, Stephen. (2013a) 'Convergence Review and Finkelstein Inquiry', March 12, Minister for Broadband, Communications and the Digital Economy, accessed May 25 2013 from www.minister.dbcde.gov.au/media/speeches/2013_-_minister_speeches/005

—— (2013b) 'Government response to Convergence Review and Finkelstein Inquiry', March 12, media release.

Coonan, Clifford. (2009) 'Crazy for English!', *The Weekend Australian Magazine*, September 19 & 20, News Limited, Sydney.

Copyright Act (1968) Commonwealth of Australia, Canberra.

Copyright Agency Ltd. (2009) 'Copyright for journalists', accessed June 11, 2009 from www.copyright.com.au/assets/documents/Copyright%20for%20Journalists.pdf

—— (2012) 'Copyright in Australia', accessed June 29, 2013 from www.copyright.com.au/get-information/about-copyright/copyright-in-australia

The Courier-Mail. (2003) 'Cretin slur worth jail, says judge', September 13.

Craftsman Homes Australia Pty Ltd v TCN Channel Nine Pty Ltd [2006] NSWSC 1297.

Cramp, K. (1939) 'From autocracy to federation', *The Sydney Morning Herald*, January 24, p. 19.

Crime and Misconduct Commission. (2007) 'The Fitzgerald Inquiry (1987–89)', accessed March 21, 2010 from www.cmc.qld.gov.au/asp/index.asp?pgid=10877

Crimes Act (1914) Act No. 12 of 1914 as amended (Cth).

Criminal Law (Rehabilitation of Offenders) Act (1986) Office of the Queensland Parliamentary Counsel.

Crowe, David. (2013) 'Press tsar to regulate standards', *The Australian*, March 13, p. 1.

Crowley, David & Heyer, Paul. (2007) *Communication in History*, fifth edition, Pearson Education, Inc., Boston.

Cryle, Denis. (1997) *Disreputable Profession: Journalists and Journalism in Colonial Australia*, Central Queensland University Press, Rockhampton.

Cuillier, David & Davis, Charles, N. (2010) *The Art of Access: Strategies for Acquiring Public Records*, CQ Press, Washington, DC.

Cusick, James & Milmo, Cahal. (2013) 'Surrey police officers accused of "collective amnesia" over failure to check 2002 report that Milly Dowler's phone was hacked', *The Independent*, April 24, accessed May 24, 2013 from www.independent.co.uk/news/uk/crime/surrey-police-officers-accused-of-collective-amnesia-over-failure-to-check-2002-report-that-milly-dowlers-phone-was-hacked-8585769.html

Dagan, Ross. (2010) Personal communication, February.

Dart Centre for Journalism and Trauma (2005) 'Self study unit 1: Journalism and Trauma', accessed October 17, 2009 from http://dartcenter.org/content/self-study-unit-1-journalism-trauma-2

—— (2009) 'Journalists and tragedies', tip sheet, accessed October 17, 2009, http://dartcenter.org/content/tragedies-journalists-3

Day, Mark. (2004) 'Condescending journalism graduates way out of touch', *The Australian*, Media section, November 11, p. 22.

—— (2012) 'Bad news belies the future', *The Australian*, June 20, p. 13.

de Burgh, Hugo. (ed.) (2000) *Investigative Journalism: Context and Practice*, Routledge (Taylor and Francis Group), London & New York.

DeFleur, Margaret. (1997) *Computer-assisted Investigative Reporting: Development and Methodology*, Lawrence Erlbaum Associates, New Jersey.

Defoe, Daniel. (n.d.) *The Life and Surprising Adventures of Robinson Crusoe of York; Mariner*, republished by Hamlyn Classics, London.

Denholm, Matthew. (2005) 'High price of snail's pace justice', *The Weekend Australian*, February 26–27, p. 1.

Department of Broadband, Communications and the Digital Economy. (2012) *Convergence Review Final Report*, March, Department of Broadband, Communications and the Digital Economy, Canberra.

Department of Infrastructure, Transport, Regional Development and Local Government. (2012) 'Road Deaths Australia April 2012 Statistical Summary', Australian Government, Canberra.

Department of the Premier and Cabinet, Queensland. (2011) 'Premier's Disaster Relief Appeal Distribution Committee Report', Queensland Government, October, accessed June 10, 2012 from www.premiers.qld.gov.au/publications/categories/reports/assets/premiers-disaster-relief-appeal.pdf

Dickenson Quinn, Sara. (2012) 'New Poynter Eyetrack research reveals how people read news on tablets', accessed March 12, 2013 from www.poynter.org/how-tos/newsgathering-storytelling/visual-voice/191875/new-poynter-eyetrack-research-reveals-how-people-read-news-on-tablets/

Director of Public Prosecutions v Luders (unreported) Court of Petty Sessions (WA), November 27, 1989.

Dixon, Susan. (1993) 'Democracy past and present—2500 years on', *Social Alternatives*, July, vol. 12, issue 2, pp. 41–43.

The Dominion Post. (2008) 'Erebus crash: myths and reality', February 12, accessed March 20, 2010 from www.stuff.co.nz/dominion-post/archive/national-news/265485

Drechsel, R. (1998) in J. Douge, *The Writer and the Law, Study Guide and Reader*, second edition, Deakin University, Geelong.

E Hulton & Co v Jones [1910] AC 20

Eismann, Katrin, Duggan, Sean & Grey, Tim. (2004) *Real World Digital Photography*, second edition, Peachpit Press, Berkeley, CA.

English, Peter. (2010) Personal communication, April 28.

Ericson, RV. (1996) 'Why law is like news' in David Nelken (ed.) *Law as Communication*, Dartmouth Publishing Co. Ltd, Aldershot.

Evans, Harold. (1978) *Pictures on a Page: Photojournalism, Graphics and Picture Editing*, Heinemann, London.

EyeTrack. (2007) 'Key findings', Poynter Institute, accessed August 1, 2008 from http://eyetrack.poynter.org/keys_01.html

Feneley, Rick. (2009) 'It's not Hanson: expert's verdict', *The Age*, March 18, www.theage.com.au/national/why-hanson-scoop-may-go-belly-up-20090316-8zwc.html

Ferguson, Sarah. (2009) 'The dishonouring of Marcus Einfeld', *Four Corners*, ABC Television, transcript, March 23.

FindLaw. (2008) 'Tort', accessed March 1, 2009 from http://dictionary.lp.findlaw.com/scripts/results.pl?co=findlaw.com&topic=71/71cf401e8052ec0c1c26e498c20fb9c3

Finkelstein Inquiry. (2012) *Independent Inquiry into the Media and Media Regulation, Report to the Minister for Broadband, Communications and the Digital Economy*, February 28, Media Inquiry Secretariat Department of Broadband, Communications and the Digital Economy, Canberra, ACT.

Fitzgerald, Shane. (2009) 'Lazy journalism exposed by online hoax', IrishTimes.com, June 21, 2009, www.irishtimes.com/newspaper/opinion/2009/0507/1224246059241.html

Frank, Phillip. (1947) *Einstein: His Life and Times,* Alfred Knopf, New York.

Franklin, Benjamin. (1729) 'The printer to the reader', *The Pennsylvania Gazette*, October 2.

—— (1731) 'An apology for printers', *The Pennsylvania Gazette*, May 27.

Fynes-Clinton, Jane. (2009) Personal interview, October 29.

—— (2010) Personal communication, March 6.

Gallagher v Durack (1983). HCA 2; (1983) 152 CLR 238, February 15.

Galtung, Johan & Ruge, Mari. (1965) 'The structure of foreign news: The presentation of the Congo, Cuba, and Cyprus crises in four Norwegian newspapers', *Journal of Peace Research*, vol. 2, no. 1, pp. 64–91, Sage Publications, Ltd, London.

Gardiner, Tom. (2012) 'RIP Mr Bean: False rumour of actor Rowan Atkinson's death trends worldwide on Twitter', *Mail Online*, 27 February, accessed 18 June 2012 from www.dailymail.co.uk/news/article-2106780/Rowan-Atkinson-death-hoax-trends-worldwide-Twitter-RIP-Mr-Bean.html

Garrison, Bruce. (1998) *Computer-Assisted Reporting*, second edition, Lawrence Erlbaum Associates, Mahwah, New Jersey.

Gawenda, Michael. (2012) 'Newspapers must get back to their core business', *The Australian*, Media section, June 4, pp. 29 & 32.

Global Press Freedom (2008), 'Mobile telephone', 16 January 2009, from www.freedomhouse.org/uploads/fop08/FOTP2008Tables.pdf

Goldner, Viva. (2006) 'The respected judge, the dead professor and a speeding fine', *The Daily Telegraph*, August 8, p. 9.

Graham, Caroline & Luck, Adam. (2010) 'Dirty money', *The Weekend Australian Magazine*, March 6–7, p. 17.

Grattan, Michelle. (2007) 'Michelle Grattan, Radio National Breakfast', accessed April 21, 2010 from www.abc.net.au/rn/talks/brkfast/grattan.htm

Gregory, Peter. (2005) *Court Reporting in Australia*, Cambridge University Press, Port Melbourne.

Griffiths, Emma. (2013) 'Media bosses put their case against media law shake-up', March 19, accessed May 24, 2013 from www.abc.net.au/news/2013-03-18/stokes-criticises-intrusive-media-reform-laws/4579872

Hartigan, John. (2009a) 'The future of journalism', an address by John Hartigan Chairman and Chief Executive,News Limited, National Press Club, Canberra, Wednesday July 1.

—— (2009b) 'John Hartigan address to the National Press Club', HeraldSun.com.au, September 9, 2009, www.news.com.au/heraldsun/story/0,21985,25718006-661,00.html

Haworth, Abigail. (2103) 'Culture shock', *QWeekend*, February 23–24, p. 10.

Hemingway, Ernest. (n.d.) Quotes.net, STANDS4 LLC, 2010, accessed January 26, 2010 from www.quotes.net/quote/769

Hennessy, Brendan. (1997) *Writing Feature Articles: A Practical Guide to Methods and Markets*, third edition, Focal Press, Jordan Hill, Oxford.

Henningham, John (ed.). (1999) 'The media' in *Institutions in Australian Society*, Oxford University Press, Melbourne.

Hepting, Daryl. (2004) 'The history of a picture's worth', accessed October 30, 2009 from www2.cs.uregina.ca/~hepting/research/web/words/history.html

Higgins, Ean. (2008) 'Hardie in secret move to the US', *The Weekend Australian*, April 19, accessed March 20, 2013.

from www.theaustralian.com.au/news/hardie-in-secret-move-to-the-us/story-e6frg6o6-1111116103947

Hilliard, Robert. (2008) *Writing for Television, Radio, and New Media*, ninth edition, Thomson Higher Education, Boston.

Hohenberg, John. (1983) *The Professional Journalist*, fifth edition, Holt, Rinehart and Winston, New York.

Hohenboken, Angus. (2010) 'Grim find for residents of upmarket block', *The Weekend Australian*, February 20 & 21, p 7.

Honours and Awards. (1967) 'James Douglas Campbell, 161 (Indep) Recce Flt 06 Sep 66–16 Sep 67', accessed January 26, 2010 from www.161recceflt.org.au/Honours/DFC/James_Douglas_Campbell/James%20Douglas%20Campbell.htm

Hough, George. (1984) *News Writing*, third edition, Houghton Mifflin, Boston.

The House, Government and Opposition. (2008) Infosheet, House of Representatives, No.19, March.

Hurst, John & White, Sally. (1999) *Ethics and the Australian News Media*, Macmillan Education Australia Ltd, South Yarra.

Ingelhart, Louis, Edward. (1998) *Press and Speech Freedoms in the World, from Antiquity Until 1998*, Greenwood Press, Westport, CT.

International Federation of Red Cross and Red Crescent Societies. (2009) World Disasters Report, accessed September 23, 2009 from www.ifrc.org/Docs/pubs/disasters/wdr2009/WDR2009-full.pdf

Internet World Stats. (2008) 'Australia', accessed August 10, 2008 from www.internetworldstats.com/sp/au.htm

—— (2012a) 'Internet usage and population statistics for Oceania', accessed January 27, 2012 from www.internetworldstats.com/stats6.htm

—— (2012b) 'Internet world users by language', accessed March 14, 2013 from www.internetworldstats.com/stats7.htm

—— (2012c) 'Top 50 countries with the highest internet penetration rate', accessed January 27, 2012, from www.internetworldstats.com/top25.htm

Invasion of Privacy Act 1971, Queensland Government, Brisbane.

Irby, Kenneth. (2004) 'Beyond taste: Editing truth', Poynter Online, March 30, accessed April 4, 2010 from www.poynter.org/content/content_view.asp?id=63131

Jackson, Sally. (2008) 'Seven Network settles with Corby's mum', *The Australian*, July 19, p. 3.

—— (2009) 'PR driving up to 80pc of content', *The Australian*, May 4, www.theaustralian.news.com.au/business/story/0,28124,25422943-7582,00.html

—— (2012) 'Journos face being outnumbered by merchants of spin', *The Australian*, May 7, p. 3.

—— (2013) 'Job numbers rise despite big cuts at newspapers', *The Australian*, Media section, January 18, p. 26.

Janda, Michael. (2009) 'James Hardie to try its luck in Ireland', ABC News, June 24, accessed March 30, 2010 from www.abc.net.au/news/stories/2009/06/24/2606901.htm

Jane Doe v Australian Broadcasting Corporation, Terence Rickard & Valerio Veo (2007) VCC 281.

Johnson, JT (Tom). (1994) 'Applied cybernetics and its implications for education for journalism', *Australian Journalism Review*, vol. 16, no. 2, pp. 55–66.

Jones, H & Benson, C. (2002) *Publishing Law*, second edition, Routledge, New York.

Jones v Hulton & Co (1909) 2 KB 444.

Kamper, Angela & Gearing, Amanda. (2002) '"My judgments have not been perfect"— Answers fail to ease the pressure', *The Daily Telegraph*, February 21, p. 5.

Kaplan, A. (1964) *The Conduct of Inquiry: Methodology for Behavioral Science*, Chandler Publishing Company, San Francisco.

Kelly, Paul. (2007) 'Honorary Awards: Paul John Kelly', accessed April 21, 2010 from www.usyd.edu.au/senate/Kelly.shtml

Kelly, Roz. (2010) Personal communication, April 30.

Kipling, R. (1986) 'The elephant's child', in Rudyard Kipling, *Just So Stories*, Exeter Books, New York.

Kirkpatrick, Rod. (2000) 'Chronic circulation decline: Regional dailies succumb to metropolitan virus', *Australian Studies in Journalism*, no. 8, pp. 75–105.

—— (2003) 'Pacific Rim cultures in newspapers' in M. Shannon & D. Copeland (eds) *The Function of Newspapers in Society: A Global Perspective*, Praeger Publishers, Westport, CT, Ch. 5.

Kiss, Jemima. (2003) 'Horses for courses', journalism.co.uk, accessed September 11, 2009 in www.journalism.co.uk/features/story591.shtml

Knight, A. (2000) 'On-line investigative journalism', *Australian Journalism Review*, vol. 22, no. 2, pp. 45–58.

Kohler, Alan. (2002) 'Cultures of journalism', *Lifelong Learning*, ABC Radio National, November 20, accessed April 28, 2010 in www.abc.net.au/rn/learning/lifelong/stories/s1174639.htm

—— (2009) 'Fairfax needs to digest net facts', *The Australian*, August 31, p. 32.

Lake, Chloe. (2009) '"Leaked list of banned websites" was not the ACMA blacklist, says Stephen Conroy', News.com.au, accessed June 12, 2009 from www.news.com.au/technology/story/0,28348,25210931-5014239,00.html

Lamb, Christina. (2010) 'Deadly simple', *The Weekend Australian Magazine*, March 13–14, pp. 21–23.

Lamb, Mathew. (2006) 'Sedition laws in Australia here to stay or about to go?', *PANPA Bulletin*, April, p. 22.

Lamble, Stephen. (2002) 'Freedom of information, a Finnish clergyman's gift to democracy', *Freedom of Information Review*, no. 97, February 2002. Clayton: Legal Service Bulletin Co-operative Ltd, Faculty of Law, Monash University, pp. 2–8.

—— (2003) 'United States FoI laws are a poor model for statutes in other nations', *Freedom of Information Review*, no. 106, August, pp. 51–5.

—— (2004) 'Media use of FoI surveyed: New Zealand puts Australia and Canada to shame', *Freedom of Information Review*, No. 109, February, pp. 5–9.

The Law Reform Commission [of Ireland]. (1991) 'Consultation paper on the civil law of defamation', St Stephen's Green, Dublin, accessed February 8, 2009 from www.lawreform.ie/_fileupload/Reports/rDefamation.htm

Leigh, J, Davidson, P, Hendrie, L & Berry, D. (2002) 'Malignant mesothelioma in Australia, 1945–2000'. *American Journal of Industrial Medicine*, vol. 41, pp.188–201, cited in Pennman, Andrew, (n.d.) 'Environmental Carcinogen Control in Australia: the Need for a Strategy', NSW Public Health Bulletin, vol. 13, nos. 9–10, pp. 199–201.

Leys, Nick. (2009a) 'Pauline Hanson secret nude photo shoot revealed', *The Sunday Telegraph*, March 15, p. 1.

—— (2009b) 'So who is the mystery girl?', *The Sunday Telegraph*, March 22, p.14.

Leys, Nick & Sexton, Jennifer. (2009) 'Hanson pics were one giant con', *The Sunday Telegraph*, March 22, p. 14.

LGA. (2009) 'Australian Local Government Association', accessed November 18, 2009 from www.alga.asn.au/about/

Lidberg, Johan. (2001) 'Freedom of information as a journalistic tool—a comparative study between Western Australia and Sweden', *Freedom of Information Review*, no 95. Legal Service Bulletin Co-operative Ltd, Monash University, Clayton pp. 42 & 43.

Ligertwood, J & Jackson, M. (2007) 'Whistleblowing, confidentiality and the McCabe case', *Commercial Law Journal*, vol. 2, no. 1, August, Thomson/Law Book Company, Melbourne, pp. 21–3.

Macnamara, Jim. (2003) 'The impact of PR on the media', accessed 26 September 2009 from www.mediastandardstrust.com/System/aspx/GetFile.aspx?id=14

Making Laws. (2008) Info sheet, House of Representatives, no.7, September, accessed November 19, 2009 from www.aph.gov.au/house/info/infosheets/is07.pdf

Marcus, Caroline. (2009a) 'A lost jacket and a stolen heart', *The Sydney Morning Herald*, January 18, accessed June 14, 2009 from www.smh.com.au/news/technology/web/a-lost-jacket-and-a-stolen-heart/2009/01/17/1232213424300.html

—— (2009b) 'You've been had: Sydney Cinderella's "jacket man" exposed as viral ad', *The Sydney Morning Herald*, June 14, 2009,

Masterton, Murray. (1995) 'Writing development stories', paper no. 8, AMIC Workshop on Editorial Management for Women Journalists, Singapore, May 24–31.

Mayer, Henry. (1968) *The Press in Australia*, Lansdowne Press, Melbourne.

McKinnon, Ken. (2004) 'Philosophy of press self-regulation', 1 February, accessed October 18, 2009 from www.presscouncil.org.au/pcsite/activities/meetings/asiapac/ken.html

—— (2008) 'State of the news print media in Australia report 2008', Australian Press Council.

McKnight, D. (2000) 'Scholarship, research and journalism', *Australian Journalism Review*, vol. 22, no. 2, pp. 17–22.

McLeod, Chris. (2005) 'Paying for the news', *Australian Press Council News*, February, pp.1–2.

—— & Lockwood, Kim (eds). (2009). *Style: The Essential Guide for Journalists and Professional Writers*, fourth edition, News Custom Publishing, Southbank, Vic.

McLuhan, Marshall. (1964) *Understanding media: The extensions of man*, fourth printing with introduction by Lewis H. Lapham, The MIT Press, Cambridge, Massachusetts.

Media, Entertainment and Arts Alliance. (2013a) *Journalists' Code of Ethics*, July 1, 2013, www.alliance.org.au/code-of-ethics.html

Media Entertainment and Arts Alliance. (2013b) 'Shield laws and confidential sources', Media Entertainment & Arts Alliance, March, May 19, 2013, www.pressfreedom.org.au/2013-report/protection-and-principles/shield-laws-and-confidential-sources

Media Watch—20 Years. (2009) 'Media Watch—20 years: Stuff ups, beat ups & barneys', accessed October 14, 2009 from www.abc.net.au/mediawatch/transcripts/s2563301.htm

Medsger, B. (2002) 'Getting journalism education out of the way', *Essays*, accessed February 6, 2009 from http://journalism.nyu.edu/pubzone/debate/forum.1.essay.medsger.html

Mencher, Melvin. (1997) *News Reporting and Writing*, seventh edition, Brown and Benchmark, Toronto and London.

Merritt, Chris. (2007) 'Judge's uppercut gives Canberra a black eye', *The Australian*, June 26, p. 3.

—— (2008a) 'Labor shelves privacy tort plan', *The Australian*, March 13, p. 5.

—— (2008b) 'Vic court expands scope of an old tort', *The Australian*, December 15, accessed January 17, 2010 from www.theaustralian.com.au/business/media/vic-court-expands-old-tort/story-e6frg996-1111118315261

—— (2013) 'Labor shelves privacy tort plan', *The Australian*, March 13, accessed June 29, 2013 from www.theaustralian.com.au/media/labor-shelves-privacy-tort-plan/story-e6frg996-1226595931407

Meyer, P. (1979) *Precision Journalism: A Reporter's Introduction to Social Science Methods*, second edition, Indiana University Press, Bloomington and London.

Mindframe (2013) 'Journalism and trauma', accessed June 16, 2013 from www.mindframe-media.info/for-universities/facts/journalism-and-trauma

Miniwatts World Stats. (2012a) 'Internet usage statistics—the internet big picture', accessed May 25, 2012 from www.internetworldstats.com/list2.htm

—— (2012b) 'Top ten internet languages', accessed May 25, 2012 from www.internetworldstats.com/stats7.htm

—— (2012c) 'World internet users and population stats', accessed May 25, 2012 from www.internetworldstats.com/stats.htm

Moeller, Susan. (2004) 'Media coverage of weapons of mass destruction', March 9, International and Security Studies at Maryland, accessed September 19, 2009 from www.cissm.umd.edu/papers/files/wmdstudy_full.pdf

Morris, A J. (2005) Bundaberg Hospital Commission of Inquiry, Commissions of Inquiry (no. 1) 2005, Brisbane.

Mott, F L. (1962). *American Journalism. A History: 1690–1960*, third edition, Macmillan, New York.

Nafziger, R & Wilkerson, M. (eds) (1949) *An Introduction to Journalistic Research*, Greenwood Press, New York.

Natoli, Rosanna. (2010) Personal communication, February.

News.com.au. (2009) 'YouTube Heidi Clarke lovelorn plea wears thin', June 14, 2009, www.news.com.au/technology/story/0,28348,24941189-5014239,00.html

News.com.au. 10.45am. (2013) 'Mother accused of poisoning daughter, 4', accessed 11 April 2013 from www.news.com.au/breaking-news/mother-accused-of-poisoning-daughter-4/story-e6frfku0-1226618009066

News.com.au. 1.26pm. (2013) 'Qld mum appears in court over poisoning', accessed 11 April 2013 from www.news.com.au/breaking-news/national/qld-mum-in-court-over-poisoning/story-e6frfku9-1226618104395

News.com.au. 2.50pm. (2013) 'Mother accused of poisoning daughter, 4, with alleged chemotherapy drugs bought online', accessed April 11, 2013 from www.news.com.au/breaking-news/mother-accused-of-poisoning-daughter-4/story-e6frfku0-1226618009066

Newspaper Publishers' Association. (2010) 'Most local news still originates from newspapers, not internet', Newspaper Publishers' Association, February 5, www.panpa.org.au/Public/Template5/ThreadView.aspx?tid=26047#post_26047

Nielsen, Jakob. (1996) 'Inverted pyramids in cyberspace', accessed September 17, 2009 from www.useit.com/alertbox/9606.html

—— (2005) 'Why web users scan instead of read', accessed September 12, 2009 from www.useit.com/alertbox/whyscanning.html

—— (2007) 'Blah-blah text: Keep, cut, or kill?', accessed September 12, 2009 from www.useit.com/alertbox/intro-text.html

—— (2009) 'World's best headlines: BBC News', accessed September 17, 2009 from www.useit.com/alertbox/headlines-bbc.html

NPPA. (1999) 'Ethics in the age of digital photography: Credibility', National Press Photographers' Association, accessed April 3, 2010 from www.nppa.org/professional_development/self-training_resources/eadp_report/credibility.html

NSW *Crimes Act 1900*, Section 312, Public Justice Offences.

NSW *Crimes Act 1900*, Section 529. April 26, 2009, www.austlii.edu.au/au/legis/nsw/consol_act/ca190082/s529.html

NSW *Defamation Act 2005*. Act 77 of 2005, New South Wales Parliamentary Counsel, Sydney.

NSW Legislative Assembly *Hansard*. (2004), p. 7134.

ntnews.com.au 11.41am. (2013) 'Stay away from the water', April 11, www.ntnews.com.au/article/2013/04/11/319495_ntnews.html

Oakes, Dan. (2012) 'Google hit with $200,000 damages bill over Mokbel shots', November 12, accessed May 18, 2013 from www.smh.com.au/technology/technology-news/google-hit-with-200000-damages-bill-over-mokbel-shots-20121112-297gk.html

Oakes, Laurie. (2010) 'Laurie Oakes, political editor', accessed April 21, 2010 from http://news.ninemsn.com.au/article.aspx?id=449276

O'Donnell, Penny, McKnight, David & Este, Jonathan. (2012) 'Journalism at the speed of bytes: Australian newspapers in the 21st century', The Walkley Foundation,

University of New South Wales, Media Entertainment and Arts Allliance, accessed January 10, 2013 from www.walkleys.com/files/media/SpeedofBytes.pdf

Office of the Privacy Commissioner. (2010) 'IPPS—Plain English summary', accessed June 12, 2010 from www.privacy.gov.au/materials/types/law/view/6892

O'Neill, Patrick & Prince, Peter. (2005) Asbestos-related Claims (Management of Commonwealth Liabilities) Bill 2005, Bills Digest, June 2, nos. 175–176, 2004–05, ISSN 1328-8091, Commonwealth Parliamentary Library, Canberra.

O'Neill, Rob. (2004) '2004: The biggest cases', *The Age*, November 30, accessed March 20, 2009 from www.theage.com.au/articles/2004/11/29/1101577387280.html

Our Electoral System. (2008) 'About Australia', accessed November 15, 2009 from www.dfat.gov.au/facts/electoral_system.html

Outing, Steve & Ruel, Laura. (2004) 'The best of Eyetrack III: What we saw when we looked through their eyes', Poynter Institute, accessed June 4, 2010 from www.poynterextra.org/eyetrack2004/main.htm

Owen, Peter. (2010) Personal communication, email, February 2.

Packer v Peacock. (1912) HCA 8; (1912) 13 CLR 577, March 13, 1912.

Packham, Ben. (2012) 'Mandatory web filter "would never have worked"', *The Australian*, November 10, accessed May 21, 2013 from www.theaustralian.com.au/national-affairs/mandatory-web-filter-would-never-have-worked/story-fn59niix-1226514016339

PANPA Bulletin 2003, 'Defamation capital? It's Sydney,' July/August, p. 9.

Papps, Nick. (2005). 'General under fire for "hoot to shoot" talk', *The Courier-Mail*, February 5, p. 19.

Parliamentary Privilege. (2008) Infosheet, House of Representatives, No. 5, March.

Pearson, Mark. (2007) *The Journalist's Guide to Media Law,* third edition, Allen & Unwin, Crows Nest, NSW.

Pelly, Michael (2009a) 'Einfeld gets three years', *The Australian*, March 21 & 22, p. 3.

—— (2009b) 'Ex-judge Marcus Einfeld jailed for speeding fine perjury', *The Australian*, March 20, accessed September 27, 2009 from www.theaustralian.news.com.au/story/0,25197,25214980-601,00.html

Penberthy, David. (2009) 'Justice has been served and shamed by Marcus Einfeld', The Punch, *The Australian*, July 25, accessed October 10, 2009 from www.theaustralian.news.com.au/story/0,25197,25831073-5015664,00.html

Pew Research Centre for the People and the Press. (2004) 'Bottom line pressures now hurting coverage, say journalists', 'Views', May 23, accessed March 26, 2005 from http://people-press.org/reports/display.php3?PageID=826

—— (2012a) 'State of the news media 2012', Major Trends, March, accessed July 7, from http://stateofthemedia.org/2012/overview-4/

—— (2012b) 'Trends in news consumption: 1991–2012: In changing news landscape, even television is vulnerable', September 27, accessed December 17, 2012 from www.people-press.org/files/legacy-pdf/2012%20News%20Consumption%20Report.pdf

Phillips, Gail & Lindgren, Mia. (2013) *Australian Broadcast Journalism*, third edition, Oxford University Press, South Melbourne.

Pollak, Michael. (1990) *Sense and Censorship: Commentaries on censorship violence in Australia*, Reed Books Pty Ltd, Balgowlah, NSW.

Pollard, A F. (1920) *The Evolution of Parliament*, Longmans, Green & Co., London.

Porter, Claire. (2013) 'ASIC "stuff up" marks return of internet filter—experts', News.com. au, May 17, accessed May 21, 2013 from www.news.com.au/technology/asic-stuff-up-marks-the-return-of-internet-filtering-experts-say/story-e6frfro0-1226645178443

Preston, John. (2007) 'Nick Ut: Double Negative', TheTelegraph.Com, December 30, accessed April 2, 2010 from www.telegraph. co.uk/culture/3670224/Nick-Ut-Double-Negative.html

Privacy Act 1988, Act No. 119 of 1988 as amended, Attorney-General's Department, Canberra.

Pullman v Hill & Co. [1891] I .Q.B. 524, p. 527, Lord Esher, as cited in *Philip M Godfrey v. Demon Internet Ltd* (1999), p. 6.

Queensland Flood Commission of Inquiry. (2012) Final Report, accessed 10 June 2012 from www.floodcommission.qld.gov.au/ publications/final-report

Quinn, Stephen. (2001) *Newsgathering on the Net*, second edition, Macmillan Publishers Australia, South Yarra.

Quinn, Stephen & Lamble, Stephen. (2008) *Online Newsgathering: Research and Reporting for Journalism*, Focal Press, Burlington, MA.

R v Gray. [1900] 2 QB 36. Queen's Bench, United Kingdom.

R v Nationwide News. (1997) Unreported, Supreme Court of Vic., February 22, 1997 (liability) and February 18, 1998 (penalty), per Gillard J.

Radford, Anthony. (2012) 'Despite gloom, regional papers thriving', *The Australian*, Media, July 9, p. 24.

Reddick, R & King, E. (1997) *The Online Journalist: Using the Internet and Other Electronic Resources*, Harcourt Brace, Fort Worth, Texas.

Reece, Stephen, D. (1999) 'The Progressive Potential of Journalism Education: Recasting the Academic versus Professional Debate', *The Harvard International Journal of Press Politics* vol. 45, no. 4, pp. 70–94.

Response Ability. (2009) Home page. November 1, 2009, www.responseability.org/

Reuters. (2007) 'Reuters toughens rules after altered photo affair', January 18, accessed April 4, 2010 from www.reuters.com/article/ idUSL18678707

Reuters India. (2009) 'Oddly enough', September 23, in.reuters.com/news/oddlyEnough

Rich, Carol. (2003) *Writing and Reporting News: A Coaching Method*, fourth edition, Wadsworth/Thomson Learning, Belmont, CA.

Richard, Carl. (2003) *Twelve Greeks and Romans who Changed the World*, Rowman and Littlefield Publishers Inc., Lanham, Maryland.

Richards, Ian. (2005) *Quagmires and Quandaries: Exploring Journalism Ethics*, University of New South Wales Press Ltd., Sydney.

Ricketson, Matthew. (2004) *Writing Feature Stories: How to Research and Write Newspaper and Magazine Articles*, Allen & Unwin, Crows Nest, NSW.

Robinson, Natasha. (2007) 'Journalists escape jail for contempt', *The Australian*, June 26, p. 3.

Rolph, David. (2008) 'A critique of the national, uniform defamation laws', *Torts Law Journal*, V.16(3), Sydney Law School Research Paper No. 09/05, University of Sydney, pp. 207–48.

Ryall, Julian & Demetriou, Danielle (2012) 'Japan earthquake and tsunami: 478 bodies remain unidentified one year on', *The Telegraph*, 9 March, accessed 10 June 2012 from www.telegraph.co.uk/news/worldnews/asia/ japan/9132634/Japan-earthquake-and-tsunami-478-bodies-remain-unidentified-one-year-on.html

Ryan, Inez. (2006) 'New Defamation Laws: A Guide', Australian Press Council, March 15, 2009, http://www.presscouncil.org.au/pcsite/apcnews/feb06/defamation.html

Samford, Karen, Dixon, Nicolee, Gastaldon, Renee, Westcott, Mary & Longworth, Kelli. (2012) *Shield Laws for Journalists*, Queensland Parliamentary Library and Research Service, February.

Schechter, Danny. (1999) *The More You Watch, The Less You Know: News Wars/(Sub)merged Hopes/Media Adventures*, Seven Stories Press, New York.

Schultz, Julianne. (1998) *Reviving the Fourth Estate: Democracy, Accountability and the Media*, Cambridge University Press, Cambridge, UK.

Seekamp, Henry. (n.d.) *Australian Dictionary of Biography: Online Edition*, October 6, 2009, http://adbonline.anu.edu.au/biogs/AS10430b.htm

Sheridan Burns, Lynette. (2002) *Understanding Journalism*, Sage Publications Ltd, London.

Simper, Errol. (2005) 'Class acts from ABC radio', *The Australian*, Media section, March 10, p. 22.

Simpson, James, B. (1988) *Simpson's Contemporary Quotations*, Houghton Mifflin Company, accessed January 18, 2009 from www.bartleby.com/63/9/8109.html

Smith, Frank. (1992) *To Think: In Language, Learning and Education*, Routledge, London.

Spry, Max. (2000) 'Executive and High Court appointments', Research Paper 7 2000–01, Parliament of Australia, accessed December 5, 2009, www.aph.gov.au/library/pubs/RP/2000-01/01rp07.htm

Starke, Petra. (2013) 'Police see mixed blessings in social media missing persons campaigns' January 5, News.com.au, accessed May 19, 2013 from www.news.com.au/national-news/police-see-mixed-blessings-in-social-media-missing-persons-campaigns/story-fncynjr2-1226547804937

Startt, James & Sloan, William David. (1989) *Historical Methods in Mass Communication*, Lawrence Erlbaum Associates, New Jersey.

Steele v Mirror Newspapers Ltd [1974] 2 NSWLR 348.

Stempel, G & Westley, B. (eds) (1989). *Research Methods in Mass Communication*, Prentice-Hall, New Jersey.

Stephens, Mitchell. (1997) *A History of News*, Harcourt Brace and Company, Orlando, Florida.

Stovall, James. (2005) *Journalism: Who, What, When, Where, Why and How*, Pearson Education Inc., Boston.

The Sydney Morning Herald. (2009). '*The Sydney Morning Herald* code of ethics', October 16, www.smh.com.au/ethicscode/index.html

'Talking turkeys'. (2008) *The Australian*, Media section, February 28, p. 36.

Tanner, Stephen (ed.). (2002) *Journalism Investigation & Research*, Pearson Education Australia Pty Ltd, Frenchs Forest, NSW.

TCN Channel Nine Pty Ltd v Henry Alfred Anning [2002] NSWCA 82 (March 25), Australasian Legal Information Institute, May 20, 2013, http://www.austlii.edu.au/au/cases/nsw/NSWCA/2002/82.html

TCN Channel Nine Pty Ltd v Ilvariy Pty Ltd [2008] NSWCA 9 (February 19).

Thayer, W M. (1897) *Benjamin Franklin: From Printing Office to the Court of St James*, Hodder and Stoughton, London.

The Sunday Telegraph 7.45am. (2009) 'Two men bashed in gang attack', September 13, www.dailytelegraph.com.au/news/breaking-news/two-men-bashed-in-gang-attack/story-e6freuyi-1225772302678

thewest.com.au 7.58am. (2013) 'Baby survives mum's suicide plunge', March 15, accessed March 16, 2013 from http://au.news.yahoo.com/thewest/a/-/breaking/16372991/baby-survives-mums-suicide-plunge/

—— 11.22am. (2013) 'Samaritan saves kitten from blowtorch', March 15, accessed March 16, 2013 from http://au.news.yahoo.com/thewest/a/-/breaking/16375674/samaritan-saves-kitten-from-teens-cruelty/

Thomas, Hedley. (2007) 'Can Dr Patel be tried justly?', *The Australian*, June 28, accessed March 18, 2010 from http://blogs.theaustralian.news.com.au/yoursay/index.php/theaustralian/comments/can_dr_patel_be_tried_justly/

Thucydides. (1972) *History of the Peloponnesian War*, translated by Rex Warner, Penguin Classics edition, Penguin Books, London.

Tiffen, Rodney. (1989) *News and Power*, Allen & Unwin, North Sydney.

Trkulja v Google Inc LLC & Anor (No. 5) [2012] VSC 533 (November 12, 2012).

'Truth is paramount' (2009) *The Australian*, April 6, accessed October 10, 2009 from www.theaustralian.news.com.au/story/0,,25294443-25209,00.html

Universal Declaration of Human Rights, 1948, The United Nations, accessed May 27, 2009 from www.un.org/en/documents/udhr/

US Constitution, Primary Documents in American History, accessed 16 October 2009 from www.loc.gov/rr/program/bib/ourdocs/Constitution.html

Ut, Nick. (2005) 'Picture power: Vietnam napalm attack', *The World Today*, BBC World Service, accessed April 1, 2010 from news.bbc.co.uk/2/hi/asia-pacific/4517597.stm

Waley, Jim. (2010) 'What I've learnt', *The Weekend Australian Magazine*, April 10–11, p. 6.

Walker, Sally. (1989) *The Law of Journalism in Australia*, The Law Book Company Limited, Melbourne.

The Washington Post. (n.d.) 'The Post investigates', accessed March 20, 2010 from www.washingtonpost.com/wp-srv/politics/special/watergate/part1.html and www.washingtonpost.com/wp-srv/politics/special/watergate/part4.html

Waterford, Jack. (2002) 'When a public figure's private life is public', *The Canberra Times*, July 5, accessed October 23, 2009 from www.canberratimes.com.au/news/local/news/columns/when-a-public-figures-private-life-is-public/659907.aspx?storypage=0

—— (2004) Personal interview, November 22.

Weaver, Belinda. (2000) 'Journalism students and information literacy', email communication with bweaver@library.uq.edu.au, November 7.

The Weekend Australian. (2012) 'What if the "hate media" had been brought to heel?', July 14 & 15, p. 23.

Weinberg, Steve. (1996). *The Reporter's Handbook: An Investigator's Guide to Documents and Techniques*, third edition, St Martin's Press, New York.

Wheeler, M. (1997) *Politics and the Mass Media*. Blackwell Publishers Ltd, Oxford, UK.

White, Sally. (1996) *Reporting in Australia*, second edition, Macmillan Publishers, South Yarra.

Wilkinson, Earl. (2004) 'Defining marketplace value for newspapers', *PANPA Bulletin*, no. 240, December, pp.76–8.

Windschuttle, Keith. (1998) 'Cultural studies versus journalism' in Myles Breen (1998) *Journalism Theory and Practice*, Macleay Press, Paddington, NSW.

—— (1999) 'Journalism and the Western tradition', *Australian Journalism Review*, Journalism Education Association, Australia, vol. 21, no. 1, July 1999, pp. 50–67.

Worcester Society of Antiquity. (1908) Proceedings for the Year 1907, Volume XXIII, published by The Society 1908, USA, CXXXII, accessed January 14, 2009 from www.archive.org/stream/proceedingsofwor01worc/proceedingsofwor01worc_djvu.txt

World Association of Newspapers. (2005) 'Newspapers: 400 Years Young!', March 1, accessed April 5, 2010 from www.wan-press.org/article6466.html

Yes Men. (2005) 'Dow', accessed May 29, 2010 from www.theyesmen.org/hijinks/dow/

—— (2012) 'Identity correction', June 18, http://theyesmen.org/

INDEX